D1615939

A. Philip Randolph

A. Philip Randolph

*The Religious Journey of an
African American Labor Leader*

Cynthia Taylor

NEW YORK UNIVERSITY PRESS

New York and London

NEW YORK UNIVERSITY PRESS
New York and London
www.nyupress.org

© 2006 by New York University

Library of Congress Cataloging-in-Publication Data
Taylor, Cynthia, 1954–
A. Philip Randolph : the religious journey of an African American
Labor Leader / Cynthia Taylor.
p. cm.
Includes bibliographical references and index.
ISBN–13: 978–0–8147–8287–3 (alk. paper)
ISBN–10: 0–8147–8287–6 (alk. paper)
1. Randolph, A. Philip (Asa Philip), 1889– 2. Randolph, A. Philip
(Asa Philip), 1889– —Religion. 3. African Americans—
Religion—History—20th century. 4. Civil rights—United States—
Religious aspects—Case studies. 5. Religion and politics—United
States—Case studies. 6. African Americans—Biography—Juvenile
literature. 7. Civil rights workers—United States—Biography.
8. Labor unions—United States—Officials and employees—
Biography. I. Title.
E185.97.R27T39   2005
323'.092—dc22   2005010772

New York University Press books are printed on acid-free paper,
and their binding materials are chosen for strength and durability.

Manufactured in the United States of America

10 9 8 7 6 5 4 3 2 1

For Michael,
    who believes all things
        are possible

The critics of religion are the allies of the prophets.

—Harvey Cox

Contents

Acknowledgments

So many people that have helped me with this book. First, thanks to Jennifer Hammer at New York University Press who perceived the value of my doctoral dissertation and turned it into a book. I would like to thank all my professors at the Graduate Theological Union, Berkeley, California, who encouraged my interest in religion and the civil rights movement, including Randi Walker, who taught me about religious biography; Eldon Ernst, who explained the complexities of American Protestantism; James Noel and his expertise on black church studies; and Thomas Buckley, for giving me my topic in the first place. Without their guidance and expertise, I could never have completed this book.

Special thanks goes to two Berkeley professors, Waldo Martin and Leon Litwack. From the outset of this project, Waldo trusted me to do the work, generously giving me his time. Leon Litwack's seminar during my first semester at Berkeley taught me the importance of getting to the sources. Fortunately, Dr. Litwack introduces all his students to Phyllis Bishof, the librarian for African and African American Collections at the University of California at Berkeley. Phyllis provided me with invaluable help throughout the writing of this book, and we share a passion for progressive religion. I must acknowledge three special history professors at San Francisco State University (the best history department around) who taught me the basics of American history: Robert Cherny, Jules Tygiel, and William Issel. Thank you for encouraging my love of historical research. For my dear friend and colleague Susan Englander at the Martin Luther King Jr. Papers Project at Stanford University, thank you so much for everything. Annie Russell, an expert editor, gave me a great deal of help in revising my manuscript, at a very busy time in her life. Elaine Caldbeck also deserves thanks for lending her advice at crucial moments. My friends Kevin Massey and Chris Anderson provided useful support with my computer questions, with great patience. Thanks also to my friend, Margaret Rogers, whose help was most appreciated. Last but not least, all my thanks to Michael, my husband and best friend, who has taught me never, never, never give up. You make everything possible.

Many valuable papers and oral histories were made available to me while I was doing the research for this book. Thanks are due to the following institutions: the A. Phillip Randolph Institute and LexisNexis Academic & Library Solutions, for the A. Phillip Randolph papers; the Bancroft Library of the University of California at Berkeley, for its oral history with C. L. Dellums; the Chicago Historical Society, for the First Series of the Brotherhood of Sleeping Car Porters Manuscript Collection; the Columbia University Oral history Research Office Collection, for transcripts of interviews with both Randolph and Rustin; the Estate of Bayard Rustin and LexisNexis Academic & Library Solutions, for the Bayard Rustin Papers; and the NAACP, for numerous materials from the NAACP papers.

Introduction

The Religious Journey
of A. Philip Randolph

Edwin Embree, the author of several books on "brown America," was waiting outside A. Philip Randolph's office for an interview. In 1944, at the height of his popularity, Randolph was busy as both the international president of the Brotherhood of Sleeping Car Porters and the national director of the wartime march on Washington movement. Embree was waiting because he needed to interview Randolph for his book *13 against the Odds*, a story of the "struggles and achievements of thirteen Negroes who are tops today."

Embree described Randolph as a "fighter and mystic, who [had] merged the Negro's cause with the general struggle of the common man." He conferred on Randolph the title "Saint Philip of the Pullman Porters." Embree presented Randolph as a serious, earnest person "given to long periods of brooding," quick to speak eloquently on the "wrongs of Negroes and all downtrodden people," but unwilling "to give details about himself." This last trait makes it difficult to decide whether Embree's portrait reflected what Randolph actually said and believed or whether Embree reported only the public opinion of the day regarding the labor leader, combined with his own personal impressions of his one interview with Randolph.[1]

In the early 1940s, much was written about Randolph. Embree borrowed liberally from Roi Ottley's best-selling book *"New World A-Coming": Inside Black America*, which had been published the year before and featured Randolph as one of the important leaders of black America. Ottley also noted Randolph's brooding intensity, as a person "free from scheming or duplicity, honest to the point of being almost naïve." He found Randolph to be "no conversationalist—but always the public speaker with a vast audience." Embree quoted Ottley's observation that "what seems to captivate Negroes" about Randolph was "the impression he gives of being all *soul*" as the basis for his identification of Randolph as a "mystic and dreamer." Beside the repeated references to the words *mystic* and *saint*, Embree used other religious terms to describe Randolph, including *prophet* and *modern Messiah*. Nonetheless, his influential essay reinforced Randolph's reputation as a "doubter" of Christianity and one who stood "against all religion." In contrast to Ottley's views of Randolph's integrity, however, Embree described Randolph as duplicitous, especially in his references to religion, arguing that he used religious imagery in his rhetoric only as a way to influence his followers in his labor and civil rights activism.[2]

For fifty years, scholars have dutifully repeated this characterization of Randolph and religion. Indeed, Embree's statement exemplifies the common perception that has been passed down for decades, that Randolph was extremely honest on all fronts except religion. As Embree wrote,

> While uncompromising in his public stand and honest almost to the point of fanaticism, Randolph was not above appealing to the porters in their own terms. Though he was an atheist, he knew that many of the Negro workers came from deeply religious homes. So in his speeches and in the Brotherhood paper, the *Black Worker*, he fell back on the Biblical language and imagery he had learned from his father. He spread at the top of his bulletins the Bible text, "Ye shall know the truth and the truth shall make you free." He pointed out that the church should support labor "since Jesus Christ was a carpenter." He was called "a Moses leading the people from the Land of Bondage into the Promised Land."[3]

This common interpretation of Randolph as an atheist and antireligious distorts the complexities of his relationship to African American religion. Therefore, the goal of this book is to set right what authors and scholars like Embree keep getting wrong. By examining Randolph's life at critical stages of his career, I show Randolph's generally positive relationship to religion and religious institutions, which never strayed far from his African Methodist roots.

A. Philip Randolph lived a long time, his ninety years coinciding with some of the most contentious events in African American history during the twentieth century. Born in 1889, Randolph's life coincided with the onset of the American system of legal segregation until its eventual demise by the time of his death in 1979. Growing up in the urban south of Jacksonville, Florida, Randolph lived through both the success and the failure of Reconstruction. Searching for economic opportunities, he migrated north with thousands of other black southerners before World War I and took part in the Harlem Renaissance that followed the Great Migration. After leading the black opposition to World War I, Randolph provided early support for Marcus Garvey (from whom he later split) and, with his partner, Chandler Owen, edited the *Messenger*, a magazine that profiled the Harlem radicals and the Harlem Renaissance. As he gained political power, his enemies began calling him "the most dangerous Negro in America."[4]

Through his support for black workers, first as a journalist and later as a labor leader, Randolph became best known for organizing the Pullman porters, the first successful black trade union, during the tough years before the New Deal changed the course of labor union politics in America. He was a pioneer of civil rights strategies, emboldening black citizens to march on the nation's capital to demand jobs in the burgeoning defense industries in the months before Pearl Harbor. In fact, his wartime efforts led President Franklin D. Roosevelt to sign an executive order banning discrimination within the government and in the defense industries that won government contracts. Then, in the 1950s and 1960s, sharing the wisdom and experience of decades of labor and civil rights leadership, Randolph passed the torch of social activism against American apartheid to the next generation of civil rights activists.

Of the numerous works on various aspects of Randolph's activism and leadership, none considers his religious life or its influence on his work.[5] This book, however, places A. Philip Randolph in the context of American religious history and seriously considers Randolph's complex relationship to African American religion. An understanding of the religious undercurrents of Randolph's career as a radical journalist, labor leader, and civil rights activist is essential to an understanding of how they intertwined with his political activities. This book therefore challenges the common perception of Randolph as an "avowed atheist," as recently stated in Clarence Taylor's *Black Religious Intellectuals*, and Paula Pfeffer's claim that Randolph possessed strong "anti-institutional leanings" toward the black church. Rather, this book demonstrates that Randolph's religiosity covered a wide spectrum of liberal Protestant beliefs, from a religious humanism on the left to orthodox theological positions on the right, as evident in African Methodism, one of the great religious traditions of the black church. I argue not that Randolph was in fact a deeply religious man but that a more nuanced view of his connections to theology, his use of religion as an organizing tool, and his complex relationships with organized religious communities provide a fuller picture of the man and his activism. I show that he consistently allied himself with the black Christian community, as well as with the larger liberal Protestant, Catholic, and Jewish communities, demonstrating his conviction that "true religion" was concerned with the things of "this world."

Randolph's foundational religious perspective, inherited from his African Methodist Episcopal (AME) parents, reflected a strong social gospel with an emphasis on "this world," a viewpoint compatible with his conversion to American socialism. At the core of this common misunderstanding of Randolph's relationship to religion is the ahistorical argument that keeps him tied to the most radical period in his life, the years from 1911 to 1921. In the 1920s and 1930s, Randolph abandoned his radical activities as a soapbox orator to become a labor activist and, in the 1940s and 1950s, a civil rights activist. Seen from this larger perspective, Randolph's religiosity reflects general patterns of liberal American Protestant thought influenced by the democratic American enlightenment.

Chapter 1 explores Randolph's religious upbringing by African Methodist parents in the AME tradition. From his parents, Randolph inherited a missionary zeal and racial pride that obligated him to "uplift the race." This religious zeal was transformed into deeply held political and sociological perspectives, since Randolph belonged to a generation that witnessed the collapse of the hopes raised by Reconstruction and the establishment of the Jim Crow system of segregation. Hoping to regain what was lost soon after the Civil War, Randolph moved north to Harlem, where he became involved in one of the most radical black communities in the United States. His conversion to socialism was a natural evolution from the social gospel message of his parents' African Methodism.

Chapter 2 explores Randolph's years as part of a radical group of black socialists who produced one of the great magazines of the Harlem Renaissance, the *Messenger*. Although many scholars have studied the *Messenger* as a political and cultural phenomenon, this book focuses on what the magazine reveals about a little-known area of African American religion of the 1920s, the progressive or liberal wing of black Christian ity. An analysis of the magazine through the three major phases of its eleven-year existence shows a wide spectrum of liberal religious thought, from atheist positions to the most theistic and orthodox religious perspectives. This chapter demonstrates how Randolph distanced himself from the label *atheist* as early as 1925, the period in which the *Messenger* became the mouthpiece for Randolph's new labor movement, the Brotherhood of Sleeping Car Porters.

Chapter 3 examines Randolph's work with progressive black religious communities to establish the Pullman porters' union, tearing down the traditional barrier between the black church and organized labor. The religious communities' support of Randolph's Brotherhood shows that he regarded it as a practical religion for working-class people, based on his belief that the black church's background was proletarian. By the late 1930s, Randolph's success as a labor organizer enabled him to achieve a national reputation as an important leader in black America.

Chapter 4 explores Randolph's rise to national prominence through his leadership of a popular wartime social movement, the march on Washington movement (MOWM). As was his labor activism of the 1930s, the MOWM was enthusiastically supported by black religious communities throughout the nation. This chapter focuses on the lesser-known aspects of the MOWM, such as Randolph's experiments with "prayer protest" demonstrations in 1942, during the highpoint of the movement's popularity among black communities. These prayer protests produced early versions of liberation theology thirty years before the noted theologian James H. Cone published *A Black Theology of Liberation*. I contend that Randolph's incorporation of the Gandhian notion of *satyagraha*, or nonviolent protest, in his civil rights activism proceeded from his religious impulses, which should not be divorced from his political activism. I disagree with those scholars who suggest that Randolph's interest in Gandhian *satyagraha* could not have come from religious motivations. In this light, it becomes clear that nonviolent protest tactics, usually considered a major innovation of the later modern civil rights movement of the 1950s, had a precedent in an earlier period.

Chapter 5 moves forward ten years, when Randolph was respectfully known as the "dean of Negro leaders." With the 1954 *Brown* decision, a new era had begun in African American history. This chapter focuses on the momentous events from 1954 to 1957, when Randolph responded to the unexpected emergence of a powerful liberation movement in Montgomery, Alabama, and the rise of one of the greatest leaders in American history, Martin Luther King Jr., a southern black preacher. In this late phase of Randolph's religious activism, he enthusiastically embraced King's leadership as a natural consequence of the many years of organizing progressive black religious communities, especially evident in their first joint venture, a national demonstration for civil rights in America, the prayer pilgrimage for freedom in 1957. The Montgomery movement inspired Randolph to join formally the Bethel AME Church in Harlem, in which he remained a member during the last years of his life. By the 1960s, Randolph's life had come full circle, in his definition of himself as "one of the sons of African Methodism."

1

One of the Sons
of African Methodism

When Asa Philip Randolph was a nine-year-old boy in Jacksonville, Florida, his father, "a highly racially conscious" African Methodist Episcopal minister, aborted the lynching of a black man charged with molesting a white woman. The Reverend James Randolph, aided by his wife, Elizabeth, organized a few community members to stand vigil all night at the local jail to protect the man. In the late 1890s, the Jacksonville black community was incensed over a general wave of antiblack propaganda and activities, especially by the lynch mobs organized by the local Ku Klux Klan. When the Klansmen saw Rev. Randolph and his companions walking up and down the sidewalk in front of the jailhouse late at night and fully armed, they stopped immediately, consulted with one another, and left. Randolph recalled how "all of a sudden they decided that something was important for them to do somewhere else." Meanwhile, Elizabeth Randolph sat up all night at home with a rifle across her lap, ready to shoot anyone who tried to harm her or her two young sons. This incident taught the young Asa Randolph that if "a people who [were] victims of racial hatred and persecution" united to protect themselves against injustice by standing firmly and holding their ground, "in the long run you'll win." When asked whether his family feared reprisals from this incident, Randolph replied, "We were always armed" and "Our father, though a preacher, was . . . determined to protect his family, and he . . . stood his ground."[1]

This incident instilled in Randolph a lifelong admiration of the militant Christian message of African Methodism in the closing days of Reconstruction. It also was why, more than sixty years later, Randolph still identified himself as "one of the sons of African Methodism." The emergence of African Methodism in the postwar South gave the Randolph family strength and dignity, important values for people in the early years of Emancipation. James and Elizabeth Randolph impressed on young Randolph their religious conviction of the importance of working collectively and solving problems in "this world" rather than in the next, and the right to human dignity and self-defense. Years later, when recalling the lynching attempt in his hometown, Randolph found it amazing that "there was complete silence. . . . Nobody talked about it. No writing in the newspapers." This incident, however, remained with the few determined people who stood their ground with Rev. Randolph that night against another southern lynching. Randolph grew up determined not to remain silent about the injustices inflicted on African Africans, and this determination shaped the course of his life.[2]

Randolph said nothing affected him as deeply as his relationship to the AME Church. He and his brother "grew up under it and in it, and our father was a part of it, and our mother was quite religious." His parents' African Methodist values included love and devotion to family, the importance of church affiliation, a sense of dignity and pride in oneself and one's race, the necessity of fighting and demanding civil rights as being integral to possessing human dignity—not just independently but also collectively and as a community—and love and admiration for learning and education. These values provided the foundation for Randolph's lifelong commitment to fighting racial prejudice and conditioned him for a life of service to others. As a young man, he dreamed about "carrying on some program for the abolition of racial discrimination" because his generation had an obligation to engage in pursuits that would benefit all people, regardless of color. "I got this from my father," Randolph observed, "that you must not be concerned about yourself alone in this world."[3]

In 1889, when Asa Randolph was born in Crescent City, Florida, the state legislature enacted a poll tax and instituted a voting system of separate ballot boxes which voters, especially new black voters, found confusing. Authorized by the new state constitution of 1885, voting practices like these were Florida's first steps toward abolishing the Reconstruction constitution of 1868, which challenged the basic Jeffersonian and Jacksonian values of antebellum days: limited government, decentralization of power, strong local authority, and white supremacy. The Reconstruction constitution created a strong executive who appointed the cabinet and county officials, enfranchised blacks, and established a system of public schools and institutions for the insane, blind, and deaf. Nonetheless, the majority of Floridians viewed the 1868 constitution as a failure and part of the most "ignominious era in the history of the state," which tainted everyone and everything associated with it. With the poll tax as the central issue at the 1885 constitutional convention, Florida's Democrats reconfigured the legislative apportionment that favored small counties, thus eliminating blacks and Republicans from the political process altogether. The effect of the poll tax was felt immediately: whereas in 1888, the Republicans won 26,000 votes, by 1890, they could count on only 5,000. By 1900, the Republican Party was dead in Florida, and the reigning political order was based on a one-party system and Jeffersonian values.[4]

In 1891, the Randolph family—Asa, his parents, and his brother— moved to Jacksonville, one of three large urban areas in Florida. The move was part of a larger black migration to southern cities in the decades after Emancipation. As blacks flooded into Jacksonville to take advantage of cheap land and economic opportunities during Reconstruction, the city became a focal point for African American hopes and Northern reformers' efforts. Before the Civil War, the free black population, about 9 percent of the city's total black population, lived in the segregated residential area known as "Negro Hill." During this period, both free and enslaved blacks made up the bulk of the local workforce performing the semiskilled and unskilled tasks of an urban economy. After the war, as in other southern urban centers, black working-class neighborhoods were established on the periphery of the commercial districts. By the 1880s, there were eight black neighborhoods on Jacksonville's northeast side, compared with the one neighborhood before the war. Residential segregation continued after the war, with white-owned wharves, businesses, and warehouses surrounding the black communities. Former slaves joined free blacks in their own independent society, in which churches, mainly Protestant, were the centers for an increasingly diverse community of institutions. Blacks built their own educational institutions. Schools supported by religious denominations included Florida Baptist Academy; Boylan Home Industrial Training School for Girls, whose courses included college preparatory classes and grammar school education; and Cookman Institute, a Methodist institution that significantly affected the young Randolph's life.[5]

Jacksonville's blacks accepted segregation in residency and education, but political segregation remained unacceptable. Scholars of Florida's history note that "Reconstruction died a slow death in Jacksonville." The size and strength of the African American community made it difficult for the Democrats to "redeem" the city quickly. In fact, between 1887 and 1889, the only delegates representing Jacksonville in the Florida House were African American. It was not until 1907, the year that Randolph graduated from high school, that black political fortunes declined in the city because of changing political conditions. Therefore, from the time that young Asa Randolph moved to Jacksonville in 1891 until his high school graduation, he did not come under the sway of the Jim Crow system. Instead, it was the later development of Jim Crow in Jacksonville after 1907, in contrast to the earlier black expectations of the southern political reconstruction, that later radicalized Randolph.[6]

The failure of the Republican reconstruction in Jacksonville eventually drove Asa Randolph out of the South in 1911, but not before he had experienced its successes, which positively influenced the rest of his life. During his childhood, Randolph had a taste of the real hope and possibilities that Reconstruction offered to formerly enslaved people, and he spent the rest of his life trying to recapture this hope, as personified in the life of an influential Jacksonville politician, Joseph E. Lee. From the late 1860s until the 1890s, Lee, who held the position of deputy port collector in Jacksonville, was known as the "Chief Ring Negro lieutenant" in Florida's Republican Party. In the early 1890s, Asa's father took him and his brother James to a political meeting held out in the open. The two boys were so young that Rev. Randolph had to carry them to the meeting. On the platform sat twenty-five to thirty people, all white, "except one man," Joseph E. Lee, who chaired the meeting and "made the introductory remarks." Randolph described him as "a fine type of person . . . [with] the spirit of an artist . . . [who] spoke well."[7]

Along with Lee's political standing in the community, Randolph was equally impressed by the fact that he was a minister. Rev. Lee was the minister of Mount Olive Church, the African Methodist Episcopal church that his mother attended in Jacksonville. Because James Randolph was the minister for several rural churches outside Jacksonville, the Randolph children attended Rev. Lee's church with their mother. Consequently, Lee made a dual impression on the young Randolph, from both the political world introduced to him by his father and the religious world identified with his mother. From an early age, Randolph studied Rev. Lee's deliberate, quiet speech and diction. Asa and his brother listened carefully to the sermons, because they had been "trained . . . to know when someone was using the wrong term." Because Lee had an outstanding reputation in both the city and the state, Randolph imagined that if he had not been the collector of the port, he might have become a bishop, because he was educated.[8]

By taking his sons to political meetings, Rev. Randolph instilled in them a sense of pride in their African heritage. From his father, Randolph also learned that some of the great men in history were men of color. Besides citing historical figures like Hannibal, Crispus Attucks, Nat Turner, Denmark Vesey, Toussaint L'Ouverture, Frederick Douglass, Richard Allen, and Henry McNeal Turner, the Reverend Randolph could also point to the living example of Joseph E. Lee. Rev. Randolph used Lee's political position as an example to his sons, saying, "Now, here is a . . . Negro . . . serving as the chairman of an important political meeting." More impressive to young Asa was the day his father took him to Rev. Lee's office in Jacksonville, where they were greeted by his secretary, who was "a white girl." Rev. Randolph's purpose in taking his sons to Lee's office was to teach them that they, too, could attain similar positions of authority. Randolph remembered this period in Jacksonville as a time when there was "the feeling and the determination and the spirit . . . on the part of a number of white people that this attitude of being just to people [was] mandatory." Randolph recalled other families in Jacksonville's black community who exhibited the same courage and determination to fight for their rights, because like the Randolphs, they were "deeply racially oriented."[9]

As the Reconstruction era evolved into the Gilded Age, the number of social, economic, and political opportunities for blacks in Jacksonville declined. The rise of Democratic politics in Florida in the 1880s and 1890s coincided with Florida's emergence as a modern industrial economy, most notably in the spread of railroads. By 1891, as public lands and grants were handed out to several new railroad companies, 2,500 miles of rail were built in Florida, the start of a new industrial order for the state. Although men like Hamilton Disston and Henry M. Flagler, influential industrialists in Florida history, never held political office, they determined the course of its politics after the 1880s. Indeed, the emphasis on successful industrial capitalists like Flagler overshadowed the social accomplishments of several Northern reformers, such as Harriet Beecher Stowe and her brother Charles Beecher; Chloe Merrick Reed and her husband, Governor Harrison Reed; the crusading Methodist minister John Sanford Swaim; and a host of other Yankee schoolteachers, social reformers, aspiring politicians, and enterprising businessmen.[10]

As a child, Asa Randolph directly benefited from their reforms. Believing that this generation of reformers had not received proper historical attention, Randolph observed that "the history of New England schoolmarms who came South during the War has yet to be written." The Jacksonville fire of 1901, a devastating event in the city's history, obscured Florida's progressive Reconstruction heritage from a new generation of Floridians adapting to the modern Jim Crow era. That is, in the new postwar era, the Swaims, Reeds, Beechers, and Stowes became "carpetbaggers," and their efforts for social reform were forgotten. As long as political conditions delayed the arrival of a strict Jim Crow system, Randolph and other blacks benefited from the social, economic, and educational advantages of Reconstruction Florida. If the Jacksonville fire divided the old Florida from the new, certainly the older history of Joseph E. Lee and the Yankee schoolteachers had the most decisive influence on young Asa Randolph. The fire, which physically changed old Jacksonville, symbolized the death of the radical hopes for freedom and equality engendered by the Civil War, ideals that A. Philip Randolph spent his lifetime trying to restore.[11]

Randolph's birth in 1889 also coincided with the twenty-fifth anniversary of African Methodism in the South. Reconstruction enabled African Methodist Episcopal churches to flourish in the South, and Asa was reared in the radical African Methodist tradition practiced by his parents. In honor of the anniversary, the noted AME Bishop Daniel Payne himself presided over a "quarto-centenary" program held at the Mount Zion AME Church in Jacksonville. The May 1890 program included various talks on the founding of African Methodism in east and west Florida; a review of its educational work, especially Edward Waters College; and a special emphasis on the accomplishment of pioneer AME women in east and west Florida, a literal testament to the postwar struggle to establish African Methodism in the South. African Methodists like the Randolph family had personally witnessed great progress since slavery, and they prided themselves on their material and spiritual achievements. They felt connected to the great institution that W. E. B. Du Bois, in the first scientific study of the black church, called "the greatest voluntary organization of Negroes in the world."[12]

As a young man, Randolph shared with other black leaders and intellectuals of the turn of the twentieth century the conviction that the African Methodist Episcopal Church, with its history dating back to the American Revolution, was a high point in black organizational ability.

Du Bois's study confirmed the black community's generally high regard for the AME Church in the nineteenth century, praised the *Christian Recorder* as "the oldest Negro periodical in the United States," and cited the AME's board of bishops as the "salt of the organization." Even when the AME Church lost its preeminent standing within African American religion later in the twentieth century, Randolph's childhood admiration of the institution remained with him throughout his life. Du Bois noted that the origins of the African Methodist Church "had a tinge of romance," owing to Richard Allen's legendary act of walking out of the segregated St. George Methodist Church in Philadelphia in 1787. Randolph, comparing Allen with Martin Luther, declared that Allen's "action had greater nobility of spirit and entailed more personal sacrifice than that of Martin Luther who nailed his ninety-five theses to the church door at Wittenberg, or when he stood before the Diet of Worms." Randolph connected personally with the "romance" of African Methodism, since Allen's "wrath against religious jimcrow . . . struck a blow for civil rights and first-class citizenship" and served as a role model for his own lifework fighting for black civil rights.[13]

Randolph's parents and grandparents had lived through the cataclysmic events of the 1860s and the subsequent changes the Civil War brought to the South. When African Americans created their own churches during and after the war, Randolph's parents chose African Methodism. After the 1863 Emancipation Proclamation, thousands of black Methodists left the Methodist Episcopal Church, South, although even before the war, many black Methodists worshiped separately within the established white Christian communities. These black Methodists exhibited the characteristics necessary for self-government: a rudimentary sense of group self-consciousness, procedures and methods for decision making, and charismatic group leaders. The war had created a liberal climate that emboldened former slaves to make the final break from the ME Church, South: a black Methodist connection with which to affiliate. Although the initiative taken by southern blacks in establishing African Methodism was a key aspect of the southern black Methodist movement, equally important was the denominational emphasis on racial uplift, education, and political activism as embodied by AME missionaries like James Lynch. Randolph's parents were the first generation of newly emancipated slaves to participate fully in this religious revolution and transition in the South.[14]

James Lynch's experience in one South Carolina town of eight hundred "colored" inhabitants and two churches, both abandoned by whites during the war, reflected this period of religious transition. Rev. Lynch occupied a church once inhabited by white Episcopalians but now filled with a mixed denomination of black Methodists, Baptists, Presbyterians, and Episcopalians. Lynch's appearance among these ex-slaves as an educated, self-confident black preacher so affected them that he recalled that "the first Sabbath I preached to them, they began to wonder among themselves as to what denomination I belonged." Since none had heard of the AME Church, Lynch told them he had been instructed to organize an African Methodist church. Except for a few dissenting Baptists, the majority of the mixed congregation voted to join his church, illustrating how missionaries and willing congregations were able to change the southern religious landscape. Moreover, the AME denomination's highly organized polity, run by educated bishops, brought respectability to its members.[15]

Another source much closer to Randolph's personal history is Charles Sumner Long's "Founding of the A.M.E. Church in Florida." Long, an AME minister and historian of African Methodism in Florida, explained that from their headquarters in South Carolina, African Methodist missionaries used Florida as a missionary field. His account starts with the great bishops of African Methodism and the usual recording of church conferences and meetings: "The history of the African Methodist Episcopal Church in Florida began June 22, 1865, with the appointment of Rev. William G. Steward as pastor of Florida." Then he interrupted his chronicle with a story "worth mentioning" about Henry Call, a slave from a small settlement in Cottondale, Jackson County, two counties away from James Randolph's boyhood home of Jefferson County. Since James Randolph's recorded birth date of 1864 places him within the time frame of the establishment of the AME Church in Florida, Call's story sheds light on how Randolph's father may have become affiliated with the African Methodist Church.[16]

In November 1863 in west Florida, Rev. Henry Call, "a local preacher among his people under the M.E. Church, South," accompanied his young master to Tennessee and watched the battle of Chattanooga behind Confederate lines. On the Union side was a large contingent of black troops. After the battle, Call searched for his dead master and came across a dead black soldier with a paper sticking out of his pocket. Because his master had secretly taught him to read, he recognized the word *Herald*, an early name for the AME publication, the *Christian Recorder*.

According to Long, "President Lincoln had thousands of copies printed for the black soldiers." The young slave noticed pictures of Richard and Sarah Allen on the front page. "It was the first time brother Call had ever seen the pictures of Negroes in a paper." Impressed by what he saw, Call "folded it carefully, put it in his bosom and continued his search for his master." Returning to Cottondale, Call took a month to read the entire issue, since he had to read it secretly when he was not working. The paper recounted how missionaries of the AME church followed the Union army, "planting the church and housing the people." Announcing the appointments of the Reverends James Lynch and D. S. Hall of the Baltimore Conference as missionaries to South Carolina, the paper boasted that black bishops would cover the whole South as soon as the Union armies occupied it. Unable to keep the news to himself, he read to three other men what he had found out. Call announced that "he was going to lead prayer meetings on Thursday night, and when they got through they were to have a general hand shaking, which meant that they had joined the A.M.E. Church."[17]

Long emphasized the secrecy of the three men's plan of action. Since blacks could not meet without a white man present, if they were discovered, they would be hanged or sold to New Orleans slave traders. Long described how "Henry Call and his three companions organized the A.M.E. church, while the white overseer looked on unaware of anything more than a prayer meeting or a hand shaking was going on." Long's story of Henry Call shows that ordinary people left the Southern Methodist Church even before the war ended, and it confirms the critical role of lay black Methodists in establishing independent black churches in the South:

> Had Henry Call had authority as Rev. Hall and Rev Lynch had in South Carolina, he would have superseded Pearce and Steward, but William G. Steward [was] the first AME Minister appointed to Florida; while in Henry Call's case it is as our Master said, "He that is for me cannot be against me." As soon as William Steward landed in Jacksonville and Brother Call heard of it, he walked from Marianna to Jacksonville to get Rev. Steward, and took him to Marianna where he and all the members were taken into our Church.[18]

Previous denominational affiliations helped determine the eventual settlement of the South's religious map after the war. William Steward established African Methodist churches in other northern Florida communities, such as Monticello, the home of the young James Randolph. In fact, Jefferson County was an active center for AME missionary recruitment during and after the war. Like Henry Call, James Randolph's family may have joined the AME Church as an alternative Methodist connection that freed them from their subordinate position within the church without disturbing their theological beliefs.

Randolph's childhood was spent in several communities near Jacksonville: Baldwin, fifteen miles east of Jacksonville; Crescent City, to the south; and Monticello to the west near Tallahassee. In Monticello, James Randolph attended a grade school that white northern Methodist missionaries opened after the war for the children of ex-slaves. When he was unable to continue his education, James's parents apprenticed him to a tailor, but the AME church in Monticello appointed him, a promising student in his early teens, as a Sunday school teacher. As a result, by the time he was twenty, James Randolph was both a self-trained preacher and an accomplished tailor. When he informed the presiding elder of the church district that he felt a "call to preach," he was ordained into the AME ministry.[19]

It was in Monticello that James Randolph befriended James and Mary Robinson, the parents of his future wife, Elizabeth. In the early 1880s, when the Robinsons moved to Baldwin, Mary Robinson, a member of the African Methodist congregation in Monticello, transferred her membership to the Campbell's AME Chapel in Baldwin. Mary Robinson urged the Baldwin congregation to appoint the newly ordained James Randolph, and the Robinsons welcomed him as one of their own. Rev. Randolph was the pastor of Campbell's Chapel, a small congregation of fifty people, preaching on the first and third Sundays of the month, leading prayer meetings on Wednesday nights, and teaching Sunday school. In 1885, a year after he moved to Baldwin, James Randolph married Elizabeth Robinson, then a thirteen-year-old pupil in his Sunday school. When he was called to be the minister of a larger congregation in Crescent City, Florida, some sixty miles south of Baldwin, James Randolph moved there with his wife and first son, James Jr. There Asa Philip Randolph was born in 1889, completing the family. After two years in Crescent City, the Randolph family moved to Jacksonville. "You remained at these churches at the most two years," Randolph later recalled, because African Methodist ministers were under the authority of presiding elders who "had a right to shift you."[20]

James Randolph's "adoption" and eventual marriage into the Robinson family greatly influenced the course of young Asa's life, as the Randolphs maintained close ties to the Robinsons in Baldwin. Elizabeth Randolph impressed upon her sons "that the family was a factor of great importance" and that the Robinsons were "highly respected by the white
people in the community." Once a month, Asa went with his mother on
the three-hour drive to visit his grandparents. Mary Robinson, an imposing woman of 250 pounds, was very devoted to her grandsons. With her
fiery temperament, she ran her household like a tyrant, and whatever she
"said[,] you had to do," according to Randolph. He described her as
being "highly spiritualized," and she held morning prayer meetings at
which attendance was mandatory for the two Randolph boys. "She
would sing and . . . preach . . . about what everybody had to do to get to
heaven." Praying together as a family was also a priority in the Randolph
home. One cousin remembered that "come dinnertime, we used to say,
'Well, it's almost time to eat and almost time to pray.'"[21]

But it was not the prayer meetings' spiritual message that affected Asa
as much as the personal example of his "superreligious" grandmother. It
was her powerful physical presence, her concern for her grandsons' well-
being, and her total commitment to the African Methodist church community that most impressed him. He noted, however, that his grandfather
"never attended church" and completely disregarded all aspects of religion. James Robinson, a hardworking, well-respected man in the Baldwin
community, devoted himself to his wood-gathering business and raising
hogs. Stern and aloof, James Robinson was uncommunicative, even with
family members. With no interest in the church, Robinson shunned the
singing and praying that went on in the cabin every night before bedtime.
Both the superreligious example of his grandmother and parents and the
complete disregard of religion by his hardworking grandfather equally affected Asa Randolph.[22]

When the Randolphs moved to Jacksonville in 1891, they settled in a
tough section of town called Oakland. As a youngster, Randolph's life revolved around his mother, and Elizabeth Randolph's life revolved around
the family and church. She socialized with church people and attended religious affairs, funerals, and weddings or traveled to see her parents in
Baldwin but had no other social life. She was born about 1872, in the
early days of Reconstruction and also of the establishment of African
Methodism in the South. Typical of African Methodists, Elizabeth Randolph preferred her religion quiet and dignified; she was "not of the

shouting type." Convinced that good citizens were connected to a church, she wanted her sons to have "the type of life that the church was supposed to give." Elizabeth Randolph expected her children "to be spotless" and maintained a meticulous household. Randolph emphasized that the day-to-day disciplining came from his mother, since his father "wasn't around enough to keep track of us." Randolph often spoke of the joys of childhood play but his unhappiness over not playing in the streets as other children did, because of his mother's disapproval. She carefully inspected her sons' playmates, often asking them about their family backgrounds. Randolph remarked that "our father never gave us any chastisement, of any physical nature, but . . . would tell us, 'Now you must obey your mother because if you don't she is going to give you a whipping.'" Later, Randolph appreciated the "rigidness of [his mother's] disciplinary policy" because it taught him responsibility, all within the context of a caring family life.

> I . . . don't know . . . any two youngsters [who] were more meticulously raised than we were, although there was not money of any consequence in the home, but we knew that there were certain things we had to comply with. They usually were things that related to your conduct, building up your habits, . . . and giving you a sense of responsibility. We had that sense of responsibility.[23]

Rev. Randolph's tailor trade was the main source of the family's income. As a working man, he usually dressed in ordinary working clothes and wore his ministerial garb only "when he attended the church at the end of the week." Since "the income from churches was negligible," the Randolphs depended on the food given to them by members of his congregations, as well as food they grew themselves. But they were always in debt. It was Elizabeth Randolph, an effective business woman, who made sure her husband's clients paid their bills. Although her husband tried other businesses, selling wood and running a small meat market, both were financial disasters. Making money was never a priority for either James or Asa Randolph, and indeed, Asa took pride in the fact that he "came through the type of home that we did have, although it was without money."[24]

Rev. Randolph's new congregation in Jacksonville was smaller than his Crescent City congregation and lacked its own place of worship. Eventually, under his supervision, the congregation built the New Hope AME

Chapel, one of several churches with which he was affiliated, since "one wasn't sufficient to give him anything to go on." His other responsibilities included churches in Green Cove Spring and Palatka, Florida, which he visited on Saturdays. He also preached once a month in Baldwin, where in addition to being a preacher, he also worked as a schoolteacher. Asa Randolph attributed his later civil rights activism to the lessons he learned while accompanying his father on his circuit. Randolph got to know his father's parishioners and their children, and from them, he learned about blacks' working conditions and the racial prejudices they faced each day. Jacksonville, situated on St. John's River, provided Rev. Randolph with reliable transit to visit his congregations in Palatka, twenty-nine miles away, and Green Cove Spring, fifty-six miles away. Randolph appreciated the historical significance of the southern river boat system but noted that travelers were divided by race, since it was a "Jim Crow arrangement [in which] Negroes had a little compartment where they had their bags and sat." Rev. Randolph went as far as he could by steamboat and then finished his journey by foot, often wading through streams to get to the churches. At his destination, the minister and his son were met by church members in oxcarts and spent the evenings there in a log cabin. Although James Jr. accompanied his father reluctantly, Asa went along enthusiastically, for to him these trips were unforgettable and enjoyable experiences.[25]

Rev. Randolph handled all aspects of church business. His main responsibility was the annual collection of "a dollar for every member in [the] church," a difficult assignment given the poverty of his congregations. The challenge, therefore, was to collect "the dollar money" from people who were "too poor to keep up their contributions" and who often needed to "receive some support from the church" themselves. The "dollar money plan" had been started in 1868, with the tremendous growth of the AME Church in the South after the Civil War, to meet the costs of the General Church. Under this plan, each pastor was required to secure from or pay for each of his members one dollar per year. W. E. B. Du Bois cited the "dollar money law" as evidence of the economic cooperation possible among black people. Since a "dollar went quite a long way, in the life of poor people," the plan impressed Randolph as "quite an ingenious thing," not only for its financial implications, but also "because they could count the members." These were instructive lessons for Randolph, who spent his life mobilizing people and resources for labor and civil rights causes. His father's financial obligations were connected to the Methodist system of annual conferences and ministerial alliances required of an AME minister. As a minister participating in the annual conference with other ministers from his area, Randolph explained that "our father knew that this was one of the obligations of his ministry and he always saw to it that the dollar for each member was given to the conference."[26]

Methodism appealed to many in the nineteenth century because the self-study it promoted enabled them to rise within the institution, regardless of whether they had a formal education. Likewise, African Methodism offered Rev. Randolph a prescribed method of study and a way to educate himself, which was critical to blacks in the early days of Reconstruction. For ministers of his generation, one's "calling" to the ministry was just as important, if not more so, than a formal education. Randolph explained the importance of his father's "calling," since "preachers in those days . . . depended on the call," which was "the real religious background and foundation" for a minister. Unless a minister got the "call," he could not be "a preacher of any consequence." Benjamin Mays, a scholar of the black church, confirmed Randolph's explanation, that in the nineteenth century "the minister was specially 'called' of God, and that if God 'called' him he needed little or no academic preparation." In fact, Mays argued that "some of the most progressive and effective Negro ministers [were] men whose academic training [had] been limited." In the 1920s, scholarship on the black church noted a generational shift in thought regarding "a calling" versus "formal education" as the proper preparation for the ministry. As Randolph noted, both his father's calling and his continual efforts at self-education constituted his formal ministerial training.[27]

James Randolph's self-education reflected his religious and political beliefs, shaped in the days of radical reconstruction in Monticello, Florida. There, black people armed themselves to defend their right to vote. Randolph wrote, "My father was strongly committed to the Republican Party" and well versed in its history, since "he was part of it though not a leader, and because he had the soul of a fighting revolutionist." Although Rev. Randolph believed that the Republican Party had failed in its mission to the former slaves, "it was, politically, the ship, and all else the sea for the Negro freedman." Besides his interest in radical politics, he enjoyed reading the religious history of African Methodism and about the lives of its founding fathers and influential bishops in the AME Church's two major periodicals: the weekly *Christian Recorder* and the quarterly *AME Review*, as well as the radical journal the *Voice of the Negro*. Asa Randolph inherited his father's interest in African American religious history and, through him, met several of the great African Methodist bishops. Randolph described to his biographer the memorable childhood experience of meeting his father's boyhood hero, Bishop Henry McNeal Turner. Rev. Randolph took his sons to meet Bishop Turner at an AME convention in Jacksonville, and Randolph recalled his elation when Bishop Turner patted them on their head, telling them their father was a fine man. Another story Randolph remembered about the great Bishop Turner was at another AME convention in the South, when Turner "pulled two revolvers from his pockets, slapped them down on the Bible, and declared, 'My life depends on the will of God and these two guns.'" From Bishop Turner's example, Rev. Randolph developed his own "soul of a fighting revolutionist" and taught his sons to do the same.[28]

Rev. Randolph taught his sons that they were connected to a "great church family." Although from time to time he allowed his sons to visit the Bethel Baptist Church to hear the Reverend John E. Ford preach, they understood that no faith took precedence over African Methodism. Their father believed that unlike the African Methodist Church, with its formal national structure, "anybody" could start a Baptist church. Rev. Randolph preferred African Methodism's emphasis on practical and ethical issues and its de-emphasis on the emotional aspects of evangelical Christianity. In keeping with the dignified aspects of the AME doctrine and traditions, Rev. Randolph remained a composed and soft-spoken man. When asked his impressions of his father's preaching style, Asa Randolph replied: "Well, he was a preacher who was not . . . a high spiritual arousing type of man. . . . He was modest, soft-spoken, a person who was devoted to his Christian ministry in the African Methodist Episcopal Church."[29]

Because of his limited education, James Randolph did not advance to better positions within the church. In Jacksonville and other urban areas, wealthier and more sophisticated middle-class congregations demanded better-trained ministers. Nor did he display a desire to advance in the church hierarchy. Although well-respected by his elders, his son believed that he "put his whole time into his family" at the expense of his personal and professional ambition. Rev. Randolph was not a "political spiritual maneuverer." Elizabeth Randolph supported her husband's position of remaining independent. At the same time, his father's itinerant ministry kept Asa Randolph from becoming a typical "preacher's kid." He could choose which church to attend: Rev. Randolph's New Hope Church, his mother's Mount Olive AME Church, or the Mount Zion AME Church.[30]

Randolph's weekly church life revolved around his mother's, at Mount Olive AME Church. Starting Sunday school at an early age, Randolph called Sunday a "pretty religious day . . . everybody knew just what he was supposed to do." As a youngster, Randolph objected to the long Sunday hours, consisting of several services with Sunday school and the Christian Endeavor League, although he viewed Sunday school as interesting, since his brother, a good student, "was quite argumentative." Often they waited for their mother to finish her own service "against our will," but they obediently observed this "ritual . . . from year to year." Through his experiences at Mount Olive and his parents' instruction, Randolph early learned the importance of church membership. Your name was "put in a book and . . . [you were] called upon to make contributions to the church from time to time." Randolph respected his parents' demand that they contribute money to the church on their own, and "the fact that there wasn't much money around was no excuse for our not making some contribution." This was another way that his parents instilled in Randolph a sense of responsibility and "that we shouldn't expect everything to be given to us." In hindsight, Randolph believed that "was a good policy for youngsters."[31]

As his parents were "religious and devoted to the things of the family," the Randolph family home attracted people in trouble, especially parents concerned about their children. Rev. Randolph spent much of his time helping young men stay out of jail. Surrounded by poverty-stricken people, he was regarded as a person with the "highest level of character" and one that others turned to for help. "Nobody ever said anything against him," Randolph remembered. Looking back on his childhood in a family devoted to serving their poor, defenseless neighbors, Randolph remembered not the poverty and despair but that "we had a beautiful life." The social gospel his father preached and practiced was the type of religion that Randolph most admired. He agreed with the AME tradition that emphasized uplifting social morale over saving souls.[32]

The social conscience of the AME tradition clashed, however, with the general trend of southern religion from the antebellum period known as "getting religion." According to two early studies of black southern religion, Randolph's postslavery generation grew more impatient with the "shouting" and frenzied religious ecstasies of religious worship. The analysis of southern black churches by the African American sociologist

E. Franklin Frazier explains that southern ministers had traditionally emphasized the "mystical aspects of religion" in their other-worldly sermons and that "getting religion" was a prerequisite to church membership. Hortense Powdermaker's anthropological study of southern culture also observes that "getting religion" remained a part of black revival meetings, although for many young black people this type of religion was losing favor. During Randolph's youth, the revival continued to be an important part of church services, but Randolph and his generation increasingly shunned the emotional religiosity of revival meetings. Indeed, Randolph never "got religion" nor received a religious calling, as his father did, but he did adopt his father's sense of social justice. Randolph linked his father's ministry to pride in his racial heritage, often mentioning both his parents' "unusual sense of racial pride." He defined the family's spirituality as "this interest in [the] progress of Negroes" and took great pride in being a minister's son, once remarking how others treated him with deference and respect. In fact, Randolph intimated a certain superiority, since his playmates "felt that we had some type of education they didn't have."[33]

Randolph remembered his father as deeply concerned about his sons' future, knowing that he could not help his sons' education beyond high school. Both James and Elizabeth Randolph stressed the importance of education, especially community service. Randolph reminisced that "she always wanted to think of us in terms of the higher educational activities, where people considered us as responsible parts of the community." Randolph attributed his interest in and lifelong yearning for books to his father's influence. James Randolph frequently visited old bookstores to look for books he believed his sons ought to read. His chief interest was biographies of the African Methodist bishops, but he also wanted his sons to know about black leaders in America, such as Frederick Douglass, as well as African leaders. Rev. Randolph insisted that his sons read every day. Indeed, neighbors recalled seeing both James and Asa reading every afternoon on the porch. One of Asa's playmates, Beaman Hearn, recalled that "those boys did practically nothing but read. Matter of fact, if Asa and I were burying a cat behind the house, he wanted to read a service."[34]

James and Asa first attended a public school in the Oakland district. But when they became dissatisfied with public education, the Randolphs moved the boys to Edward Waters College, an AME industrial school. In 1903, the boys moved once again, to the Cookman Institute, a high school run by the Methodist Church, North. A memorial to the northern white Methodist concern for educating black children in the South, Cookman was named for Rev. Alfred Cookman, a white Methodist, who donated the funds for its construction. Founded in 1872, Cookman was the first high school for blacks in Florida and part of Charles Beecher's reform of the public school system. After Reconstruction, because Florida's state government failed to provide schools for African Americans, the Baptists, Methodists, and African Methodists moved in to fill the educational vacuum.[35]

The young Randolph boys attended the new Cookman Institute rebuilt after the 1901 Jacksonville fire, which in the 1920s merged with Mary McLeod Bethune's school at Daytona Beach to form Bethune-Cookman College. Randolph considered it unusual that he attended Cookman as an African Methodist, but his presence there indicated how highly James and Elizabeth Randolph regarded Cookman and their desire to give their children the best education they could. Randolph appreciated his time at Cookman, calling it "quite an institution." Cookman's faculty consisted of southern black teachers and northern Methodist teacher-missionaries. James excelled in Latin and mathematics under Miss Lillie Whitney, while Asa shone in literature, public speaking, and drama under Miss Mary Neff. Active in the school choir and a member of the baseball team, on which he excelled as a catcher and first baseman, Asa Randolph felt for the first time that "I was important in my own right."[36]

Randolph's entrance into the Cookman Institute in 1903 coincided with two critical developments in African American history: the establishment of legal segregation in the South and the debate over national black leadership between Booker T. Washington and W. E. B. Du Bois. As he matured, Randolph's memories of the lessons on self-defense learned at home, coupled with his introduction to Du Bois's *Souls of Black Folk* while at the Cookman Institute, prepared him in his fight for social equality and justice. For Randolph's generation, the second after Emancipation, a formal education became even more important.[37]

Although his parents raised Randolph with expectations for a better future, these did not include the opportunity for a college education. In his high school valedictory speech, "The Man of the Hour," Randolph spoke of his generation's quest for a better future, even though he himself was uncertain about his own career. Advancement within the African Methodist Church required more formal education than Randolph could afford. James Randolph hoped one of his sons would go into the ministry, but both refused. When asked if his father wanted him to become a minister, Randolph replied that above all his father encouraged him to use his remarkable gifts to "create conditions that will help the people farther down" who did not have his opportunities. Rev. Randolph taught his son that "the problem of one Negro is the problem of all Negroes" and that as long as one black person remained "subjugated and brutalized by white people," all black people would be the objects of attacks and persecution. But he was also taught not to judge white people solely on the basis of skin color, since there were "white men and women who have as deep a sense of Christianity" as did African American people. As Randolph prepared himself for his future, he knew he would pursue "issues . . . that have social significance." Born into a generation with greater political options than his father's, Randolph eventually chose political activism as his lifework, stating, "So this became a part of my life, and I've always spent my time . . . in collective struggles."[38]

Without prospects for further education, Randolph worked at a variety of odd jobs and manual labor. During these four years, Jacksonville offered him opportunities to pursue his interest in the arts, especially acting and public speaking. But when Jim Crow policies narrowed his career options in the South, Randolph headed to New York, with dreams of becoming an actor. Randolph's journey to Harlem in 1911 predated the great exodus of African Americans out of the South before World War I. During this period, Jacksonville, New Orleans, Birmingham, Savannah, and Memphis served as urban concentration points for black migrants traveling north. Black migrants from the southern coastal states—Florida, South Carolina, Virginia, and Georgia—usually ended up in Philadelphia, New York, and Boston. Carter Woodson called this early migration the "Northern Migration of the Talented Tenth," placing the migrants into three groups: black politicians, educated blacks, and the intelligent laboring class. In several ways, Randolph fit Woodson's profile of those migrants motivated to leave the South for political and ideological reasons.[39]

Randolph's arrival in Manhattan coincided with an inner-city migration occurring within New York's black religious communities. The Reverend Dr. Adam Clayton Powell Sr. cited 1911 as the year when he realized Harlem would be the final destination of his Baptist Abyssinian church. In the late nineteenth century, the black churches followed the movement of their members to uptown Manhattan, and in the early twentieth century, the black churches moving into Harlem made large profits from selling their property in midtown Manhattan. In 1911, the largest black real-estate deal in the city's history up to that time was St. Philip's Protestant Episcopal Church's purchase of the entire row of buildings on West 135th Street, which it rented to black tenants. Two other distinguished churches, Bethel AME and Mother Zion (AMEZ), emulated St. Philip's move. As the "On to Harlem" movement reached other downtown churches, wealthy congregations built new churches and bought up local real estate, transforming Harlem into a black residential community. By the early 1920s, almost every established black church in Manhattan was situated in Harlem, occupying large beautiful buildings. Besides these geographical changes, black churches responded to modern, secular changes in their urban environments by expanding their activities and social programs to attract members. As in Jacksonville, black churches in Harlem supported youth organizations: the Mount Olivet Baptist Church sponsored the Baptist Young People's Union; St Mark's Methodist Church sponsored the Lyceum; Bethel AME Chapel supported the Allen Christian Endeavor League; and Salem Methodist Church sponsored the Epworth League.[40]

As a newcomer, Randolph gravitated toward Salem's Epworth League, which he found to be a good place to meet other young people "deeply concerned and interested in anything related to the stage." Through his contacts there, Randolph met many of the actors and actresses associated with the great Lafayette Theater, one of the cultural centers of the later Harlem Renaissance. As Randolph settled into Harlem life, he became increasingly involved in radical politics while at the same time struggling to find "the means of life, which couldn't come [from] the stage." For the first few years, Randolph continued to find the Epworth League, which sponsored a wide range of social activities, a good place from which to express his radical ideas based on his militant African Methodist heritage and his reading of Du Bois. Salem's well-known minister, Frederick Cullen, who later supported Randolph's political and labor activism, welcomed his participation in the league. At these meetings, Randolph met Theophilus Lewis, a close friend and later collaborator in his radical activities. Lewis described Randolph at this period as an "outstanding member" of the Epworth forums, who kept the meetings alive with controversial subjects, and even after the meetings, "he still had us arguing passionately through the streets, on our way home." Except for a few radical-minded individuals like Lewis, the majority of Epworth members disliked Randolph's political agenda because it distracted the group from its biblical discussions and also its theatrical and social concerns. Accordingly, Randolph reformulated his African Methodist sense of social justice into the prevailing social scientific language and looked for other role models to emulate. In addition, through Epworth, he learned he could attend New York City College at little cost, and so he enrolled in evening public-speaking courses, as well as history, political science, philosophy and economic courses.[41]

The single most important friend and ally Randolph made during his radical period had an Epworth connection: his future wife, Lucille Green. Impressed by Randolph's speaking abilities at one of the league's political gatherings—Ernest T. Welcome, whom Randolph recognized as a "power in the church"—approached him about his "Brotherhood of Labor," an employment agency for southern migrants looking for work in the homes of wealthy northerners. At the same time, Welcome approached Lucille Green, a widow from Washington, D.C., and a former schoolteacher, who operated one of Madame C. J. Walker's beauty salons. Because she was a successful businesswoman and well connected to Harlem's elite society, Welcome sought out Mrs. Green's assistance. He also introduced Randolph and Lucille Green, both of whom eventually left Welcome's "Brotherhood" because of his questionable business ethics. Their marriage, however, lasted for fifty years.[42]

Lucille Randolph belonged to the fashionable St. Philip's Protestant Episcopal Church, the wealthiest and most prominent black church in Harlem. After their marriage, as Randolph's reputation for radicalism grew, Lucille Randolph supported him financially and was not swayed by her husband's critics. Randolph recalled that Hutchens C. Bishop, the rector of St. Philip's, often dropped by her shop to warn her about associating with the young radical, but she remained undisturbed. In fact, she became a radical herself and was "nominated on the Socialist ticket for a member of the New York legislature." Randolph proudly recalled that Eugene V. Debs himself came to Harlem to speak on her behalf during the election, amazed that a black woman could represent the Socialist Party.[43]

Randolph's first ten years in Harlem as a radical journalist is when he acquired his reputation as an atheist and severe critic of all institutional religion, a label that persists to this day. The view that Randolph entirely abandoned his attachment to the black religious tradition of his youth because of his "conversion" to socialism during this period does not take into account Randolph's entire career. Although these years were critical to Randolph's religious development, they were only one phase in a long, productive life. The rise of industrialism by the late nineteenth century resulted in the surge of popular support for the radical Socialist Party in America (SPA), most notably in the 1912 presidential election. Randolph's "conversion" to socialism, primarily as a political and economic ideology, was not in opposition to his previous religious training but complementary to the traditional religious reformism of African Methodism. Although socialism appealed to Randolph as a solution to the problem of a rapidly expanding black labor force in the industrial North, it also appealed, for other reasons, to a variety of American citizens, including social democrats in Wisconsin, radical syndicalists in the West, tenant farmers in Oklahoma, and Jewish immigrants on Manhattan's Lower East Side. In the United States, adherents to socialism represented a variety of religious viewpoints, from believing Christian socialists to orthodox Marxists, who eschewed religion altogether.[44]

The regional diversity of American socialism was, to a great extent, bridged by the leadership of Eugene V. Debs, the national figurehead for the Socialist Party. Randolph joined the Socialist Party in the "era of Debs," who attracted thousands of socialist and working-class New Yorkers when he spoke in New York's Rutgers Square. Debs, like Randolph, has been branded as an enemy of all religion and morality because of his sharp attacks on church institutions and the clergy. This outdated view of Debs has been shifting, however, as recent scholarship has rightfully placed him in a revised, religious, context. By tracing the "spiritual communion" between Debs and other socialist Christians of this period, scholars have demonstrated that Debs's character and behavior can be "framed in a Christian idiom . . . from the beginning of his radical career."[45]

By admitting the diversity of the Christian presence within American socialism, it becomes clearer why socialism attracted such a wide cross section of the American public. Debs's ability to speak "the language of commitment and duty" appealed to many of his contemporaries, who perceived him as a prophet and saint. Randolph himself viewed Debs from his own religious perspective, referring to him as "a spiritual type of revolutionist . . . a great spiritual character." At the time of Debs's death, Randolph commented that the "Grand Old Man's" passing robbed the world of an outstanding figure "whose life and deeds were much akin to that of the Carpenter of Nazareth." Randolph considered Debs a close personal friend from the day they met outside the offices of the *Jewish Daily Forward*, a center of New York socialist activity. Although Randolph thought that Debs lacked the intellect for revolutionary theory, he viewed him as "just like the Bible preacher in the South" who had the ability to move ordinary people to understand their exploited social condition and take action against great powers of wealth. In that sense, Randolph maintained, he was "every bit as prominent as any of the great revolutionists of Europe at that time." Randolph admired Debs's selfless disinterest in amassing a personal fortune, as well as his spiritual strength, the same qualities he had valued in his father.[46]

In June 1918, Eugene Debs addressed twelve hundred members of the Ohio Socialist Party in Canton, delivering his famous antiwar speech that eventually landed him in prison for violating the Espionage Act. Six weeks later, Randolph and his partner, Chandler Owen, followed him to Ohio, and in Cleveland, they also spoke out against the war. Randolph believed that the "same government agents who locked [Debs] up and put him in prison locked us up and put us in prison," although Randolph's and Owen's stay in prison for two days was considerably shorter than Debs's. Randolph's recognition of Debs's spiritual strength and his commitment to "the principle of equality among human beings, regardless of race, color, religion," was an important influence in Randolph's own adherence to socialism during his early years in New York.[47]

In the 1930s, Randolph had a similar, even closer, friendship with Norman Thomas, the next generation's leader of the Socialist Party. As Manning Marable, a noted authority on Randolph's socialism, wrote, "Like his friend Norman Thomas, Randolph's socialism was never rooted in an atheistic outlook." Marable's analysis of Randolph's socialism, which he described as "an uneven combination of traditional religious reformism, economic determinism, fervent internationalism, and Karl Marx," captures the complexity of his religiosity, especially its relationship to his political beliefs. Marable explained that Randolph "rejected the orthodoxy of the cloth, but not the meaning of black spirituality in his politics." Marable's scholarship remains the clearest statement of Randolph's unique blend of socialism and religious reformism, illustrating his thesis that "there is much greater continuity of political ideology and practice from the younger to the older Randolph than is usually thought."[48]

Hubert Henry Harrison, known as the "father of Harlem radicalism," was another critical influence on Randolph's socialism. Randolph considered Harrison in the "vanguard" of Harlem's black socialists and "far more advanced" than his own group. As black socialists, Harrison and Randolph never joined forces politically, but their common experiences in adapting to Harlem's social and political life reveal how black churches and urban religious communities enabled these young radicals to assimilate into their new environment. Randolph's disapproval of the Epworth League's political quietism paralleled Harrison's own experience. By 1911, Harrison, an immigrant from the Virgin Islands, was already a well-known Harlem soapbox orator, addressing audiences all over New York City as a representative of the largest local branch of the Socialist Party, Local New York. As a newcomer to the city, Harrison's social and political connections began in two of Harlem's well-established religious societies: St. Benedict's (Roman Catholic) and St. Mark's Lyceum (Methodist).[49]

Besides making contact with the noted progressive black intellectuals of the day, such as journalist John Edward Bruce and scholar Arthur Schomberg, Harrison received valuable educational assistance from St. Benedict's Father Thomas M. O'Keefe, who helped him overcome a serious speech impediment to become a formidable speaker. Randolph particularly remembered Harrison as a "brilliant chap and quite articulate." Whereas St. Benedict's provided the base for his future work as a lecturer and debater, St. Mark's Lyceum, under the direction of the political activist Rev. William Henry Brooks, a founding member of the NAACP, prepared Harrison for his later activism in radical politics.[50]

Although nurtured in church lyceums, Harrison and Randolph eventually left them to pursue their radical politics. In 1908, Harrison joined the Sunrise Club, a freethought and interracial forum that invited leading black intellectuals to regularly scheduled dinners at midtown Manhattan hotels. Freethought, with a strong base in New York, circulated a weekly newspaper called the *Truth Seeker*, to which Harrison contributed articles. As radicalism waned in the 1920s, Randolph said that Harrison "developed some kind of church," which was a short-lived venture but nonetheless an indication of the connections between black socialist and black religious communities in the early twentieth century. But in the heyday of radicalism and the Harlem of 1917, Harrison, Randolph, and Owen, as black socialists, eagerly responded to the invitations by "some of the churches to come and speak at their literary societies," where they found themselves involved in a "challenging endeavor, a creative struggle, entirely new to black people."[51]

Randolph's migration to the North before World War I, just as Harlem was developing into a black community, coincided with an even larger movement of Eastern Europeans flooding into New York through Ellis Island, drawn by the advantages of the United States' industrial economy. Living at the intellectual center of Jewish socialism, especially as a student at City College, Randolph read Marxist and socialist literature under the guidance of influential Jewish professors such as J. Salwyn Schapiro and Morris R. Cohen. Randolph likened his introduction to Marx as "running into an idea which gives your outlook on life." He described *Das Kapital* as an "analysis of all the revolutions of the world," which provided a basis for "social change." According to Randolph, no group was in more need of social change than American blacks. Randolph read Marx critically "with the recognition . . . that nothing that comes out of a human being [was] absolutely perfect." Randolph's activism on behalf of the Socialist Party during these years reflected the influence of a non-Christian Marxist community when he was "preaching atheism" as a soapbox orator in the streets of New York.[52]

What Randolph meant by the term *atheism* remains unclear. In the available sources, Randolph never mentions a disbelief or doubt in God or a Supreme Being. Rather, the words and actions of his later career suggest the opposite. By the late 1920s, Randolph flatly denied he was an atheist when he defended himself against those who criticized his union organization of Pullman porters. During the years just before and after World War I, Randolph apparently absorbed the humanistic values of his Jewish mentors, which he filtered through his African Methodism. In his writings on African Methodism, Randolph himself connected these two worldviews with the term *Christian humanism*, and he did not see any contradiction in combining them.[53]

Throughout his life, Randolph remained committed to both humanist and African Methodist beliefs. In 1973, when he signed the *Humanist Manifesto II*, he also belonged to an African Methodist church. Like many other black religious humanists, Randolph did not find it necessary to question God's existence but instead demanded that the status of black persons be raised to that of white persons. Closely allied to Randolph's Christian humanist inclinations was his adherence to a personalist philosophy. Personalism, a form of idealism, holds that the universe is a society of interacting selves or persons, united by the will of God, the creator and sustainer of all things. As a philosophy, especially in its theistic form, personalism provides an individual-social conception of reality, persons, and God, emphasizing human dignity and self-worth. Although African American personalism is usually identified with prominent religious thinkers such as Martin Luther King Jr. and the black theologian J.

Oldest-known photograph of A. Philip Randolph. It was taken in 1911 or 1912, the year after he moved to Harlem and started attending classes at City College, when he became a part of Harlem's radical scene and a member of the Socialist Party. Photographed by K. C. Harrison. Reproduced from the Collections of the Library of Congress.

Deotis Roberts, A. Philip Randolph demonstrated in his speeches and writings that he was a committed personalist, which constituted an important aspect of his religious worldview. During the ten years of Randolph's most radical activism, his fusion of humanism, African Methodism, and personalism became an important development in his religious nature.[54]

Besides attending classes at City College, Randolph frequently visited the offices of the *Jewish Daily Forward*. Edited by Abraham Cahan, the *Daily Forward* was an influential Yiddish newspaper in the Jewish community and a mouthpiece for socialist ideology. Randolph called the *Daily Forward* the "heart of the Jewish radicals," and there he found fellow radicals willing to finance his own magazine, the *Messenger*. Describing these days, Randolph underscored the shock to his Jewish associates "to find that Negroes had any concept whatever of Socialism." With their encouragement, Randolph addressed large white audiences on the benefits of socialism.[55]

Another center for New York's young radicals was Cooper Union, the birthplace of the NAACP. Randolph organized socialist activities and a series of lectures at both City College and Cooper Union while at the same time he was forming his own political movement, the Independent Political Council. When Morris Hillquit, a leading socialist in New York, ran for mayor of New York City in 1917, Randolph and his friend Chandler Owen were appointed to run Hillquit's campaign in Harlem, where the black community usually voted Republican. Although Hillquit lost the election, he had the largest vote a Socialist candidate had ever received, including 25 percent of the Harlem vote. In this cosmopolitan and non-Christian community, Randolph felt a part of the larger revolutionary struggle also taking place in France, England, and Germany. Throughout his life, Randolph regarded socialism as the economic answer to problems between management and labor, and the trade union as the tool with which the working class obtained decision-making power within the means of production. While his Jewish comrades welcomed his participation as an American black, Randolph perceived his role as primarily a messenger of a philosophy explaining the problems and providing the solutions to the "struggle of the black people."[56]

Lucille Randolph introduced her husband to Chandler Owen, who, next to herself, became Randolph's closest confidant during this period. Randolph's partnership with Owen was the first of several that Randolph developed during his long career. Owen's aggressive nature and caustic wit contrasted sharply with Randolph's reserved personality. Randolph's reminiscences about their different styles and approaches to situations sheds light on his own radical religiosity. According to Randolph, Owen "was much more of the atheist turn of mind . . . than anybody else in the group," the one who was "anti-church and anti-religion." Despite these differences, Randolph and Owen worked well together as journalists.

Owen introduced Randolph to Lester Ward's writings on sociology and participated in Randolph's weekly political meetings and other Socialist Party activities. With Owen's help, Randolph expanded his political contacts at the Epworth League into the radical group that formed the *Messenger*'s staff: first Chandler Owen and Theophilus Lewis and then later George Schuyler, Joel A. Rogers, William Colson, and W. A. Domingo. But no one was closer than Chandler Owen:

> We went everywhere together. . . . he and I suffered together, and we many times didn't have much to eat, but we were not too bothered about that. . . . We knew that if we could get to the people, that we could develop their interest in this movement. It was what you might call . . . a revolutionary evangelism that had come into the life of the Negro.[57]

As "revolutionary evangelists," Randolph and Owen believed that as victims of slavery, blacks were "spiritually prepared" to receive socialism and that the experience of the black man in America was a fertile field for socialism. As Randolph recalled, "We left the tables and rooms in which we carried on our discussion . . . and went to the streets of Harlem." Randolph and Owen became a constant presence on the Harlem streets, preaching their modern social economic theories and organizing their Independent Political Council.[58]

The first *Messenger* appeared in November 1917, the year the United States entered World War I. The group of radicals following Randolph and Owen consisted of Americans and West Indians from the Caribbean. The fact that many in the radical press were West Indians prompted Kelly Miller, dean of Howard University, to characterize a "Negro radical as an over-educated West Indian without a job." Others in the group included Rev. George Frazier Miller, William H. Ferris, William Bridges, Richard B. Moore, Cyril Briggs, and Claude McKay. As part of the radical community "in the vanguard," Randolph described his *Messenger* group as "various leaders of radicalism, Communism, Socialism, [and] unionism" who wanted to express the ideas of a "new generation" and to awaken American blacks to a wider worldview than the general outlook "circumscribed within a narrow area of Negro life." In American politics, Randolph believed, no group at that time was "more left" than they were, for even the Industrial Workers of the World came to them to get their message out to the black community. Randolph attributed the small size of the *Messenger*'s staff to the "scarcity of writers of Socialist philosophy." In addition, the editors did not want to "adulterate" their philosophy by limiting it to racial issues alone, for as young intellectuals they wanted the magazine to reach a broader audience regarding the inequities created by a capitalistic society. Randolph admitted that "there was no particular group among black people" that fully accepted them. Whether it was W. E. B. Du Bois, Kelly Miller of Howard University, or influential leaders of the black churches, the *Messenger* attacked anyone it considered "ignorant of the economic problems of black people." As the magazine's influence grew, some black leaders, including "churchmen," eventually cultivated a friendship with the magazine and its staff because they admired the magazine's message.[59]

Owen became the first supervisor of the magazine because of his organizational skills and meticulous attention to detail. As other editors joined the group, they met to decide on the magazine's layout and to assign articles to the appropriate writers. Randolph wrote that Owen "stood out as the person who could organize and develop a powerful, aggressive attack on a given situation" and was unafraid to take on the Negro Church. Later, George Schuyler joined Owen, often using his sarcastic wit to deflate the hypocrisy of black and white religious communities. W. A. Domingo admired "Chandler's ruthless exposure of things" and the magazine's socialist philosophy. Because he was "part of the Garvey movement and . . . one of the editors of the *Negro World*," Domingo eventually left the *Messenger* staff when the magazine attacked Garvey.[60]

Randolph had a closer relationship with J. A. Rogers and Theophilus Lewis, neither of whom he perceived as strongly antichurch. Randolph considered Rogers, from the West Indies, as the historian of the group, whose contributions to the *Messenger* reflected an international perspective "not only in America but in Africa and everywhere else in the world." A frequent traveler, Rogers addressed the larger historical and international problems that people of color faced throughout the world. Randolph associated Lewis, his old friend from the Epworth League, with the group of "Catholics who were dedicated to the fight for Negro rights." Eventually Lewis converted to Catholicism and, according to Randolph, joined the "propaganda side of the Catholic Church" that fought for black rights. Lewis became a "force and a factor in this forum that the Catholics were conducting, and they had great respect and love for him." Through Lewis, Randolph met John LaFarge, a "clerical poet" who joined Randolph in his civil rights activism of the 1940s.[61]

Randolph described his own position in this group of black socialists as somewhere in the middle. He maintained friendly relations with all of them by never taking a "position about a question from a personal point of view." Sometimes, however, this upset Owen, for Randolph commented that "Chandler didn't always feel that my approach was vigorous enough." Nevertheless, Randolph participated in any movement "in which you had the opportunity of expressing your honest views about the problem of the Negro," especially based on trade unionist and socialist principles. Randolph recognized how his "whole life, so far as seeking to help solve the problem of black people stemmed from the *Messenger* magazine."[62]

Randolph's recollections of a childhood steeped in African Methodist values reveal that a religious worldview remained part of his character throughout his life. Combining a socially conscious African Methodism with the failed promise of Reconstruction, A. Philip Randolph brought a crusading zeal to Harlem as part of the great migration of African Americans from the South before World War I. Randolph's migration from Jacksonville to Harlem should not, therefore, be viewed as a radical break from or abandonment of his religious upbringing in African Methodism. Similarly, Randolph's reminiscences of his radical associations in his early Harlem years display a continuity with his religious heritage as he adapted to his life in New York. His Christian humanism evolved as he sought more effective ways to challenge the Jim Crow system emerging in the South. Arriving in Harlem during one of its most radical periods, the ambitious young Randolph saw Marxist socialist philosophy from the lens of his own cultural experience in the urban South, which gave him a new "outlook" on how to fight for the political, social, and economic rights of African Americans. Inheriting the "soul of a fighting revolutionist," Randolph fused his father's black religious radicalism with a socialist philosophy during his first ten years in Harlem, and in the words of Manning Marable, he "deliberately used religious principles of brotherhood and humanism in organizing black workers" throughout a long career of social activism.[63]

2

The *Messenger*
A Forum for Liberal Religion

Between 1935 and 1939, the Federal Writers Project, an extension of the New Deal's Works Project Administration (WPA), employed thousands of American writers to produce guidebooks describing the distinctive folkways and histories of rural and urban regions in the United States. The New York Project hired several talented black writers, including Richard Wright, Claude McKay, Ralph Ellison, Henry Lee Moon, Ellen Tarry, and Roi Ottley. Roi Ottley's project, under the working title of "Harlem—The Negroes of New York (An Informal Social History)," contained a chapter on postwar Harlem between 1918 and 1925 when, as Ottley wrote, "Harlem was being excited by the Back-to-Africa propaganda of Marcus Garvey after the [first world] war." He also reported that a "strong radical press, concentrating on injustices to the black man, sprang up in Harlem." At a time when even the more conservative black periodicals "spoke more boldly," the names of the new radical publications captured the "public temper" of anger and unrest in Harlem's black community: "the *Challenge*, the *Crusader*, the *Emancipator*, the *Messenger*, the *Voice* and the *Negro World*." Ottley observed that the "vitriolic utterances" of the black radical press drew the notice of Attorney General A. Mitchell Palmer and the Department of Justice, which, in their attempt to suppress it, wrote a report entitled "The Radicalism and Sedition among the Negroes as Reflected in Their Publications." In New York State, the Lusk Committee submitted its own forty-four-page investigative report on "Negro radicalism," which declared that Randolph and Owen's *Messenger* magazine was "by far the most dangerous of all the Negro publications." Ottley focused on the *Messenger* magazine as the "most widely circulated" of all the radical publications during this period, and many of the black radicals he named were associated with Randolph and Owen's group of black socialists.[1]

Every issue of the early *Messenger*s demanded a "new Negro leader-ship," since the "old crowd Negroes" remained ignorant of modern so-cial scientific thought, but after 1922 "the *Messenger* had a change of heart on social questions." According to Ottley, the magazine's shift away from radicalism "dovetailed with the split in the radical ranks, when the socialists divided into right and left, the left becoming the Communist Party." From that time on, Ottley wrote, "the philosophy of the 'New Negro' was then presented to Negro America, which, according to Ran-dolph's explanation, was 'A Formula of Practical Righteous Idealism.'" By 1924, little was written on the radical movement, the Socialist Party, or the struggles of the working class, and by 1928, the *Messenger* had "passed quietly into oblivion."[2]

Studies of Randolph and Owen's magazine supports Ottley's early ob-servations that the *Messenger* had distinct periods in its eleven-year exis-tence: a radical period from November 1917 to November 1921, a cul-tural period during the Harlem Renaissance from December 1921 to June 1925, and a labor period from July 1925 to 1928, when the magazine be-came the official organ of Randolph's new trade union, the Brotherhood of Sleeping Car Porters (BSCP). If the *Messenger*, founded by a group of "religious skeptics"—to use Randolph's own words—shifted away from its original radical socialist message, how did this change affect the mag-azine's position on religion and religious institutions? Was the magazine atheistic and antireligious in tone, as is usually assumed? How did the change in the magazine's political position affect its position on religion? By tracing how religion was treated in each phase of the *Messenger*'s evo-lution, this chapter shows that the magazine actually was a forum for var-ious liberal and unorthodox Christian viewpoints. Indeed, when the mag-azine became the voice for the BSCP, Randolph openly denied he was an atheist, for to be labeled an atheist in a predominantly religious culture would have automatically shut him out of the political debate. By under-standing the *Messenger*'s stance on religion, Randolph's own personal views on religion also come into sharper focus, for he believed that in a democracy, everything, even religion, was open to debate. His insistence that all religious perspectives had merit was the first step in the develop-ment of a progressive civil rights agenda for the Negro Church. The *Mes-senger* was more than a forum for disbelievers and skeptics; it demanded respect for all religion on the left and was a way for Randolph to advo-cate his "practical righteous idealism."[3]

The Messenger's *Radical Years, 1917–1921*

With their reforming zeal, the *Messenger* editors fought to bring their readers into the twentieth century by explaining the modern views of the political, economic, and social events of the day. As the *Messenger*'s mission statement makes clear, the remedy for society's problems was the radical shift from prayer to scientific education: "Our aim is to appeal to reason, to lift our pens above the cringing demagogy of the times." Maintaining that "prayer is not one of our remedies," the editors advocated scientific education as the way to eradicate racial prejudice in America. To this end, they attacked everything "narrow and medieval in religion" that justified the status quo in American race relations.[4]

Especially objectionable to Randolph and Owen was the uninformed way that the "Negro press, pulpit and school," fearful of offending white capitalists, prosecuted "all liberal and democratic opinions." They argued that the monetary contributions from white capitalists to black churches, schools, and charities were the reason that the black community remained ignorant and obligated to whites and rejected radical measures to improve social and economic conditions. Randolph and Owen ridiculed one "Negro minister of reputed light and leading in the city of Savannah" who reflected the general ignorance and "intellectual pabulum served up to Negroes on problems of world moment." According to the editors, the minister preached that "Bolshevism was begotten in Germany . . . from a man named Bolsheviki, an insurrectionist or rioter, who raised an army to overthrow the recognized government of Russia" and concluded that all radicalism was analogous to anarchy, lawlessness, and disorder. From the outset, the *Messenger*'s purpose was to educate the ignorant black masses, starting with the preachers, as one early news item revealed:

> A very interesting report was made on the Negro preachers' stand on Unionism, which showed a lamentable incapacity on the part of Negro Apostles of Christ to appreciate the most elementary phases of the question, and their disinclination to look kindly upon the working class of the Negro receiving more wages. Let our so-called ministers of human suffering take note. Poverty is the most appalling kind of suffering. Low wages produce poverty. The Union is the only remedy for low wages.[5]

As the editor, Randolph's radical agenda focused on his two interests: trade unionism and socialism. In this period, critics of radicalism often lumped trade unionism and socialism with agnosticism, as Randolph and Owen often pointed out: "There is much opposition nowadays to the very word—radicalism. The radicals are hunted, outlawed and jailed for propagating, as it were 'dangerous thoughts.' Whoever seeks to find out the root-cause of social diseases is a radical. Hence socialism and industrial unionism and agnosticism are radical."[6]

Still, the *Messenger* editors embraced agnosticism, along with unionism and socialism, as a legitimate approach to fighting injustice. The boldest statement of the *Messenger*'s agnosticism was the *Messenger*'s credo, published in a special supplement entitled "The Negro and the New Social Order: A Reconstruction Program, Prepared by Chandler Owen and A. Philip Randolph." The *Messenger*'s "Reconstruction Program of the American Negro" was a nine-page economic, political, and social program for the "new Negro" in light of postwar conditions. The credo, written in large type covering a full page, advocated iconoclasm, anarchism, and agnosticism as means of critiquing the traditions, creeds, and customs that crossed the "path of the light of Liberty" and obstructed the "reign of Right." In other words, it was not agnosticism for the sake of agnosticism but an attack on hypocritical religious customs that sanctioned Jim Crow in America.

Credo

I am an Iconoclast.
I break the limbs of idols
And smash the traditions of men.

I am an Anarchist.
I believe in war and destruction,—
Not in the killing of men, but
The killing of creed and custom.

I am an Agnostic.
I accept nothing without questioning.
It is my inherent right and duty
To ask the reason why.

To accept without a reason
Is to debase one's humanity

And destroy the fundamental process
In the ascertainment of Truth.

I believe in Justice and Freedom.
To me, Liberty is priestly and kingly.
Freedom is my Bride, Liberty my Angel of Light,
Justice my God.

I am opposed to all laws of state
Or country, all creeds of church and social orders,
All conventionalities of society and system
which cross the path of the light of Liberty
Or obstruct the reign of Right.[7]

The *Messenger* editors adopted the credo's author, Walter Everette Hawkins, as the *Messenger*'s "poet." Hawkins published several poems in Randolph and Owen's magazine that were often religious in tone and content. Like the credo, Hawkins's poetry criticized traditional and orthodox religion, which preferred liturgical practices and doctrinal formulas to social justice. Hawkins's poetry was a revolt against all that was hypocritical in religious institutions and complemented the *Messenger*'s editorial policy of attacking everything "narrow and medieval in religion." For example, Hawkins's poem "Too Much Religion" protested black traditional ideas of religion and God while opposing the white man's God. In another poem, "Here or Hereafter," Hawkins denounced the "other-worldliness" emphasized in contemporary black religion, a complaint voiced by other black intellectuals of this time. Moreover, Hawkins's poetry inferred that the true God was a god of social justice and that "good" religion had to improve the quality of human life in the here and now. Like the Old Testament prophets Amos and Micah, Hawkins was concerned with the ethical and social welfare of man here on earth. His poetry thus reveals a yearning for true religion rather than no religion at all.

Too Much Religion

There is too much time for doctrine;
Too much talk of church and creeds;
Far too little time for duty,
And to heal some heart that bleeds.

Too much Sunday Church religion,
Too many stale and bookish prayers;
Too many souls are getting ragged,
Watching what their neighbor wears.

There is too much talk of heaven,
Too much talk of golden streets,
When one can't be sympathetic,
When a needy neighbor meets;
Too much talk about the riches
You expect to get "up there,"
When one will not do his duty
As a decent Christian here.

And you needn't think the angels
Have no other work to do,
But to stitch on fancy garments
To be packed away for you;
For some people live so crooked
Those robes may refuse to fit;
Let us have less talk of heaven
And do right a little bit.

Here and Hereafter
Now you preach a lot of Heaven,
And you talk a lot of Hell,
But the future never troubles me—
'Tis plain as tongue can tell;
And it's mighty poor religion
That won't keep a man from fear;
For the next place must be Heaven,
Since 'tis Hell I'm having here.[8]

Other poetry from the *Messenger* revealed the magazine's war on traditional religion, and one poem by Claude McKay catches the overall tone of religious despair felt by Randolph and other African Americans at this time, when the dominant Christian community remained unresponsive to their suffering:

J'Accuse

The world in silence nods, but my heart weeps:
See, welling to its lidless blear eyes, pour
Forth heavily black drops of burning gore;
Each drop rolls on the earth's hard face, then leaps
To heaven and fronts the idle guard that keeps
His useless watch before the august door.
My blood-tears, wrung in pain from my heart's core,
Accuse dumb heaven and curse a world that sleeps:
For yesterday I saw my flesh and blood
Dragged forth by pale-faced demons from his bed
Lashed, bruised and bleeding, to a piece of wood,
Oil poured in torrents on his sinless head.
The fierce flames drove me back from where I stood;
There is no God, Earth sleeps, my heart is dead.[9]

The circulation of the *Messenger* depended on other freethought and radical communities in the United States, most notably in Seattle. La Verne F. Wheeler, the editor of a Seattle freethought magazine called the *Crucible*, wrote to the *Messenger* editors praising them for producing a "journal that any race should be proud of." Calling it "discriminative, justly critical, far seeing and tolerant," Wheeler could not "find one paragraph in the *Messenger* that [struck] a false note." Wheeler and his business manager, C. D. Raymer, offered to distribute Randolph and Owen's publication on the West Coast. At the same time, Wheeler sent a bundle of *Crucible* magazines for distribution in New York, and both parties exchanged mailing lists and ads. C. L. Dellums, a Pullman porter, recalled buying the *Messenger* in Seattle, since he couldn't "buy it any other place on the coast." Later Dellums learned that the *Messenger* had a circulation of five thousand people in Seattle, an amazing fact, since there were not "a thousand Negroes in Seattle including women and children." That is, the *Messenger* was reaching a broader liberal audience, and Dellums recalled that "it had the rating as being the number one liberal and socialist magazine in the nation for several years."[10]

The *Messenger* advertised the *Crucible* as a "Red Hot Agnostic Paper" or the "hottest paper published" which combated all religious dogma. Because the *Crucible* was connected to Raymer's Old Book Store in Seattle, these ads featured the work of Annie Besant. In addition, Wheeler, using the pseudonym Bertuccio Dantino, contributed several poems and short stories to the *Messenger*, all on controversial topics of interest to radicals: "Call off Your Dogs of War," "Conscientious Objectors," and "Race Hatred Shall Die." In a two-part fictional piece entitled "A Bronzed God," a black socialist protagonist stirs up trouble in the "lumber and turpentine camps." Written as an allegory, its socialist message groups black Christian ministers with all the "priests [who] have stupefied our people with their lies and helped to keep them bound in the chains of servitude . . . all for commercial reasons." The story's second installment censures black "priests" who aim "to keep the Negro satisfied with his lot under intolerable conditions, no matter how degrading those conditions may be." By aligning with Wheeler's anticlerical writings, which reflected his European socialist perspective, the *Messenger*'s antireligious rhetoric often inaccurately portrayed the African American religious experience.[11]

During the *Messenger*'s radical period, the magazine often alluded to well-known freethinkers and atheists such as Thomas Paine and Robert Ingersoll. In fact, Randolph compared his partner, Chandler Owen, with Ingersoll, saying, "Chandler was more anti-church than I was[,] . . . like Ingersoll." Although according to Randolph, Owen "considered Ingersoll as being backward, so far as economic deliverance of the masses was concerned," Ingersoll's modernist ideas were still worth publishing. Other evidence of the *Messenger*'s place in the larger freethought community, especially in its protest against racial discrimination, was Lovett Fort-Whiteman's brief stint in 1918 as the *Messenger*'s dramatic editor. Randolph and Owen met Fort-Whiteman, an aspiring actor and writer, when he joined the Harlem socialists associated with Hubert Harrison. Fort-Whiteman's review of Tom Brown's irreverent play *The Eternal Magdaline* praises it for "uncover[ing] the snobbery, the hypocrisy, the selfishness of the prevailing Church, the bigotry of our moral precepts, and the lie upon which our social order is supported." Fort-Whiteman's political experience with the Industrial Workers of the World and the Harlem socialists trained him as a writer and speaker, talents he later used when he joined the Communist Party.[12]

Like other periodicals of freethought communities, the *Messenger* promoted the progressive ideas on religion found in the new social sciences. As a forum for "scientific education" rather than prayer, Randolph and Owen suggested books for reading by well-known radical and social scientific authors. According to the editors, the following books were "of high social value": Jack London's *The Iron Heel*, Bertrand Russell's *Problem of Philosophy*, Scott Nearing's *Wages in the United States*, Thorstein Veblen's *Theory of the Leisure Class*, Walter Weyl's *The New Democracy*, and H. G. Wells's *New Worlds for Old*. They also added two books on religion: Upton Sinclair's *The Profits of Religion* and Simon N. Patten's *The Social Basis of Religion*. Both these books supported the *Messenger*'s general complaint against the Christian community and the Negro Church that sanctioned the Jim Crow system.[13]

Upton Sinclair's attack on supernaturalism was related to his growing disillusionment with the traditional church, which in turn paralleled Randolph and Owen's own disappointment with black churches. Simon Patten's sociological interpretation of religion belonged to an earlier generation of social scientists, socialists, Populists, and progressives, such as Edward Bellamy, Henry George, Richard Ely, Lester Ward, and Herbert Croly. *The Social Basis of Religion*, which Patten wrote before the war, showed late-nineteenth-century social science as still in harmony with the basic tenets of Protestantism. Even so, it still complemented the *Messenger*'s editorial policy that religious institutions were like any other political and social institution, which had to be held accountable for unsound and unjust policies that hurt society.[14]

Randolph and Owen's associate Wilfred A. Domingo contributed regularly to the early *Messenger* while at the same time producing his own radical paper, called the *Emancipator*, and serving as editor of Marcus Garvey's *Negro World*. Domingo, who worked on the periphery of the Communist Party but never joined it, associated with the Harlem radicals who became the first black communists: Otto Huiswoud, Grace Campbell, Hubert Harrison, Claude McKay, and Cyril Briggs. In the summer of 1919, when the socialist left realigned with the communists, Domingo urged *Messenger* readers to embrace socialism, arguing that Christianity as taught by Christ centuries ago resonated with twentieth-century socialism.[15] In matters of religion, Domingo wrote, blacks responded "logically and naturally" to the "religion of Christ, the lowly Nazarene," to bring "definite assurance of surcease from earthly pains and the hope of celestial readjustment of mundane equalities." Domingo challenged Christianity's "present day emphasis upon an after-life enjoyment of the good things denied them on earth," which revealed a general dissatisfaction with social conditions in America and a "susceptibility to socialism, which intends to do for human beings what Christianity promises to do for them in less material regions."[16]

Domingo reasoned that ignorant and unscrupulous black leaders supported oppressive institutions, and as blacks learned to think independently, "without the aid of preacher, politician and press," they would understand the value of socialism. While accusing black preachers and churches of purposely misleading blacks about socialism, Domingo used the *Messenger* as a forum to educate blacks on true Christian socialism, as the following statement indicates:

> Socialism as an economic doctrine is merely the pure Christianity preached by Jesus, and practiced by the early Christians adapted to the more complex conditions of modern life. It makes no distinction as to race, nationality or creed, but like Jesus it says "Come unto me all ye who are weary and heavy laden and I will give you rest." It is to procure that rest that millions of oppressed peoples are flocking to the scarlet banner of international socialism.[17]

In early *Messenger* magazines, Randolph never argued from a Christian socialist perspective. Instead, when he asked why Negroes should be socialists," he urged them to join the Socialist Party for pragmatic political and economic reasons. When well-known black ministers like Reverdy Ransom and George Frazier Miller ran on independent or Socialist Party tickets in local elections, Randolph endorsed them without emphasizing their religious profession. During this period, Randolph also supported Christian-based trade unions, especially one known as the Brotherhood Workers. The *Messenger* advertised and "heartily endorsed" the National Brotherhood Association's convention held in Washington, D.C., on September 8, 1919. Randolph judged this group as being made up of mature "people of some experience," who based their union on "the religious concept of brotherhood" and Christianity: "Of course we wouldn't argue with them about that because . . . there's . . . some truth to it." But at the same time, Randolph, Owen, and other *Messenger* contributors demanded the right to state publicly that the Christian community remained part of the problem. As Randolph explained, "We wanted to talk with them about the basis of the exploitation and oppression of the Christian community."[18]

The *Messenger*'s policy against all that was narrow and medieval in religion continued in 1918 and 1919, the high point of radicalism in America. During this period, the *Messenger*'s editors, like Young Turks, attacked the Negro Church as a "citadel of superstition." In January 1918,

Randolph and Owen declared war on "old crowd Negroes." Owen wrote, "Negro leaders have failed. It is hard to admit. Race-pride revolts against it. But the remedy lies in recognizing the condition and setting out to remedy it." He denounced several significant political and intellectual black leaders as "a discredit to Negroes and the laughing stock among whites." For the next eighteen months, Owen harangued those who "preached a gospel of satisfaction and content." The *Messenger*'s postwar reconstruction program on the "things essential for the thoroughgoing improvement of the Negro's status after the war" included a better school system, an enlightened press, wholesome recreation places, new radical leadership, revolt against the present "Negro leaders with their white friends," and a revolutionary church as a "forum for the dissemination of useful knowledge." Owen complained that the "revolution in the Negro Church, while essential and sure to come," was too slow in coming. Ignorant black ministers were delaying the transformation of a racist America, despite Owen's insistence that the "revolution must proceed from the masses in the church."[19]

Corruption was another charge that Randolph and Owen leveled at black ministers, who could be bought for a "very small pecuniary purchase." Several references to a Mitchell slush fund scandal appeared in the *Messenger*. Apparently, several ministers in New York were caught taking bribes during a local New York election in 1917, leading the editors to conclude that "the discovery of the Negro Baptist ministers of New York tied up in the Mitchell slush fund has greatly confirmed the suspicions which the young colored men and women had in the growing worthlessness of the Negro pulpit." The editors complained that the disgraceful Mitchell slush fund stained the character of every Negro minister in New York, with the exception of one or two. Over the next several years, the *Messenger* cited this incident as evidence against black preachers. The editors prided themselves on the fact that they steered clear of the Mitchell slush fund and "brought education into Negro politics."[20]

For his part, Randolph, ever the analytical intellectual, compared the corrupt "old crowd," those "prophets and high-priests of the old order" in America, with the fallen Russian ruling class during the early days of the 1917 Russian Revolution. Randolph predicted that with the rise of the working class, the "old crowd" would pass out of the picture, along with "its false, corrupt and wicked institutions of oppression and cruelty; its ancient prejudices and beliefs and its pious, hypocritical and venerated idols." Just as new revolutionary leaders overthrew the older regimes in

Russia, Hungary, England, France, and Italy, Randolph urged young black leaders to do the same for "black men and women who are over-worked and under-paid, lynched, Jim Crowed and disfranchised—a people who are yet languishing in the dungeons of ignorance and superstition." Frustrated with black ministers who cautioned blacks to be conservative "when [they had] nothing to conserve," Randolph ridiculed the ineffectiveness of a Negro Church that continued to preach "the meek will inherit the earth," "if the enemy strikes you on one side of the face, turn the other," and "you may take all this world but give me Jesus." Until a "new crowd" of young, educated, radical, and fearless black leadership controlled the press, the church, and the schools, as well politics and labor, by forming "an alliance with white radicals such as the I.W.W., the socialists and the Non-Partisan League," Randolph believed that "a society of equals, without class, race, caste or religious distinctions" would not be possible.[21]

The 1919 September issue of the *Messenger* promised several "gripping and scintillating" articles, including one entitled "The Failure of the Negro Church." But when the "red summer" of 1919 erupted into violence and race riots, the editorial on the Negro Church was replaced by the September "riot issue." From June to the end of the year, there were approximately twenty-five race riots in several U.S. cities. W. A. Domingo observed that a "new spirit animating Negroes is not confined to the United States, where it is most acutely manifested, but is simmering beneath the surface in every country where the race is oppressed." Domingo cited biblical authority for self-defense and physical retaliation, which reflected the "new Negro's" willingness to fight and die in defense of his rights. He wrote,

> Justification for this course is not lacking, for it is the white man's own Bible that says "Those who live by the sword shall perish by the sword," and since white men believe in force, Negroes who have mimicked them for nearly three centuries must copy them in that respect.

Domingo repeated Claude McKay's "If We Must Die" poem to emphasize the point that the "new Negro has arrived with stiffened back bone, dauntless manhood, defiant eye, steady hand and a will of iron."[22]

Self-defense became the *Messenger*'s rallying cry. When the editors asked an eyewitness of the Chicago riots, "What did the Negro preachers and Negro leaders do?" he told them that preachers and social workers met daily during and after the riot to handle emergency matters. The eye-witness noted that "preachers were especially active in making statements to the press stating the Negro's point of view and counseling order" and, along with aldermen and assemblymen, had frequent conferences with the mayor, chief of police, and representatives of the stockyards.[23]

Despite this positive report, Randolph and Owen judged the Negro Church's apolitical, antiradical position as a contributing factor in the riots. The editors took on this hot issue in the context of the *Messenger*'s ongoing invective of failed "Negro leadership": the "old crowd Negro" versus the "new crowd Negro." To that end, the *Messenger* printed two large political cartoons to accompany the text of its riot article. Above the caption "Following the Advice of the Old Crowd Negro" are three fig-ures: Booker T. Washington saying, "Be modest and unassuming"; W. E. B. Du Bois saying, "Close ranks. Let us forget our grievances"; and a third figure in clerical collar and garb saying, "When they smite thee on one cheek—turn the other." The second cartoon above the caption "The New Crowd Negro Making America Safe for Himself" depicts a young Negro driving an armored car while shooting at soldiers, saying, "Since the government won't stop mob violence I'll take a hand."[24]

According to Randolph and Owen, race prejudice in America caused the riots, and American institutions like social clubs and groups, schools, newspapers, and the Christian Church were longtime sources of racial prejudice. Ever since the Civil War, when the "Methodist Church split over the issue of slavery," the cause was economic "pure and simple," they argued, for the southern church "preached for the victory of the cot-ton kings," and the northern church "blessed and anointed the industrial capitalists." As part of the Christian Church, the Negro Church was just as guilty:

The church is usually reactionary. The Presbyterian church invested $93,000 in the slave trade. In 1830, all the white churches met in confer-ence in Charleston, SC, and issued a manifesto stating that the Negro had no soul. The Church was a bulwark of slavery. It taught them "ser-vants obey your masters." It preaches a doctrine of humility. It is seldom that a white minister preaches a sermon against lynching. In the Negro Church, the ministers are largely ignorant, venal or controlled. (There are certain marked exceptions, of course.)[25]

The editors' parenthetical note—that some black ministers stood above corruption—reflected their belief that the Negro Church could be redeemed. Although implicating the Christian Church, both white and black, the editors urged that black churches "be converted into an educational forum." Alongside the economic and political remedies of socializing industry and enfranchising all citizens, the editors advocated a revolutionary curriculum that included "more economics, history and sociology and the physical sciences" and "less Latin, Greek and Bible." The September 1919 riot issue, deemed by federal authorities as "more insolently offensive than any other" because of its justification of force, retaliation, and self-defense, revealed the intensity of American race relations in the summer and fall of 1919. Randolph and Owen courted real danger in their militant advocacy of force, with the justification that "a bullet is sometimes more convincing than a hundred prayers, editorials, sermons, protests and petitions."[26]

The controversial and delayed editorial, "The Failure of the Negro Church," finally appeared in October 1919, when the *Messenger* editors were battling the federal government and radicalism was tearing apart the black communities in New York and Chicago. As the only direct attack on the church in the magazine's eleven-year tenure, "The Failure of the Negro Church" was written at an extremely violent period in American history, as reflected in Owen's opening volley: The "Negro Church [had] failed . . . in a great crisis." Actually, the editorial, often cited as evidence of Randolph's antichurch and atheistic position, did not repudiate the institution itself but advocated a progressive program for the Negro Church, including a social gospel emphasis on "this-world" concerns. The editorial can be viewed as prophetic, since the program outlined in the *Messenger* was later adopted by black churches in the decades following the Great Migration, in response to constructive criticism on how to meet the social, economic, and spiritual needs of its members. Randolph and Owen's editorial exposed the economic and other problems that had weakened the Negro Church's effectiveness and suggested how to improve the institution.[27]

The *Messenger*'s accusation that "the chief cause of the failure of the Negro Church [was] economic" was an attack on the whole Christian community, including black churches incorporated in the white Protestant establishment. The editors condemned the Christian Church as a segregated institution created in the days of slavery. By using a socialist analysis, the editors charged that the church was governed by capitalistic interests, for "the church, now as then, [was] using its power to defend poverty, crime, prostitution, war, ignorance and superstition which are outgrowths of the system that allows one man to live off another's labor." Trinity Church, located at the head of Wall Street, served as their example of "one of the biggest corporations in America." Trinity Church controlled "a large number of apartment houses from which it reaps blood money in the form of extortionate rents from the working people," and the "white ecclesiastical oligarchy" that dominated the church opposed the people's interests. Just as Jesus threw the money changers out of the temple, the editors condemned the church as materialistic big business. They noted that even trustee boards of the smallest churches, "comprised of the most prosperous church-members," set church policies and organized rallies and events to "induce" members to give money to the church. Randolph and Owen explained the recent proliferation of denominations and independent churches in black religious communities as motivated by economic reasons. Opportunistic preachers avoided the "fat charges" and restrictions of established churches by setting up their own storefront churches. Church services and sermons, mostly concerned with collecting money, revolved around the "blessedness" of giving money to the church.[28]

Second, the *Messenger* editors cited several noneconomic issues that were harming independent black churches. Foremost, black churches were failing to educate their people because of their clerics' ignorance of the modern problems of capital and labor. The editors decried the ministry's disinterestedness in unionism as a way of securing better working conditions for their members, stating that "no conference of Negro churches has ever gone on record as endorsing the principle of unionism." They criticized the lack of political discussions in the churches "unless some good, old Abraham Lincoln Republican" wanted the black vote and was willing to pay for educational propaganda. The result was that the church had "failed to use its power to rouse the Negro against disfranchisement and lynching."[29]

As "new Negroes," the *Messenger* editors offered their own constructive program for the Negro Church, similar to a social gospel program advocated by a progressive minority in the church. According to the editors, "new Negroes" wanted a modern church that served as the center of their social, economic, and political hopes and strivings. They demanded a new "educated, fearless and racial ministry" to replace the education of inspiration with the education of information, which meant "less Bible and more economic, history, sociology and physical science." The editors recommended expanding the Negro Church into an open forum in which specialists on hygiene, labor, government, racial relationships, and national and international questions could educate the people. They even suggested that churches be transformed into cooperative stores to help reduce the high cost of living. Finally, "the church must become something more than a temple of prayer to a people who are lynched, disfranchised and Jim Crowed. Prayer has been tried for over fifty years. In short, the church must set its face against a philosophy of profits to a philosophy of service."[30]

This editorial, appearing at a time of considerable upheaval in black urban communities, immediately forced Randolph and Owen to rethink their radical attack on the Negro Church as a failure. Given the political situation in the summer of 1919, the convergence of the recent urban riots with the government crackdown on radicalism, a radical critique of the Negro Church proved to be a tactical error for a budding Socialist Party for blacks. George E. Haynes, the newly appointed secretary of the Commission on the Church and Race Relations of the Federal Council of the Churches of Christ in America (FCCC), noted the rupture that opened between the black religious community and the *Messenger* editors at this time. Randolph and Owen, perceived as atheistic troublemakers, struggled to keep their radical movement afloat as the black community's negative reaction to their tactics grew more apparent. The moderate Haynes, often described by Randolph and Owen as one of the "old crowd Negroes," described them as "a socialist group which [was] just beginning, since the World War, to secure recruits among Negroes." Haynes noted how effectively Randolph and Owen "utilized the dissatisfaction which Negroes have felt because of the evils of lynching, mob violence, disfranchisement and other things about which the race has been restless." Haynes believed their propaganda generated interest in the black community for publicizing black grievances but not for their socialist message. In his pamphlet describing recent trends in American race relations, Haynes explained that the *Messenger*'s double attack on the Negro Church and the traditional black leadership had backfired, "since . . . an attack upon the Negro Church and upon other Negro leaders has seemed to weaken greatly the influence of their published organ and their speakers."[31]

By the end of 1919, the *Messenger* editors were looking for a new focus and direction for the magazine, for as radicalism was receding in America, so was the *Messenger*'s original purpose. Accordingly, with the

February 1920 issue, the *Messenger*'s subtitle "The Only Radical Negro Magazine in America" was changed to the scientific-sounding "A Journal of Scientific Radicalism," since "its writing was recognized as so scientific and generally interesting that it applies to all races, as shown by its more than ten thousand white readers." The *Messenger*'s hard-hitting policy regarding the Negro Church and religion changed as well. The editors started inviting black churches, along with clubs and labor organizations, to participate in a series of educational lectures. Brief notices, sprinkled throughout the *Messenger* pages, announced Randolph's and Owen's availability for speaking dates on the East Coast, which led to a "successful" tour of speaking engagements in Boston, Washington, D.C., and Detroit. On January 4, 1920, Chandler Owen finished his series of lectures at the Boston School of Social Science in Tremont Temple. Earlier Randolph addressed the American Negro Academy, presided over by Archibald H. Grimké, at the Lincoln Congregational Church in Washington, D.C., on "The Negro and the New Radicalism." On January 20, 1920, Owen joined Randolph in Washington, and together they spoke at the John Wesley Church on "The New Education." In Detroit, they spoke to a variety of groups, including the Labor Forum, the Labor Lyceum, Rev. Bagnall's Episcopal church, a banquet at the Crisis Café, a group of Detroit's white teachers, and the Bethel AME Church, on the following subjects: "The Americanism of Tomorrow," "The New Education," "The New Emancipation," "Socialism and the Negro," and "The Negro and the New Social Order." The editors boasted of standing ovations at their lectures, as evidenced in their claim that the January 20 lecture in Washington was "an event in the Negro's life in this country":

> Assembled in the John Wesley Church there, was the largest group of intellectual and thinking Negroes who probably ever gathered in the United States. Nearly all the professors of Howard University, a majority of the colored teachers of Washington, together with the most celebrated physicians, surgeons, publicists, business men and lecturers of the city, constituted the audience. Not only was there quality, but quantity. By eight o'clock, nearly every seat was filled, and each seat cost fifty cents! *This, too, in a city where it is hard to get people to listen to a lecture which is free!*[32]

The *Messenger*'s reports of Randolph's and Owen's lectures show progressive black ministers contributing to the success of this endeavor. For example, the "New Education" lecture on January 20 in the John Wesley Church was originally scheduled to be given at the local Dunbar High School, followed by a social dance in the high school auditorium. When Senator Reed Smoot, "the arch-reactionary Republican of Utah," and his "lilliputian Negro lackeys" heard that the *Messenger* editors were the guest speakers, he threatened to cut off the school's appropriation if the meeting was held at the high school. When he was told about this, Chandler Owen traveled to Washington to enlist the support of John Wesley Church's pastor, Rev. Brown. Owen reserved the church for the lecture, thereby enabling it to be given on the scheduled date. The *Messenger* described the audience as "thinking and serious people," who bought 490 subscriptions to the magazine "on the spot." When voluntary donations were requested, the editors noted that "ten and five dollar bills were interspersed." After the lecture, a common question asked was, "Why isn't the school the proper place for a lecture in which there was so much education?" The editors reported similar experiences in Detroit.[33]

The *Messenger* praised the Reverend Robert Bagnall of the Episcopal church and the Reverend Joseph Gomez of the Bethel AME, who could not be "intimidated or misled by the insidious misrepresentations of that time-serving, capitalist tool among Negroes—the Urban League." According to the editors, Bagnall and Gomez "opened their churches to let the people hear the truth, their actions resulting in almost unanimous approval." Another ally in Detroit was Rev. Bradby. Apparently, Bradby had come to hear the radical speakers after the trustees of his church canceled a meeting scheduled there. After hearing Randolph and Owen speak, Bradby concluded that the editors had been misrepresented, and he invited them "back to Detroit to lecture before his congregation, at his expense." The editors praised Bradby "as a broad man" yet concluded that his action was "the exception rather than the rule."[34]

With the success of their lecture tour, Randolph and Owen created a new *Messenger* forum based on Randolph's old Independent Political Council, called the Friends of Negro Freedom (FNF). Calling for a convention in Washington, D.C., the editors received positive responses from such Washington progressives as Archibald Grimké; Nevel H. Thomas; Carter G. Woodson; Carl Murphy, editor of the *Baltimore Afro-American*; and Edgar P. Benjamin, a successful Boston lawyer. The editors listed several others who responded to the call for a national organization of, by, and for blacks, since "at the present time there is not a national organization alleged to be fighting in the interest of Negroes, which is controlled, in any considerable degree, by Negroes." Settling on Tuesday, May 25, 1920, as the starting date for the conference in Washington, D.C., the editors explained: "We had first thought of Monday morning, May 24, for the convention opening, but so many scholarly and reputable ministers have stated their desire to be present through the entire affair, that the promoters changed the date to allow them to preach Sunday and travel Sunday night and Monday."[35]

Randolph and Owen envisioned the FNF as a revolutionary movement of local, nonpartisan groups made up of men and women, young and old, in various cities and towns, organized to gain political power and equality. Although an essentially political and economic endeavor by the *Messenger*, the editors' change in policy toward religion also signified an important shift in their attitude toward the black Christian community. After the debacle over the attack on the church in 1919, which branded them as religious outcasts and atheists, the *Messenger*'s editors clarified their position on religion as they organized the FNF. At the same time, they did not want religious denominational differences to hamper the FNF's development. In the clearest statement yet of the *Messenger*'s attitude toward religion, the editors wrote: "The organization will be non-denominational and non-religious, but not anti-religious. Persons of any denomination and religion, or of no religion, shall be eligible."[36]

All persons, whether believers or unbelievers, were admitted to their new civil rights organization. Although the cornerstone of each FNF group was educational propaganda, each local organization revolved around four political and economic functions: labor unions, tenants' leagues, cooperative businesses, and boycotts. The editors encouraged the observation of international holidays, parades, and mass meetings, as in labor and socialist movements, since "twenty-five cities in which there are large groups of Negroes [holding] such parades and celebrations, the news will spread over the whole world." Each organization was to be managed by blacks, although members of other races could join, thus encouraging an "international" scope for local FNFs, because Randolph believed that "the success of Negroes in one place encouraged and embolden[ed] Negroes in another." By August 1920, the *Messenger* reported on the "splendid convention" in Washington attended by the ablest thinkers and scholars in the Negro race. Progressive Episcopalian ministers Reverend Robert Bagnall of Detroit and George Frazier Miller of Brooklyn played prominent roles in the convention. Unfortunately, however, the FNF's revolutionary agenda was never realized. During the 1920 national election, as the *Messenger* editors busied themselves promoting Eugene V. Debs for president, they temporarily laid aside their plans for the FNF. By December 1920, the FNF's activities were confined to the economic concerns of their cooperatives and the organization's educational aspects, and eventually FNF news items disappeared from the *Messenger* pages altogether.[37]

The Messenger's *Middle Years, 1921–1925*

With the demise of radicalism in the new decade, the *Messenger* entered the second phase of its existence. Randolph explored new avenues in which to take his magazine while his partner, Chandler Owen, increasingly distanced himself from the day-to-day operations. During this exploratory time, the magazine reacted to some of the greatest events of the 1920s affecting African American communities: the Garvey movement, the reemergence of the Ku Klux Klan, the Harlem Renaissance, as well as the most significant religious debate of this period, the fundamentalist-modernist controversy. In 1921 and 1922, the *Messenger*'s editorials and articles concentrated on two developments that greatly affected the black community during the early postwar years: Garveyism and the revitalization of the Ku Klux Klan. The antireligious rhetoric in the *Messenger* during this period often pertained to one of these two political movements.[38]

Marcus Garvey first appeared in the October 1920 "Who's Who" column of the *Messenger*. At first, Randolph's analysis of Garveyism, which he labeled as "an upshot of the Great World War," was impartial, even laudatory. Although he opposed its economic implications, he was not threatened by it as a serious political movement, since "Garveyism [was] spiritual." The *Messenger* still believed that the best answer for racial equality was a "renaissance in scientific thought." According to Randolph, Garveyism had "inculcated into the minds of Negroes the need and value of organization," since it effectively organized "large masses" of blacks by blacks, adding, "Of course, the A.M.E. Church has done as much." But when the Garvey movement linked up with the Ku Klux Klan and "embarked upon a queer but interesting mission—the preaching of Negro inferiority to the white and Negro peoples of the world," the *Messenger*'s attitude toward Garvey shifted dramatically.[39]

By December 1920, fully aroused by the reports of the recent reorganization of the KKK in the southern states, Randolph and Owen fired their first shot at the 1920s Klan in an "open letter." Under the auspices of their Friends of Negro Freedom forum, the editors compared the present-day Klan with the "same murderous marauders" of the past Klan, except that now it was not only antiblack, it was also antilabor, anti-Jewish, and antiforeign and used mob violence to divide the American people. Moreover, the new organization threatened "religious liberty," most evident in its anti-Catholicism:

> Already Georgia (its seat), Florida, the back door to Georgia, and Alabama have passed anti-Catholic laws. These night riders are burning Catholic churches, persecuting the priests and threatening the very life of the Catholic church in the South. Very shortly this rabid anti-Catholic spirit will result in the lynching of Catholic priests, laymen and nuns; their churches and convents will be burned down; their communicants run out.[40]

By the fall of 1921, *Messenger* editorials constantly reported on the Klan's activities, linking it with mob violence and race riots across the country. The September cover page declared, "The New Negro Ready for the Ku Klux Klan."[41] During this period, the *Messenger*'s antireligious remarks often were applied to "gullible" black churches and preachers who endorsed the Garvey movement, now linked to the KKK. Rev. W. H. Moses, a favorite *Messenger* target, received front-page coverage with the bold headlines: "Big Negro Preacher Endorses Ku-Klux-Klan." Randolph and Owen castigated Moses for his letter to the *Philadelphia Record* entitled "In Defense of the Ku Klux Klan." The editors supposed that its "readers would be shocked to learn that any Negro could be found . . . who will defend the notoriously lawless and criminal organization known as the Ku Klux Klan." The editors expressed disbelief that Rev. Moses was pastor of a large Baptist congregation, "not in Macon, Georgia, or Houston, Texas or Pensacola, Florida,—but in Philadelphia," surrounded by new Negroes, Quakers, Catholics, Jews, and "many abolitionists." Outraged by Moses' claim that the new Klan was not dangerous, the editors listed its past and current crimes and compared Moses, with "all [his] fallacious assertions," with Pontius Pilate. Moses was just one more case of "the old school, me-too-boss, hat-in-hand, good 'nigger' preacher, ready willing, nay, eager to sell his race for a 'mess of pottage.'"[42]

The *Messenger* reported an FNF record-breaking meeting at St. Peter Claver's Hall in Philadelphia, held on September 23, 1921, when the Reverend W. H. Moses was given much needed chastisement for his defense of the Ku Klux Klan. Careful not to include his congregation, the editors challenged the Zion Baptist Church, if it had "any self-respect, an iota of decency, a scintilla of racial pride, a remaining spark of manhood, a lingering bit of character, a widow's mite of dignity," to drive from its pulpit "the minister who so cowardly and ignobly has disgraced it." The editors advised the Zion Baptist Church to "go and sin no more" yet remained hopeful that a "conscientious, hard working group of Negro men and women in the Zion Baptist Church" still existed.[43]

The *Messenger* attacked other notable black preachers besides Moses, often using sarcasm to make the point. For example, Rev. J. C. Austin of Pittsburgh was identified as a "preacher and banker; [he] pledges that if you will let him save your money, *he will save your soul.*" Rev. J. R. L. Diggs of Baltimore was called "a Negro minister and teacher who claims to believe in the soundness of Garvey's empty and nebulous schemes, *but who ought to know better and does know better.*" Rev. T. H. W. Gibson of Cavalry Baptist Church in Muncie, Indiana, the center of new KKK activity, allowed a Klan organizer to address his congregation and even accepted his $40 donation. When Gibson and the congregation kept the donation, the *Messenger* had this to say about him and his church:

> The only way we can interpret the action of this belly-crawling Negro preacher is that he and his church are members of the Garvey Movement. It makes no difference where this preacher comes from it is time for this Negro and all those members of his congregation who supported him, to go with lightning speed. We have not heard of their equal in Georgia or in any part of the South.

The editorial also reported that the KKK organizer told a Catholic layman that he "could buy all the 'niggers' in the country with a little money."[44]

At the same time the *Messenger* excoriated all religious groups that supported the Garvey movement or caved into pressure exerted by the KKK, it praised churches and religious groups that condemned the Klan and Garveyism. At the outset of their anti-KKK campaign, the editors had called on more than fifteen labor organizations and twenty political, civil, and religious organizations, including the Interchurch World Movement and "white and Negro churches of all denominations," to join them in condemning the new Klan. The *Messenger* reported three FNF meetings against the KKK in Philadelphia, Washington, and New York, where Randolph and Owen explained to various clubs and groups their "new interpretation" of the Klan.[45] The editors reported the formation of a united front of Chicago "lay and clerical leaders of all racial, religious and political groups" against the KKK. Bishop Samuel Fallows of the Reformed Episcopal Church, chosen as the honorary chairman of this "militant organization," stated, "The Klan is a menace to religious freedom, a source of danger to the state, and its growing strength should be curbed through the United Effort of all true Americans, regardless of creed, race or condition of life." When the House of Deputies of the Protestant Episcopal Convention, in Portland, Oregon, denounced the KKK, the *Messenger* singled out two ministers from Georgia, "the home of the KKK," for their courageous positions: Rev. John W. Wing wrote up the resolution denouncing the KKK, and Rev. C. B. Wilmer of Atlanta drew up a resolution denouncing the lynch law. The editors expressed amazement that these actions came from the South and the church, since "both have been bulwarks of compromise and winking at evil. As a rule, one propagated and the other condoned."[46]

Randolph interpreted these events as hopeful signs that things were changing in the church. He proclaimed that the "Church has recently been manoeuvring to the front line of democracy," by citing the activity of several religious organizations: the Inter-Church World Movement for its "great report on the Steel Strike," the National Catholic Welfare Council for placing "itself squarely on the side of labor," and the Federal Council of Churches and the Methodist Federation for its "intelligent and sympathetic effort to study and fight race prejudice." Randolph concluded, "As Lester Ward would say, the Church [was] representing utility produced from error. Certainly the institution [was] rising in civilized decency when two ministers from Georgia,—white Protestant ministers— will rise in open convention and condemn the invisible government of their state."[47]

When the bitterness and turmoil of the "Garvey Must Go" campaign subsided in late 1922, Randolph and the new *Messenger* editor George

Schuyler refashioned the magazine, giving it a slick, modern format reflecting the stylish 1920s Harlem culture. With the January 1923 issue, the subtitle "New Opinion of the New Negro" revealed its new focus. The format emphasized up-to-date topics with special issues such as the educational number, the new Negro woman's number, the Labor Day number, and the Negro business achievement number. A regular feature called "These Colored United States," written by well-known black authors about their native states, appeared throughout this period, sometimes commenting on black religious and church activities. By 1924, the editors finally settled on the subtitle "World's Greatest Negro Monthly." By then, the political editorials, once located at the front of the magazine, had been moved farther back. Although Randolph's articles on political campaigns and his radical rhetoric were downplayed during this period, civil rights issues remained in evidence. Several columns devoted to children, women, and family issues were featured in 1925. Large, elaborate advertisements displayed consumer products of local businesses and services in a modern art-deco style.[48]

During this period, ads, editorials, and articles offered positive information about black churches, something unimaginable a few years earlier. For example, one elaborate seven-page *Messenger* ad ran for two months, soliciting contributions for the Sesqui-Centennial Memorial Bronze Tablet sponsored by the Mother Bethel AME Church in Philadelphia. The proposed bronze tablet, designed by noted black artist H. O. Tanner (son of an AME bishop), featured the images of Richard and Mary Allen, along with names of prominent black leaders. The tablet commemorated not only the 150th anniversary of the signing of the Declaration of Independence but also the founding of Mother Bethel AME Church in Philadelphia in 1787. The ad included a large photograph of Mother Bethel's pastor, Rev. H. P. Anderson; pictures of the bronze tablet; editorial comment; and four pages of mimeographed letters of prominent supporters of the project. In this way, the *Messenger* combined modern advertising techniques to remind its readers the place of African Methodism in the fight for racial progress.

It will be remembered that Afro-Methodism was begun one hundred and thirty-nine years ago by Richard Allen in a blacksmith shop upon the spot where Mother Bethel now stands. Rev. Anderson has conceived the idea of erecting a bronze tablet, eight by eight feet, to the memory of Richard

Allen and immediately associating with this idea other racial pioneers such as Absalom Jones, Peter Ogden, Frederick Douglass, B. T. Washington and others who helped to make history and have been a credit to the race.[49]

Another positive reference to African Methodism was made in a *Messenger* editorial regarding a resolution passed at the twenty-seventh quadrennial session of the General Conference of the AME Church. According to the editorial, the conference condemned the Republican Congress for not acting to protect African American rights, and this, the editorial stated, from the "the most powerful single body of Negroes in the world . . . composed of churchmen and laymen of recognized ability and leadership." Because this editorial and the bronze tablet advertisement revealed so much inside knowledge of the AME Church, it was undoubtedly Randolph's contribution. To him, the AME resolution represented "some progress":

> As a church we cannot keep silent while those whom we supported turn the swords we put into their hands against us. We cannot for ever vote for a party because of its past history; but must vote for those who act in our interest. We cannot longer be satisfied with the Republican Congress meeting year after year and adjourning without passing one protective measure.[50]

The most conspicuous example of an editorial policy favoring the Negro Church's progressive element was a modern four-page layout of Olivet Baptist Church, a "community serving church in Chicago." Olivet was the only black church to be so prominently featured in the *Messenger*'s eleven-year history. Billed as the "largest Protestant church in the world," with nearly eleven thousand members, Olivet was located in the middle of a dense black populace and combined the preaching of "pure religion" with the "practical illustration of these Christian doctrines." The article stressed Olivet's size, the complexity of its organization, its yearly budget, and the many services it provided for the community, such as a medical clinic, educational classes for women, sewing circles, nurseries and a kindergarten, boys' and girls' clubs, recreational facilities, and "timely civic and good government meetings." Included was a full-page picture of Olivet's beautiful gothic structure on a corner lot, which had been bought from the Methodist Episcopal denomination for $85,000 in

1918. Olivet's pastors, the Reverends Lacey Kirk Williams and Joseph H. Branham, offered "wise and altruistic leadership" in a social gospel vein:

> Acting under a profound conviction that it is her mission to be a concrete expression of the social gospel, Olivet believes that polished orations and striking epigrams are meaningless in the present-day church unless, in addition to ministering to spiritual needs, the social and economic needs of humanity also find consideration.[51]

In the May 1923 educational supplement, the editors boasted of "blazing a trail in Negro journalism" by presenting the "'best minds' of the race in review of the latest and most important works in bookdom." Under the topic of religion, one book appeared: Carter G. Woodson's *The History of the Negro Church* (1921). The *Messenger*'s review, written by Robert W. Bagnall, a minister of an Episcopal church in Philadelphia and the current director of branches for the NAACP, appears to be the only contemporary book review of Woodson's groundbreaking work.[52]

Woodson's historical study was the first to integrate the black religious experience into the story of American Protestantism. In addition, his last two chapters offer a contemporary analysis of the Negro Church of the early 1920s. "The Negro Church . . . had some difficulty in finding itself. There was still some question as to what its functions and ideals should be, and this very question all but divided the church into conservative and progressive groups." Woodson's modern analysis of the Negro Church complemented the *Messenger*'s editorial perspective on religion. In fact, Bagnall's review concentrates on Woodson's last chapters, "The Negro Church Socialized" and "The Negro Church Today":

> [Woodson] pictures how the Negro Church has been the one institution which has largely trained the masses in government, organization, business, public expression, and culture, as well as in religion. He cites instances of the modern movements toward institutional and socialized churches which will serve the life here fully as well as the life hereafter, caring for recreation, culture and employment, as well as religion. . . . But it must be a Negro Church, he asserts, free from outside interference, modern in its methods, and conscious of its relation to the whole of life.[53]

Randolph and Woodson endorsed and supported each other's political and literary endeavors. Woodson attended the first FNF Conference in Washington, D.C., in May 1920. When Woodson gave Randolph his approval for forming the FNF into a national body, he wrote, "If my name will be of any service to you, you are at liberty to use it." Another *Messenger* editorial praised Woodson's Association for the Study of Negro Life and History and its publication the *Journal of Negro History*, calling Woodson "the best Negro historian up to the present time." One "Who's Who" column in the magazine also featured Woodson and praised his "quiet, industrious and unassuming" character as one of "the most prolific producer of serious works in the Negro race." Woodson shared the *Messenger*'s hope that a "new ministry [was] in the making, which will grapple with the social, political, economic and racial problem of the world in general and [in] America." Two ministers whom Woodson admired for their forward-thinking positions in the church were Robert W. Bagnall, mentioned earlier, and the "fearless" George Frazier Miller, both contributors to the *Messenger* and active supporters of Randolph's FNF forums. Woodson wrote that they "actually preached the use of force and encouraged resistance to the mobs," the only way, he believed, that black churches could effectively counteract the evil influence of the revived Ku Klux Klan. Finally, Woodson's conclusion that the black church's "preaching of the fatherhood of God and the brotherhood of man" would continue to play a vital role in the social welfare of black Americans because "the white people of this country are not interested in the real mission of Christ" complemented Randolph's own views of the situation.[54]

George Frazier Miller's name appeared as one of the contributing editors on every *Messenger*'s masthead from March 1919 until 1925, just below Randolph's and Owen's names. During this period, he wrote on such radical topics as "Socialism and Its Ethical Basis," "Uncle Sam: No Land Grabber?" "Enslavement of the Worker," "Drama of the Bombs," "The Awakened Oppressed and the Disturbed Oppressors," and "The Social Value of the Uncultured." Miller, a graduate of Howard University, had been the rector of the St. Augustine Protestant Episcopal Church in Brooklyn since 1896. He used his pulpit as a political forum, preaching a revolutionary Jesus Christ who addressed the social needs of the poor. Such radical political views made him an independent voice in the black community and one whom Randolph and Owen praised as "the most fearless and . . . intelligent of the elderly Negro radicals." In 1918, Miller served as the Socialist Party's congressional candidate for New York's Twenty-first District. During the *Messenger*'s most radical period, Miller was "one of the few elderly Negroes who has given constant aid and comfort and support to the radical work being carried on by the young New Crowd Negroes."[55]

The *Messenger* also participated in the great American religious debate of the 1920s known as the fundamentalist-modernist controversy. Between 1923 and 1925, the *Messenger* offered its own interpretation of what Randolph called the "creed conflict." From this period until the *Messenger*'s demise in 1928, its editorial policy reflected Randolph's conviction that religion was open for debate and intelligent discussion. As an educational forum, the *Messenger* offered its readers a variety of perspectives on modern religion. Although the magazine professed to be fair, it was clear that Randolph and other *Messenger* contributors leaned toward modernist religious views while holding up conservative positions to ridicule.[56]

Randolph remembered one *Messenger* article written by NAACP activist William Pickens that set off a storm of controversy in the Harlem religious community. The article "was criticized . . . on account of the general tenor of the article against the church." Randolph explained that Pickens "was . . . critical of the church," but usually regarding a social or political issue "in relation to a given question." Moreover, Pickens had a friendly way of persuading people, and people seemed to trust him because "he was an NAACP man."[57]

Pickens's article "The Things Nobody Believes: A Lesson in Religion" resulted from his visits to the *Messenger* office when Pickens, Randolph, and Owen would "sit down and talk." Randolph asserted that "Pickens was in our corner, although he was not as aggressive as we were." Although Pickens was not a socialist, "he was not anti-Socialist," an important factor in Randolph's and Pickens's work relationship. Pickens's article described a local controversy between Rev. Percy Stickney Grant and Bishop William T. Manning, affiliated with the Episcopal Church in New York City. When Rev. Grant "stirred a sensation by saying from the pulpit what he *really believes*," he was reprimanded by Bishop Manning, who stated that "Mr. Grant can enjoy his personal liberties *outside the church*." Pickens called the Episcopal Church "a leader" in the war against orthodoxy and "a sign of the brain capacity of that Church," and sided with Rev. Grant. The *Messenger* also called Grant one of the great progressive ministers in New York, along with John Haynes Holmes, Allen McCurdy, Bishop Paul Jones, and Irwin St. John Tucker. Pickens commended Grant's "almost unheard-of audacity, even in the twentieth century" for bravely speaking his mind, since it was a known fact that "preacher's 'beliefs' [were] supposed to be ready-made in 'creeds,' 'disciplines,' 'dogmas,' 'catechisms,' and other catalogs of 'the chief end of man.'" Yet as Pickens observed, preachers who were obligated to stay within certain boundaries of orthodox belief were losing followers who questioned orthodox or literal interpretations of the scripture and were causing a crisis in the church. Pickens wrote:

> Intelligent people now-a-days do not believe half of what any "orthodox" preacher says. And a worse result is, *that intelligent people are getting further and further from the church,*—and although the dogmatists seem to know that the people are leaving off the church (for they complain against the growing lack of interest), *still they do not seem to know what is the matter.* Some of them are even so mentally lame as to lay it to the mere cussedness of human nature,—*instead of to increasing human intelligence and self-respect.*[58]

Identifying himself with the heretical tradition of John Huss, Martin Luther, and Galileo, Pickens listed all the "things" that nobody believed anymore, including the historical veracity of biblical stories like Adam's rib, Jonah and the whale, the sun standing still, a material heaven or a material hell anywhere, the parting of the Red Sea, defying gravitation, the flood that covered the whole earth, miracles that violated the laws of nature, or the chance that human bodies would ever rise from the dead. Moreover, Pickens declared that no intelligent person believed that anybody else with intelligence could believe such absurdities and concluded by praising the "rebellious and unorthodox" for making true progress both inside and outside the church. Pickens's final words provide a good indication why the *Messenger* editors agreed to print his article:

> And the sooner we *think, act and live the truth* toward ourselves and our fellows, the sooner will we be set right toward the Cosmos and toward God. *Any just God* would certainly be on the side of the man who had courage enough to be true to *his own conscience* rather than to anybody's creed. So far, the rebellious and the unorthodox (that is, *the fellows who disagreed with the bosses*) have been *responsible for all real*

progress in state and church. God is not against science,—He is not on the side of ignorance and bigotry,—He has not appointed ultimate and inviolate authorities among men. Every brave and *intelligent* man is his own mediator.[59]

Pickens's article, like Rev. Grant's sermon, created a controversy in New York's religious community, especially among black preachers. Although the *Messenger*'s "Open Forum" column never printed any letters critical of Pickens's piece, the editors fueled the controversy with this sensational notice in the next issue, revealing the public's negative reactions to Pickens's article: "NEXT MONTH: PROFESSOR WILLIAM PICKENS will answer 'Preachers Who Defend Hell.' This fire is drawn from Mr. Pickens because of the sensation created by his article in the February MESSENGER, entitled 'Things Nobody Believes.'"[60]

Pickens's second article, entitled "Intelligent Christianity: Not the Fear of Hell," was billed as his "reply to Preachers Who Defend Hell." Randolph's editorial comment preceding the article announced: "This brilliant and scintillating article . . . answers the preachers" who revealed they knew "neither their theological authorities nor their Bible—to say nothing of science." Apparently, their main objections revolved around Pickens's denial of a material heaven and hell and the doctrine of a general resurrection. Pickens refuted his detractors with four arguments. First, as a member in a Christian church for twenty-three years, Pickens shared the "belief of intelligent Christians" and ministers who interpreted the scriptures from a "spiritual" or figurative perspective. "The best mark of an intelligent Christian is tolerance and generosity of spirit," Pickens stated. Second, stressing that the "acts of a life like that of Jesus of Nazareth" were worth more "than all the terrors of a million hells," he cited Henry Ward Beecher, dead for more than thirty-five years, as his authority. Pickens quoted several passages from an unidentified sermon by Beecher in which the famed Congregational preacher refuted hell as a pernicious doctrine.[61] Third, concerning the ministers' fears about how such radical religious ideas affected young people, Pickens replied that "in the long run (and it will be *short*) hypocrisy and pretense will have the more disastrous effect upon the young mind." Finally, Pickens cited philosopher David Hume's advice to never refute "any hypothesis, by a pretense of its dangerous consequences to religion and morality." Pickens believed that the application of the "doctrines of fear have lost power with real men" and that religion, in "accord with reason and science," would prevail. Pickens' second article concluded:

> Science is of God, and reason is as sacred and divine an attribute as the soul of man has. . . . There is no prospect that man will ever be without religion, but there is every prospect that he will soon be beyond our present religious conceptions and beliefs. The letter killeth—The spirit maketh alive.[62]

The *Messenger*'s "Open Forum" column published four letters commending Pickens's first article. Kelly Miller of Howard University praised him for writing "the right stuff, although you didn't say half enough." J. W. Glover expressed surprise at the existence of a "southern-born Negro with such advanced liberal ideas, and not afraid to publicly express them," since all the southern black educators he knew were "decidedly narrow and cramped on religious matters." Freethinker J. H. Clinton hoped the article would lead to "endless discussion" and arouse the spirit of inquiry which "alone makes the discovery of truth possible." The longest reply, printed in full, came from Joseph C. Carroll, a theological student at the Virginia Theological Seminary and College in Lynchburg. Carroll hoped that the *Messenger* would print his response to Pickens's article so that "anyone who may be trying to form a positive faith in the universe and God" could be helped. Randolph printed Carroll's response in its entirety because it supported Pickens's modernist position at the same time that it critiqued his argument, thereby producing the sort of intelligent discussion that Randolph encouraged. Carroll's analysis provided insights into how the younger generation was reshaping the religious debate in the 1920s. First, Carroll faulted Pickens's distance from progressive religious thought: "Dean Pickens is one of our best informed men, he knows the race question, he is a fine linguist, but when he attempts to discuss religion he is out of his field, and thus his ignorance of progressive religious thinking was apparent in every line of his article."[63]

Carroll suggested that a better approach would start from a positive statement of what religious people currently believed. For example, everyone understood that the Bible was a "record of the religious experiences of Jews and Christians" and that it was not intended to be understood and interpreted literally. For Carroll, whether or not Bible stories were facts or myths was insignificant as long as they served their purpose.

He compared the biblical Jonah with Harriet Beecher Stowe's Uncle Tom character, for both served as a "vivid personification of an actual social condition." Carroll then criticized certain key theological points "of which Dr. Pickens [spoke] so disparagingly": heaven, hell, and the resurrection. According to Carroll, "nobody believes in a material hell that burns with fire, nor a material heaven with gold-paved streets, long white robes and so on. But everybody believes in the survival of human personality." Carroll concluded, "All human personalities are finite aspects of the infinite personality, God. At death we go back to the infinite, and without losing our identity we continue our existence in the Infinite God."[64]

Carroll, like Pickens, supported Grant in his clash with Bishop Manning, but Carroll, as a student of theology, provided *Messenger* readers with the broader social and religious context of their struggle. Carroll agreed that orthodox interpretations were outmoded and ineffective. For him, the "good Bishop represents that old-fashioned, outgrown, antiquated type of orthodoxy which makes one say that he believes that which he knows is not true, [whereas] Dr. Grant represents the new theologian who believes in calling a name by its right name." Although Carroll agreed with Pickens's conclusion, he disagreed "with him in respect to methods." Carroll believed that the modern theologian's task, as well as his own, was to restate "religious faith in terms of the twentieth century culture and learning, rather than holding up to public ridicule the mistakes of the past."[65]

Randolph and the *Messenger*'s editorial position backed Pickens's and Carroll's religious argument in support of Grant. Like Carroll, Randolph offered *Messenger* readers a broader context of the local controversy, though from a socialist interpretation of the conflict. The *Messenger* editorial declared that the "war of the theologians [was] on" and used the conflict to go beyond the religious rhetoric of Pickens and Carroll, in order to effect far-reaching social change. Comparing the current crisis with an earlier religious conflict, Randolph argued that the Protestant Reformation was only superficially creedal, for the heart of the struggle was a political and economic battle among the princes. Randolph believed that today's creed conflict also was economically based, a "reflex of our world-wide economic chaos." The Harlem controversy between Grant and Manning, and its larger religious context, represented to Randolph deeper economic, social, and material conditions needing solutions. He explained:

Under the impulse of democracy, inspired by the World War, powerful ministers whose parishes are economically independent, as the barons of old opposed the kings, are denouncing the ecclesiastical despotism of bishops. The bishops, in the main, are the representatives of the thought of the mighty financial and industrial kings in America, while the ministers are seeking to articulate the aims, aspirations and hopes of the small business interests, the farmers and trades peoples who are in revolt against the oppression of the money oligarches.[66]

Randolph found merit in the fundamentalist-modernist controversy in the hope that debate would effect political change. During the *Messenger*'s second phase, the magazine offered articles on progressive religious themes, which continued the theological debate that Pickens had fueled. Rev. Ethelred Brown contributed articles that supported Pickens's views. Like Hubert Harrison from the Virgin Islands, Brown was a radical immigrant whose name appeared on Socialist and Communist Party tickets. As the minister of the Harlem Community Church, Rev. Brown found the *Messenger* useful as he worked to establish liberal religion and Unitarianism among African Americans. Arriving in Harlem in 1920, Brown used a forum format for his religious services, to discuss social justice and political-social equality for black Americans with other socialists, communists, and Garveyites in Harlem.[67]

Other *Messenger* articles on religious subjects had proscience or antifundamentalist messages, such as Howard University professor Kelly Miller's remarks about the current debate over evolution and creation. Pointing to the conflict between science and religion, Miller warned that "if religion [was] to be an effective agency in the future it must be adapted to suit the conditions of the time." He urged readers to "follow the lead of science and range themselves in . . . defiance of these fundamentals." In another "Open Forum" column, Pickens described the "church wars" as the victory of the unorthodox over the orthodox, since unorthodoxy was only hope for a universal religion. He congratulated one Episcopal church "in the Bowerie" for celebrating Confucius's birthday. For Pickens, the creed wars signaled an intellectual and spiritual rebirth, as "science and common sense will profit by religious volcanism." George Schuyler, now assistant editor of the *Messenger*, complained that the "Negro clergy will not discuss the Fundamentalist-Modernist question of which we have read so much in the papers lately. The last thing desired by these gentlemen [was] discussion. It might start the herd to thinking!"

J. A. Rogers, the intellectual and historian from the West Indies who had his own column in the *Messenger*, had little use for fundamentalists: "Imagine an organism that never threw off any of its excrement, and you have a fundamentalist. The fundamentalist are suffering from constipation of the brain." Of course, Rogers as "the critic" knocked everyone, from the fundamentalism of William Jennings Bryan and John Roach Straton to that "backwash of civilization . . . in California, that paradise of freak faiths." As the minister of the Calvary Baptist Church in New York, Straton often clashed with fellow Baptist (later Presbyterian) Harry Emerson Fosdick of the Riverside Church, both of whom personified the liberal and conservative Christian forces in New York. According to the *Messenger*, Rev. John Roach Straton typified all fundamentalists, referring to Straton as demagogic and dangerous.[68]

The Messenger's *Labor Years, 1925–1928*

The *Messenger*'s editorial policy as a forum of liberal religion open to intelligent debate continued into the magazine's third metamorphosis as the official organ of the Brotherhood of Sleeping Car Porters. In July 1925, Randolph joined the Pullman porters' fight for an independent trade union. With the *Messenger*'s more intense focus on trade union and labor issues, the magazine's role as a forum for unorthodox and liberal religion helped Randolph connect with the progressive thinkers in those black churches that supported his labor movement. During this period, the *Messenger* once again initiated several forums for religious debate. In January 1927, the editors announced that Ira de A. Reid's article had won the prize of ten dollars in the *Messenger*'s "Why I Like Harlem" essay contest. Over the next six months, the *Messenger* staff invited its readers to address such controversial topics as "Is Marriage a Failure?" "Should the Negro Be Patriotic?" "Can the American Race Problem Be Solved?" and "What Good Are College Fraternities?" No topic launched more debate than the third one, "Is Christianity a Menace to the Negro?" Randolph's contribution was evident in the contest's organization. Together, Randolph and George Schuyler established the contest's rules and format, with Schuyler in charge of the details. Essays were directed to his attention, and "all answers" were to be addressed to him. In their advertisement for the contest, the editors identified three views of Christianity in the black community. The first view accepted Christianity as a white man's religion which taught the "philosophy of slavery, meekness and submission," including the worship of "a white God, a white Jesus, white angels and cherubs." The *Messenger* editors regarded this position as a needless consumption of "the Negro's time, money and energy." The second view was that of those who argued that "Christianity has been a blessing," proving itself to be "a rock . . . during the time of great trial; . . . a comfort in the hour of distress." According to them, "the Christian church was the Negroes' first means of getting together and building race solidarity." Finally, there were those who took "the ground that Christianity is all right," since "people *will* have *some* religion. Yet the present 'Negro Church' was too "archaic in form, structure and policy . . . [to] hold the Negro of intelligence and education."[69]

Apparently, "a large number of answers" arrived at Schuyler's office, who declared John Baddy of Washington, D.C., the winner. Schuyler, the avowed atheist on the *Messenger* staff, admitted that the "selection of the winner was very difficult because of the excellence of so many." Baddy's conclusion corresponded to the first religious position described in the contest's announcement: "If the Negro desires to live an intelligent, happy and comfortable life, he must of necessity regard Christianity as more of a menace than a blessing." The *Messenger* editors judged Baddy's essay as the most logical and valid. Baddy, the editor of a new magazine called the *Aframerican Digest*, was admired by the *Messenger* editors as "as a keen, courageous, unbiased thinker and journalist." Using a Marxist analysis, Baddy focused his critique on Christianity as an illegitimate religion for the American Negro. First, Baddy claimed that Christianity's dogmatic beliefs—an incarnate God, Jesus as Son of God, Heaven, Hell, personal immortality, ethereal phenomena, and the Bible's infallibility—could "no longer be accepted by any intelligent person." Once scrutinized in the "critical light of reason and scientific inquiry," Christianity did not stand up to "modern scientific knowledge." Calling it an opiate that kept its believers oppressed and exploited, Baddy connected black acceptance of Christianity to "the period of slavery in this country," which has persisted "in a slightly modified form up to the present." Here, Baddy only reiterated what William Pickens had argued earlier in his *Messenger* essay. Second, Baddy argued that since blacks were primarily working-class people, their best interest was whatever provided a "more desirable plane of existence." Since the fundamentals of Christianity kept him in a "very low economic status," once again it was "tried and found wanting." True advancement for the black worker rested on his labor power as a skilled worker, "mastering the principles of mechanical devices." On this point, Baddy's views coincided exactly with the *Messenger*'s prolabor position. Baddy's third point, not as well developed, questioned the "passive morality" of the Christian church. He asked: How many Christian ministers worked for the abolition of slavery? How many Theodore Parkers were there? How many today speak out against "lynching, peonage, economic oppression or the innumerable social injustices of which Negroes [were] victims?" Once again, Baddy described the *Messenger*'s advocacy for a viable and responsible social gospel. And his basic contention that Christianity with its emphasis on "an alleged future life" was "more of a menace than a blessing" complemented the *Messenger*'s editorial position on religion.[70]

Following up on the interest generated from the essay contest, the *Messenger* advertised a religious debate scheduled at the Community Church in Harlem, on Sunday, April 24, 1927. The topic this time was "Is Orthodox Christianity a Handicap to the Negro's Progress?" Held under the auspices of the *Messenger* forum and organized by Abram L. Harris, the new emphasis on "orthodox" Christianity significantly altered the debate.[71] The *Messenger*'s advertisement announcing the debate encouraged its readers to "Come Hear This Great Debate" in John Haynes Holmes's Community Church. Holmes's willingness to sponsor a debate on orthodox Christianity indicated the independence of the Community Church's pastor and congregation. Previously, the *Messenger*'s editorials had singled out Holmes as one of the outstanding progressive ministers in the city and recognized him as a reliable ally in radical politics. One of several liberal Protestant ministers advocating a social gospel, Holmes had embraced socialism and its principles before World War I. In the 1920s, Holmes participated in the "labor church" movement, which recognized the alienation between many Protestant churches and working-class people. According to historian Donald Meyer, Holmes's Community Church forsook "any recognizable Protestant character, to become a kind of lower or lower-middle-class variation upon the religion of community service and humanism." Naturally, Holmes enthusiastically supported Randolph's BSCP activities from the outset and was indignant at the "steps taken by the Pullman Company to break up" Randolph's budding movement. The Community Church's debate featured Kelly Miller on the "no" side supporting orthodox Christianity and V. F. Calverton on the "yes" side denouncing orthodox Christianity. The magazine staff declared it a success, hoping that it would stimulate "a nationwide discussion of a very basic question among the white and colored people of the world today."[72]

Doing its part to encourage this discussion, the *Messenger* announced its intention to publish Miller's and Calverton's views along with a third perspective from sociology professor Gordon B. Hancock of Virginia Union University. Randolph's editorial decision to expand the religious debate to three views corresponded to the *Messenger*'s essay contest, which identified three modern views of religion found in the black community. A review of each of the three positions reveals, however, that the *Messenger* did not offer its readers a true debate on the pros and cons of orthodox Christianity but, rather, a forum presenting three liberal religious perspectives for the edification of the African American community.[73]

V. F. Calverton represented the radical viewpoint of those "who say that Christianity is a white man's religion; that it teaches the philosophy of slavery, meekness and submission." V. F. Calverton, a pseudonym for George Goetz of Baltimore, was a white radical and editor of the socialist magazine called the *Modern Quarterly*, which regularly advertised in the 1926 and 1927 *Messenger*s as the "One Realistic, Radical and Revolutionary Magazine in America." In his brief life, Calverton (1900–40) was at the center of American radicalism, influencing radical thought on the topics of sexuality, radical literature, and Socialist Party politics. For him, one of the most grotesque, spectacular, pathetic and tragic "contradictions in American life [was] that of a black man worshiping a white man's God in a black man's church." Although arguing that religious influences were declining in white culture, Calverton believed that black religiosity, the result of economic oppression, had persisted in black culture because of the strong influence of the Negro Church. The "result [was] timidity in emotional approach and compromise in intellectual conclusion." Developing and tracing the economic roots of black religion, Calverton believed that submerged classes always adopted the religion of the ruling class. But when southern plantation owners acquired a "this-worldly" construction of Christianity to enslave the "heirs of Ham," American blacks adopted an "other-worldly" Christianity to escape their oppression. Calverton argued that a religion "that visioned heaven as its millennium and earthly struggle as a futile delusion" reflected the escape mechanism, anomie, and the despair of slave Christianity, which continued to the present day.[74]

As a borrowed religion with an obsessive orthodoxy, Christianity harmed blacks, acting as a "chaotic, centrifugal influence" in black society and obscuring the struggle that was the inevitable concomitant of a competitive, capitalistic society. Blacks could not escape the conflict of the class struggle any more than whites could. Orthodox religion, backward and unprogressive, created myths instead of science and promoted Jesus instead of Marx and Darwin. Calverton's Marxist analysis of religion insisted that "the hope of the Negro [was] economic," whose salvation rested on uniting with the working class in a new economic order. Since blacks must challenge, not tolerate or submit to, the present order, Calverton urged blacks to leave the white man's conservatism and join the radical movement. "It is not against the white man, but against the ruling economic class that the new Negro must focus his assault." Calverton concluded:

> Orthodox religion, by its very philosophy, handicaps the growth of this attitude. In this respect, it handicaps not only the progress of the Negro but the progress of the entire proletariat. It handicaps the process of social change and economic revolution. Can we allow orthodox religion to impede the advance of a people and a proletariat?[75]

Randolph's inclusion of Calverton in the *Messenger*'s forum on orthodox Christianity not only reflected Randolph's connections to the freethought community in New York but also revealed the common way in which atheistic radicals like Calverton presented their unorthodox religious views to the general public. In this case, Calverton's participation in the *Messenger*'s debate allowed him to present his radical views to a black audience. Later, in 1934, Calverton published the *Passing of the Gods*, a fuller treatment of the Marxist interpretation of religion that he argued in John Haynes Holmes's church. To promote his book, Calverton arranged a symposium with Reinhold Niebuhr, Sidney Hook, and A. J. Muste at the Christ Presbyterian Church on the topic "Religion vs. Marxism." Calverton and Hook treated Niebuhr roughly. The *Messenger*-sponsored debate revealed that the radicals argued among themselves as well. The magazine printed an ongoing battle between the two Marxists V. F. Calverton and John Baddy, the contest winner. Baddy's attack on Calverton's essay revealed the deep divisions among radicals on religion, and their debate ended only with the *Messenger*'s demise. More important, the second debate elevated to a respectable level the atheistic perspective on religion.[76]

Kelly Miller, a professor of sociology at Howard University, represented the moderate wing of "Negroes who say . . . that the Christian church was the Negroes' first means of getting together and building race solidarity." During the *Messenger*'s radical period, Miller's moderate positions often irritated Randolph and Owen. In one early editorial, the editors observed that Miller "has made young Negro men and women think that he was radical, . . . and they will not stop now at his standard, but will press on to real radicalism." During the *Messenger*'s second phase, the editors' critical remarks about Miller lessened, especially when he publicly supported the magazine's liberal views of religion in its first religious debate and contributed articles advocating scientific evolution. Miller's support of orthodox Christianity in this current debate still proceeded from a progressive position, as the *Messenger* staff fully recognized. His support for traditional black Protestantism from a progressive position won the approval of the *Messenger* editors, who called it "one of the best things he's written," especially in his advocacy for science.[77]

First, Miller analyzed Christianity's role in modern civilization, making no attempt to dispute the "superhuman assumptions and metaphysical speculations which underlie all religion." For him, Jesus' influence was "greater than that of Alexander, Caesar, Napoleon, Washington and Lincoln rolled into one and manifolded a hundred times." Miller cited the progressive benefits of Christianity throughout its history in the development of ethical codes and human fraternity, as well as in the advancement of the great Western nations, and wondered how it could possibly "retard the Negro race in its upward struggle to attain the level which they have already reached through the beneficence of its influence?" He perceived the Christian Church as divided into "two conflicting camps from its very incipiency": the reactionary and the progressive. Understanding that "the leaven of the progressive spirit has ever been at work," he argued for the compatibility of science and religion, even religion's adaptability to science: "Moses could not wait for Copernicus, Sir Isaac Newton, Darwin and Einstein. But as fast as science fully demonstrates that any of the assumptions of religion are false or erroneous, religion has never failed to adjust itself to the fuller discovery of truth." In fact, it was the backward, reactionary faction of the church that "refused to follow the light of science." Miller conceded that the Christian Church had made mistakes, yet "the Christian Church in America lives as near to the fullness of the stature of the Sermon on the Mount as the state does to the doctrine of the Declaration of Independence." Miller thereby held to the optimistic conviction that the progressive wing in Christianity was triumphing over the more conservative elements.[78]

Second, Miller admitted that blacks encountered Christianity "when religion was in a reactionary mood," yet by using what St. Clair Drake identified as a "providential design" argument in black religious thinking, Miller asserted that "slavery was a school of learning, as well as of labor." He shared the same Eurocentric values of other progressives of his time, especially in his perceptions of the backwardness of Africa as a jungle or a heathen and benighted nation. According to Miller, the Fourteenth Amendment enabled Africans to be incorporated into the "most coveted citizenship of the world," possibly because former African slaves, as Christians, shared the same religious tradition as the dominant culture. Miller wrote that "a race within a race constitutes a problem of great complexity; but when the issue of race becomes complicated with the difference of religion the problem takes on a double order of difficulty." As part of the dominant Protestant Christian tradition, Negroes had one less form of discrimination with which to contend. He elaborated:

> Through its cruel discipline the Negro learned the language, the industrial method, the moral code, and the cultural canons of the most advanced section of the human family. . . . The African has caught the secret and method of European culture. The enslaved Negro has become the most advanced section of the two hundred millions of his blood. If the continent of Africa is ever to be redeemed, it will be through the enslaved fragment in Christian lands. The enslavement of Joseph made for the salvation of the Israelitish race. It may prove so with the enslavement of the African.[79]

At the same time, Miller argued that Christianity had not conditioned blacks to servility, since Christianity's teachings of the fatherhood of God and the brotherhood of man doomed human slavery. He cited Denmark Vesey, Nat Turner, Frederick Douglass, and thousands of slaves who "rushed to the Union lines in quest . . . of freedom," as not submissive but Christian men of progressive spirit. Moreover, "religion was essential to the Negro's well-being" because it offered him solace from the inescapable ills "which he must needs suffer here." As for being "otherworldly," Miller believed in the "inherent wisdom" of an apocalyptic philosophy that "transfers to another world the joys which are forbidden in the vale of tears." The black man's yearning for heaven, which Miller de-fined as a place of justice and equality, was based "in the deeper recesses of his being," and he hoped that eventually justice "would be prevalent here on earth." Miller insisted that all "overborne and heavily laden peoples" embraced an apocalyptic philosophy to sustain them in the "darker days of trial and tribulation."[80]

Miller's final point centered on the Negro Church. Christianity had not handicapped black progress but in the "sphere of religious activity" blacks had made the "greatest headway" and demonstrated "the greatest executive ability and effective concerted will." The Negro Church, had "organized four millions of his race in definite religious denominational allegiance," building "thirty thousand churches" and ordaining "forty thousand priests of God," at a property value of "eighty millions of dollars." Noting the complex organization of the Negro Church, Miller explained that it provided a stable base for American blacks, establishing numerous schools and colleges. In politics, business, and in "movements for political and civic reforms," black ministers led the way. Harking back to his providential design argument, Miller believed that without this religious encumbrance, "there would be a rapid relapse back towards the jungle level of heathenism and barbarianism from which the Christian religion has rescued" the black man. With one last comparison with the "native African," Miller argued that contact with Christianity had been the chief agency in this salvation, not merely in the salvation of his soul in the future world, but also in his social salvation in the world that was here and now.[81]

According to the *Messenger* editors, Gordon B. Hancock, a sociology professor at Virginia Union University, represented the viewpoint of those "who take the ground that Christianity is all right . . . but that the Negro Church is just archaic in form, structure and policy." Since 1925, Hancock had served as pastor to the Moore Street Missionary Baptist Church in Richmond, Virginia. Hancock's biographer Raymond Gavins stated that "Moore Street teachers and students from Union rubbed shoulders with hundreds of uneducated workers, while the church's day care center, industrial school, and adult education program offered strong testimony to the idea of betterment in this world." Hancock believed in an earth-centered church and "expected Moore Street to play an even greater role in providing social services and promoting social justice." Randolph and the *Messenger* staff saw Hancock's position in their debate as between Calverton's "yes" and Miller's "no." As a socially conscious Baptist minister, Hancock was the type of young progressive minister that Randolph needed to support his labor activism.[82] Hancock stimulated intellectual inquiry among his Union students, who made a significant contribution to the "Talented Tenth." Chandler Owens had been a Virginia Union student, as had been Abram L. Harris, the debate's organizer. Apparently, Harris invited Hancock to participate in the *Messenger* debate, as well as another "Unionite," sociologist Charles S. Johnson, who presided over the debate at the Community Church.[83]

Unlike Calverton and Miller, Hancock distinguished liberal orthodoxy from conservative heterodoxy, since "this lack of definite distinction makes neither the affirmative or negative position necessarily conditional." In a two-part argument, Hancock demonstrated his position that the benefits of a liberal orthodoxy effectively counteracted the handicaps of an illiberal orthodoxy evident in the Negro Church. Defining black progress as the ability to partake in the larger life of the society, Hancock argued that the essentially conservative religion of the Negro Church encouraged white philanthropy, a poor substitute for social justice. At the same time, Hancock cautioned against precipitously casting away the old institution for new and doubtful radical elements, as Calverton suggested. Hancock emphasized that "the radical element" had little or nothing to offer, truly an ironic position to take, considering the *Messenger*'s support of radicalism and freethought. But it underscored Randolph's commitment to an open debate, even when it criticized a position supported by the *Messenger*'s editorial policy. Hancock elaborated on his indictment of atheism:

> Although there are some Negroes who inveigh against religion itself and apparently incline themselves to atheism and irreligion, thanks be, their number is inconsiderable when compared with the great masses of Negro who seem neither capacitated nor inclined to dispense with the solace of religion. Atheism is negative and progress is positive and the progress of a race cannot be intelligently predicated upon a negation. Atheism, therefore, is subversive of the Negro's highest aspiration.[84]

Hancock believed that the Christian message found in scripture, which advocated the fatherhood of God and the brotherhood of men, contributed to the physical and spiritual emancipation of black people in America but that the centripetal forces of the conservatives balanced the centrifugal forces of liberals in the Negro Church, only as social justice prevailed in society.[85]

Hancock perceived several dangerous tendencies in an illiberal interpretation of Christianity. An orthodoxy that inflated a false distinction between reason and faith or science and religion often deflected "spiritual energies that might be used for more fruitful purposes." He cited current efforts to introduce "monkey bills" into some state legislatures over the "celebrated Scopes trial in Tennessee," and those "fundamentalists" who attempted to discount scientific progress. From Hancock's perspective, "the Negro has nothing to gain by a disbelief in science and in so far as orthodox religion seeks to cultivate the age-long enmity between religion and science it certainly is a serious handicap to the Negro's progress." The religious dogmatism that accompanied much of orthodox religious thinking only incapacitated the black freedom of thought and expression that was "so essential to any program of social betterment." By an overemphasis on doctrinal issues, arguing the finer points of the Atonement, the Trinity, and the Virgin Birth, ministers became caught up in heated wrangles and pointless controversies, especially when "the Negro needs a social gospel and not a theological gospel as some erroneously postulate in the name of orthodoxy." Besides, illiberal orthodoxy's attack on liberal religion contradicted historical evidence, and Hancock cited such examples as Martin Luther, John Huss, St. Paul, and John Brown, who "dared put his head into a hangman's noose in holy mockery at the monster of human slavery." Moreover, Jesus himself was a liberal thinker, "crucified by orthodox Jews of his day," as were today's "white men and women of the north and south who believe that the Negro is entitled to every right granted other races." In his advocacy for a liberal orthodoxy, Hancock concluded,

> Any suppression of liberal thought is subversive of the interests of society and certainly it tends to contravene the aspirations of black men. . . . A race religiously trained to narrow thinking will be . . . handicapped in a world where progress lies along the path of liberal thought . . . through which submerged groups may hope for relief.[86]

Unlike the earlier religious debate, the *Messenger* offered no clues to the public's reception to its three-part debate on orthodox Christianity, perhaps due to the increasing editorial preoccupation with BSCP matters.

There were several similarities between the 1923 and the 1927 *Messenger* debates on Christianity and the black community. Both showed that the magazine consistently endorsed liberal and unorthodox religious views. Although the editors claimed they presented all sides of the debate, the content of both debates never offered the conservative, orthodox side of religion. William Pickens and Kelly Miller represented the progressive views in the Negro Church circulating before World War I, which critiqued it as an archaic institution. John Carroll and Gordon Hancock represented a younger generation, well educated and conversant with modern theological trends and supportive of a more liberal orthodoxy in black Protestantism.

Randolph used his *Messenger* magazine to educate the black community about new religious alternatives available to African Americans in the new postwar world order. This liberal approach demonstrated that he and his colleagues objected to the orthodox religion of the Negro Church but not to religion or religious institutions themselves. For them, religious orthodoxy stifled and denied black people their social, economic, and political rights as American citizens. Throughout the magazine's existence, Randolph became more adept at targeting his opposition to the orthodoxy of the Negro Church, which tacitly accepted a secondary and segregated role in American Christianity.

As if heeding Gordon Hancock's admonition that atheism subverted "the Negro's highest aspiration" and that "the progress of a race cannot be intelligently predicated upon a negation," during this period when the *Messenger* took up the Pullman porters' cause for better working conditions, Randolph began to deny publicly that he was an atheist. From 1925 to 1937, while Randolph fought for recognition of a Pullman porters' union, his opponents often accused him of being a communist. Randolph hoped that with the number of ministers and other social and civic associations that supported the Brotherhood, the "old bogey, manufactured out of whole cloth, that [the] movement was 'red,' inspired by Moscow, [had] been completely exploded and retired forever." Often linked with communism were charges of atheism, a label Randolph had more difficulty refuting. An analysis of the *Messenger*'s religious content reveals that charges of Randolph's atheism started early and came up frequently. Randolph, angry that his opponents continually classified his socialist beliefs as disloyal and atheistic, reprinted the *Social Service Bulletin* of the Methodist Episcopal Church in the *Messenger*, which en-

dorsed the BSCP as a "bona fide labor organization." The report shows
that the Pullman Company attempted to discredit Randolph by labeling
him an atheist:

> The Pullman Company is actively opposing the union. . . . A company
> representative states emphatically that the Pullman Company has done
> more than any other agency for the negro in this country. A. Philip Ran-
> dolph, editor of the *Messenger* is in his estimation, "socialistic" and
> "atheistic," an organizer for the union is an undesirable character,
> porters who join the union are "disloyal."[87]

Several early *Messenger* articles reflected Randolph's sarcastic and vitriolic attitude toward his opponents, especially their charges of atheism.
At first, he regarded the charges as too absurd for consideration. His
replies to the prominent Perry Howard, a Republican national committeeman from Mississippi, suggested that such a ridiculous accusation
hardly merited a reply:

> Not satisfied with his nameless puerilities, misnamed economic view-
> point, he labors to drag in some half-wit comment on the movement to
> organize the Pullman porters denying the existence of God. And this is
> supposed to be a lawyer, too. The charge is so groundless that it does not
> merit a decorous reply.[88]

In another article singling out Howard, Randolph attacked his opponent's logic, which not only stereotyped political and religious beliefs but
also confused them.

> You say that my philosophy will convert the race into atheists, commu-
> nists, and agnostics. This is unworthy of a man of your alleged intelli-
> gence. You ought to know better. It is so ridiculous, inane and preposter-
> ous that it hardly merits a decorous reply. It is the last refuge of a man
> without arguments, principles or facts.[89]

Randolph's reply to Joe Bibb, the editor of the *St. Louis Argus*, used
the same sarcastic tone, implying that his reputation made it unnecessary
for him to offer a serious reply: "And as the last refuge of an impotent intellect, you attempt, in the absence of facts and argument, to drag in some

talk about unbelief in a God. This is so irrelevant and immaterial, puerile, pusillanimous and absurd that it does not justify any serious consideration."[90]

But as Randolph and his labor movement progressed and personal attacks on his character continued, he was forced to answer the charge of atheism directly. In a long response to a Boston-based group called the Industrial Defense Association, Randolph spoke out on what he perceived as an attack on his character and good name. According to him, the Industrial Defense Association, created at the height of his BSCP organizing efforts, was a front for the Pullman Company and part of its propaganda efforts against the BSCP. In his reply, Randolph identified ten specific charges made by the association against him: he was a believer in Negro social equality, miscegenation, and free love; an atheist, a communist, and an anarchistic socialist; an advocate of violence and riots; a race leader intent on dominating the world; a publisher of indecent literature; and a draft dodger. Randolph pointed out that all the charges made against him were "predicated upon alleged opinions of mine appearing in the *Messenger* . . . some eight or ten years ago." He argued that the "objectionable opinions," which had appeared recently, had not been written or "spoken by me in eight or ten years." Randolph believed that "terrifying and subversive opinions" were sent to leading citizens and papers because he was then "actively organizing the Pullman porters and maids." On the specific charge of atheism, Randolph made this comment:

> I am charged with the belief in freedom from all religious inhibitions and restraints and the adoption of atheism as a means to freedom. This, too, is a definite mis-representation. I have never advocated any such opinions. I attend churches, although I am not a member of any particular church. I was raised in the African Methodist Episcopal Church, my father being one of its oldest ministers. I am not an atheist. I am fully appreciative of the social and spiritual value of the Church of all faiths.[91]

Randolph further argued that church membership was not a reliable indicator of one's character and named several prominent unchurched citizens—all white—who were not attacked because of their personal views on religion. In so doing, Randolph implied that charges of atheism covered up a latent racism, as well as a historical antipathy to trade unionism in America: "It is a matter of common knowledge that some of our most useful citizens are not churchmen. Thomas Jefferson, Thomas A.

Edison, Clarence Darrow, Henry Ford, and others. But I have heard of no attack upon these characters by the Industrial Defense Association."[92]

Randolph and other Americans who challenged the Christian Church's obvious weaknesses and inconsistencies put themselves in dangerous positions and became vulnerable to personal attack. Randolph's refusal to be labeled an atheist was linked to his conviction that it obscured his unequivocal stand against the racial discrimination practiced by white America and long sanctioned by the American Christian community. Historians of American religion have observed that "liberal religionists have often been perceived by their more conservative compatriots as not only unsound in belief but as scarcely distinguishable from unbelievers." In a religious community, the charge of "unbeliever" and "infidel" often serves as a straw man to arouse the conservative or orthodox faithful to be on guard against anyone tainted with "unbelief." Randolph recognized charges of atheism as a ploy by those against his positions on trade unionism and Jim Crow laws and as a way to cut him out of the debate on these social and economic issues. From this time on, Randolph either denied he was an atheist or just gave up trying to explain his own religiosity.[93]

This exploration of the *Messenger*'s religious content shows how A. Philip Randolph and a group of Harlem radicals used the magazine to express a variety of liberal black Protestant viewpoints. Unlike Randolph's other unsuccessful and short-lived attempts to organize political forums during this period, such as the Independent Political Council and the FNF, the *Messenger* existed for more than a decade as a forum for liberal and progressive ideals, finding an appreciative, national audience. Although in the beginning the *Messenger* editors set out to attack all that was "narrow and medieval in religion," especially the Negro Church's accommodation to Jim Crow, Randolph himself redirected this counterproductive editorial policy in religion in order to reach out to progressive-minded allies inside and outside the Negro Church. With the demise of radicalism by the 1920s, Randolph and other *Messenger* editors nonetheless kept up the debate on "orthodox" black Christianity by offering religious alternatives to their readers adapting to new industrial environments. In this process, Randolph insisted that religious ideas and institutions were not so sacrosanct as to be excluded from democratic debate. As a forum for various religious viewpoints, the *Messenger* should not be overlooked as a powerful mouthpiece for modern religious reform, especially for black religious communities.

In the *Messenger*'s last phase, as Randolph deliberately moved to organize the Pullman porters into an independent labor union, he consciously distanced himself from accusations of atheism while still challenging the Negro Church's status quo position regarding Jim Crow. Nonetheless, Randolph's advocacy of liberal religious ideas left him consistently branded as an unbeliever, an atheist, and one opposed to all religious institutions. Friends and opponents alike continued to label him in this way, little understanding the complexity and genuineness of his Christian beliefs, albeit unorthodox. Over the next thirty years, as Randolph organized the Brotherhood of Sleeping Car Porters in the 1930s, led a civil rights movement in the 1940s, and served as a pioneering architect for the modern civil rights movements of the 1950s, he consistently adhered to his own liberal religious beliefs, rooted in the socially conscious African Methodist traditions of his parents.

3

The Brotherhood
Religion for the Working Class

On April 5, 1930, two white boys in Locust Grove, Georgia, discovered the dead body of a black man tied to a small tree, his knees touching the ground. The man's white coat, the uniform of a Pullman porter, had been used to tie the man's neck to the tree. The boys reported their gruesome find to city officials, who identified the man as John H. Wilkins, a Pullman porter for the Southern Railway's Kansas City Special, who had been reported missing when the train reached Atlanta at 5:25 in the morning. Except for Wilkins's identity, everything else about his death remained a mystery. On closer examination, Wilkins's skull was found to be fractured in two places, and there was a deep wound under one of his arms. Ordinarily, the Kansas City Special ran nonstop between Macon and Atlanta, but railroad officials reported that on this particular run, the train had stopped at Juliette and then again in Sandy, seventeen miles south of Locust Grove. One report said the train went through Locust Grove at high speed, never stopping until it reached Atlanta. Another unconfirmed rumor circulated that the porter was killed on the train, taken from it when it slowed down in Locust Grove, and then carried more than a quarter of a mile from the tracks to the woods where the body was later found. At the coroner's inquest three days later, J. F. Busbee, the Pullman conductor on the train, stated that the train never stopped at Locust Grove, nor could he understand how the porter's body could have been taken from the train and lynched without Busbee's knowledge.[1]

Wilkins's mysterious death left many questions unanswered. His coat pocket contained $58.60, so robbery was eliminated as a motive for the murder. Speculation ranged from suicide to Wilkins's implication in such illegal activities as bootlegging and the theft of Pullman property, yet the dead man was considered an old and faithful employee of the Pullman Company, whose clean record left train officials completely baffled as to why he had been lynched. One possible motive for Wilkins's death was his membership in the Brotherhood of Sleeping Car Porters (BSCP). The BSCP quickly claimed Wilkins as one of its own, declaring that it intended to "place its entire resources behind this case" and to bring the guilty to justice. Wilkins's murder occurred in the formative years of the BSCP when A. Philip Randolph and a handful of disgruntled Pullman porters formed an organization that would represent the interests of Pullman porters.[2]

Since 1925, Randolph had begun to expose the difficult conditions in which black porters worked: low wages, unregulated work hours, unreasonable working conditions, tensions between white train conductors and black porters, and a poor pension plan. Randolph and the BSCP argued against probusiness practices such as the company-run union called the Pullman Porter Benevolent Association (PPBA), the company-controlled employment plan, nonmonetary rewards for worker recognition, and the appointments of token black leaders loyal to the company. Pullman porters needed their own independent trade union. Over the next several years, Randolph attacked Pullman's policies in the *Messenger*, especially the PPBA and the Employment Representation Plan, as falling far short of meeting the porters' economic needs. Randolph promised his readers that this was "only the beginning of the biggest fight ever waged in the interest of the down-trodden, exploited, starved and enslaved Negro workers."[3]

In the early twentieth century, the relationship between blacks and organized labor was tense, with deep racial animosity separating white and black workers on a number of working-class issues. The BSCP thus faced the daunting task of changing black public opinion from a bitter and hostile perception of trade unions to a recognition of the advantages that trade unions could offer black workers. The black religious community was divided between the independent BSCP union and the company union, so the BSCP worked quickly to galvanize black ministers and churches behind its fight for recognition. As far away as New York City and Oakland, California, black churches sponsored large "mass meetings" to protest John Wilkins's death. At St. Luke's Hall in New York, A. Philip Randolph, Roy Lancaster, and Ashley Totten, representing the BSCP, joined Walter White of the NAACP in a protest meeting on the evening of April 11, 1930, presided over by Rev. William Lloyd Imes. Outraged by Wilkins's murder, "a big mass meeting staged by the preachers of New York for the Brotherhood" was held on June 15 at the Salem

Methodist Episcopal Church, presided over by Randolph's old friend, Rev. Frederick Cullen. Through their efforts, the ministers' committee raised $175 in cash and secured pledges of more than $200.[4]

As a result of this meeting, a citizens' committee was formed, chaired by Rev. Imes, which issued a public statement, "To Our Fellow Citizens," stating that "a black man, a Pullman Porter . . . has been done to death" and that another "monster demonstration of the Brotherhood," organized by Ashley Totten, would soon follow. The statement demanded that porters be given not only a fair and decent wage with tolerable working conditions but also a safe working environment so that "this shocking, nameless and outrageous crime and murder SHALL NEVER HAPPEN AGAIN!" Nine more clergymen joined Imes and Cullen in protest: John Robinson of St. Mark's ME Church, Adam Clayton Powell of Abyssinian Baptist Church, W. A. Byrd of Community Church in Jersey City, A. C. Garner of Grace Congregational Church, D. Ward Nichols of Emanuel AME Church, W. P. Hayes of Mount Olivet Baptist Church, E. T. Clark of Bethel AME Church, Thomas J. B. Harris of Randall Memorial Church, and J. W. Broth of Mother Zion AME Church. In stirring religious rhetoric, the ministers endorsed Randolph's Brotherhood movement to organize Pullman porters into an independent trade union:

> "Son of man stand upon thy feet and I will speak unto thee," was a prophetic injunction given a GREAT SOUL when cast down in apparent hopeless dejection and despair. And in these trying times of storm and stress such a call to black men and women has come to stand upon thy feet and fight for the cause of TRUTH and RIGHTEOUSNESS—economic, political and religious, and, we, as a great race, shall not fail, for the God of Power and Progress will aid us. One such cause is the Brotherhood of Sleeping Car Porters, a movement to organize the Pullman Porters and Maids for a living wage and to make the life and limb and labor of BLACK MEN on Pullman cars, in the south, as safe as they are for White men.[5]

Supported by the black religious community, one ad in the *Black Worker* graphically depicted a lynching with the warning "This May Happen to You" and publicized the preachers' endorsement with a bold caption that read "Negro Ministers Join Fight." By June, the BSCP had organized the Wilkins Lynching Investigation Defense Fund. Rev. Cullen, representing the Interdenominational Ministerial Alliance, headed the

Wilkins Fund's ministers' committee. For the next several months, the
BSCP paper updated their readers on the state of the Wilkins Fund, often
specifying what various congregations contributed: St. Mark's Church,
$32.25; St. James Presbyterian Church, $40; a New York AME church,
$12; Emanuel Church, $10; Grace Congregational Church, $12. In Oak-
land, California, a mass meeting in Beth Eden Baptist Church was held to
raise money for the Wilkins Defense Fund. Other BSCP divisions rallied
behind the fund, demonstrating the issue's nationwide appeal to all black
Americans.[6]

On the same day that the New York preachers formed a citizens' committee in Rev. Cullen's church, the PPBA, the Pullman Company's union
for black porters, held its own religious "memorial services" at the
Abyssinian Baptist Church for porters who had died. This service was an
established custom reflecting the loyalty of the nation's black communities to the PPBA, an association they had always considered to be favorable to blacks.[7]

Ashley Totten's attack in the *Black Worker* on the PPBA meeting in the
Abyssinian church showed that the Brotherhood offered a fresh alternative to the black community to represent Pullman porters: the independent BSCP or the traditional PPBA. Totten argued that since the "services
were held under the auspices of the Pullman Company Union Benefit Department and . . . not by any of the Negro officials," this proved that the
Pullman Company's benefit association and the Employee Representation
Plan were "born of the same mother." Moreover, Totten claimed that the
memorial service failed even to mention the name of "J. H. Wilkins, the
Pullman porter who was lynched at Locust Grove, Ga., while on duty,
among the dead," a sure sign that the PPBA did not have the true interests of black people at heart, whereas the BSCP did. Although Totten concluded that the memorial service attendees were "stool pigeons, uncle
toms, enemies of their own race progress . . . without guts and manhood,
spies, spotters and sneaks," acting as slaves bowing to their masters, he
avoided blaming Adam Clayton Powell Sr., Abyssinian's minister who
hosted the event, or "an innocent congregation [that] did not know that
the worshipers of mammon had occupied the pulpit to perpetuate the system of long hours, low wages, little or no rest, frame-ups, slugging by the
underworld, lynching and other outrages by taking texts from the religion
of Jesus Christ." Totten contended that such burlesque shows put on by
the PPBA drove "the youth from the church and served to build up a race
of weaklings." In addition, Totten's sources claimed that even efforts to

get members of the audience to testify on behalf of the PPBA failed. Rev. Powell's "sermon was exceedingly short," which disappointed the PPBA group that "he didn't deliver a long pean [*sic*] of praise on the Pullman officials and welfare workers." He concluded that "Dr. Powell probably thought that it was an outfit which couldn't be blessed anyhow." Totten ended his attack by observing, "Perhaps the kindliest comment which might be made [was] that Negro churches should close their doors to that branch of the Pullman family which uses Christianity to fool the public."[8]

Five years before John Wilkinson's murder, Randolph had transformed the *Messenger* into the official organ of the fledgling union and a powerful tool for propaganda. But within weeks, Randolph's new organization faced opposition not only from the Pullman Company but also the black community. In the early days of labor organizing, Randolph claimed that he rarely found a black preacher committed to the philosophy of labor unionism but that white preachers did not "champion the cause of the trade union" either. Accordingly, Randolph and the BSCP had to fight antiunion sentiment both inside and outside the black Christian community.[9]

From the outset, Randolph and the Brotherhood organizers worked discreetly within established boundaries of black religious institutions to gain the porters' allegiance to their trade union. BSCP propaganda in the *Messenger* usually identified three groups in the black community as their main opposition: black leaders affiliated with the Pullman Company, the black press, and the Negro Church, but when BSCP organizers accused this corrupt triumvirate of selling out the race "for a mess of pottage," they carefully singled out individuals who opposed their labor union–organizing efforts. In the Pullman Company, the BSCP targeted Perry Howard, Melvin Chisum, and Perry Parker, the head of the PPBA. In the black press, the *Chicago Whip*, *Chicago Defender*, and the *St. Louis Argus* represented the opposition. The BSCP targeted Bishop A. J. Carey and Rev. I. Garland Penn as symbols of the Negro Church. When organizing the local BSCP divisions, the national BSCP sent questionnaires and surveys to the local divisions, asking them to assess the attitude of the black press, the church, and other black leaders toward the Brotherhood and to rate them as poor, fair, or good. The following statement is typical of how the BCSP attacked its opponents individually:

Since the Brotherhood of Sleeping Car Porters was organized on August 25th, 1925, the Pullman Company has done everything imaginable to kill it. It bought up the so-called big Negro leaders like Perry Howard,

Melvin Chisum, Claude Barnett, Bishop A. J. Carey, Rev. I. Garland Penn, and a number of others, but found to its utter regret that they didn't lead anybody. It chloroformed some of the alleged leading Negro papers with gold, such as the *Whip*, the *Defender*, the *St. Louis Argus*, *Heebie Jeebies*, etc., but soon saw that these journals of deceit, ignorance and venality were forthwith discredited and condemned by the porters in particular and the public in general. Today these men and these papers are only a by-word and a hissing in the minds of respectable Negroes.[10]

During the BSCP's first year, the *Messenger* ran a negative campaign against these "big Negro leaders," using cartoons portraying them as fawning "hat-in-hand" Uncle Toms. Pullman employees Perry Howard and Perry Parker often appeared in minister's garb, on their knees petitioning "to the Lawd" to save their jobs. Although one cartoon depicted the Pullman Company as a large octopus grasping a symbolic church building labeled "Negro Churches," most cartoons were aimed specifically at Bishop Carey and Rev. Penn. One cartoon showed them slinking out of a Pullman office, their Bibles dropped on the floor, which suggested they had sold out their religious principles to the Pullman Company. Another cartoon summed up the BSCP's position on the "most notorious" event connected with Bishop Carey: the infamous 1925 Washington, D.C., conference. The Pullman Company, depicted as a giant, pot-bellied, double-chinned white man handing a bag of money to three little black figures, fat and thick lipped, is saying, "Take this money and get your race leaders in conference in Wash., D.C.—supposedly to fight segregation but actually to condemn the porters' organization movement." The money was spent on transportation, hotel bills, a big banquet, and a "little something" for themselves. The three black figures, identified as Bishop Carey, Perry Howard, and Melvin Chisum, replied, "Yas sir, yas sir boss,—and we don't mean maybe."[11]

Bishop A. J. Carey of the African Methodist Episcopal Church remained the biggest target for attack by Randolph and the BSCP. During the early years of the Brotherhood, no one personified old "Uncle Tom" preachers better than this powerful AME bishop. Randolph described Carey as both "against the movement" and "against me." The fact that Carey knew Randolph's father through the AME Church connection and was outspoken in his disapproval of Randolph's new socialist ideas put the young radical on the defensive. Moreover, Bishop Carey's powerful opposition kept the BSCP from securing the endorsement of the AME Church. Indeed, at the 1925 Southwest Missouri Conference and annual convention, the African Methodist Episcopal Church passed a resolution unequivocally opposing black membership in the American Federation of Labor (AFL). Bishop Carey himself guided the resolution through the convention, instructing the ministers under his jurisdiction that "they had a responsibility to caution their membership against the pernicious influence of labor leaders."[12]

Three years later, the BSCP tried again to secure the endorsement of the General Conference of the AME Church, which was convening in Chicago. Again, Randolph blamed the lack of success on Bishop Carey's domination of the conference. In the summer of 1926, Randolph wrote in frustration of the Brotherhood's inability to secure the endorsement of the Baptist ministers' alliance from Rev. L. K. Williams, also president of the National Baptist Convention (NBC). Randolph complained that no minister at the meeting could offer any reason why the alliance would not endorse the BSCP. Randolph concluded that the Baptist alliance depended on the Pullman Company for travel passes, which Rev. Williams passed on to ministers to help defray travel expenses to church conferences and to conduct church business. Two years later, one supportive Baptist minister in Detroit suggested that the Brotherhood ask L. K. Williams for an opportunity to address the Baptist convention meeting in Louisville in September 1928. Milton Webster, a top BSCP official, agreed to write Rev. Williams, although he believed it was useless. But Randolph encouraged Webster to try, since the NBC was a "very powerful group." But like Webster, Randolph was not too hopeful about gaining Williams's cooperation. As he wrote to Webster, "If you can get the ear of Rev. L. K. Williams, it will go over; but he is a hard-boiled reactionary, and I don't know what can be done with him."[13]

The 1925 Washington conference, presided over by Bishop Carey, epitomized the antagonism between the BSCP and black religious leaders, an event that Randolph called the "most notorious example of Negro preachers taking the side of the Pullman Company against the porters' organization." The conference's organizers hoped to demonstrate that black leaders supported the Pullman Company's policies. According to the union's propaganda, the mastermind behind the Washington conference was not Bishop Carey but Melvin Chisum, an employee of the Pullman Company. In this case, Bishop Carey was only one of Chisum's "handy men." *Messenger* editorials described Chisum as a devious "Iago-type character few could trust," who intended "to glorify" the Pullman Company at the expense of the independent BSCP by getting black preachers and other leaders to endorse the Pullman Company's own employee plan.[14]

Chisum, "pulling the wool over the eyes" of those who attended the conference, claimed that the purpose of the meeting was to fight segregation. Carey was able to mobilize many of the ministers in his diocese to the Pullman cause because transportation and hotel expenses were defrayed by the Pullman Company and paid for by Melvin Chisum. In addition, the Pullman Company broadcast through the black press that black leaders endorsed the conference, but rumors circulated that this was not the case. For the next several months, the BSCP officials urged the conference attendees to have "guts enough to protest" the Pullman Company's unscrupulous tactics. Randolph wrote to several prominent ministers and conference participants, including Hutchens C. Bishop and Reverdy Ransom, demanding they explain why they had been "shamelessly manipulated by the Iago of the race to subserve the interest of the Pullman Company in its fight against the Pullman porters organizing for a living wage."[15]

Randolph's letter had an effect. By early 1926, new information regarding the conference led the BSCP to conclude that the majority of the participants had been lured into it "wholly unaware of its purposes and aims." As the BSCP circulated reports about the conference's real purpose—to discredit their union—the participants claimed they "knew nothing about resolutions sent out by the Associated Negro Press blessing the Pullman Company and damning the Pullman Porters' Union."[16]

Randolph believed that opposition to the BSCP was fueled by ignorance, especially in the case of most black ministers, since the average preacher, "white or colored," misunderstood the difference between a company union, in which membership was mandatory, and a trade union. Black ministers had traditionally viewed company unions as a "form of a beneficent economic philanthropy," to be accepted with gratitude and without condemnation. As Randolph explained,

> Because the Negro preachers regarded the industrial paternalism of the Pullman Company, manifested in its Employee Representation Plan and the Pullman porters Benefit Association, as a generous concession to the race, they viewed the rise of the Brotherhood of Sleeping Car Porters in August, 1925, with mingled suspicion, distrust and fear. What [was] true

of the attitude of Negro preachers was characteristic of most Negro leaders toward the porters' union."[17]

Randolph's correspondence with the highly regarded AME minister Reverdy Ransom confirmed the Brotherhood's position that many attendees at the conference had been deceived. Ransom told Randolph he had refused to attend, since he did "not care to attend meetings at the expense of anybody I do not know." Ransom's admission that he knew "nothing about the deliberations of the Conference held in Washington" agreed with other reports that Randolph received from other prominent individuals who attended the meeting. When the conference's true purpose was exposed, several of the attendees disavowed it and its program.[18]

Randolph respected Ransom's progressive positions in the AME Church, which helped counterbalance Carey's conservative actions, so far removed from Randolph's perceptions of the AME Church's activist tradition. Randolph emphasized that Ransom, "when approached to lend his name and influence to the above-named conference, definitely refused and sharply condemned its purpose," adding that the "Brotherhood count[ed] him among its most powerful champions in the ministry." Yet Ransom stopped short of openly endorsing the Brotherhood. Like other black religious leaders of his generation, Ransom had reservations about trade unions' organizing black workers. Randolph's conviction that black preachers were not committed to the cause of labor unionism because of the inherently racist practices of most unions was born out in Ransom's response to Randolph:

I did not and do not understand this movement pro and con. I feared on the one hand that there was an effort to organize the Pullman porters into a labor union and then that designing labor leaders may call a strike and white porters be substituted. On the other hand, I have understood that the aim of the Pullman Company is to seek to foster some sort of organization of the porters in connection with their company. You see by the foregoing that I am quite hazy as to the business, but I am not hazy on the question of permitting myself to be used in any interest affecting the race that is not strictly on the square.[19]

Randolph's and the BSCP's negative campaign against Bishop Carey continued throughout the first year of the BSCP's existence. But once the Washington conference controversy died down, the BSCP also toned down its anti-Carey rhetoric, claiming that it had "silenced" the opposition. One full-page cartoon portraying Bishop Carey, Melvin Chisum, and Perry Howard being plowed underground by a powerful BSCP tank driven by "General Organizer Randolph" illustrated that the "silenced" opposition signaled an end to any significant opposition by black churches. By June 1927, the BSCP reported a "new point of view among Negro churchmen," in which Carey and Penn stood virtually alone as "defenders of the rich Pullman Company."[20]

Still, the Washington conference remained a sore point for Randolph during the early days of the Brotherhood. In one letter to Webster, Randolph explained that the "conference of the 'big Negroes'" coincided with the "inspired propaganda" the Pullman Company had sent out to alienate him from the "the leaders of the American Federation and the standard railroad unions" and to weaken the Brotherhood. Randolph was referring to the charges, mentioned earlier, made by the Industrial Defense Association of Boston for the Pullman Company, which included the accusation that he was an atheist. Randolph sent Webster a copy of his reply to the association, to set the record straight once again.[21]

Besides the notorious Washington conference incident, the debate between Randolph and Perry Howard has gone down in Brotherhood lore as the time when clergymen generally changed their position toward the union and churches were no longer closed to the organization, indicating, from the BSCP's perspective, that opposition to Randolph's labor-organizing efforts in the black religious community was short-lived. In a 1934 article, journalist John L. Leary described the early days when the Pullman Company still enjoyed the backing of the black press and the clergy. But this all changed when a big break, "in the form of a challenge" to Randolph to debate Perry Howard, a Republican National Committeeman from Mississippi and an employee of the Pullman Company.[22]

The debate took place in Chicago, the center for the Brotherhood's organizational activity, when Randolph and Milton Webster, the organizer for the Chicago division, "began a series of meetings for putting the BSCP on the map." Webster faced considerable opposition from Chicago's black leaders, yet the Metropolitan Community Church "hall was packed, and hundreds of porters, with upturned faces and eager eyes, were awaiting the long expected emancipation" from the Pullman Company. Webster claimed that Pullman detectives "dogged our every step" in order to keep the local porters in line. When the Pullman Company ordered Howard to debate Randolph, the church was packed with "workers, business people, and the professional group." Randolph and Howard each spoke for forty minutes, and at the end Randolph claimed victory. Leary described Milton Webster's version of the story:

> Randolph and I were holding a lodge of sorrow when that challenge came. . . . We were pretty nearly down and out. We couldn't pray hard enough that the Lord would preserve Mr. Howard's good health until the night of the meeting, and not allow him to change his mind about meeting Randolph. The Lord was with us. Howard showed up all right, in the biggest hall in the Negro section. In almost less time that it takes to tell, Randolph ran him out of gas. I got my coat ripped off, helping the police get Howard out.[23]

Believing that the opposition was effectively silenced, Randolph embarked on a constructive campaign to educate the black community about the positive aspects of trade unionism. Like missionaries in uncharted territory, the BSCP began a campaign to create a "new" Pullman porter. Believing that the public was on their side, Randolph described the BSCP's strategy to mobilize black opinion into "an active force behind us." They planned "to acquaint every social, civic and religious organization with the aims and methods of the Brotherhood" and obtain their endorsements. Recognizing the support of black religious leaders and communities as critical to changing public opinion regarding unionizing, Randolph devised several strategies to win them over to his cause. First, he sought alliances with like-minded progressive or liberal ministers and ministerial associations throughout the various BSCP divisions as he toured cities setting up forums and "mass" meetings. Second, he involved black preachers and churches in labor conferences featuring educational talks on labor and the church. In this way, Randolph broadened the BSCP's base of support by building strong alliances with social gospel advocates in white Protestant circles, as well as affiliating with a black ecumenical movement in the black church and still in its formative stages in the 1930s. Finally, as Randolph worked to integrate black religious communities into his labor-organizing activities, he searched for a religion suitable for working-class people, a religion based on the idea of brotherhood.[24]

Randolph's compatibility with "outstanding, independent, progressive, intellectual Negro preachers" not only reflected his own religious nature but also demonstrated Carter G. Woodson's observation that by the mid-1920s, the black church contained an influential progressive force. The alliances that Randolph formed with progressive leaders in the black church from this period remained with him throughout many years of his civil rights activism. BSCP propaganda in the *Messenger* and later in the *Black Worker* showed how progressive ministers and their churches often defined the path that Brotherhood organizations would follow.[25]

The "BSCP Notes" were often vague on the exact location of meeting places, since union organizing in the early days was dangerous work, but it is clear that all six original BSCP divisions started in black churches or religious communities. The BSCP did not provide the names of porters, either. After the first successful "mass meeting" in Washington, D.C., the first BSCP divisions were established in Boston, Chicago, St. Louis, Kansas City, and Omaha. By 1928, BSCP organizations had been organized into larger regions on the East Coast, the Midwest, the Northeast, the Northwest, the West, and West Coast. The BSCP's strategy of meeting in black churches as often as possible had political and psychological as well as economic advantages. The BSCP gratefully accepted the use of a church building free of charge, for it saved the Brotherhood money. For Randolph, this situation was critical to the movement's beginning:

> In the beginning of the movement, every effort was made to close the doors of churches throughout the country to the porters' fight. In every city, however, the organization was able to secure a large prominent church for its meetings, though sometimes it was necessary to pay fifty dollars therefor. In some instances, the use of the churches was given the union without any cost.[26]

The BSCP campaign on the East Coast concentrated on Washington, D.C., Boston, and New York City. Washington was "the first in the organization campaign drives to put the Brotherhood over the top." There, Randolph described one event when the pulpit of the John Wesley Church was filled with white labor leaders. At this early meeting, several union leaders of the "Big Four" railway unions appeared alongside the leader of the AFL, William Green. A close associate of Randolph during this time, Green had an important influence on the Brotherhood's development. Besides his connections to the labor community, Randolph related to Green as a former Methodist preacher. Randolph worked closely with the Negro

International Ministers' Alliance in Washington, which unanimously endorsed the Brotherhood in the early stages of its organization.[27]

In Boston, Randolph recounted that "a series of meetings had been prepared by some of the bolder spirits of the porters in the colored churches." Although Boston had a "superconservative" reputation, the Brotherhood movement gradually took hold. When BSCP organizer Ashley Totten arrived to "awaken Boston" on a second tour of the city, he found receptive audiences in such groups as the Twentieth Century Club and the League of Neighbors, as well as in religious groups like the New Thought Forum. One influential Bostonian named John Orth, described as "a humanist and champion of the rights of all oppressed peoples," helped stage a Brotherhood meeting at which Randolph's speech, "stirred all Boston" in "one of the largest mass meetings" held there. So successful was the campaign drive that Brotherhood propaganda claimed its opposition had been "completely routed" so that "men in Boston [were] flowing into the Union."[28]

One effective strategy Randolph used in this period was mobilizing "various liberal persons" into "citizens' committees of one hundred" to educate the public about "the drastic policy of reprisals" practiced by the Pullman Company on porters suspected of belonging to the Brotherhood. Organized in large cities, Randolph wanted each committee to cooperate with its local BSCP division. By mobilizing the community's support of the Brotherhood, Randolph believed that the "Company cannot stand up against the Brotherhood and the Community too." Progressive-minded ministers constituted an important base for these citizen committees. Professor Orth served on Boston's citizens' committee, composed of seventy-four white and black men and women who proclaimed their "faith in the justice of the cause of the Pullman porters and maids" by publishing a small pamphlet entitled "The Pullman Porters' Struggle." The pamphlet advertised the Brotherhood's fight for decent wages and employment conditions for Pullman porters, listed their demands, and provided a brief history of several early BSCP events. In an early endorsement, the Boston committee identified with Randolph's labor movement from a neoabolitionist perspective, in the tradition of the New England antislavery movement, as its pamphlet explained:

> We are but continuing the glorious and illustrious tradition begun by self-sacrificing schoolmarms, the flower of New England life, who left

their comfortable home surroundings, and went to the aid of the freed-
men after the Civil War, carrying the torch of education and religious
training, as well as the matchless heroism and noble devotion to principles of her sons.[29]

The membership list included at least thirteen clergymen, including its
chairman, Rev. Sidney Lovett. Cassius A. Ward, of Ebenezer Baptist
Church in Boston, chaired the finance committee. Other notable members
included Rabbi Samuel J. Abrams, Professor Felix Frankfurter, and
William Monroe Trotter. Trotter, an influential black journalist before
World War I, was well known for his radical opposition to any form of
accommodation to Jim Crow policies. Randolph had long admired Trotter's radicalism, even though it "was chiefly racial," reflecting an older
school of thought among black intellectuals unlike the modern views of
Randolph and other black socialists. Years later, when asked whether
Trotter supported the Brotherhood, Randolph replied, "Yes, he'd come to
the meetings in Boston, and I had meetings in the churches chiefly, and he
would agree to be on the program and speak."[30]

New York City, Randolph's home base, was the intellectual center of
the Brotherhood. During his years in Harlem, Randolph had formed
friendly relationships with several of the city's most progressive ministers
through his political activism. He therefore was able to mobilize an impressive group of ministers behind his union in the very early days of
Brotherhood organization, well in advance of other BSCP divisions,
which still had to educate their ministers on the advantages of labor
unions. Randolph described the Interdenominational Ministerial Alliance
as "an outstanding instance of stalwart, honorable, progressive Negro
clergymen . . . who endorsed the BSCP and agreed to preach Brotherhood
sermons on its behalf." To Randolph, they represented the "new point of
view among Negro churchmen."[31]

New York City's porters support of the union developed slowly in the
first months of 1925 until Rev. Adam Clayton Powell Sr. of the Abyssinian Baptist Church "unequivocally and clearly registered his support and
endorsement of the Brotherhood," which Randolph perceived as "an action demonstrating growing BSCP support in the city." On June 13,
1926, a "mass meeting" arranged by Rev. Powell proclaimed Randolph
"as a prophet," and Powell's church "packed enthusiastic weekly meetings" in support of the Brotherhood. Rev. Powell's name appeared on
New York's "committee of one hundred," including several other clergy-

men and seminarians—William Lloyd Imes of St. James Presbyterian Church, Edwin Fairley, Clarence Howell, John H. Robinson of St. Mark's Methodist Episcopal Church, George Frazier Miller of St Augustine Episcopal Church, John Haynes Holmes of the Community Church, and Robert Bagnall, associated with the NAACP. Randolph stressed the "public prominence" and respectability of the men and women on the committee:

> It certainly speaks definitely for the responsibility of our movement. None of the persons, who are members of the Committee, can be accused of readily affixing their names to anything in which they have no confidence. Especially, would they be hesitant about venturing into the Brotherhood, implicit with big and far-reaching principles, unless they were committed to its program.[32]

Early BSCP campaigns in the Midwest were carried out in St. Louis, Kansas City, Omaha, and Chicago. In St. Louis, without any advance agent to secure accommodations and make arrangements for meetings, Ashley Totten did everything himself. The local paper, the *St. Louis Argus*, a staunch opponent of the BSCP, hampered local organizing. Although Totten secured a centrally located church and advertised a Brotherhood meeting, he found "the work was uphill and difficult for the first week." But an interest in their efforts developed as the "pall of fear was gradually being dissipated by the constant hammering of facts and arguments on reasons why every porter should become a member of the Brotherhood." Although the *St. Louis Argus* had "already sold out to the Company," Randolph sent out his own bulletin "setting forth the truth about the movement." He recorded that "one preachers' organization, after a short presentation of the work before it, endorsed the movement." In this first report, Randolph seemed convinced that by the campaign's end, "a vigilant and able organizing committee was established" and the "the spirit of St. Louis has grown rapidly in favor of the Brotherhood."[33]

Although it is not clear to which "preachers' organization" in St. Louis Randolph was referring, the "able and vigilant" local committee was certainly E. J. Bradley. Inspired by Randolph's first article on the Pullman porters, Bradley joined the Brotherhood early in November 1925, after working twenty years for the Pullman Company. Bradley organized the BSCP in St. Louis at great personal risk: his wife left him, he was never paid, and he was constantly harassed by the Pullman Company. Although constantly pressured to close his Brotherhood office, especially later during the Depression, Bradley managed to hold on. Two preachers came to his aid despite Bishop Carey's powerful influence. In November 1925, just as the Brotherhood started actively recruiting porters, Bradley reproted how "Bishop Carey held a Methodist conference and warned all of his local preachers to discount the 'Randolph Movement' and they did just as they were advised." To make matters worse for Bradley, "the *St. Louis Argus* printed a very bad article against our organization." Still, two of St. Louis's "big Negro churches," Rev. George Stevens's Central Baptist Church and Rev. Jackson's Metropolitan AME Zion Church, obviously not under Carey's influence, opened their doors to the Brotherhood.[34]

For the most part, however, Bradley struggled alone, especially while the negative ad campaign sponsored by the Pullman Company continued. According to Bradley, during the early stages of the BSCP's organizational drive, the Pullman Company circulated in its local offices editions of "five of the largest Negro newspapers" carrying weekly articles "written by some preacher or educator advising Pullman porters to beware of that 'Randolph Union.'" Bradley found that many black ministers "accepted $300 to keep any and all of us out of their churches." Since St. Louis was the Pullman Company's third largest district, Bradley feared its loss would give the company a signal victory and weaken the Brotherhood. Randolph, too, worried about St. Louis in the early days, as this letter to BSCP organizer Roy Lancaster indicates:

> The situation in St. Louis is quite discouraging. I am writing brother Bradley for a list of his members so that I may send them a personal letter . . . to stimulate them. . . . I will inform brother Bradley unless some improvement can be made in the production, we will be compelled to close the office there. It is unfortunate that he has been unable to do better, St. Louis being such a large district.[35]

The Brotherhood traveled to Kansas City by invitation; in fact they were "urged to hasten there," for "rumors were afloat everywhere that the field was ripe." By the time Randolph arrived, Ashley Totten had secured a meeting place for a BSCP rally and had already spoken in several churches. The local YMCA provided space for "meetings day and night." Randolph reported that Kansas City "men showed little or no fear" on hearing the Brotherhood's message. He applauded "the splendid assistance" of Rev. D. A. Holmes, "who gave me the opportunity to address his large Sunday morning service on the objects and aims of the movement." Holmes remained a loyal BSCP supporter throughout the tough years of BSCP organizing, and the BSCP recognized him as one of the "first of the leading ministers of the country to come out boldly and openly and champion the cause of the porters' right to organize." BSCP organizer Bennie Smith recalled one local porter's funeral service in which Rev. Holmes "preached the sermon" in a "real Brotherhood funeral and the stooles [*sic*] were taken to task by Rev Holmes." It was in Kansas City that Randolph directly confronted "four of the prominent leaders of the city" whom Melvin Chisum had talked into attending the Washington conference. Randolph claimed that the conference had created a "considerable stir among the people" in Kansas City, and when he confronted several of the community leaders involved, they "protested their innocence pointing out that they had no idea of the purpose of the conference."[36]

From Kansas City, Randolph and Ashley Totten went to Omaha, Nebraska, where despite the very cold weather, "the people turned out in large numbers to the meetings." In Omaha, Randolph began organizing citizens' committees. As they had in Kansas, they vigorously assaulted Bishop Carey for his "action in betraying the porters for the Pullman Company." Since they were in Bishop Carey's diocese, this "caused citywide talk . . . [and] was the subject of bitter comment by the people." But Omaha's "high militant spirit" made it a BSCP stronghold.[37]

Chicago, headquarters of the Pullman Company, was another center of Brotherhood activities, primarily because of the critical leadership of Milton Webster. Webster's powerful influence in the Brotherhood was second only to Randolph's, and their partnership made the Chicago division the heart of the international BSCP. Historian William Harris described the effectiveness of this partnership despite the two men's entirely different personalities and styles of leadership. Like many local BSCP organizers, Webster experienced more of the day-to-day hardships of union organization, especially in the first years of opposition to the Brotherhood's message. As "an old-timer in Chicago," Webster knew everyone "from the crooks up to the preachers." When Webster started organizing, he "started first on the preachers." Of the "35 or 40 top Negroes" whom Webster approached, five agreed to participate in a planned BSCP meeting, yet only one actually showed up. Because Chicago had a notoriously antiunion history, the BSCP's eventual victory was all the more significant. But in the early days, with "much of the influential Negro leadership in the community" lined up behind the Pullman Company, Webster found "not every preacher, but many of them, the biggest ones; not every politician but many of them, the biggest ones; not all the newspapers but most of them, the biggest ones, were lined up on the other side."[38]

Fortunately for Webster, one minister went out of his way to endorse, cooperate, and present "the organization to the people of Chicago": Dr. W. D. Cook. Just as Webster played a critical role as Chicago's local BSCP organizer, Dr. Cook played a central role in Chicago's black religious community in encouraging support for the BSCP in its early days. According to Randolph, Dr. Cook served as "one of the outstanding instances of a Negro preacher resisting the corrupting influences of the Pullman company." Dr. Cook, a former pastor of the Bethel AME Church, founded the Metropolitan Community Church in 1920, reflecting a new religious trend of "community churches" that started with the Great Migration when black churches proliferated, owing to church "splits or schisms."[39]

Benjamin Mays, scholar of the early black church, wrote that some churches in Chicago, Baltimore, and Detroit broke from the autocracy and oppression of denominational authorities. For example, the Metropolitan Community Church in Detroit described itself as "a church of the people, by the people, and for the people." The People's Community Church of Christ in Chicago organized "for religious liberty and freedom of action." Dr. Cook's position as an independent minister of a community church freed him from the ecclesiastical authority of church leaders like Bishop Carey. Indeed, Cook's independence from denominational authority partly explains his fearless support of the BSCP and demonstrates how new religious developments in the black community made labor union activism more acceptable. One of Cook's church members was Ida B. Wells-Barnett, also a former member of Chicago's Bethel AME Church, who joined the Metropolitan Community Church the year Cook founded it. Together he and Wells-Barnett supported the fledgling union. Webster expressed gratitude for Wells-Barnett's "noble assistance when we were passing through our most critical period" when the union "met the most strenuous opposition."[40]

The critical period to which Webster was referring was in December 1925 when he and Randolph were seeking the support of several women's organizations in Chicago that "showed intense interest and expressed deep disgust and amazement at the treachery, duplicity and venality" of the BSCP's vocal opposition, Perry Howard, Melvin Chisum, and Bishop Carey. At one "pink tea parlor social affair" hosted by Ida Wells-Barnett, Randolph addressed a Chicago women's forum of twenty-five persons. Originally Wells-Barnett wanted Randolph to address the forum at the Appomattox Club but was refused because many of the club's members had ties to the Pullman Company. Webster considered the Appomattox Club the "home of all our enemies." Wells-Barnett could not conceive "of Negro Leaders taking such a narrow and selfish view of such vital problems affecting the Race." Wells-Barnett, active in the adult Sunday school and president of the Sunday Evening Forum of Dr. Cook's Community Church, regularly presented "outstanding speakers and engaged in discussions of religious, civic, and social importance." At the tea, Wells-Barnett introduced Randolph by saying:

> Inasmuch as we have heard so much propaganda directed against the organization of which our distinguished speaker is the head and being unable to find anything in our press favorable to this movement, I am frank to state that our curiosity became aroused. It is therefore, through a desire to hear the other side of the case that we have invited Mr. A. Philip Randolph to address us on this occasion.[41]

Randolph's brief outline of the Brotherhood's aims and purposes was received by the group "with enthusiasm," and after answering some questions, the group endorsed the Brotherhood. Cook, who shared the platform with Randolph at the afternoon tea, was impressed with Randolph's "eloquence and his use of the King's English, likening him to Wendell Phillips, Lloyd Garrison and Frederick Douglass, in their zeal for the Abolition Movement." After the tea, Randolph addressed the Metropolitan's Sunday Evening Forum of five hundred people on "Industrial Democracy and the Negro."[42]

Over the next three years, Webster organized a series of "monster mass meetings" in the face of "aggressive and determined opposition," eventually turning public opinion in favor of the Brotherhood. The first mass meeting, scheduled for October 3, 1926, was actually held in the Pilgrim Baptist Church when Webster could not secure Dr. Cook's auditorium and where the Brotherhood did not have to "worry about the matter of splitting the collection." Rev. J. C. Austin, the pastor of Pilgrim Baptist, promised to give the BSCP "every possible assistance to make the meeting a success." This was the same Rev. Austin that the *Messenger* magazine had vilified four years earlier for his support of the Garvey movement. Determined to "mobilize all of the forces in Chicago, religious, social, fraternal and otherwise," Webster once again called on Ida Wells-Barnett to ask for her membership list "so he could send information to women directly about the mass meeting." Donald R. Richberg, a leading railroad labor attorney and advisor to Randolph on BSCP legal matters, addressed the church crowd, as did Miss Mary McDowell, head of the Chicago's Department of Welfare. Although the Brotherhood considered the meeting at the Pilgrim Baptist Church a "huge success in every respect," it did not generate any favorable publicity in the black newspapers, which disappointed both Randolph and Webster.[43]

One year later, another mass meeting was held with very different results. The *Messenger* reported on the big Chicago rally with "two thousand citizens of all walks of life gathered at the Metropolitan Community Church," held on Sunday afternoon, October 30. Dr. Cook gave the invocation in which "doctors, lawyers, ministers, business men, prominent members of fraternal circles, post office clerks, officials of white labor unions made up the large audience." BSCP propaganda described the event in great detail, especially the opposition by the *Chicago Defender*. Dr. Cook, considered by the BSCP as "the most outstanding figure of the meeting," made a "stirring appeal to the people" endorsing the Brotherhood and black leadership "of the type of Mr. A. Philip Randolph." Special emphasis was placed on the fact that Cook refused to be intimidated or bribed by the Pullman Company to close his church to the Brotherhood.

> Some mysterious power made a desperate effort to influence the Metropolitan Church people not to let the meeting be held in their church, but without avail. Dr. Cook has been an ardent supporter of the Brotherhood since its beginning in Chicago and in the early stages of the movement, when Big Negroes in Chicago were running away from it, he stood solidly behind it. So the mysterious power did not get very far.[44]

Chicago's second mass meeting for the Brotherhood encouraged more porters to join the union and this time generated some favorable publicity in the local black newspapers. Webster reported to Randolph that "we have public sympathy in Chicago now, as we never had before." Randolph also concluded that the Chicago meeting "was a powerful force in building sentiment for the Organization." After the big Chicago rally, the *Chicago Defender*'s manager, M. K. McGill, followed Randolph back to

New York, begging him "for a statement on the Brotherhood" so the paper could carry it. Webster believed that "the attack made upon the newspapers here was largely responsible for the capitulation of the *Chicago Defender*." From this time on, the *Chicago Defender* backed the Brotherhood.[45]

From their first organizational tour in February 1926, Randolph and several New York–based BSCP organizers, like Ashley Totten, Frank Crosswaith, and William H. DesVerney, struggled to establish BSCP divisions in St. Paul and Minneapolis and northeastern industrial centers like Pittsburgh, Cincinnati, Cleveland, Detroit, Buffalo, and Albany. In Minnesota, Randolph noted that "the ministers of the Twin Cities opened their churches freely to the union." Some of the ministers refused to charge for the use of their churches. Abram L. Harris, active in organizing the *Messenger*'s religious debate, worked with BSCP officer Paul Caldwell to stage four public meetings in the region. According to Caldwell's reports, each meeting was "big and enthusiastic," especially the ones held on Sunday. Caldwell regularly reported back to the New York office of the "steady and progressive development of the movement" in Minnesota. For one Minneapolis visit, Randolph gave Caldwell only a few days' notice that he would be in the city. Caldwell used his "close contact with the ministry of the two cities," and through "their willingness to cooperate" he quickly arranged several meetings, including two mass meetings for Sunday, and publicized the meetings "from every pulpit in the twin cities." Caldwell commented that the attendance of the meeting "proved far above expectations due to the magnetic appeal made by Mr. Randolph."[46]

Although the charismatic Randolph attracted crowds, Caldwell experienced, as did other local organizers, the Pullman Company's "usual forms of intimidation" and the local press's opposition, which in the early days kept porters from joining the Brotherhood. Caldwell found that the local Urban League, the NAACP, and the Phyllis Wheatley Community Center "put themselves to much pain to assist us in the movement," yet the local ministry offered less than full support. Regarding Minnesota's black religious community, Caldwell commented that the "ministry, although they have allowed our notices to be read and sold or gave us the use of the churches (mostly sold), has been nearer neutral than active in our activities."[47]

In Buffalo, Randolph spoke to a group at a white YMCA, "arranged by some white liberals composed of business men, professors, teachers, writers and social workers." Similarly, in Cleveland, Randolph addressed a "big meeting" successfully staged by white social workers in the Neighborhood Playhouse Settlement, "despite a terrific downpour." Since "most of the Negro leaders of Cleveland were afraid to touch it," it was left to a group of Negro social workers who "fearlessly lent their support." But one pastor, Rev. Russell Brown, "openly took a position of sympathy with the meeting," and his church choir "rendered the Negro National Anthem" at one of the Brotherhood meetings. Moving on to Detroit, Randolph held another meeting at Rev. Gomez's Bethel AME Church, which supported Brotherhood activities. Randolph commented on the "militant, fearless, and independent" spirit at Bethel which prevailed "in spite of a heavy rain."[48]

At the same time, Frank R. Crosswaith, a noted black labor activist of the time and later executive secretary of the Trade Union Committee for Organizing Negro Workers, and William H. DesVerney, cofounder of the BSCP, actively organized Pittsburgh, known as "one of the most solidly anti-union industrial centers in the eastern section of the United States." Crosswaith found Pittsburgh a "hard nut to crack" because the Pullman Company exercised an extraordinary amount of influence over its black community and institutions. He wrote, "Negro churches and social agencies were . . . influenced to such a degree that for a time it seemed as though the brotherhood's message would remain undelivered in Pittsburgh." Crosswaith believed it was the "exceedingly agile manoeuvring" of himself and DesVerney that eventually overcame the Pullman Company's influence and allowed them to make some progress "among the porters there."[49]

Crosswaith reported that the three hundred porters in Pittsburgh's Pullman district were closely supervised by Pullman employees who ruled the territory with a "czaristic philosophy." An unidentified social worker, sympathetic to the Brotherhood cause, described networks of spies in black labor organizations, "especially those with an economic program," which gave Pittsburgh the reputation as the "ancestral home of 'stool pigeons.'" In this difficult situation, Crosswaith and Des Verney contacted the Baptist Ministers' Conference of Pittsburgh and vicinity, and when it unexpectedly endorsed the Brotherhood, the Brotherhood declared that it had turned aside the tide of its opposition. The conference's resolution endorsing the Brotherhood and exhorting "Baptist Clergy and laymen everywhere to give the Pullman Porters all moral and financial support possible" was considered such a significant victory for the Brotherhood that it was printed in the *Messenger*, to encourage other porters to join.

> Whereas, We, the undersigned ministers representing the Negro Baptist Ministers' Conference of Pittsburgh and vicinity, with 150 churches and a combined congregation of approximately 45,000 persons, after hearing the address of Frank R. Crosswaith, a representative of the Brotherhood of Sleeping Car Porters, do hereby go on record unqualifiedly endorsing the gallant efforts being made by this group of Negro workers to strengthen their chances in the struggle to live by organizing a union. And, Whereas, we endorse this movement because we feel that in organizing a union, through which to protect their interest, they are doing no more than workingmen of other races have done and are doing. We also endorse this movement because we believe that if these men succeed with their program their success will tend to encourage race workingmen everywhere to harness their producing powers for the purpose of improving their economic, social and educational status, making generally for the betterment of the human race. And, Whereas, we unhesitatingly condemn those who, being devoid of vision and race pride, have lent their time, ability and their position to misrepresent this great movement and thwart its progress, especially those ministers of the gospel who, in this instance, have substituted the Cross of Christ for a cross of gold in order that they might stand with those who would keep this body of Negro workers from exercising their inalienable right to life, liberty and happiness. Therefore, be it Resolved, That we, the Baptist ministers of Pittsburgh and vicinity in conference assembled, do hereby pledge unstintingly our moral and financial support to the manly and courageous efforts being made by the Pullman porters to organize themselves into a union, to be known as the Brotherhood of Sleeping Car Porters. And we appeal to our brethren everywhere to aid them in every way possible.[50]

During the early battles of labor organization, the Brotherhood developed an effective tactic that branded ministers not receptive to the Brotherhood's message as "sell-outs" to the race, often juxtaposing good ministers with bad ministers "who pawned their souls to wealth and greed." In his organizational drive in the Northeast, Crosswaith praised the ministers who supported their efforts, such as Rev. C. A. Jones, pastor of Central Baptist Church, and Dr. H. P. Jones of Euclid Avenue Church, who "with a few others, stood out among the ministers of Pittsburgh like a beacon light at night on a dark and storm-swept sea." When Crosswaith and Des Verney failed to obtain an endorsement from the "Washington Conference of the ME Church," presided over by a Bishop Claire, they broadcast the rude treatment they received at the hands of the bishop who "absolutely ignored" Crosswaith's requests to address the gathering. Not only were the BSCP representatives unable to speak, but "those who controlled the publicity of the Conference saw to it that all other visitors were announced in the press except the representatives of the Brotherhood." Crosswaith sarcastically observed that "the learned ministers . . . considered themselves rendering a great service to God and their race." Apparently, the Baptist organizations in these northeastern centers appeared to be more open-minded to the early labor-organizing efforts than Methodist groups were. Through the BSCP's efforts, Crosswaith reported that the porters of the Pittsburgh district were "steadily coming into the Organization" and the Cincinnati, Detroit, and Cleveland districts appeared receptive to the Brotherhood message. The organizers believed even small meetings provided "propaganda value" to the cause. Considering their northeastern tour a "splendid triumph for our cause," Crosswaith described their victory in religious language, proclaiming that black workers were now ready for "the gospel of economic emancipation." "The spiritual and educational gains of this trip" defied description, but through the Brotherhood's efforts, "workers generally . . . [were] spiritually richer."[51]

Crosswaith's early labor activism in Detroit for the Brotherhood apparently laid the groundwork for the future activism of Horace A. White, minister of the Plymouth Congregational Church. Besides his ministerial duties, White was a member of the NAACP, active in the National Negro Congress, and a member of the Michigan State Legislature in 1941 and 1942. Twelve long years into the struggle for an independent black union, White and a "group of progressively minded" blacks invited Randolph to address a large group in Detroit. Although the white community opposed their efforts, the black religious community did not. White stated that "in Detroit the people interested to see to it that the Negro stays anti-labor start with the preachers," because hiring conditions in Detroit depended on local black churches. Ordinarily, White explained, manufacturing plants hired previously employed workers or used employment agencies, "but in Detroit the procedure [was] somewhat different, especially when it comes to hiring or rehiring Negroes." When the Ford plant planned to hire blacks, "the Negro preacher [was] asked to send men from his church with a letter. On days when men [were] needed at the plant the offices of the Negro churches [were] full of men seeking to get letters for work at Ford's." In making the arrangements for Randolph's visit, White secured the largest church, but within twenty-four hours of securing the church, church members employed by the Ford plant were "threatened by their bosses . . . that if they permitted Mr. Randolph to speak, they would be the first laid off and their minister would not have the privilege of securing them another job." But the "liberal-minded" pastor of the church refused to be intimidated by the Ford Company, and the meeting took place as planned. While Detroit's black religious community accepted Randolph by the late 1930s, other labor organizers such as the more militant Detroit Scottsboro Defense Committee were not on board. Nonetheless, after twelve years of BSCP organizing, Randolph and his organization had made significant inroads into Detroit's black religious community.[52]

In the early years, Randolph and BSCP organizers successfully mobilized black communities in the "far west" regions of Spokane, Seattle, Portland, Oakland, Berkeley, and Los Angeles. In Washington, the BSCP's activities included "two large enthusiastic meetings" in Spokane, and in Seattle, "known for its extraordinary union spirit among both white and black workers," the BSCP organizers were welcomed by the city's mayor, and "all the meetings were huge." For the most part, sympathetic white labor movements provided the necessary locations for meetings, especially in Seattle where the "fire and zeal which characterize the labor movement" existed. In Portland, Oregon, where "rumors were rife that the Company's propaganda would be hard to overcome," Randolph and Totten found just the opposite: a strong company of men ready "to fight with us." Randolph's old Cookman classmate Clarence Ivey, a board member of the largest black church in Portland, arranged the Brotherhood meetings in Portland. The *Messenger* news described Ivey as one of the "brilliant, progressive and promising" citizens of Portland and well connected in the city's fraternal, civic, and social circles. Describing large meetings that resulted in many porters joining the union, Randolph believed that "Portland like Seattle went over the top." Ivey and his wife entertained Randolph in their home and arranged a meeting at Reed College, where Randolph addressed the student body and the faculty.[53]

An "old veteran" porter, Dad Moore, spearheaded the BSCP's organizational efforts in Oakland, California. Moore, who corresponded regularly with Milton Webster in Chicago, impressed both Randolph and Webster with his dedication to the Brotherhood. As a longtime Pullman employee, Moore was drawing a company pension and was not afraid to jeopardize it by organizing the younger porters and maids. Through his encouragement, Oakland porters joined rapidly and fearlessly.[54]

In a report to Webster, Moore identified a "stool pigeon," Ben Robinson of Portland, who went to a church "here on the coast" to get permission from the pastor to make a statement for the Pullman Company during one of the services. But the pastor grabbed him by the coat and said, "Now, my dear, sir get out of this church at once. I know . . . you are here to fight the B.S.C.P. Organization." Moore also reported going to a "safety meeting" sponsored by the Pullman Company at a Baptist church. Moore and the other porters who accompanied him "went to the meeting with a chip on their shoulder" but were surprised to find that "the meeting was in our favor," and he had "no complaint to make at all." C. L. Dellums, who joined Dad Moore in organizing porters in Oakland, also encountered opposition from what he termed the "parlor stool pigeon brigade," a group of local black professionals—dentists, physicians, realtors, and so forth—who tried to "turn Negro sentiment against the porters joining or remaining in the Brotherhood through their wives in order to break up the Brotherhood. But they didn't succeed." But Dellums never included ministers or black religious communities in this category nor spoke disparagingly of any church group.[55]

While in Oakland, Randolph visited the Berkeley campus of the University of California and addressed faculty and students on black leaders' attitudes toward organized labor, in a talk, "Relations between the Black and White Workers of America." Dellums was impressed by Randolph's intellect and the fact that he was "so well-educated—largely self educated." Describing Randolph as "an unusually brilliant man" with "almost a photographic memory," Dellums watched Randolph use this intellect when addressing ministers. "Randolph had read every word in the Bible, and, I think, remembered it! I have seen him, on more than one occasion, when we'd get into a conversation or something with a minister. I never saw one yet that didn't pretty much run out of gas."[56]

Dellums met Randolph in January 1926 on an early Brotherhood tour at the Parks Chapel Church in west Oakland. Besides his intellect, Dellums admired Randolph's sincerity in fighting and sacrificing for the

Brotherhood cause. Impressed that he was "skinny as a rail," Dellums re-called how once he placed a hand on his hip, which gradually slid down as he was speaking. "He was so thin, he didn't have a hip." Indeed, since his early days as an editor and political activist, Randolph often went without eating. His sacrifices for the Brotherhood gave Dellums confi-dence, for he believed that the "real revolutionary leaders," those that paid the price and stuck "were invariably thin, like Nehru or Gandhi." In the early struggles, however, Randolph's intellect often got in the way, and Dellums discovered he "had trouble writing propaganda for porters" because he used big words the porters didn't understand. "So for quite a while when Randolph wanted to get something out, he would send it to me and I would rewrite it for him. I didn't change anything. I'd just write it in *my* language, in everyday language, language that the working man could understand."[57]

The first BSCP meeting in Los Angeles, held in the "beautiful" Second Baptist Church, was "astonishingly large." Here Randolph, sick himself, heard the news of his mother's death. Describing the "bitter tears scald-ing my inner self," Randolph continued his Brotherhood duties. He re-ported meeting with large, enthusiastic audiences, speaking to a women's group on the "New Mission of the Negro Woman," and to a University of Southern California group on the "Economics of the Negro Problem." At a Central Trades and Labor Council he described the "Brotherhood Trade Union," and at a Negro Business Men's Club, he spoke on the "Problems of Business." At one meeting of western newspapermen, Ran-dolph was surprised at the spirit of unity among the group, since he had never seen "all of the colored newspaper men get together on anything." Under a "great burden of sorrows" from the news of his mother's death, Randolph's visit to Robert Owens's magnificent ranch comforted him. His tour in Los Angeles ended with a huge mass meeting in Dr. Griffin's Second Baptist Church. George S. Grant, the local BSCP organizer, arranged several of the Brotherhood events in Los Angeles and kept the New York BSCP division constantly apprised of the situation in Los An-geles, for Grant seemed determined to make Los Angeles "the banner Dis-trict of the Brotherhood." Besides his BSCP activities, Grant ran his own real estate company and held several other jobs as well. In 1927, in honor of Ashley Totten's visit, Grant organized three "mammoth" affairs, in-cluding a meeting, a banquet, and a dance. On July 4, an "independence mass meeting" was held at the Independent Church, with the theme "In-dependence for the Pullman Porter." In honor of the BSCP's second anniversary, on August 28, an enthusiastic crowd listened to a program at the Hamilton ME Church "designed to more fully enlist the whole-hearted support for the movement." At this meeting, Rev. S. M. Beane delivered a stirring address in which he emphasized the importance of the porters' union not only to the porters but to all the black people of the United States and whose success would open the door of achievement for other underpaid and opposed black workers.[58]

Randolph and Totten also went to Salt Lake City and Denver. In the "Capital of the Mormons," Randolph noted a "high interest . . . although a few porters joined." In Denver, they encountered the most opposition on their western tour, from finding adequate transportation to opposition from the black press. Nonetheless, a meeting was scheduled at a Baptist church ministered by Rev. Dr. G. L. Prince. At this meeting, Randolph and Totten shared the podium with Denver's mayor, an ex-governor, and the president of the Colorado Federation of Labor. But the high point for Randolph was the sensation created by Dr. Prince when he "announced that he had been offered $250 to $300 to refuse Randolph and Totten his church." Dr. Prince's announcement was greeted with "deafening applause." In addition, he agreed to serve as the local BSCP secretary, and his daughter, Mrs. Floretta James, joined the local BSCP's ladies' auxiliary. Randolph made several references to Prince's "herculean service for the movement" in the BSCP propaganda, considering him in the same category as Dr. D. W. Cook, another preacher above corruption, the quality Randolph prized most.[59]

Randolph estimated in the first year alone that the BSCP carried the message of labor unionism to thousands of black and white workers in more than five hundred meetings. Ranging in size from 100 to 2,500 people, these meetings addressed people who knew nothing about organized labor. Most church leaders, Randolph believed, had heard only the Pullman Company's propaganda, that "many of the Negro preachers did not know what it was all about, except that some "black reds" were coming to town to urge insurrection among Negroes." Yet Randolph claimed that through their efforts, the "Brotherhood has secured entrance into a number of Negro churches." Randolph addressed "numerous church groups, Protestant, Catholic or Baha'i," that is, anyone receptive to the Brotherhood message. Randolph also claimed the support of the National Young People's Baptist Union, Conference of Congregational Workers, Lott Carey Baptist Convention, Conference of Congregationalists, and interdenominational ministerial alliances in Boston, Kansas City, Los Angeles, Pittsburgh, and St. Louis.[60]

As Randolph traveled across the country giving speeches for the Brotherhood, his rhetoric not only inspired Pullman porters to "keep the faith" but tapped into the "religious impulse" of workers, which was based on the BSCP's foundational philosophy: the "Brotherhood of Man." In the railroad industry, "brotherhood" was a common title for a variety of unions, but it also had deep religious connotations for African Americans and was an important element of Randolph's religiosity. Over the next several decades, Randolph conveyed the practical and spiritual meaning of the "brotherhood" for black workers in American society.

When Randolph encountered liberal religious-minded porters fearlessly joining his black trade union, he encouraged them to speak their minds. For example, George S. Grant, the BSCP organizer in Los Angeles, contributed several religious poems and articles to the *Messenger*. In the month before it appeared, Randolph advertised Grant's forthcoming article, which captured Randolph's own ideas on how religion and religious institutions had to account for working-class conditions. In "Religion and the Working Class," Grant analyzed the exploitive role of religion in ancient and modern societies. But Marxist interpretations of history failed to explain man's "religious impulse." Working-class movements gained many advantages by tapping into man's "religious impulse": they provided the basis of class solidarity, promoted education and the "knowledge of things as they are," informed the public about the working class's struggle, and publicized working-class interests. Religion freed from "upper-class psychology" had a universal appeal, and "once the religion of the working class has been perceived and realized," working-class organizations could succeed. According to Grant, the elites' selfish use of the "religious impulse" destroyed the full force of its power, and only through an effective working-class program, "with the addition of the power of truth," could "the Brotherhood of Man" be more readily recognized.[61]

Randolph motivated porters to join the BSCP by appealing to their religious sentiments. In 1927, Randolph wrote Webster several times emphasizing the importance of "ministering" the Brotherhood oath and password in a solemn and meaningful way. "It is of the utmost necessity that each brother understand the . . . significance of the pass-word in order that they will get the real meaning of the word and become Brotherhood men in deed and in spirit." When Webster was training a new man in his office, Randolph urged him to give "good instructions [on] giving the pass-word, so that he will make it impressive and also to ministering the oath." Although the mechanics of office work were important, Randolph stressed that "we must never fail to carry on constantly our educational and spiritual work." He believed that "constant educational and spiritual talk" helped the porters understand the importance of organization, since "power comes only through organization, in large numbers." The "Instructions for Giving the Pass-word to a Brother" emphasized solidarity, loyalty, and commitment among brothers, and the "Oath of Fealty to the Brotherhood of Sleeping Car Porters" began and ended with an appeal to God.[62]

Randolph's religious conviction that the Brotherhood was a righteous cause inspired men to join and stay. When Webster wrote to him about a porter named A. M. King, a company plan man who had finally decided to join the Brotherhood, Randolph remarked, "I am glad to hear that Mr. King is becoming converted to the Brotherhood religion." When some of the PPBA porters from Kansas City saw that the BSCP raised money to investigate John Wilkins's lynching, Randolph saw this as evidence of the growing perception that the BSCP was a "Christian organization devoted to the welfare of the porters and maids." The *Black Worker* informed faithful porters of the BSCP's activities and warned them about the Pullman Company's duplicitous policies, inspiring porters to "keep the faith." One regular contributor likened the BSCP to the "Three Hundred of Gideon's army," urging porters to read their Bibles, since "many points in the struggle of the Brotherhood of Sleeping Car Porter and Maids for the rights of self-determination in negotiating for better wages and working conditions are strikingly analogical to this period of Israel's history."[63]

The *Black Worker* often contained poetry and inspiring quotations to keep porters faithful to the union, such as the following excerpt from a poem entitled "Am I My Brother's Keeper":

> Am I my brother's keeper? I
> Who spurned this cod and mocked his pain?
> And from my heart comes the reply:
> The keeper of your kin—or Cain.[64]

Randolph reminded porters that union organization fulfilled the scriptural demand to be "our Brother's keeper." He believed "no man can live unto himself alone. Workers must organize, fight and hang together or they will hang separately." Under the *Black Worker*'s motto, "Ye Shall Know the Truth and the Truth Shall Make You Free," Randolph regularly contributed articles meant to inspire porters to join the union and support it financially, often using biblical and religious language but with a radical edge. Keeping faith with the Brotherhood was a common theme: "Once more Brethren, I challenge you to put on the armor of FAITH for our future struggle." The BSCP began a new drive for members in 1930 "to enlist every porter in the movement and re-fire the hearts of every delinquent member with a new zeal for the cause." Randolph wanted porters "filled with a flaming, fighting faith in the right to better conditions and in the power of organized collective action to secure recognition, better wages and hours."[65]

In one inspirational article, Randolph deprecated the Pullman Company's paternalistic philosophy which treated blacks like the children of "Mother Pullman [who] toddle along, sucking their fingers, while the other children, who have the sense to cry out and kick, are getting the milk of good wages and better working conditions." But all the efforts to organize the Pullman porters would be useless unless the "porters themselves have the courage and guts to fight for themselves." As Randolph told them, "The one lesson the Pullman porters in particular and Negroes in general must learn is that salvation must and can only come from within." Randolph lambasted all "doubting Thomases," critics, and skeptics who pessimistically predicted that a union "was bound to be short-lived because the Negro lacked spirit and character." Randolph rallied the porters by placing New Testament prophecy into a modern working-class context:

> Peace I leave with you, my peace I give unto you, not as the world giveth, give I unto you. Let not your hearts be troubled, neither let it be afraid, comes the injunction from the prophet of a new world Brotherhood, and is a challenge and a promise to the world-weary, worn and oppressed millions by the heartless hands of capitalist imperialists in our modern industrial society. Fight on brave souls! Long live the Brotherhood! Stand upon thy feet and the God of Truth and Justice and Victory will speak unto thee![66]

In 1929, Randolph collaborated with Jerome Davis of Yale Divinity School on a worldwide symposium on labor and religion, and through this effort he produced his most definitive statement on black labor and the church. In Davis's anthology of the labor symposium, *Labor Speaks for Itself on Religion*, Randolph was "the only Negro to contribute to the volume." Randolph's essay, "Negro Labor and the Church," allowed him, as the struggling leader of the fledging BSCP union, to develop his views of a working-class religion into a theology for a black proletariat. His essay coincided with Benjamin Mays's and Joseph Nicholson's research on the black church which showed that the majority of urban church members were either domestic servants or laborers, with only a few skilled tradesmen, business, or professional people. Similarly, Randolph argued that "since the Negro Church is largely composed of Negro workers there is no good reason why it should not express and champion a proletarian philosophy." Gathering labor leaders from the United States, Canada, Europe, Australia, and Asia, Davis wanted labor leaders to speak out on religion, since many religious leaders had failed "to welcome sincere criticism leveled at the church." Davis believed that "it would be a tremendous stimulus to real religion if these opinions could be read by every sincere believer." He contended that because Christians had failed so miserably in their high calling, they should welcome severe criticism. Weren't Jesus' "greatest criticisms . . . hurled against the comfortable and the hypocrites?" Davis asked, demanding that every person ask himself:

> Is labor justified in the attitude which it has taken towards the church? To what extent is their indictment true? How can we secure cooperation on the part of these men in a task that involved us all? What part should the church and religion play in helping the laboring masses?[67]

Over the next few years, Randolph and Davis continued to promote their liberal religious agenda. In 1931, Randolph and Benjamin Mays were featured speakers at a Yale Divinity School seminar called "Whither the Negro Church?" There, Randolph challenged black churches to adopt a "working class viewpoint and program." That same year, when the BSCP initiated an injunction fund to "disestablish" company unions and yellow dog contracts, Davis served on its committee with Randolph's friend Rev. Imes. While at Yale, Davis made a study of 387 church boards of the leading Protestant denominations, demonstrating that an elite class, unsympathetic to organized labor, controlled Protestant churches, an argument similar to one that Randolph and Chandler Owen had made in their *Messenger* editorial "The Failure of the Negro Church" more than ten years earlier. From the labor symposium, Davis planned to organize a "religion and labor bureau," a nondenominational and nonsectarian organization that would include both church and labor leaders on its board. Later when it was formed, Randolph served as a board member. Davis remained an active supporter of the BSCP during the 1930s and continued to work with Randolph in the 1940s and 1950s.[68]

Randolph's essay, half devoted to church history and half to his personal experiences as a labor leader in the 1920s, revealed a sophisticated understanding of black religious history as well as his own historical consciousness of the radical beginnings of what he termed the *black church*. Randolph's argument that a black church developed in opposition to the racism of the white church and "as a protest against persecution by the whites in their churches" was comparable to current dialogues about African American Christianity as a "resistance culture." Unlike Carter Woodson's history, Randolph started his religious narrative in Africa but concluded that the "dominant religion of the New World, Christianity, decreed the doom of African animism." An "alleged civilized form" of worship among the slaves began with the established white churches, albeit with rebellious undercurrents of the revolts by Gabriel Prosser, Denmark Vesey, and Nat Turner. But for the most part, "the African slave enjoyed the blessings of the Christian doctrine" given him by his white masters. Just as later scholarship identified the "invisible institution" of southern slave religion, Randolph recognized the distinctive evolution of religion in the South, where "the black and white church were practically one under the slave power." However, in the North, the "formal Negro Church" was "born as a protest against discrimination in the white church, as was the case with the African Methodist Episcopal Church," or was divided "into separate religious bodies by, for and of Negroes."[69]

Randolph characterized this black church as "both proletarian and revolutionary," proletarian since "the black proletariat . . . constituted practically ninety-nine percent of the Negro population" and revolutionary because it was fugitive and former slaves who protested against racism in churches. In the North, free blacks "prayed and struggled and fought for freedom of the slaves in the South," when probably not half a dozen churches, if any, existed in the South at that time. During Reconstruction, the early black church "championed the cause of freedom for the black bondmen," serving as centers for the enforcement of their civil and political rights. However, conditions rapidly changed with emancipation and industrialization. Booker T. Washington, with "the vision of a prophet," readied blacks for the industrial and commercial profit system, and the National Negro Labor Union, the Knights of Labor, and the American Federation of Labor tried to organize blacks.[70]

The black church did not keep pace with the new industrial order, however, for it "did not readily grasp the nature, scope and meaning of the Negro workers' economic efforts to raise their wages, shorten hours of work and improve working conditions." Randolph offered two historical reasons for black preachers' "indifference and opposition" to black labor organization. First was the fear of losing white philanthropic support for church programs, which generally opposed all working-class organizations. Second, blacks generally, and rightfully so, distrusted white labor unions, based on a long history of discrimination against black workers. Randolph optimistically believed that the "short-sighted policy of some international trade unions will be corrected by the organization of Negro industrial workers, despite discrimination," since white and black workers have common interests and are "bound irretrievably together." Randolph's narrative of black religious history ended when he and the BSCP struggled to educate the black religious community about the advantages of trade unionism and urged a Negro Church to "champion a proletarian philosophy." As for being antichurch, he explained,

> Negro labor leaders are not anti-Church, though they may not be church members. All of them feel that the Church can be of constructive social, educational and spiritual service to the Negro workers. If the Church, white or black, is to express the true philosophy of Jesus Christ, Himself a worker, it will not lend itself to the creed of oppressive capitalism which would deny to the servant his just hire.[71]

Randolph's 1929 analysis of black church history corroborated Gayraud Wilmore's later contention, more than forty years later, that the black church underwent a "de-radicalization" process during the late industrial period of American history.[72] Nonetheless, Randolph kept connecting with progressive ministers and their churches around the country, not only to combat this negative trend, but also to gain the "approval of the aims and objects of the Brotherhood" in black communities. On December 2, 1927, Randolph planned the first labor conference in New York City, to bring professional, business, religious, and educational groups "into the Trade Union Circle of interest" and to unite them behind the American black wage earner. Perceiving the labor conference movement as "something entirely new in the life and history of the Negro, for . . . not only have these groups been unsympathetic, but hostile," Randolph and other BSCP organizers saw themselves as innovators, calling the labor conference idea as "one of the most significant movements initiated in America in the last decade." The New York labor conference, held at the Urban League's auditorium filled to capacity, attracted leaders "from every section of Negro opinion" to discuss the Pullman porter movement. There, the "Church, Press, Social Service, Education Law, Politics, Medicine and Labor were prominently represented." William Lloyd Imes, the faithful BSCP activist and Presbyterian clergyman, spoke on "The Negro Worker and the Church," while Randolph addressed the interracial audience on ways "to awaken community interest in the problems of labor as they affect the Negro." Other panel discussion groups tackled issues such as workplace discrimination, health issues, civil rights, education, the press, the black worker and social service movements, cultural arts, black business, the black woman, and the Negro Church's relationship to the worker. In fact, the church was seen as foundational to mobilizing public support of the BSCP, as one editorial stated:

> Nor can the church be ignored when confronted with the problems of mobilizing public opinion in favor of the solution of the great social question. Therefore, the Conference sought to have the church represented in giving its view point on the relation of the church to the worker. When it is remembered that the National Catholic Welfare Council, the Central American Association of Rabbis, and the Federal Council of Churches of Christ, have conjointly given expression to their view points from the angle of religion on actual industrial struggles, such as the Western Maryland Railroad, the Conference considered it timely and wise to have both the Negro and white clergymen represented in handling this important theme.[73]

Randolph considered the "Conference in New York . . . a huge success," and it served as a model for similar conferences held in Washington, Boston, Chicago, Cleveland, St. Louis, St. Paul and Minneapolis, Kansas City, Denver, and Los Angeles. A common theme emphasized at all the conferences was the mutual concerns of all workers, whatever their "various social, religious, political and civic" attitudes.[74]

In January 1928, a third Negro labor conference was held at a local YMCA in Washington, D.C., composed of a racially mixed audience of labor and liberal representatives from "the church, press, business, education, fraternal societies, politics, law, social service, medicine." As in New York, Randolph organized an ambitious agenda of twelve panels, including two on the church: "The Negro Worker and the Church," led by Rev. H. T. Medford, and "Labor and Religion," led by Dr. John A. Ryan, the most persistent Catholic voice for a progressive social action program. Besides creating a favorable public opinion of the BSCP, the labor conferences were intended to improve the life of Pullman porters, to "raise funds to aid the porters' fight for the right to organize, a living wage, and the abolition of the tipping evil." At the same time, they encouraged the porters to join and support a struggling trade union. One BSCP bulletin circulated during the early years of the Depression listed nineteen reasons why porters should join the union and pay dues, including the contention that the BSCP's National Negro Labor Conference was "the only VOICE of organized Negro labor in AMERICA." In one radio address, Randolph cited the labor conference movement as part of the BSCP's agenda to educate the public on industrial and economic matters, especially the porters' "fight for a living wage."[75]

By 1929, labor conferences were being advertised as national conferences. One of the first national labor conferences was sponsored by the BSCP's Chicago division, organized by Milton Webster in January 1930. As the labor conference agendas became more complex, they often included social events like receptions and dances, which required more planning by local organizers. They also drew national figures such as George E. Haynes of the FCCC, who planned to address the Chicago labor conference on "The Negro Worker and the Church." Other panels linked social science experts discussing "various social evils" with the church, press, fraternal societies, and professional, business, and student groups. Randolph believed these groups were "not economically far removed from wage earners themselves" and that their own progress depended on the development of black workers.[76]

Through Webster's "able and energetic work," several clergymen participated in the conference, indicating the progress that Webster had made with Chicago's black religious community over the past five years. Rev. Harold Kingsley of the Good Shepherd Church, who figured prominently in St. Clair Drake's study of Chicago churches of the late 1930s, "made a real Brotherhood talk, and has endeared himself in the hearts of the Sleeping Car Porters," Webster reported. Dr. W. D. Cook of the Metropolitan Community Church participated, along with Dr. Herbert L. Willet of the University of Chicago and Norman D. Barr of the Olivet Institute, who "made valuable contributions to the conference on the question of the Church and the Worker." Rev. Joseph Nicholson, the coauthor of *The Negro's Church* with Benjamin Mays, represented the CME Church at the conference. Dr. Worth Tippy of the Federal Council of Churches in Christ stood in for George E. Haynes, who had originally been scheduled to speak at the conference. Finally, Rev. H. D. Greene of the Seventh Day Adventist Church participated. In all, two thousand people attended the conference's mass meeting held in the Metropolitan Community Church.[77]

For several decades, labor conferences became a permanent institution, an integral publicity and propaganda strategy of the BSCP, and remained a vital part of its way of gaining recognition by the public, the AFL, and the Pullman Company. Years later, Randolph described the labor conference movement as instrumental in the Pullman Company's eventual recognition of the BSCP in 1937. In nearly every Pullman district from coast to coast, local BSCP division held these conferences "to determine representation of the porters in 1935, and intermittently, thereafter." In fact, one labor conference held in Jacksonville, Florida, at the Ebenezer ME Church in early 1940, followed the same format as Randolph had planned in the late 1920s. Randolph believed that the conferences not only effectively offset "the attacks from the Negro press, church and other leaders" but that they also enabled "various groups in the communities" to acknowledge the Pullman porters' grievances and demand solutions. At the same time, Randolph believed that the BSCP organizers gained experience and confidence in planning programs, establishing contact with colleges and universities, securing the cooperation of various professors to speak at the conference, and appearing before ministers' alliances, women's clubs, and business leaders' meetings. According to Randolph, local porter officials gained "new perspectives, vision, faith and a sense of belonging . . . [to] the constructive and creative life of their community." The BSCP labor conferences educated black communities on the modern developments in the relationship between church and labor.[78]

While Randolph was promoting trade unionism in black religious groups, he also was seeking alliances with white clergymen with social justice agendas. Randolph benefited from the growing ecumenical spirit of Protestants interested in social justice. The BSCP viewed the favorable report of the independent porters' union by the FCCC as giving the Brotherhood's "fight public importance and significance." As part of its propaganda strategy, the BSCP circulated a copy of the report to "each and every porter," regarding it as one of the "most important and effective pieces of propaganda" to mobilize public support of the porters. Usually cited as an achievement by the Brotherhood, Randolph considered securing the FCCC's support to be a major "conquest of public opinion," and "both friend and foe were amazed at this notable achievement." Milton Webster, noting the tremendous influence of the FCCC, expressed his confidence in their support of the BSCP.[79]

Another indication of the liberal Protestant establishment's support was Dr. Worth M. Tippy's presence at the BSCP-sponsored 1930 labor conference in Chicago. Tippy formed the Methodist Federation for Social Service (MFSS) in 1907, a "voluntary society of those who wished to rally Methodism around the social gospel banner." Like the FCCC's report, the BSCP reprinted the favorable MFSS's social service bulletin, as it lent credibility to the Brotherhood's program. Finding the Brotherhood compatible with the Methodist Church's social creed, the MFSS was impressed with the success of the Brotherhood's establishment, "which had barely come into existence at the first of the year, [and was] rapidly attaining a vitality which indicates permanency."[80]

Besides Protestant groups, Randolph also found support in Catholic organizations. Randolph asked Webster to travel to Cincinnati to speak to the Catholic Industrial Conference. Webster reported back on how well received his Brotherhood talk went with the Catholics, which, he believed, would "radiate throughout the zone." Randolph expressed his delight at Webster's "strategic blow" of reaching Catholic priests, "who will be able to carry the message back to all sections of the country," and also at the shock of the Pullman Company representatives when Webster was introduced to speak at the conference. Randolph commented several times on the positive effect that the Cincinnati Catholic conference had had on the Brotherhood.[81]

Between the stock market crash in 1929 and the beginning of the New Deal in 1933, the BSCP struggled for survival. After the economic downturn, the BSCP sponsored unemployment conferences. By 1930, many porters still belonged to the company union, the PPBA. The *Black Worker*, the BSCP's new publication, was having difficulty staying afloat and, for several years, did not have enough money to publish it. Thus, the BSCP's investigation into the murder of the Pullman porter John Wilkins

was never completed, and the fate of the Wilkins Fund remains unknown.[82]

But as long as it could, the *Black Worker* focused on the issue of the
nation's rising unemployment rate. The Brotherhood in New York, along
with the New York Urban League, planned an unemployment conference
in the Mother Zion AME Church. The purpose of the two-day conference
was to explore unemployment among blacks. The BSCP hoped to build a
"united front among Negro organizations," including the church, the
press, fraternal societies, college fraternities and sororities, and various
Negro social service institutions. An active BSCP supporter, Rev. John W.
Robinson of St. Mark's Church, was listed along with some prominent
participants: Walter White of the NAACP, Ira D. Reid of the National
Urban League, and Harry W. Laidler of the League for Industrial Democracy.[83]

Seven years into the struggle, the BSCP declared a major victory in
Chicago when it announced that for the "first time the porters' union has
been able to enlist the unified backing of the colored ministers of
Chicago." The BSCP's efforts to align with black progressive ministers
and ministerial alliances and with the liberal white Protestant and
Catholic supporters of labor had finally paid off. Randolph and Charles
Wesley Burton, a Congregational minister and the chairman of the citizens' committee supporting the Brotherhood, appeared before the Baptist
Ministers Conference of Chicago, the AME Ministers Association, the
CME Ministers Alliance, and the AME Zion Ministers Conference to
gain their endorsement of the BSCP. Randolph reported, "In every instance endorsement was given and cooperation promised." According to
a report by the *Black Worker*, it was a white Congregational ministers'
union that persuaded other ministerial alliances to openly support the
BSCP.[84]

In 1932, several white ministers supported the BSCP in a wage-cut dispute between the porters and the Pullman Company. When Randolph
and Webster learned, from reliable sources, about two secret conferences
held by the Pullman Company, along "with its hand-picked company
union representatives," to slash the porters' wages, they acted quickly to
mobilize the Congregational ministers' union to go public about the latest Pullman policy. In an open letter, the ministers condemned the reduc-
tion in wages and at the same time alerted the porters to the situation so
that "porters every-where [were] in revolt against the recent wage cut."
Webster reported on other successful alliances in Chicago during this pe-

riod: two Congregational Forum groups, the Jewish People's Institute, and an Interracial Commission, all indicating how well the BSCP had influenced public opinion even during the tough Depression years.[85]

The BSCP's strategy of building alliances with the progressives thinkers in black and white churches indicated how attitudes toward the Brotherhood had shifted during the twelve years it took to gain recognition. As historian Eric Arnesen explained, the BSCP was successful because it championed a trade unionism that was more "about race and civil rights than it was about class." Mays's and Nicholson's study of the Negro Church in this period claimed that one of its strong points was that the church was owned and controlled exclusively by blacks, but the BSCP's demand to be recognized during the 1930s challenged this belief by asking black religious communities to question the real ownership of Negro churches. In its years of struggle, the BSCP demanded that black churches live up to their historical and radical potential and to be truly independent. Randolph and the BSCP's insistence that a "de-radicalized" black church live up to its original potential is an important aspect of the church's historical participation in the modern civil rights movement.[86]

As the BSCP was challenging the Negro Church's position on the race question, AME Bishop Reverdy Ransom founded the Fraternal Council of Negro Churches in 1934. From its inception, the Fraternal Council sought not doctrinal consensus or structural mergers but church unity based on "social action directed toward the achievement of racial justice." In her study of black ecumenism, Mary Sawyer argued that

> if the Fraternal Council was a departure from the interracialist approach of the FCC's Commission on Race Relations, it was of a piece with other black change-oriented movements and organization of its time. At the very least, the Council provided an alternative forum for church leaders who rejected the extremes of "back to Africa" advocates, but who felt the prophetic mandate to critique and to protest America's shortcomings.[87]

In many ways, Randolph's and the BSCP's efforts to build alliances with the Negro Church during the early days of union organizing anticipated the ecumenism of the Fraternal Council, the first successful black ecumenical movement. In 1936, Randolph served as the first president of the National Negro Congress (NNC), which was officially endorsed by the Fraternal Council. The NNC's early literature featured several black ministers who figured prominently in the new organization. The NNC en-

The eleventh anniversary parade (August 1936) of the New York division of the Brotherhood of Sleeping Car Porters, the year before the Pullman Company recognized Randolph's Brotherhood as the official union of Pullman porters. Photographed by Brown Brothers, 1482 Broadway, New York, N.Y. Reproduced from the Collections of the Library of Congress.

couraged blacks "to hold faith and confidence in God and the Church, as set forth in the life example and teachings of Jesus." The congress's vision for the black ministry reflected Randolph's vision formed during the difficult days of union organizing:

> WE FURTHER RECOMMEND that our Ministry, with renewed courage and uncompromising conviction shall preach an economic and social gospel as well as a spiritual gospel, for the salvation of the whole man and that the Church shall engage themselves to hold week-day schools and institutes to instruct Church members, to develop a consciousness of conditions and the best means of meeting them for general welfare. The churches are further asked to work out an adequate technique comprehending social and economic problems affecting our group and working with non-Christian groups whose economic and social ideas are of value to the solution of our economic and social problem, without [compromising] the fundamental principle of the Christian

Church. We sense a new imperative facing the Church for great consideration and challenging incentives for saving the youth for the Church. The Church must rearrange her program and machinery to be more youth-centered in her operations. Negro Christians throughout the world are urged to cease striving to widen the denominational breaches to the hindrance of the building of racial brotherhood and cooperative action.[88]

Furthermore, Sawyer argued that when Randolph left the congress in 1940, disillusioned by the infiltration of communists, he recommended that the Fraternal Council serve as an alternative to the defunct congress, since it was "committed to black development and liberation." Randolph's involvement in the NNC attracted many black churchmen, who remained wary of the congress's dangerous connection to Soviet-style communism. Accordingly, George E. Haynes's support of the NNC lasted only as long as Randolph remained in it, and when he resigned as president, many other black religious leaders left also. In 1940, when Rev. William H. Jernigan became the president of the Fraternal Council, after Bishop Ransom, Jernigan cooperated with Randolph on labor and civil rights activities, and Randolph sought the Fraternal Council's support, exemplifying the similarity of their agendas by the 1930s. Although Randolph's secular labor movement and the Fraternal Council's ecumenical movement are often viewed separately, both movements pushed the Negro Church toward its earlier purpose: to fight segregation and demand social justice.[89]

In 1950, reminiscing at the Brotherhood's twenty-fifth anniversary convention about its early struggle for survival, Randolph noted the many changes that had occurred over time and concluded that "the Negro Church, too, naturally [was] changing." Recalling the early days when "some, [but] not all, of the top-level Negro preachers" barred "the doors of their churches to the leaders of the down-trodden porters," he reminded his audience that it went against the biblical tradition of "the great prophets of Israel, Elijah, Elisha, Amos, Micaiah and Isaiah, who were poor shepherds or herdsmen." As the Brotherhood fought its way to victory, Randolph saw evidence that although black ministers continued to "preach the evangelism of Christ," they also increasingly turned their "attention to the economic, social and political welfare of their members." Randolph was encouraged that the black church was finally setting a right course.

Negro Church leaders who joined the exploiters of the Negro workers, betrayed the rich background of the Negro Church, which was born in revolt against segregation and discrimination in the white church during slavery under the leadership of such spiritual titans as Bishop Richard Allen of the African Methodist Episcopal Church.[90]

After twenty-five years of struggle for the recognition of an independent black union, Randolph believed that the Negro Church was recovering its original revolutionary message. A. Philip Randolph, Brotherhood organizers, Pullman porters, and progressive ministers and church members all knew their efforts had kept the civil rights tradition of the Negro Church alive during the darkest days of Jim Crow.

4

The 1940s March on Washington Movement

Experiments in Prayer Protests, Liberation and Black Theology, and Gandhian Satyagraha

Coinciding with the 1940 New York World's Fair, the Brotherhood of Sleeping Car Porters, celebrating its fifteenth anniversary, held its first national convention in New York since the struggle began in 1925. At the labor banquet, considered the highlight of the convention, Eleanor Roosevelt delivered the keynote address. In keeping with Randolph and the Brotherhood's history of mobilizing various groups within the black community, several fraternal, religious, benevolent, civic, and labor organizations participated in the week-long festivities beginning on Sunday, September 15. Three ministers received special commendation for their "untiring efforts and devotion" to the Brotherhood cause: Frederick A. Cullen of Salem Methodist Episcopal Church, Rev. William Lloyd Imes of St. James Presbyterian, and Rev. Paul E. West of the Lutheran Church of the Transfiguration. The black press proclaimed the Brotherhood event the "most successful convention in its fifteen years of existence" and Randolph "the most influential Negro labor leader in America." Despite the celebratory nature of the meeting, Eleanor Roosevelt's keynote address underscored some of the greater concerns facing the black community as a whole during this critical period in American history.[1]

In the two years before Pearl Harbor, several black newspapers worked "for a common cause—to secure for Negroes first class citizenship in America and human dignity for oppressed people everywhere," especially as the United States prepared for war. The most vigorous campaign was the *Pittsburgh Courier*'s "Double V" campaign: victory at home and victory abroad. On September 14, 1940, the day before the Brotherhood convened, the Selective Service Act instituted compulsory military training for a period of one year for all eligible males between the ages of twenty-one and thirty-six. In the spirit of the times, the Brotherhood demanded that the president and the Congress practice "no discrimination . . . against American citizens entering all departments of the Army, Navy and Air Corps on account of race or color." In black communities across the nation, the combination of low morale and an increasing militancy created new possibilities for social agitation and organization. In this volatile atmosphere, Randolph, now a successful and respected labor leader, was catapulted into the national spotlight between September 1940 and December 1941, demanding that blacks develop radical strategies to fight Jim Crow in the military and on the homefront.[2]

Eleanor Roosevelt urged her husband to meet with black leaders to address the growing anger in the black community regarding national defense issues. One week after the BSCP convention, Randolph joined Walter White of the NAACP and T. Arnold Hill, former industrial secretary of the National Urban League, to attend a White House conference on September 27, 1940, to discuss black integration into the military as part of the national defense program. Having just been reelected president at the BSCP convention, Randolph had earned his place as one of the "Big Three" of black leadership. As a committee, the three gave President Franklin D. Roosevelt a list of demands with respect to national defense. Before their meeting with him, Randolph, White, and Hill met in the NAACP's Washington bureau, where Hill suggested they write up a memorandum stating their position.[3]

A "wise suggestion," White later recalled, because two weeks later a White House press release confirmed its intention to keep the armed forces segregated. The War Department reasoned that since segregated regimental organization had proved satisfactory in the past, any changes would only hurt morale and impede the preparation for national defense. But when the White House press release intimated that Randolph, White, and Hill had approved the segregation policy, the news "fell like a bomb" in the black community, and angry and puzzled telegrams and letters, local and long-distance telephone calls poured into the NAACP's Washington headquarters. A *Courier* editorial claimed the White House deliberately smeared "the good name and reputations of Messrs. White, Randolph and Hill to deflect from itself the anger and rage of colored citizens over the callous and viciously reactionary statement of future government policy toward Negroes in national defense." The *Chicago Defender* also added "its voice to the nationwide chorus condemning the statement." Even though President Roosevelt attempted to smooth over the incident, the damage had been done.[4]

Randolph consequently concluded that the traditional conference method of pleading for equal consideration no longer worked. By November 1940, Randolph suggested to Milton Webster that "we ought to get 10,000 Negroes to march on Washington in protest, march down Pennsylvania Avenue. What do you think of that?" Although the usual account of the movement's origins was a conversation between Randolph and Webster while on a southern tour for the BSCP, E. E. Williams, a labor organizer for the blasters and drillers union, claimed the movement developed out of a meeting "at a cafeteria in downtown Manhattan" of himself, Randolph, George Haynes of the Federal Council of Churches, Frank Crosswaith of the Negro Labor Committee and a BSCP organizer, and Noah Walton of the Laundry Workers Joint Board, all of whom formed a combination of Randolph's labor and religious connections.[5]

However it originated, by January 1941, Randolph's idea became front-page news: "'Defense Rotten'—Randolph" declared one headline of a news article by Randolph, who urged the direct action approach of marching on Washington. Randolph intended his "pilgrimage" to wake up and shock official Washington, since "nobody expects 10,000 Negroes to get together and march anywhere for anything at any time." Using the slogan "We Loyal Negro-American Citizens Demand the Right to Work and Fight for Our Country." Randolph explained to the black public that

> Negroes are not getting anywhere with National Defense. The whole National Defense Setup reeks and stinks with race prejudice, hatred and discrimination. . . . Hence, Negro America must bring its power and pressure to bear upon the agencies and representatives of the Federal Government to exact their rights in National Defense employment and the armed forces of the country.[6]

Randolph's idea caught on quickly, and in the first six months of 1941, the black press kept the public focused on Randolph's march. In early February, a *Chicago Defender* editorial supported Randolph's proposed march and his tactic of "mass pressure as a means of stimulating social action . . . [and] one which has yielded beneficial results where other methods have failed." Calling Randolph's suggestion that ten thousand Negroes march on Washington timely, the editorial urged action "if the objectives aimed at are to be achieved before it is too late." Nonetheless, the *Defender* questioned Randolph's optimism that a march could be organized:

> It is not possible to get Negroes to march in impressive numbers for denunciation of the miscarriage of justice in the case of the Scottsboro boys; it has not been possible to get them to march in protest against lynching, against peonage and poll-tax. . . . To get 10,000 Negroes assembled in one spot, under one banner with justice, democracy and work as their slogan would be the miracle of the century. However, miracles do happen. We fervently hope this one will happen before the battle of England is over and in the manner prayed for by Mr. Randolph.[7]

Despite their early doubts, the *Defender* rallied behind Randolph's march, recognizing its historical connection to another march on Washington: "Coxey's Army." Compared with the *Defender*'s enthusiastic support of Randolph's march, the *Pittsburgh Courier* was openly antagonistic to his assumption of leadership on the national defense issue, claiming that "certain Negroes [were] setting themselves up as spokesmen for the entire Negro group." Because the *Courier* claimed to have started the "fight against color discrimination in national defense and defense industries," Randolph was perceived as seeking "another opportunity to bask in the limelight" with his most recent "crackpot proposal." As the months wore on, the *Courier* accused Randolph of being a visionary whose "crackpot schemes . . . never completely visualize the difficulties and dangers, nor the discomfort and expense to others." Other *Courier* editorials argued that as a tactic, marches on Washington always failed, since members of Congress regarded them as "nuisances organized by publicity hounds, job-hunters and addle-pates," consisting of the "mob-minded and misguided." Throughout the six months leading up to the proposed march, the *Courier* opposed the march, even when enthusiasm for the march and its numbers kept growing, warning that "far less than the heralded 50,000" marchers would show up "to pound the hot pavements and stand in the sun listening to the rounded phrases of Brother Randolph and Co."[8]

By April, Randolph, as the spokesman for militant social, civic, and religious groups who vigorously protested the Jim Crow policy of national defense, demanded that President Roosevelt "issue an executive order immediately to abolish discrimination in the Army, Navy, Air Corps, Marines and in all industries working on defense contracts awarded by the federal government." By May, Randolph had organized the "Negroes' Committee to March on Washington for Equal Participation in National Defense," headquartered in Harlem, which set July 1, 1941, as the official date for the march on the Capitol. The march on Washington committee (MOWC) consisted of longtime BSCP labor activists and friends, Rev. William Lloyd Imes and Frank Crosswaith, along with Miss Layle Lane, vice president of the American Federation of Teachers. Walter White's (NAACP) and Lester Granger's (National Urban League) presence on the committee represented the broad national support that the march received in these early days of mobilization. Other members included important individuals in the larger national defense movement: Rayford Logan, Henry K Craft, and Richard Parrish. In addition to the march on the Capitol, the MOWC urged that demonstrations be staged in front of the city hall and city council buildings. By this time, the march proposal had created so much excitement that the black press anticipated fifty thousand marchers. In late May, Randolph, now recognized as the "national director of the movement to mobilize fifty thousand Negroes to march on Washington," toured the South on behalf of BSCP business. While conducting Brotherhood business, he organized other march on Washington committees, urging them to march on city halls in support for the big march on the Capitol. Randolph envisioned a "blitzkrieg tempo to execute a maneuver of mass action by Negroes for their economic, political and social rights that will shake America."[9]

Eugene Davidson, a local MOW activist in Washington, D.C., described the MOWC's plans for a "march of mourning" to the nation's Capitol, where "Muffled Drums Will Lead Dissenters in Silent Demonstration." Marchers were to parade to the Lincoln Memorial, "where Marian Anderson sang at the feet of the great emancipator." The MOWC planned to ask the president to speak to the group assembled at the memorial. Davidson reported that the "spectacle of 50,000 Negroes silently marching through the streets of Washington, behind muffled drums, will become a reality." Not only was the MOWC's Washington branch enthusiastically preparing for the march, but in two planning sessions the committee had organized other programs, including a nationwide promotion of the march through radio, newspapers, and advertisements, as well as plans to raise money, by selling buttons, for the "cost of the hegira to the nation's capital." The MOWC stressed direct action, not business as usual. In the last weeks before the scheduled march, Davidson expressed the conviction, as well as the frustration, that a march would actually take place: "We do not want any private meetings with committees. . . . We want the President to speak forthrightly on the problem and tell the world what this administration will and can do on behalf of the underprivileged minority groups of the city."[10]

By the critical month of June, the number of anticipated marchers had grown to 100,000. Finally, Randolph and the MOWC's pressure tactics caught the president's attention. Even Eleanor Roosevelt, one of Randolph's supporters, could not have foreseen the radical turn of events since her keynote speech at the BSCP convention several months earlier. In a letter dated June 10, objecting to the march, she wrote Randolph,

I have talked over your letter with the President and I feel very strongly that your group is making a very grave mistake at the present time to allow this march to take place. I am afraid it will set back the progress which is being made, in the Army at least, towards better opportunities and less segregation. I feel that if any incident occurs as a result of this, it may engender so much bitterness that it will create in Congress even more solid opposition from certain groups than we have had in the past. I know that crusades are valuable and necessary sometimes, but undertaken when the temper is as tense as it is at present, it seems to me unfortunate, and to run the risk which a meeting such as this carries with it, is unwise. You know that I am deeply concerned about the rights of Negro people, but I think one must face situations as they are and not as one wishes them to be. I think this is a very serious decision for you to take.[11]

Following up on the letter, Mrs. Roosevelt met with Randolph and Walter White at Mayor Fiorello LaGuardia's New York office and once again urged them to call off the march. At the same time, the black press reported that President Roosevelt, fearing a mass march on the Capitol, sent a memorandum to the Office of Production Management (OPM) to halt discrimination in all U.S. defense industries. But Randolph and the MOWC insisted on nothing less than an executive order banning discrimination in the armed forces and defense industries. On June 25, President Roosevelt finally agreed to a White House conference with Randolph, White, and several key MOWC members. From this conference came Executive Order 8802, barring discriminatory practices in defense industry hiring, and the Fair Employment Practice Commission (FEPC). Having achieved his goals, Randolph "postponed" the march.[12]

Randolph's tactical decision to call off the march only temporarily was made partly to appease those who so enthusiastically responded to the call. But the "postponement" disappointed many of the marchers, especially those in the movement's New York youth division. It also signaled a shift in the development of this new social movement. Herbert Garfinkel, the first historian of the march, observed that "when the March was officially a Committee (MOWC) it possessed the attributes of a successful mass movement." But when it was transformed into the march on Washington movement (MOWM), "in actuality, it was already losing its mass movement character" and becoming one more organization competing for public attention. At this point, Randolph intended to "broaden and strengthen the Negro March-on-Washington committees all over the United States, to serve as watchdogs" to see whether industries were complying with the president's executive order. On July 2, the day after the proposed march, Randolph met with eleven of the fifteen members of the MOWC in New York to make plans for the future. However, as the MOWM became a "movement without a march," it became necessary to find ways to keep the public's interest. Randolph, as the recipient of the prestigious NAACP Spingarn Medal in 1941 for the establishment of the FEPC, now faced the daunting task of channeling this anger into effective protest, at a time of increasing patriotism in the nation. How vigorous could black protest be without appearing seditious?[13]

When the FEPC public hearings got under way in October 1941 in Los Angeles, a few months before the attack on Pearl Harbor and then later in January and February 1942 in Chicago and New York, the enthusiasm for the march was even greater. From July 1941 to the summer of 1942, as the original MOWC transformed itself into a national organization, Randolph attempted to rally the black community behind his new organization, as he had with the BSCP in the 1930s. He envisioned a series of dramatic mass rallies, in Washington, D.C., New York, Chicago, and St. Louis in the summer of 1942 to compensate for the canceled march. Randolph wanted "mammoth rallies so large and so dramatized that they might serve notice of a united community ready to go farther if the Administration did not act." Several sites were chosen for their enormous amphitheaters: Madison Square Garden in New York, the Chicago Coliseum, the St. Louis auditorium, and the Washington, D.C., ball park, which substituted for the Lincoln Memorial, off-limits during the wartime emergency. Randolph's "hands-on" management style, in which he oversaw countless organizational details, and his ability to mobilize several citizen committees largely made up of women activists resulted in three large and dramatic protest meetings. Although the movement remained closely connected with and underwritten by the BSCP organization, it was the official citywide committees in New York, Chicago, St. Louis, and Washington that made the MOWM summer rallies possible. Each committee included an enormous number of subcommittees: finance, sponsors, organizations, literature, program, publicity, coliseums, ushers, first aid, youth, speakers, and "minute men." Also included in this organizational structure were special committees designated for churches, which reveals how important they were to the rallies' success.[14]

New York's citywide committee held a conference to organize its own giant protest meeting at Madison Square Garden, set for June 16, 1942. At the outset, Randolph asked Rev. S. T. Eldridge, pastor of the Berean Baptist Church and president of the Baptist Ministers Conference of Greater New York, to be the chair of the ministers' committee for the rally. "I know that you will devise ways and means of mobilizing the Negro ministers of Greater New York behind this important struggle," Randolph wrote to him, "to break down the barriers against Negroes today in defense industries and in the Federal Government."[15]

Although Eldridge was in charge, Randolph gave him specific instructions about what the ministers' committee had to do before the rally, still more than two months away. First, the committee had to "sell" every minister in New York on the value, necessity, and possibility of a "monster mass meeting." Second, the committee needed to call immediately an early conference of "Negro ministers only" to educate them on the "political situation with respect to discrimination against Negroes today in defense industries, the Armed Forces . . and the departments of our Federal Government." Randolph believed that such a conference would prepare ministers to "be ready, able, eager and determined to put their shoulders to the wheel" to make the rally a success. Third, Randolph wanted the ministers' conference to make sure that each minister in Greater New York preach a "Madison Square Garden Protest Meeting sermon" on the first Sunday in May, because an effective sermon would generate the support of the church and the people for the protest meeting's aims and purposes. At the same time, Randolph reminded the ministers' committee to draft a letter, containing all their signatures, to every minister in Greater

New York in order to defray the cost of the mass meeting. Randolph suggested that Eldridge and other committee members be present at each church on the Sunday set aside for the rally sermon to "present the case to the members" and reminded Eldridge to meet with "the Baptist ministers . . . and the Interdenominational groups that meet every Monday" to obtain their endorsements for the rally. Finally, Randolph asked Eldridge to get out a press release "indicating that your Committee is working to the end of unifying the Negro ministers in this great effort." Randolph promised to keep in close contact with Eldridge and "make some suggestions on matters of procedures from time to time."[16]

With his knowledge of religious calendars, Randolph took advantage of spring church conferences and meetings to spread the word about the upcoming rally to religious communities. Randolph's mobilization of New York ministers for the Madison Square Garden event reveals his thorough understanding of the structure and nature of religious institutions. When Rev. T. B. Harten of Trinity Baptist Church in Brooklyn wrote to Randolph about his interest in the rally, Randolph seized the opportunity "to send a word of greetings to the great meeting you are holding." With the support of "stalwart, courageous and hard-hitting fighters" like Rev. Harten, Randolph believed that "we can make our cause heard in America and the world." His comments to Harten show how careful he had to be in the months after Pearl Harbor. Admitting that "Negroes must remember Pearl Harbor as loyal Americans," Randolph also reminded Rev. Harten of the horrible lynchings, shootings, and killings of "Negroes in Uncle Sam's uniforms." When Randolph contacted Rev. George Sims, president of the Pastors' Convention of New York State, about mobilizing 25,000 people for the Madison Square Garden rally, he wrote, "It will cost some $6,000, but it will be worth millions." Assuring Sims of the many ministers already supporting the rally, Randolph still needed the support of "a stalwart veteran pulpit orator and leader" of Sims's caliber. Furthermore, he encouraged the pastor to place the matter "before the members of the church and the ministers under [his] supervision" in support of the rally.[17]

The extensive correspondence between Randolph and the MOWM's Chicago division demonstrates not only how much organizational work went into these rallies but also Randolph's reliance on local committee members to get things done in his absence. Randolph appointed Rev. Charles Wesley Burton, an activist minister on Chicago's citizens' committee who supported the BSCP, to direct the citywide committee for the

Chicago Coliseum rally scheduled for June 26, 1942. In the early days of the movement, Rev. Burton, a Congregational minister in Chicago, as well as a "lawyer, social worker, leader and champion of civil right, labor and liberalism," served as the local chairman of the MOWC. As Randolph's personal choice for this critical position, Burton reflected the close connection among the BSCP, the new march movement, and progressive ministers in Chicago. Milton Webster referred to Chicago's MOWC as the "militant expression of the BSCP in the interest of Negro rights" and worked to form a "Brotherhood Committee of 500" to ensure that the mass meeting in Chicago was a success. In the months following the postponement of the original march, Burton actively promoted the movement, which had "received an enthusiastic response" from the Chicago black community. There, the Good Shepherd Community Church, a center for BSCP activity, and a group called the "Committee to Fight for Negro Freedom" sponsored a "mass meeting" in support of the original call to march on Washington. With the upcoming rally, Burton remained at the center of the MOWM activity in Chicago. As the official director of the MOWM Chicago division, he informed the Chicago community in an open letter of a "series of giant public mass meetings to be held throughout the nation under the auspices of the March-on-Washington Committee." Simultaneously, Burton invited a variety of local organizations to the citywide planning meeting for a "proposed Chicago Mass Meeting," at which "Mr. Randolph himself [was] expected to be present." With his help, Randolph simultaneously planned three large rallies in New York, Chicago, and St. Louis, and set up local and national committees to "unite in this effort to achieve full citizenship status" as "unrestricted Americans."[18]

Two months before the rally, Burton told Randolph that the Chicago "campaign [was] under way and gradually gaining momentum." With fourteen committees formed, Burton rattled off his accomplishments: the contract for the Chicago Coliseum signed, and the "fresh-off-the-press" placards distributed with the motto "50,000 Negroes March to the Coliseum Friday, June 26, 1942–7:00 P.M. in Mass Demonstration Against Discrimination and for Jobs—Admission Free—Auspices Chicago Division March on Washington Movement." Randolph's photograph appeared prominently in the rally's publicity. Besides the citywide planning meeting, three additional planning meetings were scheduled for a weekend in May to promote local enthusiasm for the rally: a Saturday evening and a Sunday afternoon meeting in Chicago's Morgan Park area, ending with a "special mass meeting" at St. Stephen's AME Church for Monday, May 18. Burton kept Randolph, who was busy with BSCP business in the South, informed of his progress. His letters to Randolph indicate his excitement: "I am glad to hear that Negroes in the South are taking enthusiastically to the March on Washington Movement. This indicates that we are creating a national unity among Negroes for full and complete integration in our national life without discrimination and segregation."[19]

The names of two ministers appeared prominently in the Chicago MOWM correspondence: Dr J. M. Brown, pastor of St. Stephen's AME Church, and Rev. Ross D. Brown, founder and pastor of the Truth Seekers Temple Liberal Church. The Truth Seekers Temple Liberal Church's letterhead revealed the liberal principles of the congregation: "Not the Church that tries to make you Shout, but the Church that tries to make you Think," with its motto "Religion without Superstition, Facts without Fear, Tolerance without Bigotry." Often appearing just below Webster's and Burton's names on organization lists, the two Rev. Browns played an important role in mobilizing Chicago's religious community for the rally. Rev. J. M. Brown's St. Stephen's congregation appeared to be the "West Side Division of the March on Washington Movement," a center of enthusiastic support for Randolph's program. Rev. Ross D. Brown was active in publicity and advertising, especially as an announcer over the public address system set up for the June 26 event. On the day of the Chicago mass rally, Ross Brown's liberal congregation sent Randolph $20 in support of the rally and also thanked him for "helping us out in our church drive on March 29th last." The donation for the rally came from the "pastor, officers, members, friends, and visitors of the Truth Seekers Temple Liberal Church" and urged Randolph to "keep up the good work," for "our Church and its Pastor are always with you in the struggle for the economic emancipation of the Negro race."[20]

Randolph and Burton appointed Rev. D. DeWitt Turpeau Jr., another influential minister in Chicago, to head the churches committee, and although Burton and Turpeau were listed as the organizers of the religious community, the independent women organizers, who made up the second tier of the movement's leadership, actually organized the black religious community.[21]

In particular, three women organized most of the June 26, 1942, Chicago rally: Ethel Payne, the planning committee chairman; Neva Ryan, the program committee chairman; and Georgia Eason, secretary to the citywide committee directed by Burton. Payne and Ryan were drawn into the movement because of Randolph's leadership. Payne, whose father was a Pullman porter, knew Randolph before the MOWM because of her familial connections to the Brotherhood. She gained a reputation as the "first lady of the black press" in her work as the *Chicago Defender*'s one-person Washington, D.C., bureau during the 1950s. Like Randolph, Ryan was a labor organizer, and as founder of the Domestic Workers' Union in Chicago, she also served as its president. Both experienced labor organizers, Ryan and Randolph worked closely together on the Chicago rally. While Burton officially announced the rally to Chicago's ministers, behind the scenes Neva Ryan was already planning several May demonstrations to advertise the Coliseum event. She even was considering asking author Pearl Buck and the mayor of Chinatown to appear at this pre-rally demonstration and asked for Randolph's advice: "[I see no] reason why Chinese should not be asked to participate. . . . Of course, we would not invite the Japanese. . . . This is a demonstration for Negroes, but since we want to help win this war it is an opportunity to at least show a desire for unity."[22]

As the program chairman, Ryan believed that a pre-rally meeting could "fill whatever place [was] chosen" and described to Randolph the successful base that she, Ethel Payne, and Georgia Eason had established in the communities of St. Stephen's Church on the West Side and Beth Eden Church in Morgan Park. They planned meetings in each church, with seating capacities of twelve hundred and two thousand, respectively, for two successive nights. Ryan was most excited about the donation of a car. As she wrote to Randolph, "Ethel, Mrs. Eason and I have covered so much of Morgan Park and the West Side on foot that any kind of vehicle would cause us to rave." Ethel Payne corroborated Ryan's enthusiasm about the positive response they were getting for these pre-rally meetings. Through their efforts, a group on the West Side, based at St. Stephen's Church, planned to establish a permanent organization called the Chicago Division of the March on Washington Movement. Ryan assured Randolph, scheduled to speak at these church meetings, that "their enthusiasm will inspire you."[23]

There was considerable friction between the women organizers and the male leadership of the Chicago movement, especially with Payne, who resented Burton's autocratic control of all decision making for the movement. Payne complained that Burton often rescinded the actions taken by her planning committee, thereby placing Randolph in the middle of the dispute. Burton appeared to be unaware of Payne's complaints. In his letters to Randolph, Burton remained upbeat about the Chicago division's progress. Indeed, his optimistic report that "we shall put the Chicago meeting over with a bang" contradicted Payne's pessimistic reports. Burton emphasized the "splendid cooperation" that the rally had received from the black press, as well as other enthusiastic responses from the public. Randolph avoided the squabble by relying on both Payne and Ryan to keep the peace. Instead, he focused on the larger goal of a successful rally at the Chicago Coliseum and on keeping his movement alive, as did Neva Ryan. She promised Randolph that the women organizers would not override Burton's decisions or disregard his authority, that "on June 26 the Coliseum will be filled and the meeting will be a success."[24]

As the Chicago demonstration drew near, Randolph directed his instructions to Neva Ryan, who had been promoted to "official office manager." Even Burton expressed enthusiasm for Ryan, whom he described as "busy as a bee" with activity and confidently gave "her free rein" to do "whatever she wishes to do." With the successful May pre-rallies over, Randolph sent Ryan a detailed list of things to do for the Coliseum rally.[25]

Along with his concern for publicity signs, street parades, a chorus of one thousand voices with appropriate religious music, and the decoration of the Coliseum with American flags, Randolph was worried that the planning conference for Chicago ministers had not yet taken place. He had earlier asked Burton to make the arrangements and was concerned that this important organizational meeting had not materialized. Randolph wanted a letter sent immediately to all potential participants, signed by prominent ministers such as Rev. Archibald Carey, Harold Kingsley, DeWitt Turpeau, and other "outstanding Baptist ministers." Randolph announced that he and Milton Webster would address the ministers' conference personally. Why Burton or Turpeau, the head of the churches committee, had not organized the meeting themselves is not clear. Yet with Ryan's collaboration, a ministers' conference took place on June 3, followed by Burton's official letter inviting Chicago's religious leaders to the event. Burton's report to Randolph on the ministers' meeting revealed that the Chicago ministers unanimously endorsed the movement and A. Philip Randolph's leadership. They agreed to set aside Sunday, June 21, as March-on-Washington Day, with sermons emphasizing the mass meeting and offerings to help defray the rally's expenses. To ensure that they got the money from the congregations, Randolph advised that MOWM representatives be present on the last two Sundays before the rally at every church on the south and west sides of Chicago. He even asked to "get the plates for taking up collection from the churches in advance" for the two hundred ushers at the rally. The ministers also endorsed Randolph's proposal of a "blackout" to symbolize the "disabilities heaped upon American Negroes" during this time of war. Black churches provided ushers and choir members to "join the thousand voices chorus."[26]

Randolph envisioned an ecumenical demonstration. For publicity in the black press, he asked that the names of the Baptist and Methodist ministers scheduled to give the three-minute talks be prominently listed. Randolph specifically requested that Harold Kingsley, of the Good Shepherd Community Church, give the invocation, with either a Presbyterian or an Episcopalian minister providing the benediction. In addition to his insistence on an ecumenical rally, Randolph wanted women speakers. When he directed Burton to get representatives from medical and legal professions for the three-minute talks, he added, "You also need to get a woman speaker." Ten days before the Coliseum rally, Randolph contacted Ryan, now the designated "coordinator of the citywide committee," with another detailed list—and this on the day before the monster rally in New York. As Randolph warned her, unless all arrangements were completed a week before the affair, "everybody . . . will be up a tree and helpless." Reporting on how the parade for the New York rally had "stirred up all Harlem," Randolph hoped for the same success for the Chicago event. Above all, he did not want the choir singing "any songs of resignation" and suggested an appropriate spiritual would be "Joshua Fit the Battle of Jericho."[27]

Randolph also directed the St. Louis march rally, set for August 14, 1942. Three weeks before the "great public meeting" in the St. Louis Municipal Auditorium, Randolph still expected a mass meeting to take place in the Washington, D.C., ball park on September 4. Unlike the citizens' group that organized the rally in Chicago, T. D. McNeal, a top official in the BSCP organization, directed the St. Louis rally, working closely with Randolph. Randolph instructed McNeal to form a "blackout committee" with a dynamic chairman, since Randolph found the blackouts to be a most effective part of the rallies. Randolph asked that a committee work out the details of a parade to advertise the rally, since parades were another way to attract interest. "Try to get as many people in the parade as possible, old and young, educated and uneducated, good and bad, crap shooter and preacher," Randolph instructed McNeal, "for everybody is needed in this fight for Negro rights." As with the New

York and Chicago rallies, dramatic plays and skits were used. One playlet, *The Watchword Is Forward*, written by Dick Campbell, was performed again in St. Louis, as it was in the first two rallies. The sixteen-page program for the St. Louis rally was filled with photographs of the organization committee and one of Randolph, community business advertising, an agenda of the meeting, and a complete copy of Executive Order 8802, the movement's greatest achievement. As with the other rallies, Randolph reminded McNeal to contact every church and organization, big or small, requesting contributions, endorsements, and cooperation. McNeal's top priority was to create a preachers' committee to organize "every preacher to preach a sermon before the meeting on the March on Washington fight for jobs for Negroes and against discrimination in the armed forces."[28]

The MOWM rallies in New York, Chicago, and St. Louis in the summer of 1942 were enormously successful. The New York rally mobilized eighteen thousand people; the Chicago rally overflowed with twelve thousand people; and the St. Louis rally attracted nine thousand militant marchers. The dramatic blackouts and parades before the rallies, as well as the rally programs themselves filled with music, dramatic skits, and stirring speeches by noted black leaders, gave the movement an air of excitement, urgency, and solidarity. These wartime rallies emphasized religious pageantry and language. Randolph and the MOWM organizers used radical slogans such as "Fight for Freedom," "Storm the Coliseum," "Mobilize Now!" and "Fight for Justice, Democracy and Manhood Rights," which resounded with militant and patriotic verve. Any song or spiritual that indicated resignation or weakness was rejected, but hymns like "Joshua Fit the Battle of Jericho," "Hold the Fort," and "Onward Christian Soldiers" were accepted.[29]

Theophilus Lewis, Randolph's old friend from his Epworth Society days and former drama critic of the *Messenger*, best caught the sense of religious pageantry that permeated the rallies. Lewis, a recent convert to Catholicism and a contributor to the *Interracial Review*, a Catholic "journal for Christian democracy," considered the New York rally from a drama critic's perspective. Lamenting the current theatrical season as "so barren of merit that both the Pulitzer committee and the Critics' Circle declined to make an award for the best American play of the year," Lewis declared the Madison Square Garden rally such a stirring spectacle of an oppressed people demanding justice that "even the most case-hardened critic would have been compelled to concede that the event was well staged." Lewis described A. Philip Randolph entering the Garden, with a bit of "pomp and circumstance," escorted through the auditorium by a hundred Pullman porters in uniform. At the head of the procession marched a chef, in white cap and apron, followed by fifty maids forming the rear guard. The porters' band played "Hold the Fort for I Am Coming," which Lewis described as a "martial Protestant hymn" of "militant Lutheran music," which "lifted the assemblage to a restrained state of religious fervor which was sustained until the end of the program." The number of ministers on the speaker's platform only enhanced the religious atmosphere of the rally, at which "all faiths were represented, with the Baptists predominating." Lewis called Rev. William Lloyd Imes's invocation a "gem of sheer artistry," in which he included verses from James Weldon Johnson's "Negro National Anthem," invoking patriotism and devotion "to God, a people and an ideal." On the less sublime side was the "comic relief" offered by Rev. W. C. Carrington, who, Lewis believed, "could easily qualify as a monologue artist." He especially liked his punch line: "We want it clearly understood," Carrington said, "that we are not here to embarrass the President or the administration. They have embarrassed themselves."[30]

Just like the original July 1, 1941, march, the rally scheduled for September 4, 1942, in the Washington, D.C., ball park never happened. Because the symbolic value of a successful march rally in the nation's capital was necessary for a march on Washington movement, the fact that there was no rally called into question the movement's long-term ability to mobilize followers. Garfinkel believed that Randolph's failure to give his scheduled speech at Madison Square Garden as originally planned portended the movement's "incipient decline." Indeed, Randolph's failure to deliver his address contrasted dramatically with Adam Clayton Powell Jr.'s exciting announcement to run for Congress on the night of the Madison Square Garden rally. The diminishing numbers of people at each of the summer rallies was another indication that the movement's "momentum had slowed" by the late summer of 1942 or possibly after the MOWM's first convention in Chicago in July 1943. Later, Randolph explained to Garfinkel the difficulties in putting together a wartime program comparable to the meetings staged in other cities. "Knowing the conservative climate of Washington, among both white and colored people, I was conscious of the need of a program which would touch off a rally of huge proportions and we were unable to get people of the stature we wanted for such a meeting."[31]

Randolph's controversial decision to make the MOWM an all-black organization opened it to criticism that it was Jim Crowism in reverse. At the Detroit policy conference in September 1942, when Randolph and sixty-five selected delegates came together to set up a national organization and formulate policy, establish goals, declare principles, plan programs, and discuss methods, strategies, and tactics, the first issue on the agenda was a discussion of its restrictive membership. Randolph argued that the essential value of an all-black movement was to create faith by blacks in blacks, to develop self-reliance, and to break down the slave psychology and inferiority complex that inevitably existed in mixed organizations ostensibly created for blacks. An all-black membership policy also had the added advantage of effectively shutting out communist agitators, a problem for an organization that used techniques of mass pressure and militant action to secure its objectives. Members of the movement recognized, however, that an all-black organization exposed it to charges of black nationalism. The group specifically denounced this charge in one resolution, declaring their final goal was full integration into all phases of America life. Several conference resolutions touched on religious issues, especially the MOWM's position against anti-Semitism and anti-Catholicism. The group condemned both as a "vile manifestation of Fascism" and as undemocratic, unsound, and dangerous forms of religious bigotry unworthy of a people who found themselves "victims of racial prejudices." The delegates recognized that as a mass movement composed of people of varying religious beliefs, they stood for the "democratic principles of the freedom of religious worship." By passing a "nonsectarian" resolution, the members went on record as not endorsing any "religion, denomination, or sect," although they recognized that individual members could belong to "any religion, denomination, church, or sect."[32]

Randolph sympathized with American Catholics and in his activism sought out alliances with them. The emergence of a MOWM coincided with an important interracial movement developing in the Catholic community, most notably around the Jesuit priest John LaFarge. Beginning with his missionary work in Maryland among poverty-stricken blacks in Catholic parishes, in the same year that Randolph migrated to New York, LaFarge believed that education and interracial contact could alleviate the discrimination against blacks in American society. When he moved to New York in 1926 to serve as the editor of the liberal Catholic journal *America* and, later, the *Interracial Review*, LaFarge continued developing his interracial theories. In 1934, he founded the Catholic Interracial Council of New York (CICNY), and with the establishment of the FEPC in 1941, LaFarge regarded Randolph as the black leader closest to his own philosophy. LaFarge believed he "struck a straight course" when he worked with A. Philip Randolph on the monster demonstration in Madison Square Garden. Throughout the 1930s, the CICNY opposed communism and feared that African Americans would turn to it as a political alternative. LaFarge admired the fact that the MOWM was not communist inspired, nor could the communists "take it over." He thus understood Randolph's all-black movement as a necessary restriction to keep the MOWM from communist infiltration. LaFarge particularly praised Randolph's rejection of a large contribution from a "Trotskyite faction of the Communist Party" to defray rally expenses. As LaFarge and Randolph drew close in the early days of the movement, LaFarge accepted Randolph's proposal to be the only white speaker at the Madison Square Garden rally. With LaFarge on the podium, Randolph was able to refute charges that the MOWM was both separatist and communist, and the presence of a Catholic made the program more ecumenical. As the editor of the *Interracial Review*, LaFarge brought the movement positive publicity because he devoted the entire July 1942 issue to the Madison Square Garden rally. This issue included LaFarge's address "The Spiritual Front," in which he defined a front of religious-minded men and women, "be they Catholic, Protestant, or Jew," to defend the natural rights of all children, regardless of color, for "there [was] but one front for souls in this war."[33]

Scholars have commented on the unlikely partnership of John LaFarge and A. Philip Randolph. LaFarge, the cautious, interracial gradualist, influential in crushing the 1930s black protest movement within the Catholic Church by the Catholic and black civil rights activist Thomas Wyatt Turner, would appear to have little in common with the radical Randolph and his racially class-conscious MOWM. In fact, by allying himself with Randolph's MOWM, LaFarge was taking uncharacteristic risks. However, their compatibility reflected their common values, especially during this wartime crisis: a commitment to social activism, a mutual dislike of communism, personal admiration for each other, similar economic interests, and a respectful attitude toward socially conscious religion. As the United States moved from isolationism to military preparedness, the CICNY's monthly bulletins revealed its common economic concerns with the MOWM: "Negro Employment Shows Increase," "To

Widen Negro Job Opportunities," "Crawford Clothes Company Hire 200 Negroes Survey Reveals," "Plants in Illinois Agree to Use 15% Negro Labor," and "Labor Discrimination Outlawed in Nebraska." Besides these social concerns, both LaFarge and Randolph respected the type of organized religion concerned with addressing societal problems and conditions. Randolph's friendship with LaFarge revealed his antipathy toward anti-Catholicism, which he perceived as essentially undemocratic. Years later, Randolph described Father LaFarge as "gentle, impressive and profound," with an "uncompromising commitment to the principle of the God-given right of every human being, regardless of race, color or religion, to life, liberty and the pursuit of happiness." Randolph called Father LaFarge's presence at the Madison Square Garden rally in the early 1940s a "significant slice of contemporary interracial history," a history forgotten by many because of the "Civil Rights Revolution [which] broke upon America in the early sixties." As contemporaries in civil rights activities before the 1960s, Randolph compared LaFarge's support for the MOWM in the 1940s with the later 1960s:

> The presence of Father LaFarge on the platform was an eloquent testimony to the esteem and affection the militant March on Washington entertained for this great church leader. And it is timely to note that the big march on Washington for Jobs and Freedom, August, 1963, made special preparations (a wheelchair on the platform) to accommodate Father LaFarge who was in attendance.[34]

The Detroit policy conference established a complex organization of five areas in the United States: the North Atlantic, South Atlantic, Southern, Midwestern, and Pacific regions, with each divided into smaller units of states, divisions, districts, and neighborhoods. Although this ambitious plan was never fully realized, MOWM branches were established in twenty-four cities, where some of them actively conducted local "marches" and picketed local defense industries. The MOWM's St. Louis division was one of the most active branches. Two weeks after the rally at the municipal auditorium, BSCP organizer T. D. McNeal planned to march on the Carter Carburetor Corporation, which was operating at full production capacity but still refusing to hire black workers. While McNeal planned demonstrations on other local war plants with discriminatory practices, he informed Randolph that the St. Louis division planned an "open air mass prayer meeting for Negro rights" to be held in the early part of September at a World War I soldiers' memorial on the municipal plaza. McNeal believed that a "prayer protest" struck the right balance between making a dramatic statement to the St. Louis community that blacks were fully determined to fight for their rights and doing so in a respectful way when public patriotism was so intense. The MOWM's St. Louis group successfully staged a prayer protest by two thousand demonstrators on Sunday, October 18, 1942. The mass prayer service at the soldiers' memorial was jointly sponsored by the local MOWM division and the St. Louis Inter-Denominational Ministers Alliance. Five ministers actively participated in the program: James M. Bracy of First Baptist Church, W. A. Cooper of Metropolitan AME Zion, J. Milton Thompson of Berea Presbyterian Church, N. W. Clark of Lane Tabernacle CME Church, P. A. Gray of unknown affiliation, and James W. Cook of Antioch Baptist Church and the director of the local YMCA. McNeal and other MOWM organizers arranged the prayer meeting in the "center of the business district," at the foot of the soldiers' memorial, which required that the corner of Thirteenth and Chestnut Streets be blocked off so that chairs could be set up for spectators. A platform was erected on the steps of the memorial where the speakers delivered their messages.[35]

The program, an ambitious undertaking divided into three parts, began patriotically with congregation singing of the "Star Spangled Banner" and McNeal's ten-minute speech on the MOWM's "aims, objectives and purposes." Then McNeal introduced the March Players, a dramatic group which performed a skit by David M. Grant, a local activist in the MOWM. Grant's skit, which he described as a "biblical narration partly taken from the book of Exodus" compared the ancient situation of the Israelites with the modern-day African American experience, illustrating how black religious communities articulated a theology of black liberation. Grant's seven-page narration included two voices, one from the biblical past and one from the present. The following verses provide some flavor of the narrative:

Voice I: And the children of Israel "which came into Egypt . . . were fruitful, and increased abundantly, and multiplied . . . and the land was filled with them.

Voice II: And the Negro people which were brought into America in chains, . . . made the land fruitful with their labor, and increased its yield abundantly and multiplied its wealth . . . and the land was filled with the cries, their woe, and their suffering.

Voice I: Now there arose up a new king over Egypt . . . [called Pharaoh, who] did set over them taskmasters to afflict them with burdens. And they built for Pharaoh treasure cities.

Voice II: And so too the Negro people in America did build treasure cities, and grew beautiful crops under the lashes of their taskmasters. And so too did they multiply and grow under their afflictions.

The two voices briefly summarized how Moses journeyed into Egypt, appearing before Pharaoh to demand the delivery of his people. As the two voices completed the biblical narrative, the March Players sang "Go Down Moses," which eventually faded out as two characters, representing Pharaoh in a red-spangled robe with crown and scepter, and Moses, clad in a plain black robe, appeared on the stage. Throughout their dialogue, the Moses character reiterated the plaintive cry "Let my people go!" Although Grant's script has the two actors on stage while speaking the dialogue between Moses and Pharaoh, the St. Louis version was performed offstage using microphones to project the players' voices. McNeal described to Randolph the dramatic effect this had on the audience, hearing the narration "in voice only" with the players performing their parts over special microphones installed inside the soldiers' memorial: "It was truly impressive."[36]

As the scene between Moses and Pharaoh ended, a voice repeating the refrain, "Let my people go, let my people go," was heard loudly and emphatically until it eventually faded out. Then the two voices returned to relate the Israelites' escape through the Red Sea and Moses's appointment of Joshua, who led the children of Israel to the walls of Jericho. At this point, Grant used the second voice, which represented the current situation, to compare the Joshua of the Old Testament with the modern-day MOWM. Just as Joshua led the marchers around the walls of Jericho, with trumpets blaring until the walls came tumbling down, Grant wrote,

So too, shall the walls of discrimination, intolerance, prejudice, deceit and abuse fall down before the onslaughts of truth, courage, determination and the forthright thinking of honest men, who shun the false prophets and traducers of the democratic way of life. The MARCH ON WASHINGTON MOVEMENT has set its face toward delivering the Negro people.

The skit ended with "Joshua Fit the Battle of Jericho and the Walls Came Tumbling Down," performed by a well-known tenor, Laverne Hutchinson.[37]

Twenty years later, the sociologist E. Franklin Frazier used the same biblical image in his *The Negro Church in America* to describe how by the late 1950s "the walls of segregation" were tumbling down as he observed a southern civil rights movement forming under the leadership of Martin Luther King Jr. Frazier, like David Grant, drew on a powerful theological motif in African American religious culture since colonial times. The biblical image of "walls come tumbling down" was the final theme of the St. Louis prayer protest as the program shifted to its final phase, when the ministers took charge. Rev. Bracy dedicated the service to a victory by the United Nations, the millions of black people living "on the crust of American civilization," and other enslaved peoples of the world. After Bracy's invocation, quiet meditation, and a responsive reading, Rev. Cooper gave a prayer for victory of the United Nations, followed by Rev. Thompson's act of communion and meditation. After a silent prayer, Rev. Clark contributed his own prayer for the enslaved people of the world and victory over hate and oppression. The congregation sang the "National Negro Anthem" and "God Bless America." Rev. Gray offered a responsive reading, a prayer of repentance and a brief sermon, "Breaking Partitions," harking back to the "walls tumbling down" theme. The following is the sermon as it appeared in the prayer protest's program:

Most of us live walled-in lives. Some walls are as ancient as the Chinese walls, others may be more modern. Some are racial walls, some walls of hate, others national, others social. All walls are prisons. And since most walls are built by the prisoners, themselves, they can be destroyed only by Jesus, who is the kind of truth that sets men free. When Christ becomes our innermost possession the walls, regardless of their age and origin, go down. Where man-made partitions still dominate the mind and the emotions and motivate our relations to our fellowmen, it is proof that Christ has been received by us lukewarmly and reluctantly. He is therefore unable to do mighty works in us. We must allow ourselves to be influenced by the fact that Christ can break down the grim middle walls that plague industry. He can annihilate the partition between the races. He can break down the dividing walls of hate. The walls must go down. And they will go down only when Christ is vitally in our midst. For Christ either breaks down the walls or He breaks through them and becomes the door. He is both a wall-breaker and a door-maker.[38]

McNeal planned to collect the money from the crowd of two thousand people at the end of the program, but unfortunately the weather worked against them. Steady rain fell during the latter part of the meeting, causing the MOWM to lose money on the affair. Although McNeal claimed that only a small minority of the audience left because of the weather, the MOWM collected only $80, or 40 percent of the cost to produce the prayer protest. But overall, McNeal and the local organizers considered their efforts successful and their money well spent, since the meeting, in McNeal's words, "meant much to the Movement." For one thing, the partnership between the local MOWM division and the St. Louis ministerial alliance continued after their collaboration on the prayer protest. Ten days after the event, Randolph traveled to St. Louis to address an evening mass meeting, held indoors at the Washington Tabernacle Baptist Church. Randolph joined the church's pastor, Rev. J. E. Nance, and key prayer protest organizers T. D. McNeal, Rev. James Bracy, and David Grant, in an elaborate program of speeches, an invocation and offertory, several music selections from the Legend Singers, and McNeal's report on the MOWM's position on department store cafeterias. The St. Louis MOWM benefited from an active church committee and a religious community's enthusiastic support for Randolph's movement.[39]

McNeal, always certain that the St. Louis mass prayer meeting would be successful, urged Randolph to use the "prayer protest" in other cities. For Randolph, prayer protests struck a right balance between patriotism and protest. The MOWM's experimentations with prayer meetings as a tactic of protest during a period of intense patriotism coincided with several brutal reports of lynchings in the South. In Shubuta, Mississippi, two fourteen-year-old boys named Charles Lang and Ernest Green were found hanging from a bridge across the Chickasawhay River, on October 11, 1942. A small community subsisting on a couple of sawmills and some farming, Shubuta was known for its "impressive lynch record," wrote the *Chicago Defender* reporter Enoc P. Waters, who investigated the lynching. Eager workers, Lang and Green earned money by collecting old rubber tires and scraps of iron, copper, and aluminum. Waters reported "it was this quest for vital metal to help win the war against the Axis and to make this country a better place to live" that led to the young boys' deaths. Apparently, while collecting rubber and metal scrap near the bridge, the boys exchanged innocent greetings with a young white girl returning home from school. A white man, crossing the bridge at the time, reported the incident to the girl's father, which led to the eventual lynching. Six months after the lynching, the *Defender*'s investigator concluded that it was ignorance, wartime hysteria, and a lack of cohesiveness in the black community that contributed to the boys' lynching. With wartime job opportunities opening up in Mobile and Meridian, blacks in Shubuta were becoming more prosperous, and whites in the community perceived them as "getting uppity and out of their place." Moreover, the black community lacked cohesiveness, since "not one of the ministers of the four Negro churches—two Baptists, one Methodist and one Sanctified—[lived] in the community." Without black churches as a traditional "rallying point," Shubuta's black community could not effectively counter the injustices they faced.[40]

Two days before his appearance at the Washington Tabernacle Baptist Church in St. Louis, Randolph wired Burton and the Chicago MOWM division to organize a public prayer meeting in the Loop to protest the Mississippi lynchings. He wanted Burton to mobilize a group of black and white ministers to participate in a prayer protest. He believed that prayer protest demonstrations had two great advantages: religious communities could be mobilized quickly and they introduced the MOWM to people who didn't know about the movement "through its other forms of demonstrations." Wittie Anna Biggins, a contributor to the *People's Voice*, described the philosophy behind MOWM's prayer protests, which were "being launched throughout the nation" as a way to "arouse the Christian elements of this great democracy to a full realization of the horror of lynching and the injustice of racial discrimination." By means of prayer protests, the MOWM "served notice that prayers of all the people are essential to a democratic government." The Chicago MOWM division, torn up by dissension over the "undemocratic" way that Webster and Burton were running the local movement, never held a prayer protest, but Randolph personally rallied the MOWM division in New York for a prayer protest scheduled for November 9, 1942.[41]

Randolph and the New York MOWM focused their public prayer protest on the lynchings in Mississippi, as well as two other murders in Arizona and Texas. In his letter to New York's black ministers, Randolph publicized his new project, concentrating on the barbarism, cruelty, and fanaticism he saw behind these acts of violence. He demanded decisive action from the ministers by appealing to their sense of duty as the "spiritual leaders of our people." In his mind, the New York MOWM's public prayer protest originated in the black community's view that lynchings attacked their dignity as human beings and required a spiritual response. Randolph's prayer protest equated local mob violence with the horrors of the world war in Europe and the Pacific. He juxtaposed the lynchings, which he called a "throw-back to jungle law," with the fact that African Americans were dying "upon the seven seas and upon the far flung battlefields of the world" in service to their country. The "mob violence and terrorism" in the United States was nothing more than forms of "native Nazism and Fascism in America" and no different from the "threat to American democracy which the war now waged by the united nations . . . professed to preserve." Randolph felt this was urgent and demanded that it be done "now while this war [was] going on, for if we fail, we cannot tell what the future holds." Randolph's plan included various civic and fraternal organizations as a sign of solidarity for "this Prayer must be well attended to show our determination to start a constructive movement to abolish lynching."[42]

Randolph orchestrated every phase of the prayer protest, even though he was busy with his regular BSCP responsibilities, which in the end kept him from participating in it himself. Nonetheless, Randolph mobilized New York's ministers and black churches smoothly and quickly. Randolph sought Rev. S. T. Eldridge's endorsement of "this religious effort," as he had for the summer rally in Madison Square Garden. As pastor of the Berean Baptist Church and president of the Baptist Ministers Conference of Greater New York, Eldridge had considerable influence in the black religious community. Together they worked on the prayer protest, and with Randolph often out of town, Eldridge handled many of the details. Because of some BSCP business in Canada, Randolph canceled a scheduled ministerial planning session for the public prayer meeting but was able to telephone several ministers interested in the public prayer protest and to attend the Inter-Denominational Ministers' Alliance, which endorsed the event. The president of the alliance, Rev. S. H. Sweeney of St. Mark's Methodist Episcopal Church, agreed to participate in the ceremonies. Besides Sweeney and Eldridge, Randolph once again called on his old friend Rev. William Lloyd Imes. Randolph anxiously tried to reach Imes before his Canadian trip, because he wanted representatives of each faith—Jews, Catholics, Episcopalians, Methodists, Baptists, Presbyterians—to offer a brief prayer. Imes was needed to represent the Presbyterian Church.[43]

As with the St. Louis event, the New York prayer protest was a joint effort by the local MOWM division and local ministerial alliances. Planning meetings were scheduled at the MOWM headquarters, and the ministers were instructed to send a representative if they could not attend themselves. Randolph asked the MOWM representatives to announce the event at every Sunday service before the public prayer protest. Individual ministers responded positively to Randolph's call as well. James B. Adams, the pastor of Brooklyn's Concord Baptist Church of Christ, promised to make the "necessary announcement" about the prayer protest to his congregation and to attend himself. James E. Lee, president of the Relief Association of the Baptist Church, responded promptly and enthusiastically to Randolph's call, ordering his group to be at the meeting. He expected 100 percent attendance because he and his group supported the meeting as a "religious protest" against the lynchings in Mississippi.[44]

One of the most interesting letters Randolph received regarding the prayer protest was from Shelton Hale Bishop, the prominent minister of St. Philip's Protestant Episcopal Church and the son of Hutchens Bishop, who twenty-five years earlier had opposed Randolph's radicalism. The younger Rev. Bishop endorsed, and actually participated in, the prayer protest, even though he was not "primarily a 'protest person,'" as he told Randolph. From his correspondence with Randolph, Bishop expressed his dismay that the original "intention to march on Washington had been withdrawn" and that intentions and purposes of Randolph's new "marchless" organization were not clear. Yet, he greatly respected Randolph's leadership, and his participation in the prayer protest indicated his support of the MOWM, even though it was not as radical as he had hoped.[45]

As with the St. Louis prayer protest, Randolph scheduled his demonstration to take place in front of City Hall, "in the heart of the City," on Monday at noon. Not only did Randolph want the most public place he could get, but he envisioned the protest as a "solemn petition to God to give us the faith to press forward in our struggle for justice, equality and freedom." In his call letter to black ministers, Randolph stressed the solemnity of the affair. It was meant to impress "the Christian people of America [to] feel a sense of moral responsibility . . . [and] to cure this dreadful malady of racial hate and prejudice," which not only threatened the life and property of the black community but was "a deadly threat to Democracy and our Christian way of life." He believed that only a simple and somber protest would produce the "desired effect" of impressing New Yorkers with the seriousness of their intent.[46]

The meeting was to consist of only brief prayers and four songs: "My Country 'Tis of Thee," "Onward Christian Soldiers," "Faith of Our Fathers, Living Still," and one Negro spiritual. Randolph encouraged the male protesters to wear black crepe bands on their arms and the women protesters to wear mourning dresses to symbolize the "mob murder of these boys." By keeping it a solemn and dignified affair, Randolph was also able to persuade more black ministers to become involved. Several ministers had asked how the prayer protest was to be conducted. Randolph wrote several ministers, including Rev. Charles Young Trigg of the Salem Methodist Episcopal Church, assuring them the prayer protest would be conducted in the "most solemn and respectful manner." Aware that ministers demanded that a prayer protest "reflect creditably upon the Negro churches and religious leaders of our country," Randolph tried to alleviate their concerns. To them, Randolph stressed the ecumenical nature of the protest and the solidarity of the black Protestant community that endorsed it. He assured them that only appropriate religious and patriotic music would be used and that "this program will meet and merit your approval, support and cooperation."[47]

This ecumenical and interracial public prayer gathering intended to bring white religious leaders of the Catholic, Jewish, and Protestant faiths together with Harlem's Christian community, to stir the white Christian community's "public conscience," showing how racial hatred had endangered American democratic and Christian institutions. To this end, Randolph invited several white influential ministers in New York with outstanding reputations on social justice issues: Harry Emerson Fosdick of the Riverside Church, Dr. David de Sola Pool of Shearith Israel, Allan Knight Chalmers of Broadway Tabernacle Church, and John Paul Jones of Brooklyn's Union Bay Ridge Presbyterian Church. All but Fosdick accepted Randolph's invitation. Fosdick believed strongly that racial prejudice was a critical domestic issue in the United States, but he "questioned the practical efficiency of such movements as involve a march on Washington," which were "not kindred with [his] personal way of working."[48] Allan Knight Chalmers of Broadway Tabernacle Church wrote Randolph a short note saying, "If it is held at a time when I can be there, I will be there . . . count on me." Apparently Chalmers had a scheduling conflict. David de Sola Pool, rabbi of Shearith Israel, and Rev. John Paul Jones, minister of Union Bay Ridge Presbyterian Church in Brooklyn, participated in the November 9 ceremonies. Randolph appreciated Rabbi Pool's "immediate willingness to participate in the Public Prayer." Just as Fos-

Portrait of A. Philip Randolph by Gordon Parks, the famous New Deal photographer. Taken in November 1942, the same month of the New York "prayer protest" demanding justice for two young boys lynched in Mississippi and at the height of Randolph's popularity as a national civil rights leader. Reproduced from the Collections of the Library of Congress.

dick was a well-known and respected representative of the liberal Protestant community in New York, Rabbi Pool represented New York's oldest Jewish community. As rabbi of Shearith Israel, the oldest synagogue in the United States, Dr. Pool was known for his social activism during the war when he served as chair of the National Jewish Welfare Board's Committee on Army and Navy Religious Activities. With Rabbi Pool's participation, the event could not be perceived as a Protestant affair only, which was what Randolph wanted. Unfortunately, neither Randolph nor Eldridge was able to find a Catholic representative. The final list of ministers on the prayer protest program included Eldridge representing the Baptists, Imes and Jones representing Presbyterian congregations in New

York City and Brooklyn, Shelton Hale Bishop representing the Episcopalians, Sweeney representing the Methodists, and Pool representing the
Jewish community in New York.[49]

The prayer protest took place as Randolph originally conceived it. Except for the addition to the program of Dr. J. C. Jackson, president of the
New England Baptist Conference, at the last minute, the program of brief
prayers and the congregational singing led by Merritt Hedgeman and the
YMCA Mixed Choir went off as planned. At the last minute, because of
a parade scheduled to pass City Hall at one o'clock, the sixty-minute program was shortened. As chairman of the public prayer protest, Eldridge
contacted each of the participating ministers, asking them to limit their
prayers to three minutes because Mayor Fiorello LaGuardia had cut the
program to forty minutes. Eldridge supervised the ministers and the actual program, and Lawrence Ervin, the chairman of the New York
MOWM division, handled the complicated logistics of a meeting at City
Hall. Randolph's absence, due to BSCP business, meant that the responsibility for a successful prayer protest rested on Eldridge's and Ervin's
shoulders, but Ervin kept Randolph closely informed by telegram and
telephone of the meeting's progress. Ervin's and Eldridge's partnership on
this project also showed how the MOWM could work effectively with
local and ministerial alliances, enabling it to function throughout the war
as a social movement.[50]

A second problem was Mayor LaGuardia's fear that the MOWM's
Public Prayer might establish a dangerous precedent for allowing future
prayer meetings in front of City Hall. By applying public prayer as a tactic of protest, Randolph and the MOWM were exploring uncharted territory, especially in an environment that clearly distinguished between
church and state issues. When LaGuardia resisted giving permission for
City Hall, Ervin met in the mayor's office for thirty minutes to discuss
possible alternative sites. Other sites, such as Foley Square in front of the
Supreme Court Building or Carnegie Hall, were suggested, but Ervin
overruled Carnegie Hall because of a lack of funds. When LaGuardia insisted that they use Foley Square, Ervin claimed there was no time because he needed to inform six hundred ministers of the specific plans immediately. With things about to fall apart, Randolph negotiated with La-
Guardia by telegram, and Ervin kept showing up in person at the mayor's
office until the issue was settled. Eventually Ervin reported to Randolph
that LaGuardia was "very nice and . . . sincere, and I feel that he will give
me complete cooperation." Confident of securing City Hall, Ervin con-

tacted the ministers, made arrangements for advertising the program over the local radio station, WNYC, and sent the mayor a copy of the public prayer program.[51]

Mayor LaGuardia's concerns about a religious program put on by the black community reflected his anxiety over public reaction to a black protest meeting during a period of increasing wartime patriotism. On the same day that the MOWM secured permission to use the City Hall steps, Ervin wired Randolph about a new crisis involving Rev. Adam Clayton Powell Jr. One of Ervin's contacts at City Hall, a Captain Harten, informed him that Powell had stated that the purpose of the Monday demonstration was to "protest the low morale of the colored citizens of New York City." Mayor LaGuardia demanded that Powell publicly retract his statement or he would call off the Monday event. Powell, one of the original members of the MOWC, probably felt a certain proprietary right to make public statements on behalf of the organization, especially as the public prayer was perceived as an event sponsored by Harlem's black religious community.[52]

This was not the first time that Powell had stolen Randolph's thunder, as evidenced in his showstopping speech at the MOWM Madison Square Garden rally, which marked the beginning of Powell's rise to national prominence. Some of the march organizers distrusted Powell completely. When the Chicago MOWM division came out in support of local rapid transit employee strike, Iona Morris, a MOWM activist in New York, warned Randolph about Powell and "his henchmen" coming to Chicago to "steal the show," as he had done with a New York bus strike. Ervin acted quickly to assure the mayor that Powell was not a spokesman for the MOWM, although he stopped short of demanding that Powell retract his statement. Instead, Ervin insisted that the public prayer meeting was being held to protest the lynching of the two young men in Mississippi and was not a political statement about black wartime morale. Ervin wired Randolph about the problem, and through his intervention the public prayer protest took place as planned. In personally thanking each of the ministers for participating in the event, Randolph insisted that the protest's purpose was a religious response to southern lynching.[53]

Randolph's experimentation with prayer protests in the early 1940s has been largely ignored or forgotten. Herbert Garfinkel compared the St. Louis prayer meeting with the one in New York and concluded that the New York "'prayer meeting' met with less success." A closer reading of the sources finds support for Garfinkel's assessment, but the circumstances of the New York prayer protest offer several reasons why it was less successful than the St. Louis event. Randolph and the MOWM organizers in New York faced many problems unique to their locale: church and state issues, the difficulty of staging social protests during wartime, Powell's interference with the MOWM organizers, the personal antagonism between Powell and Mayor LaGuardia, Randolph's physical absence from the protest, and logistical issues such as timing and competition with another civic event. Wittie Anna Biggins, an observer of the prayer protest, blamed Mayor LaGuardia and "several thousand white citizens, parade participants . . . and what have you in parade equipment" for occupying the space designated for the prayer meeting fifteen minutes before the meeting was scheduled to end. Given the wide publicity of the meeting and the thorough planning of the local MOWM, Biggins blamed several "short-sighted Christians" whom she interviewed after the meeting for their failure "to attend or encourage the public prayer service because they believed it the responsibility of the church rather than the March On Washington Committee."[54]

All these issues should be factored into why the New York event attracted only fifty black protesters. Still, Randolph's New York "prayer protest" showed how quickly black and white religious leaders and communities would mobilize behind him for a religious event. Randolph's experiments in prayer protests in the early 1940s foreshadowed his later involvement with the first national civil rights campaign of the modern civil rights movement: the 1957 prayer pilgrimage. In the few months since the canceled march on Washington, Randolph had moved inward, tapping his own religious impulses in order to lead this new social movement. Randolph's experimentations with prayer in the early 1940s as an effective tool of social protest contrasts strikingly with his earlier declaration that "prayer [was] not one of our remedies" in fighting social injustice. These events in late 1942 provide some insights into Randolph's next controversial tactic, of using Gandhi's method of nonviolent civil disobedience, another spiritual response to directing social movements.[55]

As the MOWM was seeking spiritual ways of challenging Jim Crow, Randolph's turn to Gandhian nonviolent civil disobedience, or *satyagraha*, is yet another example of his religious activism. Most scholars agree with Garfinkel's claim that Randolph did not possess the "religious component" to practice *satyagraha* and that he used nonviolent, direct action only as a political tactic. Randolph explained that his "advocacy of the philosophy of nonviolence as one of the highways for fundamental social change" was inspired by the life of Jesus Christ as well as by Gandhi. But even before he had heard of Gandhi, Randolph attributed his "belief in the moral and spiritual power of non-violence from his father who was a minister of the African Methodist Episcopal Church" and a man of "high moral commitments."[56]

Randolph's rhetoric and writing in 1943 anticipated a theology of black liberation which is connected to his Gandhian turn during the war. For Randolph, the MOWM was his version of a civil rights organization designed to fight for "first-class citizenship," since African Americans consistently fell short of full equality. As he was quoted in one black newspaper: for economic equality, blacks received charity grants; for political equality, they got poll taxes and white primaries; for social equality, they got Jim Crow and lynching; and "for religious equality, he has been given good will and a white God." From Randolph's perspective, the war was a world revolution that tested this double standard of citizenship. In speeches before two religious communities in Cleveland and Chicago, Randolph connected the black person's fight for "first-class citizenship" to deeper spiritual issues that plagued America. To an ecumenical Christian group in Cleveland, the American Co-operative Christianity in United Counsel, Randolph argued that racial discrimination not only insulted the black man's "soul" but destroyed the "the soul of America." Through the efforts of Rev. James Lafayette Horace, Randolph appeared as the principal speaker of Chicago's Church Federation. Before three hundred Chicago ministers, Randolph castigated the white church of America for maintaining a "religious ceremonial dualism for white and black Christians" and failing to live up to the principles of Jesus Christ. He asserted, "When the test of Christian brotherhood came upon the most humble and the weakest followers of Christ—the Negro people—a corrosive and deadening spirit of complacency seized the entire life of religious America."[57]

As the United States built up its war arsenal, Randolph focused on India's war for independence. Written into the MOWM's platform from the Detroit policy conference was the recognition that India's "world shaking, history making fight for independence" made India's fight the "Negro's fight." At AFL meetings, Randolph raised the issue of India's freedom and independence, calling it "pure hypocrisy to talk of this war as being fought for democracy while India [was] continually oppressed by British autocracy." Like other black civil rights activists of his time, Randolph was deeply affected by the situation in India. Pauli Murray expressed her dismay when she wrote to him, "Even on vacation, the Indian situation haunts me." Murray believed that "the freedom of India [was] as important to the cause of the United Nations as was the Emancipation Proclamation to the cause of the Union forces in our own Civil War." Murray urged Randolph and the MOWM to initiate a rally with other democratic groups, such as the Union for Democratic Action or Norman Thomas's Post War World Council, in order to protest India's plight more effectively. Murray believed that Randolph had to take action, since he was "the logical person to take the lead here."[58]

By December 1942, Randolph, began combining the local MOWM units into a national organization. From its New York headquarters, the MOWM planned to mobilize "five million Negroes into one great mass of pressure for freedom and democracy in America." E. Pauline Myers from Richmond, Virginia, was appointed as executive secretary. Since the early 1930s when she was a student leader and activist at Howard University, Myers had worked in a variety of democratic and liberal causes in Richmond, Washington, Philadelphia, and Chicago. From her position as the business, industrial, and public affairs secretary at the Phyllis Wheatley YWCA branch in Richmond, Myers moved into the march headquarters in New York's Hotel Theresa in January 1943.[59]

With a full-time executive secretary in place, the MOWM unveiled its next big event: a national convention scheduled for May, to explore a "broad national program on nonviolent and civil disobedience and non-cooperation" as a tactic of abolishing Jim Crowism in America. Within weeks, given the intense wartime patriotism, the May convention developed into a week-long national event with the theme "I am an American, too." In addition to the more traditional ways of direct-action protest—marching on city halls, sending letters and telegrams to government and corporate officials, and using the pulpit and the press to preach the March's slogan—"Defeat Hitler, Mussolini and Hirohito by Enforcing and Observing the Constitution and Abolishing Jim Crow"—the march organizers added the technique of nonviolent civil disobedience used effectively by Mahatma Gandhi. The MOWM perceived civil disobedience as another way to achieve liberation, which enabled trained individuals to boycott Jim Crow cars and waiting rooms in an "orderly, peaceful and quiet manner." But instituting such a radical idea, especially in wartime, proved to be easier said than done. Needing more time to make the necessary arrangements, Randolph and the national MOWM pushed back the convention, set in Chicago for June 30 to July 4, 1943, one year after the Chicago Coliseum rally had attracted almost twenty thousand people.[60]

The MOWM's new program quickly encountered opposition from the black community, particularly from the *Pittsburgh Courier*, the movement's nemesis. When *Courier* editors complained that the march's leadership was completely visionary, lacking the concrete administrative skills to sustain a responsible civil rights organization, especially with "irresponsible talk about suicidal civil disobedience and mass marches which never materialize," Randolph fought back. He retorted that the *Courier*, representing the "petty black bourgeoisie," was nothing but "Gestapo Journalism," which explained "why it cannot comprehend the deeper spiritual implications of the March Movement." In his view, the *Courier* lacked a cause, a mission, and "a dedication to an ideal or principle bigger than itself." Lacking "faith in the masses, black or white," *Courier* editorials "breathe the lifeless air of defeatism, cynicism, supersophistication" while sneering and snubbing "the people's struggles, for economic, political and social righteousness."[61]

For Randolph, the MOWM's "deeper spiritual implications" came from its roots "deep in the soil of the Negro masses." Because the MOWM had been born in a time of economic chaos, political disorder, social confusion, and revolutionary ferment, Randolph argued that policies of accommodation and appeasement were futile. His direct-action tactic of marching on Washington had inspired the African American community to abandon the traditional "conference method" of petitioning for equal rights. Since the attack on Pearl Harbor, conditions for blacks had only worsened. Randolph reasoned that unless they fought for their democratic freedoms now, "while conditions [were] fluid and unsettled," it would be too late after the war, when race relations would "become crystallized with encrusted dogmas that will resist change." Therefore, it was necessary for blacks to use "revolutionary, unusual, extraordinary, dramatic, and drastic" methods and techniques to place their minority cause into "the mainstream of national and international public opinion." But this could happen only if blacks developed "the spirit of self-reliance" and initiative for the solution of their own problems while collaborating with other oppressed minorities—Jews, Catholics, and other liberal forces—to extend the "frontiers of democracy." Randolph believed that as an oppressed people, the African American community had the spiritual capacity as Christians to withstand the suffering and sacrifice necessary to make their equality a political reality. He believed that this power resided in the masses who were waiting to be organized, mobilized, and disciplined to struggle for equality, for

> the law of the achievement of freedom, justice and equality is the law of the Seed and the Cross. This is the law of struggle, sacrifice, suffering. It is the law of death. Death precedes life. The seed must decay and die before the tree can live. Jesus Christ had to bear the cross and die in order to give life everlasting. Verily, there is no royal road to freedom.[62]

While implementing a nonviolent disobedience campaign, the MOWM propaganda reiterated the religious themes that Randolph laid out in his defense against the *Courier*: a crisis situation that mobilized an outraged black community to an acceptance of suffering, sacrificial death, and eventual liberation as blacks united together. Randolph's rhetoric during this period had a sense of urgency as he reiterated his belief that the world war was "an hour of crisis." Similarly, liberation theologians of the 1970s identified the sense of urgency or crisis felt by oppressed people fighting for their human dignity and civil rights with the biblical term "a *kairos* moment." MOWM organizers understood the black community's frustration and discontent with the old methods of doing business. The MOWM served as a forum for blacks to tell their story of oppression and exploitation. It allowed them to express outrage over the nation's indifference to their plight. Randolph reminded his readers that the original idea of marching on Washington was itself a technique of nonviolent direct action to demonstrate to the public the black community's numerical strength. Randolph and his followers always understood the movement as inspired by the protests, grievances, and injustices experienced by blacks with a "mass cry for deliverance." The march's objective was "to crystallize the mass consciousness of injustices and inhumanity." Randolph's belief that this cause was something that black Americans would "gladly and willingly suffer and sacrifice" reflected more his own deep spiritual commitment than that of his followers.[63]

Through mass meetings intended to "develop Cause Consciousness," Randolph hoped that these types of activities would provide the moral and spiritual strength needed for "our Movement and the Negro masses." Each local march division fostered the idea that each individual was important to the liberation movement. The objective was to "harness the flow of rising resentment and indignation" of blacks, intensified by the war, and turn it into a "deep spiritual force for constructive social action." During the week of the first MOWM convention, only trained black citizens would use "nonviolent, goodwill direct action," such as boycotting trains, street cars, buses, restaurants, waiting rooms, rest rooms, hotels, schools, and institutions that enforced Jim Crow laws and patterns. By turning to civil disobedience as a tactic to fight Jim Crow, Randolph and other march activists did not regard it as a dramatic departure for the movement or for the black masses. The MOWM propaganda emphasized how blacks "jumped Jim Crow" every day, although the "escape [was] often expensive, sacrificial and many times hazardous."[64]

From the MOWM perspective, enlistment into the march movement was a part of the war effort, as it defeated the "Hitlerites at home," and therefore was winning the war for democracy. It constantly turned the individual to the larger context of world events and to the need for self-reliance and individual responsibility, as exemplified in this warning to its followers:

> The anxious eyes of India and China are being turned toward America. America can no longer remain half slave and half free. The time to choose the way is now. We cannot put our faith entirely in armaments to win freedom for the world. Our faith must be fixed on truth. "Ye hereditary bondsmen, know ye that he who would be freed must himself strike the first blow."[65]

Randolph planned extensive training and educational programs to help blacks prepare the "proper moral and intellectual attitude" necessary to make the technique of passive resistance effective. He insisted that with proper training, American blacks had the capacity to carry out civil disobedience tactics but that it would take sacrifice and courage, since "justice and equality for any people were never won on flowery beds of ease." Randolph warned that "a people who have fear in their hearts are doomed to be slaves."[66]

Still, the MOWM continued to face opposition and found itself constantly defending its position. The *Courier* conducted a poll on Randolph's "noncompliance project" with the survey question "Do you believe a nonviolent, civil disobedience campaign would help American Negroes?" According to the *Courier* poll, 71.8 percent of those polled said no; 25.1 percent said yes; and 4.1 percent were uncertain. The paper provided several reasons why the black public disapproved of the march's new tactic: an "Oriental" solution that did not apply to black Americans; deep-seated fears of mob violence; concerns about losing liberal sympathy and support; and the inability of American blacks to sustain such a campaign, since many doubted "the spiritual responsibility of the Negro to successfully conduct a non-violent campaign." Another concern was that it interfered with the war effort. Owing to the provocative and hysterical articles written against the MOWM, Randolph and the MOWM activists found it extremely difficult to present their program and to awaken blacks from their docility.[67]

As news spread of the MOWM's new tactic of civil disobedience, the organization constantly refuted charges that it opposed the war effort. While MOWM propaganda declared that its civil disobedience program did not apply to blacks serving in the armed forces or defense industries, they defended it as a "form of social protest and revolt against the unjust, unfair and undemocratic laws that violate the basic moral and human citizenship rights" of African Americans. Although the MOWM remained an all-black organization, it enlisted the aid of "white liberal and Christian America" to join its nonviolent protest, which Randolph hoped would have a "profound spiritual and moral influence upon the whole social thinking of America." The MOWM's critics charged that the movement was undermining the allied war effort. Randolph defended the "passive resistance program" as a limited form of protest by selected individuals only during the week of the convention in Chicago, now called "We Are Americans, Too." Moreover, MOWM propaganda revealed how organizers planned to use the tactic differently in the North and the South. In the South, individuals would practice "negative" forms of boycotting: demanding the right to sit in white sections of trains and other forms of transportation, and parents agreeing to keep their children home from school during that week. In the northern civil rights states, individuals would use a "positive" form of boycotting: patronizing "with their white Christian friends" hotels, theaters, and restaurants not usually frequented by blacks. These explanations by Randolph and other MOWM organizers, however, never overcame the negative publicity that MOWM's civil disobedience tactic was antiwar and unpatriotic.[68]

Concerned with the unfavorable publicity the march was receiving in the black press, Pauli Murray suggested that Randolph send a copy of the proceedings of the MOWM's Detroit conference along with a copy of the Fellowship of Reconciliation's (FOR) pamphlet on civil disobedience to editors of the black press and the liberal white press to encourage a public discussion of the issue of nonviolent direct action. A close connection developed between the MOWM and FOR, especially when Randolph publicly supported nonviolent goodwill direct action. The black march rights movement attempted to reeducate white Americans, especially white "liberal and Christian America." When A. J. Muste learned from the black press that Randolph planned several nonviolent civil disobedience demonstrations, he congratulated him for his "vision, intelligence and courage" and believed the move to be "epoch-making."[69]

In the months before the MOWM convention, the MOWM and FOR worked together to devise training courses for individuals to learn how to apply nonviolent direct action. FOR and MOWM circles gathered twelve to fifteen students in close-knit, coordinated groups. From FOR, young activists such as James Farmer, George Houser, and Bayard Rustin formed the Congress of Racial Equality (CORE), one of the influential civil rights organizations of the 1960s. Formed just a year after the MOWM, CORE shared many of the same objectives as Randolph's march, but its membership was open to both blacks and whites. Randolph's foreword for George Houser's book on the early development of CORE reveals the close connection between CORE and MOWM. In it Randolph also defined nonviolent, goodwill direct action in its religious context: "It is applied Christianity. It is applied democracy. It is Christianity and democracy brought out of gilded churches and solemn legislative halls and made to work as a dynamic force in our day to day life."[70]

Besides Randolph's close relationship to FOR and CORE in these months before the June convention, two other important religious figures in liberal Protestant Christian circles came out publicly for the MOWM's nonviolent tactic: E. Stanley Jones and J. Holmes Smith. Smith, a former Methodist missionary in India, directly influenced the founders of CORE. As a leading activist in the Non-Violent Action Committee that FOR created in 1941, Smith founded the Harlem ashram, a small interracial cooperative that often served as the meeting place for the New York CORE chapter. Like Muste, Smith believed that Randolph's announcement to institute civil disobedience techniques in the march movement was a historic opportunity. During these formative months before the MOWM's first convention, Smith enthusiastically supported Randolph and viewed him as "a distinctly American Gandhi." Randolph sought Smith's advice on a variety of issues regarding nonviolent tactics and used his proposed course outlines for training programs in nonviolence as developed by the

Harlem ashram. The ashram's most notable direct-action program was a two-week "pilgrimage" from New York to the Lincoln Memorial in Washington, D.C., which coincided with the MOWM's summer rallies in 1942. The interracial Harlem ashram pilgrims hoped to dramatize the antilynching and antipoll tax bills before Congress at that time.[71]

In May, the MOWM announced that Dr. E. Stanley Jones, "the most militant internationally known white champion of the cause of the Negro people in the world today," would address the "We are Americans, too" conference. Jones, an innovative American Methodist missionary in India, had established several Christian ashrams, or retreat centers, for study and meditation, in order to share Christianity with the Hindus he encountered in his missionary work. Author of the best-selling the *Christ of the Indian Road* (1925), Jones also was well known in the West and was a popular preacher and lecturer. Randolph persuaded Jones to rearrange his busy schedule so he could address the Sunday mass meeting scheduled at the end of the MOWM conference. Randolph believed that Jones, with his international reputation for "the cause of religion and social service for the advancement of human justice," had the stature to convince others of the reasonableness of using nonviolence as a tactic. He scheduled Jones to address the mass meeting on the topic "Race and Non-Violent Solutions." After the conference, MOWM propaganda stressed the enthusiastic response that E. Stanley Jones received from the Chicago audience. There, Jones argued that nonviolent goodwill direct action required "those who take up this principle of social action" to be prepared to suffer in a "comparable manner with the capacity of the enemies to inflict suffering." Jones believed that violence and bloodshed lead only to confusion, ill will, and social chaos. For his part, Randolph wanted the audience at the MOWM convention to connect nonviolent social action with the "need for action in the Negro liberation movement."[72]

Besides Randolph's involvement in the FOR community and his controversial use of the Gandhian notion of *satyagraha*, he also worked on several projects to mobilize black and white religious individuals, communities, and churches. At the top of his agenda was persuading black ministers to sign "the call" to the "We are Americans, too" conference. Randolph wanted an "imposing group of nationally known citizens" to sign it, including Bishop John Gregg of the AME Church, Rev. D. V. Jemison of the National Baptist Convention of U.S.A., and several ministers leading local MOWM units, Charles Wesley Burton in Chicago and Horace White from Detroit. In Pittsburgh, Randolph enlisted the aid of Rev. Robert P. Johnson of the Bethesda Presbyterian Church, a young, energetic minister with the "proper attitude" who agreed to establish a local MOWM unit and send a delegate to the conference. The public announcement of the conference revealed an ambitious ten-point agenda, including the adoption of *satyagraha* as the "foundation of peace for a new world."[73]

No minister expressed the proper revolutionary spirit of the march better than David V. Jemison, pastor of the Tabernacle Baptist Church in Selma, Alabama, and president of the National Baptist Convention, U.S.A. Jemison sent Randolph several enthusiastic letters endorsing the movement, the upcoming convention, and assuring him that his four million constituents supported the endeavor. Jemison believed that any recognition that black people would get from the government would come from fighting for it, and like Randolph, Jemison understood that "anything that has value attached has a cost mark attached also." In one letter, Jemison expressed his frustration and despair with the "camouflaging and hypocrisy of whites," the very fighting spirit that the MOWM encouraged. Commenting on how southern blacks "entirely deserted the farm" because of the white man's "injustice, intrusion and imposition," Jemison perfectly expressed the sense of anger and self-sacrifice that the march was trying to instill in its followers, using Patrick Henry's demand, "Give me liberty or give me death." Randolph found Jemison's comments so true and stirring that he responded, "Now is the time for the Negro to fight for his rights because his cause is righteous and God is on his side." Since finding an outspoken, influential minister from the heart of the deep South so representative of the spirit of the MOWM was an extremely rare commodity, Randolph made several attempts to get Jemison to address the opening session of the Chicago conference, but without success. With the wartime emergency, Randolph did not expect a great number of delegates from "out of town."[74]

Several members of the Fraternal Council of Negro Churches (FCNC) corresponded with Randolph because of their interest in the march movement. AME bishop R. R. Wright from Wilberforce, Ohio, the FCNC's executive secretary, wrote on behalf of the group to learn more about the MOWM. As Wright explained, the FCNC wanted to make "more practical the principles of the Christian religion" but did not want to duplicate what other black organizations were doing. Wright asked Randolph for a clear statement of the MOWM's purposes. Other FCNC official endorsed the "We are Americans, too" convention, including Rev. William Jernigan and Bishop James A. Bray. They also supported Randolph's petition of protest to President Roosevelt regarding the recent changes in the FEPC status being put under congressional control. Bishop Bray called the change in the FEPC's status, as set up under the original executive order, "calamitous."[75]

In the months before the convention, Randolph enlisted the support of other religious groups for the FEPC's increasingly shaky status. At least twenty-five Catholic, Protestant, and Jewish leaders signed the petition protesting blacks' second-class citizenship and reaffirming the principles of Executive Order 8802. Signing the memorial were ministers who had actively supported Randolph's activism for years, such as William Lloyd Imes, and John Haynes Holmes, as well as other well-known religious figures representing the Protestant, Catholic, and Jewish faiths: Reinhold Niebuhr, John Ryan, and Sidney Goldstein.[76]

Along with the petition, Randolph's BSCP associate Ashley Totten arranged a conference to "save the FEPC" in Washington, D.C., sponsored by the Colored Locomotive Firemen's union. Once again Randolph and Lawrence Ervin mobilized the New York ministers for this campaign. Ervin informed the New York's black ministers of recent developments that had severely curtailed the FEPC's effectiveness, urging them to send representatives to the FEPC hearings scheduled for January 1943, to enlist their congregations to send letters and telegrams to the president, and to attend a mass protest meeting to hear Randolph and Dr. James Meyers of the Federal Council of Churches, speak. Randolph also contacted Rev. Eldridge concerning the crisis surrounding the FEPC and the urgent need for organizing the public to support it. Randolph warned that unless this was done quickly, southern politicians such as Governor Frank Dixon of Alabama, Ex-Governor Eugene Talmadge of Georgia, and Governor Sam Houston Jones of Louisiana, who bitterly opposed the FEPC on the grounds that it challenged "the social policy of segregation in the South," would win. Randolph suggested a "pilgrimage" of ministers, from those who attended the "save the FEPC" hearings, to march on the Lincoln Memorial as a way to protest this opposition and to generate public support for the FEPC. Randolph envisioned a pilgrimage similar to the one J. Holmes Smith and the Harlem ashram had sponsored in 1942. Randolph tentatively scheduled this "pilgrimage of citizens" to the Lincoln Memorial for February 1943. He hoped that an ecumenical body of black and white Protestant ministers, Catholic priests, and Jewish rabbis would "constitute a moral and spiritual force which the southern cracker will not be able to ignore or brush aside."[77]

The Chicago MOWM division remained the center of march activities as plans progressed for the first convention. Three months before the conference, the Chicago division opened a headquarters office and started to furnish it with equipment and an "office girl." Besides asking every MOWM member to contribute $5.00 for expenses for the upcoming convention, the group held planning meetings every Wednesday night. The Maywood area and the Lincoln Memorial Church continued to hold the larger meetings and events. Burton tried to introduce nonviolent civil disobedience to Chicago's black community and believed that "much educational work must be done to put over the non-violence program." To help Burton with the plans, Pauline Myers spent several weeks in Chicago organizing and enlisting citizens into the campaign. Outside speakers were invited to explain to the group the "Indian" concept of nonviolence. MOWM organizers worked closely with CORE activists. At Randolph's suggestion, Burton attended an institute in Detroit on nonviolent, goodwill direct action as a technique for their black liberation movement. Speakers included E. Stanley Jones and A. J. Muste. In the closing session with Muste, Burton spoke of the MOWM as a "program for today." One session erupted in controversy over the issue of using nonviolence in the MOWM when James Lindahl, of the United Auto Workers, attacked the MOWM's civil disobedience tactic as "treasonable." Coming to the MOWM's defense, Burton was interrupted by "heated discussion" on the topic. However, Burton reported to Randolph with his characteristic optimism that the session had "awakened the people" to the possibilities of nonviolence, "even though Lindahl tried to get in some C. P. propaganda." The MOWM correspondence shows the organization's confusion over how best to implement the nonviolent direct-action program. Some Chicago activists thought the nonviolent program was to be carried out before the convention, and others, after it.[78]

Randolph made several trips to Chicago before the conference, mobilizing Chicago's black churches. The influential minister Archibald Carey Jr., of the Woodlawn AME Church, asked Randolph to address his "church monthly forum," an opportunity that Burton jumped at because it allowed the MOWM to present its case before a large audience. Carey's influence in Chicago made his active support for the movement crucial. As the son of Randolph's old nemesis from his radical days, Bishop Carey,

Rev. Carey's support for his activism was especially significant and another indication of Randolph's acceptance by the black religious community by the 1940s. The MOWM also counted on Rev. Harold Kingsley's Good Shepherd Congregational Church, whose auditorium allowed the march to hold large meetings. In June, Ethel Payne arranged for Randolph's appearances at several churches in Chicago: Good Shepherd, Hope Presbyterian Church, St. Matthew's Methodist Church, and the Original Providence Baptist Church. When he was not in Chicago, Randolph kept in touch with Burton about last-minute details.[79]

In June 1943, ten days before the MOWM conference, race riots erupted in Detroit; Beaumont, Texas; and Collins, Mississippi. In this period of intense racial unrest, the first MOWM convention nonetheless went forward with its five-day program of business meetings, panel discussions, a symposium and town hall meeting, an open air prayer service, receptions, and banquets and ending with a final mass meeting on July 4. Held primarily in the Metropolitan Community Church, each day's activities included a religious component, a prayer or invocation, and music. Like the BSCP labor conferences, the opening meeting had a speech on the "Negro Church and the Race Problem," delivered by Rev. James Horace. Members of FOR played an active role in the convention: A. J. Muste addressed one session on "Race and Nonviolent Solutions"; Bayard Rustin appeared on Thursday's symposium discussing the "Program to Abolish Jim-Crow in America" and served as the cantor for Sunday's religious service; and James Farmer appeared at Friday's town hall meeting, calling for the abolition of the war's "greatest scandal": "Jim Crow in Uniform." Sunday, July 4, the final day of the convention, the mass meeting "drew thousands of friends and spectators," serving as a rally call "to the Negro people to struggle, fight, and die if necessary in the cause of their own liberation." The two main talks were E. Stanley Jones's speech on nonviolence and Randolph's keynote address on the MOWM's principles and policies. Randolph tied his topic to the recent riots, blaming them on the government's segregation policy and the FEPC weakened by the Roosevelt administration.[80]

On the final day of the convention, a Sunday morning prayer service was scheduled before the mass meeting. Advertised as "Inter-faith, Inter-denominational and Inter-racial," the event was actually a memorial service for black soldiers serving the country, with the theme "We shall not fail our boys." The well-planned religious service played an important role in keeping the tense emotions of the black community in check while

Photograph of Randolph and Milton Webster at a BSCP banquet at an AME church in Chicago in the late 1940s. Photographer unknown. Courtesy of the Chicago Historical Society.

expressing a radical message. The hour-long program included organ music, choir singing, and offerings by five black ministers. Burton had contacted ten ministers by phone in preparation for a sunrise religious service on Independence Day, and half of them agreed to participate. Longer prayers were offered by a Catholic, Protestant, and Jewish clergyman. The dramatic moment of the religious service was the "Unveiling of [a] Manifesto by Clergy of All Faiths." Pauline Myers described the manifesto as a statement "reporting the case of the Negro People to the Nation and to the World." By using the term *manifesto*, the prayer meeting was transformed into a radical religious message, with an emphasis on black liberation. Designed as a scroll, the manifesto listed nine grievances accompanied by nine demands. Randolph and the march organizers intended to print the manifesto in several white newspapers, including the *New York Times* and the *Washington Star*, after the convention.

The manifesto's demands were (1) a democratic army; (2) equal access to employment opportunity; (3) an end to disfranchisement in the South; (4) equal access to educational opportunities; (5) the end of "caricature and slander of Negroes" in newspapers, radio, and films; (6) minority-group representation in all administrative agencies that determined policies affecting all people; (7) an end to residential ghettos and "restrictive covenants"; (8) and the strict enforcement of the constitutional clause that "guarantees . . . life, liberty, or property." The Sunday morning's prayer service was followed by a "mammoth mass meeting" at which Randolph shared the stage with Dr. E. Stanley Jones. Although reports verified that the meeting was attended by a "wildly enthusiastic audience" of hundreds of delegates jamming the DuSable high school auditorium, the riots overshadowed the meeting's theme of black liberation through nonviolent means.[81]

The controversy and opposition that surrounded the MOWM's civil disobedience campaign in the months before the conference continued after the delegates went home. Randolph's tactic of nonviolent, goodwill direct action leaned too close to pacifism, a traditionally unpopular option for Americans during times of war. After the conference, Randolph and his MOWM civil rights organization never regained the popularity they enjoyed in 1941 and 1942. After Randolph's six-part series on the MOWM appeared in the *Chicago Defender*, laying out the movement's principles and philosophy, the paper withdrew its endorsement. Op-ed columnist John Robert Badger declared Randolph an "isolationist" and a "racist" who played on the "national aspirations of his people." Badger decried Randolph's program as alien to the traditions and experiences of black Americans. For the *Courier*, the MOWM conference in Chicago only confirmed its opinion that the movement was "irresponsible demagoguery," a great outpouring of words but "little sensible action." As for the civil disobedience campaign, which the MOWM had resolved to adopt, the *Courier* declared that it could only lead to disaster considering the current national state of mind. The op-ed concluded that "if the leaders of this movement are seeking martyrdom, they have certainly chosen an excellent device for achieving it."[82]

The MOWM also faced criticism from white liberal supporters such as Nancy and Dwight MacDonald, New York intellectuals who in 1943 had started publishing a leftist magazine, *Politics*. In a scathing memo on the movement's many weakness, the MacDonalds argued that the MOW had lost its radical edge and was too dependent on "Mr. Randolph, who lacks the time to give it the attention it deserves." They believed that there was an "unhealthy degree of leader-worship of Mr. Randolph," which paralyzed decision making. The MacDonalds, who had spent much time and energy supporting the movement, were disappointed that the nonviolent direct-action tactic, the center of attention for several months, was never put into effect and "dropped out of sight." The MacDonalds were most upset about the incompetent way "in which the manifesto-advertisement, 'Are Negroes Citizens?' was handled."[83]

Apparently Dwight MacDonald had submitted his own version of the manifesto because he was appalled that a "supposedly militant organization" like the MOWM had asked a "conservative Churchman, Mr. [George] Haynes" to prepare the first draft. Dwight MacDonald spent considerable time and effort formulating what he thought the document should state and submitted it to Pauline Myers for publication. In the end, MacDonald's draft of the manifesto had been altered so much that he did not recognize it when it was published in the *Washington Evening Star*, and he complained that it was worse "than Haynes' original draft." The MacDonalds ended their long memo with the recommendation that the MOWM urgently needed a "program of *action*, however modest in the beginning, and fewer speeches and manifestoes."[84]

Among the many things that the MacDonalds' memo revealed about the inside workings of the MOWM in its formative stages was Randolph's ongoing association with George Haynes of the Federal Council of Churches. Dr Haynes had been a featured speaker at the convention's Thursday symposium on "Mapping a Broad National Program in the Interest of Abolishing Jim Crow in America." Since the early 1930s, Haynes had participated in Randolph's BSCP labor conferences, supported Randolph in the National Negro Congress, and backed his formation of a civil rights organization after the march was postponed. Randolph naturally turned to Haynes as a prominent leader in the black church, and even though he might have lacked the radical credentials of the Mac-Donalds, he was a persuasive and respected leader in the black community.[85]

Randolph read the MacDonald's critical memo with interest, finding some of the comments sound and others "not so sound." Stating that "every movement must be capable of self-examination and self-criticism," Randolph wrote, "Personally, I think MOWM has inner strength and objective clarity of vision but it is young and will make mistakes and blunders which in turn will give it new strength and fresh faith and inner power." He reminded the MacDonalds that the "business of organizing anybody or anything" could not be done overnight and was "full of headaches" but that a movement's "progress must come from its own successes and defects." For Randolph, the main criticism from the white liberal community was due to his insistence that the MOWM remain all-black. Randolph met "plenty of opposition from both Negro and white on this question" but remained adamant on this principle. Despite the growing criticism of Randolph's movement, the MOWM carried on. Randolph planned an "echo meeting on the conference" to be held at the Good Shepherd Congregational Church in Chicago. Pauline Myers, left with the "dreary task" of getting national projects into immediate action, passed on to Dr. William Stuart Nelson, dean of Howard University's School of Religion, the task of chairing the National Advisory Committee on Nonviolent Good Will Direct Action. Myers hoped that under Nelson's stewardship, the committee would prove "stimulating to local branches," but with the movement in decline, its controversial civil disobedience campaign died with it.[86]

After the "We Are Americans, Too" conference, the MOWM struggled along, but without its original momentum. Randolph cochaired the National Council for a Permanent FEPC with Allan Knight Chalmers, the activist UCC minister of New York's Broadway Tabernacle Congregational Church. Rev. Chalmers, a leader in the pacifist movement, had chaired the national Scottsboro Defense Committee and was active in the NAACP. In 1947 and 1948, Randolph launched two other civil rights movements: the Committee against Jim Crow in Military Service and Training, which he cochaired with Grant Reynolds, a former minister and army chaplain, and the Nonviolent Civil Disobedience against Military Segregation, which began Randolph's alliance with Bayard Rustin, a Quaker pacifist who had served time in prison for his antiwar beliefs.[87]

Ten years after Randolph's initial experimentation with Gandhian *satyagrapha* in the 1943 MOWM conference, he received a letter from a young Jewish man named Nathaniel Cooper, who wanted Randolph's help in launching a movement that combined "the methods of Satyagraha, Christian conversion from evil to good, and Kiddush Hasham (sanctification of the name), the Jewish form of anti-violence . . . to abolish 'legalized' discrimination now oppressing the Negroes of the South." Cooper had learned from Pauli Murray, Adam Clayton Powell, Henry Lee Moon of the NAACP, Will Maslow of the American Jewish Congress, and others, of Randolph's pioneering role in using Gandhi's *satyagraha* method in opposing discrimination during the war. In his letters, Cooper described his conviction that *satyagraha* would play an important part in removing racial discrimination in 1950s America. Randolph's experience in using this method was valuable, Cooper believed, but he regretted that "unfortunately, not all of those working for equality know about the methods of Mohandas K. Gandhi; and therefore, [although] your experiments should be of the greatest value in every effort made today for human rights for all Americans, these spiritual advances you have made are too much neglected."[88]

Cooper's prediction that Gandhi's nonviolent methods of protest would play a major role in abolishing racial discrimination proved correct. Less than three years away, a civil rights movement in Montgomery, Alabama, applied Gandhi's principles of nonviolent direct action with spectacular success. In fact, all the religious strategies that Randolph used in his MOWM—experiments in prayer protests, liberation theology, and civil disobedience—were resurrected in the modern civil rights movement. By uncovering Randolph's religious activism of this earlier period, we are able to understand better the historical connection between the 1940s and the civil rights movement of the 1950s, both based in the African American religious culture.

5

The Miracle of Montgomery

In December 1957, Randolph wrote to Rev. Richard Allen Hildebrand formally asking to join Bethel AME Church in Harlem. Why did Randolph, after so many years, want to join a black church? And why Bethel? According to Rev. Hildebrand, Bethel maintained a membership of working-class people in the "lower-income brackets" and, since the days of one of its most illustrious ministers, Reverdy Ransom, had maintained a reputation as an institution with a social justice conscience. Randolph's biographer, Jervis Anderson, labeled his act ironic, claiming that "it was not any discovery of religious faith which had brought him back, but merely a wish to contribute to the church's survival as an important social institution." Anderson said that Randolph never attended services but was "satisfied to send Bethel an annual check for $350 to help carry on its work."[1]

Although the correspondence between Randolph and the Bethel AME Church centered on financial issues, it also revealed a deeper religious motivation on Randolph's part. In an exchange of letters between Randolph and Rev. Hildebrand more than a year and a half after he rejoined, Randolph responded to Hildebrand's comment that he must have joined the church for his own "personal, spiritual comfort and reassurance" with this clarification: "I am in the church because I believe in it." Moreover, Bethel was a logical choice, since he had been "born and raised in the AME Church." The correspondence also provided several reasons for his poor church attendance: his out-of-town Brotherhood business trips, and when in town, his care for his invalid wife Lucille, bedridden for several years, and, as the years went by, his own failing health.[2]

Despite his irregular attendance, Randolph was a "Bethelite" for more than sixteen years and received regular updates on church activities, on which he sometimes commented and offered advice. Rev. Hildebrand was pleased "beyond measure" to welcome such a distinguished person into membership, and the evidence suggests that other fellow "Bethelites" took pride in Randolph's affiliation with their church. According to church correspondence, Randolph regularly paid his church dues, gave generously to the church's building fund, served as Bethel's representative to the 1958 summer session of the AME Church Bishops' Council, and befriended the two ministers and their families that pastored Bethel while he was a member: Hildebrand and his successor, Henderson R. Hughes.[3]

Randolph supported Hildebrand's campaign to become an AME bishop because he believed him to be "supremely qualified intellectually, spiritually, and morally to be the recipient of this great honor and responsibility." He assured Hildebrand "that you have my prayers for success." When Hildebrand expressed his embarrassment for asking funds for himself in his campaign for bishop, Randolph gave him practical advice on when and where during the Sunday service he could collect the most money from the congregation. Hildebrand heeded the advice and advanced to the bishopric. At Randolph's death, it was Rev. Hughes who presided over his special memorial service at Bethel, and Bishop Hildebrand delivered the eulogy.[4]

Several historical developments in African American civil rights may also have been factors in Randolph's desire to rejoin the African Methodist Church in 1957, especially when a new round of civil rights activism followed the groundbreaking legislation by the U.S. Supreme Court in 1954 and 1955. The *Brown* v. *Board of Education* decision profoundly affected Randolph, as it did many other African Americans, and sparked a series of social movements and national demonstrations for black civil rights that lasted for a decade. A new era had begun. No event represented this better than the inspiring, and surprising, movement in Alabama known as the Montgomery bus boycott.

Sparked by one woman's refusal to give up her seat on a bus, a citywide boycott of Montgomery buses began on December 5, 1955, sponsored by a coalition of local civil rights activists. It lasted more than a year when the U.S. Supreme Court affirmed an Alabama state court ruling that segregation on buses was unconstitutional. Randolph, like so many other longtime civil rights activists in the north, watched in amazement as the boycott continued month after month, right in the heart of the old southern confederacy. It was nothing less than "miraculous." Ella Baker, who worked closely with Randolph to find ways of supporting the struggling Montgomery movement, caught the sense of awe that many old activists felt as they monitored the dramatic day-to-day developments of the nonviolent civil disobedience campaign in Montgomery. As the first anniversary of the bus boycott approached, Baker wrote, "The miracle of effectiveness of this form of passive resistance has involved growing sacrifice and we have been seeking ways to help." With the successful conclusion of the bus boycott, Randolph echoed Baker's observation when he called the Montgomery bus boycott "one of the great sagas of the struggle for human decency and freedom, made effective by a veritable miracle of unity of some fifty thousand Negroes under the spiritual banner of love, non-cooperation with evil and non-violence."[5]

Bayard Rustin, a key architect of the modern civil rights movement, recalled in an interview the momentum created by the Montgomery bus protest: "From the Montgomery bus boycott in 1955, for the next two years following to May 1957, the center of gravity and the center of activity for the whole civil rights movement was the church people and ministers of the south." According to Rustin, Randolph hoped to revive this same spirit in the northern black churches "as the black church had been deeply involved in most of the activities that were happening in the South." The Montgomery protest immediately led to the first national civil rights demonstration in Washington, D.C.: the 1957 prayer pilgrimage. In fact, the prayer pilgrimage celebrated the third anniversary of the Supreme Court decision.[6]

Billed as the "Prayer Pilgrimage for Freedom," the event, a joint venture of Randolph's BSCP and AFL connections, Roy Wilkins and the NAACP, and the newly emerging Southern Leadership Conference—later the Southern Christian Leadership Conference, or SCLC—brought to national prominence the charismatic black preacher Martin Luther King Jr. Rustin called the 1957 prayer pilgrimage a turning point when the growing activism among black Americans became identified as a "black revolution." The pilgrimage brought the young Martin Luther King north, which "introduced him to the labor movement in the north, which then began to put up money," Rustin explained. As a close associate of Randolph during this period, Rustin provided an insider's view of how Randolph conceived the prayer pilgrimage, as a way of bringing "the revolution" of southern "church people and the ministers" north and to achieve three goals toward that end.[7]

First, Randolph hoped, "he would involve again, in a very dramatic way, the ministers and churches of the north," as he had tried in his earlier experiments of "prayer protests" in his old MOWM days. The spectacular national success and unified support by the whole African American community behind the pilgrimage must have gratified Randolph immensely, given his memory of his earlier less than spectacular attempts at "prayer protests." Second, he wanted to provide a national "platform for . . . the spokesman of the revolution, Dr. Martin Luther King." At the prayer pilgrimage, King gave his first important national address, the "Give Us the Ballot" speech. Finally, and above all, Randolph hoped the prayer pilgrimage would "concentrate not on public accommodations but on the right to vote." Randolph believed that the vote was the fundamental issue for black Americans in 1957. According to Rustin, "from the quietude of his office in New York," Randolph laid down the strategy that enabled the young preacher to step out into the national spotlight with the ballot issue. Randolph believed that direct action, effective in achieving equity in public accommodations, had its limitations, since certain rights like housing and education depended on "having political strength" attained only "through congressional action." The prayer pilgrimage directed "attention toward the new and very necessary element of political activity."[8]

These three national events—the *Brown* decision, the miracle of Montgomery, and the 1957 prayer pilgrimage—all within a brief span of three years, preceded Randolph's joining an AME church. By analyzing in greater detail his role in these events of the early years of the modern civil rights movement, we can situate Randolph's alliance with Bethel in a fuller historical context and see it as part of his own evolving religious experience. Randolph's joining a black church at that particular point in American history speaks volumes about his perception of the black church's progress since his stinging critique of the "Negro Church" fifty years earlier. Given his experience in mobilizing black religious communities throughout his career, it is not remarkable that Randolph joined a church. Rather, the historical events between 1954 and 1957 confirmed his own perception that the black church had finally joined him in the fight against Jim Crow. Joining Harlem's Bethel AME Church was an act of faith and solidarity with the black church that had begun reclaiming its rightful prophetic role against social injustice, just as Randolph had stated thirty years before that "the early Negro Church . . . championed the cause of freedom for the black bondmen." The following describes Randolph's religious responses to the variety of political events that occurred just before his joining the Bethel AME Church.[9]

In the months before *Brown* and Montgomery, Randolph had reverted to the traditional conference method of gaining access to the new Eisen-

The official photograph of the three cochairmen of the 1957 prayer pilgrimage for freedom. From left to right: Roy Wilkins of the NAACP, Martin Luther King Jr. of the future SCLC, and Randolph representing the BSCP. Photographer unknown. Reproduced from the Collections of the Library of Congress.

hower White House. In this tradition, Randolph politely invited the president to meet with a delegation of black leaders representing several major black organizations, including Roy Wilkins of the NAACP, Lester Granger of the National Urban League, Vivian Mason of the National Council of Negro Women, Benjamin Mays of Morehouse College, Robert Johnson of the Elks fraternal order, Milton Webster of the BSCP, and Rev. Joseph H. Jackson of the National Baptist Convention. Randolph reminded them of "a background of no little experience in arranged conferences with Presidents in the White House on social issues."[10]

With the 1954 *Brown* decision, which undermined the legal system of American segregation in the South, Randolph's letters to Eisenhower took on a greater sense of urgency. Randolph warned the president of the crisis brewing in the South in reaction to the recent court decisions. He listed several areas that needed to be discussed: federal civil rights legislation, the continued use of federal funds to support segregated schools, federal funds for housing free from racial discrimination, opportunities for qualified blacks to serve in the foreign service and other governmental agencies, desegregation of the forthcoming White House conference on education, and, finally, the "threatening tides of terrorism and intimidation" that were rising in the southern states, especially with the revival of the Ku Klux Klan. When Randolph told Roy Wilkins of the NAACP about his letter to the president, he noted that the times were "pregnant with psychological disaster" for black youth unless action was taken immediately.[11]

While Randolph was pursuing the traditional method of gaining access to the executive branch, he became actively involved with a New York–based leftist organization called "In Friendship," the brainchild of Ella Baker, a former NAACP field worker; Bayard Rustin, formerly of FOR; and Stanley Levison, from the American Jewish Congress and a former secret operative in the American Communist Party. As conditions in the South worsened and the Montgomery bus boycott was in its first few weeks of operation, "In Friendship" served as a fund-raising organization to provide "economic aid to victims of race terror in the South." Baker, Rustin, and Levison organized this eclectic group of civil rights activists and sympathizers from the American Jewish Committee, the American Veterans Committee, the NAACP, the Jewish Labor Committee, the BSCP, the Workers Defense League, and a broad range of liberal religious leaders. From its inception, the organization struggled with a leadership problem. At the original conference on January 5, 1956, Randolph had agreed to chair the organization "in the interest of a quick beginning," and in the next few weeks, In Friendship struggled to establish itself while operating temporarily out of the Workers Defense League office. It quickly became apparent that Randolph had overextended himself in accepting the chairmanship. Writing to Ella Baker, its executive secretary, Randolph wrote that it was "utterly impossible" for him to continue as chairman of a fund-raising organization to support the economic boycotts occurring throughout the South, since he had just signed a letter to all the trade unions asking them to support the NAACP financially in its time of crisis. It was not just the impropriety of his soliciting more funds from the trade unions for yet another worthwhile cause that bothered Randolph, it was its ineffectiveness. In withdrawing from the chairmanship of In Friendship, Randolph looked for an alternative solution to the leadership problem, one that had to represent the organization's spiritual response to the increasing crisis in the South.[12]

Randolph believed that the way to broaden and strengthen the organization's appeal to a larger New York audience was to develop a "tripartite arrangement" among "three eminent religious leaders" in the city. Randolph asked Monseigneur Cornelius Drew of St. Charles Roman Catholic Church, Rabbi Edward Klein of the Stephen Wise Free Synagogue, and Rev. Harry Emerson Fosdick of Riverside Church to serve as cochairmen of In Friendship. Randolph wrote that "in view of the strong, spiritual overtones of the struggle in the South, it seems most fitting that our efforts to support our Southern brothers should have a similar character." Randolph assured them that the organization would confine its program to "meeting the economic needs of those integration leaders who are in distress." At the same time, he told them that In Friendship planned to cooperate fully with Dr. Oscar J. Lee of the National Council of the Churches of Christ to form a similar committee on a national level.[13]

Father Drew, Rabbi Klein, and Rev. Fosdick agreed to serve as cochairmen. Father Drew quickly agreed because of his confidence in Randolph's leadership. In fact, Drew had such complete confidence in Randolph's intelligence and integrity that he wrote, "I must go along with you in every effort for our People," since the new organization offered to "support those who without our help cannot stand up." Of the thirty-nine "sponsors" listed on the organization's letterhead from a variety of civic, labor, and academic organizations that supported In Friendship, more than 25 percent represented the most progressive religious communities in New York. Included on this list of Catholic, Protestant, and Jewish religious leaders were several ministers of the progressive wing of the National Baptist Convention: Thomas Kilgore, David Licorish of Abyssinian Baptist Church, and Gardner Taylor. In late March, Gardner Taylor invited the young Martin Luther King to address his Concord Baptist Church, where a capacity crowd of 2,500 people came to hear the young preacher speak at his first northern fund-raiser since the boycott began. Black Methodists who supported In Friendship included Randolph's future minister, Rev. Richard Allen Hildebrand, and Rev. L. S. White of Williams Institutional CME Church. Nor were religious humanists excluded, as evidenced by the inclusion of Algernon D. Black of the New York Society for Ethical Culture as a sponsor of In Friendship.[14]

The rapid formation of In Friendship in New York reflected the growing sense of crisis that many northerners felt as they watched the events playing out in the South. As Randolph increasingly threw his support behind the leadership of a church-based movement, former friends and colleagues suggested that the crisis demanded a revival of the old march on Washington movement, especially as radio reports flashed news of legal setbacks in the Montgomery boycott. Although Randolph agreed that immediate action was necessary, he resisted the idea that his tactics of 1941 could be effective in the current climate:

> While I am not certain that a March on Washington can be successfully developed today, it is the purpose of the Brotherhood to stage some big rallies here in the East to arouse the country, in the interest of getting something done for the protection of our Negro brothers and sisters in the South.[15]

For Randolph, the crisis of 1956 required a spiritual response to the events he saw unfolding in Montgomery. As the summer approached with no end in sight for the boycott, Randolph received inquiries about a passive resistance movement led by ministers backed by laypeople, as many of his former associates remembered Randolph's leadership in the passive resistance techniques in the 1940s. But Randolph came out firmly in support of Martin Luther King's leadership, responding positively to the idea that the ministers "should come out of Montgomery with the Reverend King as the guiding force." He also backed the idea of a national passive resistance conference if either King or Ralph Abernathy called for it, but "unless the Montgomery church leadership" was prepared to lead a national passive resistance movement, Randolph felt it would be "untimely for such a movement to be organized."[16]

Randolph's support for In Friendship further solidified his relationship with Bayard Rustin. Rustin had worked with Randolph several times in the 1940s, first as a leader in the youth division of the original MOWM in 1941, then as a participant in the Inter-denominational Prayer Service at the 1943 MOWM convention in Chicago, and finally with Randolph's "Committee to End 'Jim Crow' in the Armed Services" in 1948. As a member of FOR, Rustin had worked closely with Randolph's committee, which was instrumental in getting the Truman administration to act against segregation in the armed services, and also in the civil disobedience campaign instigated by activists in the League for Nonviolent Civil Disobedience.[17]

The young Rustin publicly criticized Randolph's decisions to call off the 1941 march and later to disband the civil disobedience league when he obtained executive orders from Presidents Franklin Roosevelt and Harry Truman that achieved his objectives. In the 1948 situation, Rustin recalled how "a number of 'Young Turks' and I decided to outflank Mr. Randolph" by continuing to operate the league without Randolph's backing. Rustin and friends denounced Randolph in the black press as "an Uncle Tom, a sellout, a reactionary, and an old fogey out of touch with the times" in their efforts to keep the league going, but it subsequently collapsed within weeks without Randolph's support. Afraid that Randolph would not forgive him for his "treachery," Rustin avoided him "for two whole years." When Rustin finally mustered the courage to visit Randolph in his office, he expected to be chastised for his recklessness:

> As I was ushered in, there he was, distinguished and dapper as ever, with arms outstretched, waiting to greet me, the way he had done a decade ago. Motioning me to sit down with that same sweep of his arm, he looked at me, and in a calm, even voice said: "Bayard, where have you been? You know that I have needed you."[18]

Randolph did need Rustin. August Meier, a prominent historian of African American history, noted the "symbiotic relationship" between the two men. Meier believed that the importance of their relationship to the civil rights movement was a subject that deserved more careful analysis and that Rustin's "pivotal and crucial role in Randolph's career and in the whole civil rights movement of the 1960s" had been "greatly underestimated and obscured." Until his death, Randolph's activism remained indelibly linked with Rustin's organizational genius, just as Randolph's radicalism during the World War I era remains associated with Chandler Owen, and his successful labor activism of the 1920s and 1930s depended on his partnership with Milton Webster. Although it is not possible here to analyze Randolph's and Rustin's relationship in any depth, it is important to point out their compatibility from a religious perspective, especially at the moment when the civil rights movement was being propelled forward by church people in the South.[19]

Coming from liberal Protestant traditions with a strong emphasis on social justice, both Randolph and Rustin understood and encouraged the spiritual motivations for the Montgomery movement. Rustin's Quaker pacifism complemented Randolph's African Methodism. Randolph and Rustin shared similar liberal religious sensibilities, especially in contrast to those of Randolph's former associates: the iconoclastic, materialistic Owen and the irreverent, outspoken Webster. Because of health problems, Randolph could no longer keep up his hectic schedule, and he grew increasingly dependent on Rustin to carry out the details associated with social movements.[20]

In 1953, after an incident in Pasadena, California while on business for FOR, Rustin, a homosexual, was arrested on a morals charge of sexual misconduct. This incident led to Rustin's split with Randolph's old friend and colleague A. J. Muste of FOR. When he no longer had FOR's organizational base, Rustin became an outcast among his former friends and civil rights activists. And without Randolph's friendship, support, and considerable influence in the civil rights community, Rustin might have been completely ostracized from any subsequent social activism. But when the civil rights "revolution" took off, Randolph and Rustin needed each other and worked well together. Rustin recalled how several black leaders pressured Randolph to keep his distance from him, but he paid no attention to their advice. Although Randolph could not believe that "Bayard would do anything wrong," he conceded that "if the fact is, he is homosexual, maybe we need more of them; he's so talented."[21]

When the Montgomery bus boycott continued through the holiday season and into January 1956, Randolph and the In Friendship activists soon recognized the boycott's potential to advance the cause of black civil rights. James Farmer of CORE talked about a meeting in Randolph's office where the In Friendship network met to discuss the crisis. The group agreed that Rustin, with his experience in nonviolent techniques, could best evaluate the situation in Montgomery and provide training in nonviolent direct action. Using Randolph's connections, Rustin immediately contacted the boycott's leaders: E. D. Nixon, the first person whom Rosa Parks called from jail after her arrest, Martin Luther King Jr., and Ralph Abernathy. Rustin's arrival in Montgomery came at a critical point in the boycott, on February 21 when a grand jury delivered more than one hundred indictments against the leaders of the boycott. Rustin recalled that Abernathy accepted his help only when he learned of and verified his con-

nection to Randolph. Meeting with Abernathy and Nixon, since King
was out of town, Rustin suggested a "classic Gandhian tactic": that the
leaders turn themselves in to the authorities instead of waiting to be arrested. Nixon was the first to be arrested under the boycott indictment,
and his action touched off a chain reaction until those indicted and spectators swarmed around the courthouse, creating a victory out of a cata-
strophe.[22]

E. D. Nixon, a Pullman porter, had taken a strategic role in nominat-
ing Martin Luther King Jr. to the presidency of the Montgomery Improvement Association (MIA), since his own job as a porter often kept
him out of town and unavailable. Nixon's leadership position in Montgomery's black community enabled him to play an important role in the
early days of the boycott, which was then often referred to as a movement
led by "ministers and porters." It was Nixon who originated the boycott
and who organized the ministers around his idea. Later, as King gained
national prominence as the leader of the boycott, Nixon's influential role
diminished, almost to the point of obscurity, which Nixon deeply resented. As a Pullman porter and longtime civil rights activist through his
membership in the BSCP, Nixon believed that Randolph's guidance had
done more to help him "in the field of Civil Rights" than any person he
knew. For Randolph's part, Nixon was his link to the events in Montgomery and an important connection for the northern coalition supporting the boycott.[23]

Both Randolph and Nixon recognized in the Montgomery boycott the
realization of their years of effort fighting for black rights. With Nixon's
boycott idea now in its third month, Randolph wrote to him of his "great
pride and inspiration" for "you and your fellow citizens," which indicated that Randolph understood the Montgomery battle from Nixon's
point of view. Randolph reminded him that it was a fight about "respect
and human dignity" and assured him that "justice and right are on your
side and the moral conscience of Negro and white Americans . . . who believe in God and his righteousness." He counseled Nixon that he must en-
dure suffering and sacrifice if necessary "but never give up," for by remaining steadfast "you are bound to win." He assured Nixon that he was
backed by the BSCP and all "Negro and white people who love justice
and human liberty."[24]

In the brief time that Rustin remained in Montgomery, he worked effectively with King. Although Randolph and In Friendship supported
Rustin's presence in Montgomery, his former colleagues in FOR were not

so sure. John Swomley, the new executive secretary of FOR, and Charles Lawrence, its national chairman, disapproved of Rustin's being in Montgomery and believed it would be "better if Bayard did not go South, [because] it would be easy for the police to frame him with his record in L.A. and New York, and set back the whole cause there." On the other hand, Charles Walker, a black FOR staffer, wanted to collaborate with Rustin. Glenn Smiley, a FOR staffer, already in Montgomery working closely with King, agreed that "Bayard has had a very good influence on King," writing speeches for him and sitting in on all the strategy meetings. Swomley accused Smiley of collaborating with Rustin and let him know that some of the Montgomery leaders had asked Randolph to have Rustin "called back."[25]

In New York, Swomley and Lawrence of FOR met with Randolph and about twenty other activists in the In Friendship group to discuss the growing controversy around Rustin's activities in Montgomery, since Randolph had been called "by influential leaders down there . . to find out whether Bayard was the genuine article." Bowing to the pressure by the FOR leaders, Randolph and the group agreed that Rustin should leave Montgomery. For his part, Glenn Smiley thought he was a "pore, pore substitute" for Rustin and regretted his departure, since Rustin "really could make a mark here." Within a week, Rustin's New York supporters, including Randolph, asked him to return home so as not to harm the cause in Montgomery.[26]

As the controversy between In Friendship and FOR over Rustin's role in the boycott subsided, Randolph continued to support the ministerial leadership of the boycott. When Randolph and In Friendship turned away from its original idea to have northerners "train or otherwise run the non-violent campaign in Montgomery," they increasingly looked to the southern leaders for advice on ways they "could be of help." With his confidence in the deep religious faith of ordinary people, Randolph suggested that since the Montgomery leaders had managed successfully so far without the help of the so-called nonviolence experts, northerners might "learn from them rather than assume" they knew it all. Smiley, however, believed that Randolph's confidence in the ministers was misplaced. Although the Montgomery leaders had managed a mass resistance campaign for nine weeks with little help, "it was petering out." King, inexperienced as a leader of a movement, ran "out of ideas quickly and [did] the old things again and again." Smiley argued that the new emphasis on nonviolence made the boycott newsworthy, and when the story about the "indictments and arrests . . . handled with a non-violent response" hit the press and "King suddenly remembered Gandhi," serious help from the outside finally started in the form of telegrams, letters, and checks for thousands of dollars.[27]

In fact, In Friendship had originally sent Rustin to Montgomery because Randolph had heard from one of his top BSCP lieutenants, Benjamin McLaurin, that "ministers and porters" were collecting an arsenal of weapons there. Smiley confirmed that "the place [was] an arsenal." As for King's consistent commitment to nonviolence as a tactic, Smiley observed that King "believes and yet he doesn't believe." At this point in the boycott, King still kept guns in his home and requested gun permits for his bodyguards. Smiley believed that as King grew as the leader and symbol of the movement and "won to a faith in non-violence," there would be no end to what he could do. As Rustin and Smiley knew, King's leadership of a nonviolent movement had to proceed from his own deep spiritual commitment to nonviolence in every aspect of his life, or it could not be effectively communicated to the movement's rank and file. Yet with all his confidence in the important role that FOR played in sustaining the nonviolent protest, Smiley agreed with Randolph that he and others "could learn much from the Montgomery leaders," especially from their courage and the "plain earthy devices for building morale."[28]

Smiley's observation of one Montgomery mass meeting described the tremendous inspiration that Randolph believed was at the core of the new movement:

> The mass meeting last night was like another world. 2500 people, laughing, crying, moaning, shouting, singing. Religious fervor is high and they are trying to keep it spiritual. Not once was there an expression of hatred towards whites, and the ovation I received when I talked of Gandhi, his campaign, and then of the cross, was tremendous. They do want to do the will of God, and they are sure this is the will of God.[29]

Rustin's problems in Montgomery were not just personal but those that all northern outsiders experienced as the crisis in the South grew. At this stage in their careers, both Randolph and Rustin were content to stay in the background as long as they could wield influence. From Montgomery, Randolph redirected Rustin to Birmingham to mobilize support for the boycott among black trade unionists there. There Rustin met secretly with King, who confirmed his fear that a common perception of white Southerners was that "New Yorkers, northern agitators, and communists [were] in reality leading the fight." So despite the flap over Rustin begun by his former FOR colleagues, Randolph and Rustin agreed that working in the background and directing all "communications, ideas and programs" directly to King or E. D. Nixon was a "wise and necessary procedure."[30]

As a social activist of many years standing, especially under Randolph's tutelage, Rustin directly connected the success of the Montgomery bus protest to Randolph's 1940's FEPC fight. One example he cited was at a low point of the bus protest. King was discouraged over the lack of automobiles for the local carpool. Rustin called Randolph for advice, wondering whether they could find "enough middle class people to give up their automobiles." Randolph laughed at the suggestion but guided Rustin to the Birmingham steelworkers, who made enough money to have two cars. "Ask them for their second, beat up car," Randolph advised, and the boycott continued. Rustin knew that Randolph's "fight with the AFL-CIO over the years" to get black workers into good union jobs was related directly to their ability to help the boycott financially. While Randolph and Rustin worked behind the scenes, Randolph and In Friendship worked with Adam Clayton Powell, Oscar Lee of the National Council of Churches, "and other responsible church leaders, to see whether there can be a genuine prayer meeting" as another way to support the Montgomery movement. Randolph and James Farmer called a meeting of thirty people to develop a "large prayer observance" or national demonstration featuring Powell, Joseph H. Jackson of the National Baptist Convention, the National Council of Churches, and a group of AME Zion people. Although this idea never materialized into a direct-action campaign at that time, it was the basis for the national prayer pilgrimage event a year later.[31]

As the Montgomery crisis wore on, the speeches Randolph gave in 1956 revealed his perspective on the basic religious and theological issues raised by the bus boycott and other injustices in American society of the 1950s. In that year, Randolph addressed the NAACP's annual convention, the second triennial convention of the BSCP in St. Louis, the fifty-first anniversary luncheon of the League for Industrial Democracy, a Madison Square Garden rally organized by In Friendship in New York, the "State of the Race" convention in Washington, D.C., sponsored by the BSCP, an address on "Civil Rights and the Negro" in Chicago's Orchestra Hall attended by Mayor Richard Daley, the New York Society for Ethical Culture, and the Catholic Interracial Council, also in New York.

These speeches provide insights into Randolph's personal and religious thinking inspired by the events of that momentous year in civil rights history. One underlying religious theme that emerged in Randolph's rhetoric at this time can again be associated with the biblical word *kairos*, reminiscent of the same sense of urgency Randolph felt in the early 1940s. Theologian Robert McAfee Brown explained the term: "A time of *kairos* is a time when unexpected possibilities enter the scene, brand new things can happen—and frequently do." It is when a people "discover themselves living in a situation with almost unprecedented possibilities for change." In his speeches, Randolph reminded his audiences that the "crisis" in the South was a special time, a rare circumstance, full of opportunities for African Americans to undo many of the injustices in American society if they acted now.[32]

In April, Randolph's speeches at a League of Industrial Democracy luncheon and the State of the Race convention in Washington, D.C., given ten days later, described for his audiences this "period of crisis." At the luncheon, Randolph began with a historical analysis of how the "civil rights revolution," stretching all the way back to President Lincoln's Emancipation Proclamation during the Civil War, had been disrupted by a "counterrevolution" that nullified all the progress made during Reconstruction. Randolph concluded that

> although every advance of the Civil Rights Revolution against segregation, from the beginning of the first decade of the twentieth century, was bitterly fought by the forces of southern racial reaction, it was not until May 17, 1954 that a massive, monumental and momentous blow was struck upon the citadel of segregation in the South by the United States Supreme Court.[33]

Just one month earlier, one hundred members of the House and Senate signed the "southern manifesto," which declared that the *Brown* decision was a "clear abuse of judicial power." Randolph warned his audience that this was another counterrevolution in the making unless the black community united together to fight this latest encroachment on their civil liberties. He emphasized the same sense of urgency again ten days later at the State of the Race convention:

This crisis has been sharpened and broadened by the rise, growth and spread of the White Citizens Councils and the revival of the old Ku Klux Klan and other hate groups, together with the famous manifesto, signed by 101 Southern Congressmen and Senators, designed to bring about the nullification or reversal of the segregation decision of the Supreme Court.[34]

The convention, sponsored by Randolph and the BSCP, was meant to counter the anti–civil rights legislation of the southern manifesto and its "declaration of constitutional Principles" which encouraged local and state governments to refuse to comply with the school desegregation order while at the same time uniting the "black advancement organizations," the church, civic, fraternal, and business groups representing twelve million blacks. Since Randolph recognized that anti–civil rights forces were also antiunion, he hoped that the State of the Race convention, a closed meeting of seventy-five black leaders held at the headquarters of the National Council of Negro Women, would forge a link between the civil rights struggle and organized labor.[35]

In his convention speech, Randolph described the current political crisis, calling for urgent action by the black community. He repeated the same message of hope he had offered earlier to the League of Industrial Democracy audience in New York. Using biblical imagery, Randolph foresaw that "verily, out of the darkness of racialism in the South, a stream of light and hope [was] apparent" and directed his audience to the events in Montgomery, declaring,

> 50,000 Negroes in Montgomery, in the spirit of the Sermon on the Mount, are not only achieving their internal, spiritual and moral freedom but whose philosophy of winning their rights through love and truth, good will and faith, are teaching not only the South but our entire country a new lesson in the brotherhood of man. Instead of berating, deriding and decrying their enemies, they are expressing love for them and praying that the God of Abraham, Isaac and Jacob may save them from themselves and make them instruments in the achievement of the Kingdom of God on earth.[36]

Randolph's April speeches reveal his belief that the Montgomery protest was an effective partnership of ministers and porters, in reference to Rev. King and "Brother" E. D. Nixon. Together, these men were achieving extraordinary things right in the "headquarters of the old Confederacy of the South, Montgomery, Alabama." Randolph expressed amazement at this "new spirit of passive resistance, non-violent, good will direct action" by the black community in Montgomery. Their leaders showed "great wisdom" in resisting "the hatemongers of the White Citizens Councils" and "instead of retaliating . . . on a basis of violence, seek[ing] deliverance through prayer." According to Randolph, this was a "greater shock and blow to the old Ku Klux tribal spirit of racial fanaticism in the South than any army could inflict." These momentous events in the old Confederacy also strengthened the position of the United States throughout the world, especially in its "worldwide conquest of the international Russian communist conspiracy." He viewed the civil rights battle in the nation as "a great measure and test of American democracy and American Christianity all over the world." Since "these rights [were] God-given and not man-made," Randolph claimed that the "moral justification" for their fight for equality, freedom and justice, made any "doctrine of gradualism" unacceptable. Moreover, doctrines of gradualism were in "conflict with the basic Judeo-Christian ethic which emphasizes the worth of every individual human being," and he found it "paradoxical to think of one gradually accepting the law of God or the law of the State." Randolph's April speeches referred to segregation as a sin, "and a sin should not be gradually accepted or gradually rejected."[37]

Randolph's rhetoric at this time emphasized his concern that the Supreme Court's decisions regarding desegregation were losing ground in public opinion. To reverse this dangerous trend, Randolph wanted the "realists" at the State of the Race convention to "look inwardly" to "re-examine, re-appraise and re-evaluate" the policies, strategies, and tactics of "this civil rights crisis." Randolph blamed the growing reluctance by the black community to oppose the segregationists on the lack of coordination among black organizations, the organizational strength of white citizens' councils, and the recent "southern manifesto" by leaders in the Senate and Congress.[38]

To counter these trends, Randolph recommended that the convention members first adopt the recent "Declaration of Intentions" issued by the Reverend Joseph Jackson of the National Baptist Convention. Randolph believed that Jackson's declaration was a "moving and powerful statement of the moral and religious affirmation" that justified the implementation of the desegregation decision and other civil rights legislation. Randolph argued that the adoption of Jackson's statement as their own would give them "the moral framework within which the fight for a better tomorrow for black Americans may be carried forward with assurance and faith in the ultimate triumphant of truth." Besides adopting Jackson's declaration, he also wanted the convention to adopt the "Negro manifesto" published by the *Pittsburgh Courier*. The "Negro manifesto" was the *Courier*'s "biting answer" to the one hundred signers of the "southern manifesto" who openly defied the Supreme Court's desegregation decision. This document represented hundreds of black citizens throughout the nation who pledged to uphold the Fourteenth Amendment of the U.S. Constitution and to "use all the legal and moral power we have to oust members of Congress who sit there illegally because our citizens are denied the right to vote. This is OUR manifesto," declared its signers. By asking those at the convention to endorse the *Courier*'s manifesto because of its "manifest political significance and value," Randolph added his voice to general moral outrage felt by other individuals across the country during the first months of the boycott crisis. In his convention speech, Randolph repeated his belief that Montgomery was evidence "of the Kingdom of God on earth" and encouraged the assembled group of black leaders to raise funds for the NAACP, the MIA, and black farmers boycotted by white citizens' councils in Mississippi and South Carolina.[39]

In May, Randolph delivered two more major speeches on the "raging and devastating hurricane of human hate sweeping over the land . . . below the Potomac." Randolph wanted a massive rally in Madison Square Garden to draw national attention to the crisis in Montgomery, similar to the one held there fifteen years earlier for the MOWM. Taking a two-month leave of absence from the War Resisters League, Rustin worked full time to organize the rally. Aided by Ella Baker and Stanley Levison from In Friendship and Randolph's close BSCP aide Benjamin McLaurin, the group organized a "mammoth civil rights rally" for the southern freedom struggle. Ella Baker described the rally as the first civil rights event to be held in the New York area in many years, an indication of how older civil rights activists saw the historical connection between the current crisis in the South and the sense of emergency that the social and economic conditions of World War II produced in the African American community in the 1942 civil rights rallies sponsored by the MOWM.[40]

A central feature of the rally program was to introduce Dr. King as one of the "heroes of the South." But two weeks before the rally, King told

McLaurin and Rustin that he could not make the trip north to attend the rally. As the citywide chairman, Randolph pleaded with King to make an appearance, since promotional literature publicizing King's presence had already been sent to every "major religious, labor and civic organization in Greater New York and New Jersey." Randolph found it inconceivable that King would not be present, since he had become "in the minds of Americans a symbol of the Montgomery struggle." Randolph wanted King to realize the "importance of the Rally in relation to our entire struggle for freedom." At the same time, Randolph hoped to raise $100,000 for the NAACP, the MIA, and other victims of economic boycotts in Mississippi and South Carolina. Not wanting to disappoint Randolph, King promised he would make every effort to attend the rally. But in the end, Randolph settled for Rosa Parks and E. D. Nixon to represent Montgomery. Both received standing ovations from the sixteen thousand to twenty thousand people attending the rally. Randolph shared the podium with Adam Clayton Powell Jr., Eleanor Roosevelt, Autherine Lucy, Roy Wilkins, and Rabbi Israel Goldstein, president of the American Jewish Congress. Wilkins, the new head of the NAACP, who usually regarded rallies and demonstrations with suspicion, declared the rally an "overwhelming success."[41]

Randolph's introductory remarks at the rally once again emphasized the "spiritual and moral" nature of the current struggle and the dual leadership of "ministers and porters" in Montgomery. The rally speech balanced these religious themes with a political agenda: persuading the black community to remain united behind the *Brown* decision, using the civil rights struggle to strengthen American democracy at home and abroad, rejecting support or cooperation by the "Communists, Communism, and the Russian Soviet Union's way of life," and remaining "politically uncommitted" to either national party in the presidential election until its record on civil rights could be determined. Randolph reminded his audience at the rally that American democracy was based on the religious pluralism of the Protestant, Catholic, and Jewish faiths, which condemned the "unspeakable practices" of the newest Ku Klux Klan, the white citizens' councils.[42]

The constant references in his speeches to the "Judeo-Christian" nature of American society indicate that Randolph was aware of current trends in American religious sociology, best associated with Will Herberg's 1955 book *Protestant, Catholic, Jew*. In fact, Randolph cited Catholic Archbishop Joseph Francis Rummel of New Orleans as his authority for equating racial prejudice and segregation with human sin. In three other speeches during this period, Randolph mentioned Archbishop Rummel as "the one outstanding white church leader of the South." Rummel had closed a parish for refusing the services of a black priest and threatened to excommunicate Catholics in the Louisiana legislature who voted to abolish public schools in order to evade the court decision to desegregate them. Since the main purpose of the rally was to register support for the Montgomery struggle, Randolph reiterated his "belief in the validity and effectiveness of non-violent good will, direct action and passive resistance to evil" and his condemnation of using violence to fight for civil rights. Randolph recognized that the nonviolent aspect of the struggle had become the most apparent characteristic that distinguished it from other struggles.[43]

One week before the rally at Madison Square Garden, Randolph traveled to Chicago to attend another "religious civil rights meeting," commemorating the second anniversary of the *Brown* decision. Held in Chicago's Orchestra Hall, one participant noted that "Mayor Daley remained throughout the proceedings . . . to hear himself the authentic voice of the Negro people speaking on this crisis." Of all Randolph's speeches of this time, the Orchestra Hall speech best represents Randolph's theological position as he laid out the "moral philosophy and religious foundation" of the current civil rights struggle.[44]

As in his State of the Race convention speech, Randolph began with a religious justification of the righteousness of the black civil rights cause before he launched into his seven-part political agenda. Like a sermon, Randolph began with a scriptural text, Psalm 46, to allay the fears of his audience: "God is our refuge and strength, an ever present help in trouble. Therefore, will not we fear, though the earth be removed and though the mountains be carried into the midst of the sea." He repeated the promise that "the God of Abraham, Isaac and Jacob, by the Psalmists 700 years before Christ" would sustain and deliver "us in this hour of troubles, tears and tragedies" because of "our belief in the ultimate triumph of righteousness." Second, he reminded his audience that "our dream of . . . a better tomorrow" was deeply embedded in "the great religious tradition of the prophets and our Judeo-Christian heritage." He pointed them back to the old prophets of ancient times—Amos, Hosea, Isaiah, Micah, Jeremiah, and Ezekiel—all dedicated to the "concept that relationships between men should be righteous, in order that their relations to God might be acceptable to Him." Third, Randolph argued that since the Judeo-Christian ethic and "our Christian faith" were the foundation of the American democratic society, it was a "cardinal principle that every individual [was] sacred to God; that he [had] intrinsic worth." The acceptance of the fatherhood of God led to its corollary of the brotherhood of man and the "recognition of the equality of the children of God [as] mandatory and inevitable." With these comforting assurances, Randolph concluded the religious portion of his speech by connecting it with the unjust social and political conditions of American society. Randolph's theistic argument, with its notion of the "sacredness of the dignity of the human personality," reflected the theological viewpoint known as personalism, as evidenced in the following:

> Thus, if the children of God are equal before Him, segregation of God's children on account of race, color, religion, national origin or ancestry, is not only artificial but constitutes a rejection of the idea of the fatherhood of God, and is, thus, sacrilegious. It is the negation of the principle of human solidarity which springs from the doctrine of one Creator of all mankind. One cannot accept the idea of the sacredness of the dignity of the human personality and also sanction segregation of individual human beings because of differences in the color of skin or the possession of varied superficial physical characteristics; for such segregation attaches stigma and inferiority to peoples and serves to degrade, demean and demoralize their human dignity.[45]

Personalism, a popular American philosophy and theology from the late nineteenth century through the 1960s, has been identified with Boston University, the great bastion of personalist studies in the United States. Two American theologians associated with personalism are Borden Parker Bowne (1847–1910) and his student Edgar S. Brightman (1884–1953). Bowne, a Methodist, has been credited with liberalizing American Protestantism, by emphasizing that religion is concerned primarily with the pursuit of righteousness. Professor Brightman of Boston University's School of Theology, who upheld the ultimate value of all human beings, was a major influence on Martin Luther King Jr.'s theological development and his own adherence to personalism as a way of encountering God.[46]

Although King is usually cited as the principal African American associated with personalism, recent scholarship has expanded the field of African American personalism to include John Wesley Edward Bowen, the first African American to earn a Ph.D. from Boston University, and black theologians J. Deotis Roberts, and James H. Cone. Harry Emerson Fosdick, the influential New York minister and popularizer of modernist religious ideas, assigned a high value to human personality in his sermons and has been identified with the theological position of personalism. Given the proximity of and interaction between Fosdick and Randolph during these years, it is highly likely that Fosdick influenced Randolph's absorption of a personalist theology.[47]

Randolph's emphasis on the "sacredness of the human personality" could also be attributed to another New York friend, Algernon D. Black, president of the New York Society for Ethical Culture. Ethical Culture, still in existence today, is a religious humanist and educational movement inspired by the ideal that the supreme aim of human life is to create a more humane society. A basic principle is the worth and dignity of every person. When Black became the society's leader in the 1930s, he actively worked against racial discrimination in housing, just as Randolph struggled to organize the Pullman porters.[48]

Through the society, Black directed a youth program called "Encampment for Citizenship." This group, limited to young people between the ages of seventeen and twenty-three, conducted a workshop on civil rights that explored ways to advance the cause. Ella Baker and Stanley Levison hoped to make Black's youth group a kind of blueprint for a youth arm of In Friendship. Several months after the Madison Square Garden rally, Black asked Randolph to address the society on Labor Day. In his speech, Randolph reiterated his belief in the "dignity of the individual personality," compatible with a religious humanist perspective:

> It is pertinent to note that the religion of Jesus, planted and nurtured by a manual laborer, formed the basis of hope from which stems the great labor movement of our time. This movement has been severely attacked and misrepresented and branded as calamitous because, in an organized and consistent manner, it openly struck a blow at the cruel system of masters and slaves, ever emphasizing the principle of human equality— the dignity of the individual personality. This is the heart of the Judeo-Christian ethic.[49]

In his Chicago speech, Randolph's sermon on the religious principles of the current black liberation struggle ended with a list of the specific political actions that black citizens needed to take: unifying their support of

Brown; finding money and members for the NAACP, the Montgomery boycott, and the "farmers, business people, discharged workers, dismissed teachers and militant leaders in Mississippi, South Carolina, Georgia and Alabama"; and initiating a nationwide "register and vote crusade." Randolph claimed that all these ideas were sanctioned by Rev. Joseph Jackson's "Declaration of Intentions" adopted at the recent BSCP State of the Race convention. Randolph urged his audience to support the fifty thousand people in Montgomery in their "gallant walk for freedom" under the leadership of Martin Luther King Jr. and "an humble Pullman porter, Brother E. D. Nixon." Randolph concluded his political remarks by comparing the current situation with the Old Testament days of the prophets Amos and Micah. As the prophets demanded righteousness from the rulers of their day, so must black Americans.

> "But let judgment run down as waters,
> and righteousness as a mighty stream."
> And the counsel of another great prophet, Micah:
> "He hath shewed thee, O man, what is good;
> And what doth the Lord require of thee,
> But to do justly, and to walk humbly with God?"[50]

On February 2, 1956, Randolph had sent a telegram to President Dwight D. Eisenhower expressing his outrage at the bombing of King's and Nixon's homes, "obviously because of their leadership in a boycott by Negro citizens." Randolph reminded the president that as citizens, King and Nixon deserved "protection in the lawful exercise of their right to boycott an agency of transportation which [offered] insult to the dignity of their personalities." He demanded that immediate steps be taken "in the interest of justice and Christianity" for the preservation of democracy. After the State of the Race convention in Washington, Randolph had resumed his efforts to gain a White House audience with President Eisenhower. Explaining that the convention, a meeting of seventy-three black leaders representing organizations with a "combined membership of twelve million Negroes," unanimously voted to seek a White House conference, Randolph laid out their central grievances: the resistance to the recent *Brown* decision; the attempt by antidesegregation forces such as the white citizens' councils to "sever the northern educational, church and liberal forces['] . . . involvement in the racial desegregation movement"; the attempts to encircle, isolate, and annihilate the NAACP in the

South; and, finally, the "attempt to create a cheap labor market and attract northern anti-union business interests" to the South. Randolph wanted to give the president a "firsthand account" of the reasons for the rising tensions African Americans were experiencing in the South.[51]

Throughout 1956, Randolph sent three more requests for an audience with the president and eventually heard from a White House representative that Eisenhower "expressed friendly interest in arranging a conference." Randolph persisted in his efforts and by early 1957 had selected sixteen black leaders to join him in a White House meeting: Roy Wilkins, Thurgood Marshall, and Loren Miller from the NAACP; Lester Granger from the National Urban League; C. B. Powell and Carl Murphy from the black press; Irene McCoy Gaines and Vivian Carter Mason from national associations of black women; Benjamin Mays from Morehouse College; F. D. Patterson from the Phelps-Stokes Fund; and Milton Webster from the BSCP. Representing the black church, Randolph asked Joseph Jackson of the National Baptist Convention, David Licorish from Abyssinia Baptist Church, Bishop D. Ward Nichols of the AME Church, and Martin Luther King Jr. Bishop Ward and Martin Luther King affirmed their interest in participating in the conference, but Jackson refused, believing that it was "far better to have some one man . . . to go in and plead the cause of the race than to confront the president with a committee of sixteen people." Once again, Jackson rebuffed Randolph's efforts to include him in his political activism. Because of their mutual interests in bringing the religious message of the black church to the political arena of civil rights, Randolph increasingly threw his support to the young Martin Luther King Jr. However, serious talk about Randolph's White House conference plan was delayed until after the prayer pilgrimage.[52]

Randolph supported King because he epitomized the emergence of a new militant black church, something he had hoped for since his radical activism in the days before World War I. With the successful, though not official, ending of the bus boycott in December 1956, one year after it started, the MIA sponsored an "institute on nonviolence and social change," an entire week of seminars and church services in several of Montgomery's Baptist churches. The institute attracted the most powerful leaders of the Black Baptist Church: William Holmes Borders from Atlanta, Gardner Taylor from Brooklyn, T. J. Jemison from Baton Rouge, and Joseph H. Jackson of Chicago, who had never openly endorsed the boycott but who made an appearance at the Sunday service that closed the institute. White liberal supporters who spoke included the novelist Lillian Smith and the Unitarian minister Homer Jack.[53]

King opened the institute with a sermon on the "six lessons" he had learned from the Montgomery bus boycott. The basis of the sermon came directly from an article that Bayard Rustin had written for his New York pacifist journal, *Liberation*. Rustin asked King's permission to use his name as the author of the article, which appeared in the magazine's April 1956 issue entitled "Our Struggle." According to Rustin, *Liberation* readers included "many important leaders of the church" intensely interested in nonviolence. King claimed authorship of the *Liberation* article, as Rustin had suggested, and used Rustin's words as his own for his opening speech at the institute. King described how the boycott taught blacks that they could stand together in a common cause, without their leaders selling out or being intimidated by threats and violence. He learned that "our church [was] becoming militant, stressing a social gospel as well as a gospel of personal salvation," and by gaining a new sense of dignity and destiny they discovered a new and powerful weapon—non-violent resistance.[54]

In the article "Our Struggle," Rustin explained how "Montgomery [had] broken the spell and [was] ushering in concrete manifestations of the thinking and action of the new Negro." If King was borrowing Rustin's words for his "six lessons" sermon, then Rustin was certainly borrowing from Randolph's old *Messenger* rhetoric of the "new Negro." Since the 1920s, Randolph had expressed his desire for a militant church with a social gospel. As a longtime activist, Randolph found in Martin Luther King Jr. and "the miracle of Montgomery" the emergence of his long-awaited dream that the black church was becoming militant. This had a powerful effect on Randolph, especially when articulated by a younger generation represented by King and Rustin, as their article "Our Struggle" states:

> Twenty-four ministers were arrested in Montgomery. Each has said publicly that he stands prepared to be arrested again. Even upper-class Negroes who reject the "come to Jesus" gospel are now convinced that the church has no alternative but to provide the non-violent dynamics for social change in the midst of conflict.[55]

From this time on, Randolph and King worked together. King and the Southern Negro Leaders' Conference called for another institute on "transportation and nonviolent integration," scheduled for January in King's father's Atlanta church. Along with others in In Friendship, Randolph planned to attend the conference, but a scheduling conflict with the Railway Labor Executives' Association made it impossible for him to attend. In a hastily drafted note to the senior Reverend King, Randolph wrote of his "deep affection and faith our people and millions of liberty-loving white people" had for his dedication in "waging the great moral and spiritual offensive against the sin and evil of segregation of God's children." Randolph assured him, "We are with you in spirit and we are with you financially. It is written in the stars that love will conquer hate, justice will overcome injustice, and truth will triumph over error and thus our great crusade . . . cannot fail."[56]

The group of ministers at the Atlanta conference agreed to meet again in Rev. A. L. Davis's New Zion Baptist Church in New Orleans. At this meeting, ninety-seven ministers, dropping the word *Negro* from their name, called themselves the Southern Leaders' Conference (only later was *Christian* added) and resolved to sponsor a pilgrimage, not a political march, to Washington, D.C. The group insisted that the event "be rooted in deep spiritual faith."[57]

While the progressive group of ministers organized, Randolph and Stanley Levison obtained a $4,000 grant from the Christopher Reynolds Foundation to enable King "to visit India and Africa for the purpose of broadening the Reverend King's educational background on Gandhi's teaching and to study actual conditions in these countries first hand." In his requests for the grant, Randolph stressed King's role "in the great struggle . . . for human dignity" and King's need to learn more about "biblical and Gandhian concepts of nonviolence." The Reynolds Foundation, the American Friends Service Committee, and Montgomery's Dexter Avenue Baptist Church jointly sponsored King's trip. During Ghana's independence celebrations in Accra, King and Randolph—who accompanied King on that part of the trip—talked about pooling their resources for the next national civil rights event: the prayer pilgrimage. For the first time in his religious activism, Randolph had found the perfect spokesman for a progressive civil rights agenda: a minister of the church.[58]

On March 26, 1957, Randolph, Roy Wilkins, and King, representing the newly formed SLC, met in New York to discuss their first joint venture: the prayer pilgrimage. Randolph and King came to the meeting with their own agenda for some sort of direct-action campaign. Randolph revealed the blueprint for a mass meeting in Washington for civil rights. Given the success of the boycott, King supported the idea of mass direct action, but Wilkins remained cool to the idea. Although the NAACP convention in San Francisco demanded an appropriate observance of the three-year anniversary of the *Brown* decision, Wilkins did not share Randolph's and King's enthusiasm for mass demonstrations.[59]

Randolph's and King's united front, beginning with the prayer pilgrimage and continuing into the next decade, revealed a compatibility based on similar religious principles. But both depended on the expertise, financial support, and organizational clout of the NAACP to mobilize the fifty thousand pilgrims they expected to attract to the steps of the Lincoln Memorial in six weeks. In order to reassure Wilkins, Randolph and King emphasized that this was not a "march on Washington" but a "pilgrimage" to "awaken the nation's moral consciousness" of the plight of black people in America. Regarding May 17, 1954, as a "second American Emancipation," there were to be no "picket lines, resolutions, or attempts to call on the President." This was the emphasis in most NAACP reports on the upcoming pilgrimage, as in a memo from Rev. L. Sylvester Odom of the San Francisco NAACP regional office: "We are going to pray at the Lincoln Memorial for deliverance from the cancer of racism at the precise movement the segregation decision was handed down three years ago." Throughout the preparation for the pilgrimage, Wilkins and other NAACP organizers consistently rejected the notion that this was another "march on Washington," since it had "none of the implications of either the original March on Washington, or of those which have been subsequently proposed."[60]

Given the Red scare of the 1950s, the cochairmen faced concerns about the demonstration's attracting communist agitators and fears of a communist takeover. When Jewish activist Kivie Kaplan wrote to Roy Wilkins about "rumors that the communists are trying to horn in on our Prayer Meeting," Wilkins reported that he and Randolph had released a statement one week before the event that "the Prayer Pilgrimage for Freedom will be a spiritual assembly, primarily by the Negro Clergy, and the NAACP." There was to be "no place for the irreligious," nor had any communists been invited to "participate in the program either as a speaker, singer, prayer leader, or scripture leader." Wilkins added there was to be "no picketing, no poster walking and no lobbying" at the pilgrimage.[61]

The NAACP files verify its extensive and foundational role in the prayer pilgrimage. With Randolph's BSCP base shrinking economically and politically by the mid-1950s and the fact that King's SLC, or "ministers' group," was still in its formative stages, the more powerful NAACP provided the financial (estimated at $25,000) and organizational resources to stage the affair. It took more than a month to persuade the National Park Service to let them use the Lincoln Memorial, as it was concerned about blocking a famous tourist attraction. After being turned down once, Clarence Mitchell of the NAACP persisted by emphasizing the symbolic value that the memorial had had for the pilgrimage, to counter the "despair, disillusionment and anger . . . generated by recent acts of racial violence and intimidation in the South." The NAACP spent time, money, and labor on advertising, program arrangements, travel arrangements, and the mobilization of individuals and groups to attend and donate money to the cause.[62]

When trying to schedule Marian Anderson for the pilgrimage, Wilkins, Randolph, and King asked Sol Hurok to intervene. Although Anderson's schedule did not allow her to appear, Wilkins was able to engage Mahalia Jackson, who signaled the growing popularity and respectability of black gospel music. According to black sociologist E. Franklin Frazier, by the early 1960s, the increasing influence of gospel singers like Mahalia Jackson, Rosetta Thorpe, and the Ward sisters represented "the attempt of the Negro to utilize his religious heritage in order to come to terms with changes in his own institutions as well as the problems of the world of which he is a part."[63]

By late March, In Friendship was spending all its resources on making the pilgrimage a success. Rustin's, Levison's, and Baker's names appeared along with those of several NAACP field-workers and labor activists who had been assigned to the staff organizing the pilgrimage. An early planning memo by the group shows that the philosophy of the pilgrimage was based on mobilizing the newly aroused southern black clergy in a series of direct-action activities. Since his return from Montgomery and Birmingham, Bayard Rustin had worked behind the scenes bringing together the three organizations. As the key organizer, Rustin had to think through the many details necessary to launch the event. Regarding the directives from the SLC's meetings in Atlanta and New Orleans on the aims, purposes, and emphasis of a Washington, D.C., mass demonstration, Rustin wrote,

The prayer pilgrimage was first mentioned at the New Orleans Conference. The implication, if not precise wording, of the press release (issued
at the end of the conference) tied the proposed Pilgrimage to President
Eisenhower's failure to come South to speak out for law and order. *It is
now generally conceded that the Pilgrimage should not center on the
President but should be broadened*—with emphasis on the four political
aims outlined above.[64]

The first aim of the event was "moral and spiritual," as "experience
with many of the southern leaders at the Atlanta and New Orleans Conference" suggested the importance of clear moral objectives. The other
three aims were organizational, political, and psychological. Since the
SLC's first meetings, Rustin felt that the political climate had changed
from its and Randolph's original Washington mass-action plan:

> In the first place, the center of gravity has shifted from the prevalence of
> violence in the south to attention on the civil rights struggle in Congress.
> Secondly, to continue to press the President to come south at this time
> may be viewed in some quarters friendly to the civil rights struggle as ha-
> rassment of a singularly popular president. For those who argue that in
> any case pressure should be kept on the President, it should be noted
> that Mr. Randolph's request for an interview with Mr. Eisenhower is still
> under advisement.[65]

With this change in the political climate, Randolph and Rustin
planned their strategy, taking "great care" that the pilgrimage achieve
"the greatest sense of unity and urgency in the Negro community." Rustin
reasoned that Wilkins, King, and Randolph were the "three leaders in-
dispensable to the success of the Pilgrimage" because it brought together
"the NAACP, the preeminent mass membership organization, with the
leaders of the southern struggle whose ties are with the church masses,
and both are connected with organized labor through Randolph. It was
felt that if these men agree on aims, approach, tactics, time, and so forth,
success was assured."[66]

The letter from Randolph, Wilkins, and King announcing a meeting of
black leaders on April 5 emphasized the crisis of the struggle in the South
and the need for support of the national leadership in the fight for legislation requiring dramatic, unified action. The letter underscored the effort to secure "the active involvement of church leaders who have recog-

nized ability in developing mass action of this type." When the three cochairmen decided that a clergyman must head the pilgrimage staff, Randolph settled on his associate from In Friendship, Thomas Kilgore, as the national director of the pilgrimage, and Ralph Abernathy as the southern director.[67]

As the NAACP worked to secure the Lincoln Memorial site, Thomas Kilgore organized a "prayer pilgrimage for freedom tour" for himself, Rustin, and Baker. Working with NAACP organizer Gloster Current, Kilgore arranged three "city organization" trips between April 22 and 26. Designed to "whip up support" for the prayer pilgrimage, Ella Baker concentrated on the states of Virginia and Maryland, the cities of Baltimore and Richmond, and the Chesapeake Bay communities of Norfolk, Portsmouth, and Newport News. Kilgore covered the large northern cities of Detroit, Cleveland, and Chicago, while Rustin toured Boston and Philadelphia. Kilgore extended the trip into the South to mobilize pilgrims in Charlotte, Winston-Salem, Greensboro, Raleigh, and Durham. With Ella Baker's efforts, citizens in Raleigh and Durham promised to set a quota of 250 pilgrims from each city, and Norfolk and Richmond set a quota of 500 pilgrims each. In each city, Current wrote to the local NAACP organizer to make speaking and living arrangements for Rustin, Baker, and Kilgore. Baker reported that the prayer pilgrimage tour found a gratifying response in each area, where black communities responded to the slogan "Give a day for freedom" and willingly agreed to support the effort financially if they could not send pilgrims. At the same time, Baker mobilized In Friendship members to join the pilgrimage, reminding them that the round-trip train fare from New York to Washington, D.C., was only $9.50, and the bus fare, $5.50.[68]

With little more than three weeks remaining before the event, Rustin told Wilkins, Randolph, King, and Kilgore that critical decisions had to made about the pilgrimage program itself so that the staff could "begin the tremendous amount of work required." Rustin listed several categories about which the staff remained uncertain, for example, the "major talks," the use of ministers for the prayers and scripture readings, and the music to be used. With Rustin's guidance, the cochairmen decided to limit their own speeches but to include congressional leaders who supported civil rights legislation.[69]

The staff argued about the best ways to present and include all the ministers involved in the program. Should the ministers, wearing their clerical garb, assemble together before the meeting and march to the memorial in a body? Some of the staff suggested having the ministers perform a "dignified worship service" at the beginning of the program and a "response-litany" between the clergy and assembly at the end. Eventually the staff decided that six ministers, designated as honorary cochairmen, would say a brief prayer or give a scriptural reading between the three major speeches by Randolph, Wilkins, and King. The staff worried about Rev. Jernigan's penchant for making strong political statements and Rev. Joseph H. Jackson's change of mind at the last minute, expecting to be on the program. The staff eventually assigned scriptural selections to the ministers so as to avoid repetition. Besides the problems organizing the black clergy, Randolph expected that an "important white" Catholic priest, Jewish rabbi, or Protestant churchman would take part in the ceremony, as had been the tradition since his MOWM days.[70]

There also were questions about whether the congregational singing by the audience should include only simple hymns and well-known spirituals, in order to avoid hard-to-sing songs like "Lift Every Voice and Sing," or whether a band should play hymns like "Onward Christian Soldiers" at key spots throughout the meeting. Most agreed that the music should be both religious and patriotic, like "The Star Spangled Banner" and "America the Beautiful." Rustin considered the greatest concerns to be the introduction of the southern "freedom fighters," students like Autherine Lucy attending white colleges, and the ministers whose churches had been bombed.[71]

The "official call" signed by Randolph, King, and Wilkins emphasized that the pilgrimage was a celebration of the three-year anniversary of the May 17 *Brown* decision as a "new Emancipation." As the catalyst of a crisis that involved the whole nation, the pilgrimage was meant to arouse its conscience. Although nine states and the District of Columbia were moving toward desegregation, Randolph, King, and Wilkins warned that "eight states have defied the nation's highest court and have refused to begin in good faith, with all deliberate speed, to comply with its ruling." Furthermore, the "governments of these states have joined the assault on democracy by moving to put the National Association for the Advancement of Colored People out of business." Stressing the NAACP's historic role in the life of American Negroes, especially in fighting for their constitutional rights, the pilgrimage cochairmen contended that the current resistance confirmed that "some states today are seeking to wipe out history and to restore to force the Dred Scott decision of 1857." Connecting their constitutional concerns to the tenets of American religious freedom, the three cochairmen reached out to all Americans with these final words:

> We believe Americans are deeply religious and wish to order their lives and their country according to the great moral truths to be found in our common religious heritage. As the Founding Americans prayed for strength and wisdom in the wilderness of a new land, as the slaves and their descendants prayed for emancipation and human dignity, as men of every color and clime in time of crisis have sought Divine guidance, we now, in these troubled and momentous years, call up all who love justice and dignity and liberty, who love their country, and who love mankind, to join in a prayer pilgrimage to Washington on May 17, 1957.[72]

The response to the call by progressive ministers, both black and white, was immediate. Both northern and southern ministers contacted the three cochairmen regarding the initial planning meeting in Washington, D.C., on April 5. Rev. William Herbert King of Grace Congregational Church in New York looked forward to "thought-provoking discussions and prayerful planning." William Holmes Borders of Wheat Street Baptist Church in Atlanta believed that the pilgrimage would be "intelligent, objective, comprehensive, deeply religious and effective," but he wondered "where will we go from the prayer pilgrimage," since there were bus fights to finish in Atlanta, Tallahassee, and Birmingham; voting issues that had to be addressed; and continued agitation for the implementation of the *Brown* decision. Borders insisted that the demonstration lead to future action. Reinhold Niebuhr sent his support for the pilgrimage, believing that it would have a positive "impact on the mind and conscience of the nation." Rev. Henry Koch of the Washington Federation of Churches commended the "leaders of the prayer pilgrimage for the spiritual depth" they brought to their struggle for freedom. Representing Catholic support for the pilgrimage, the Very Reverend James A. Pike of New York's Cathedral Church of St. John the Divine expressed disappointment that the pilgrimage was not being held farther north because of the segregation there but agreed that a dramatic gesture of a prayer pilgrimage would "disturb the complacency about this crucial problem of Christian ethics." Randolph's old friend John LaFarge wrote directly to him with his blessings for "this great occasion." The black press published the NAACP's press release to show that "outstanding ministers of all races and creeds," such as Niebuhr, Pike, and LaFarge, endorsed the prayer pilgrimage. Both Eugene Carson Blake and Oscar Lee of the National Council of Churches of Christ supported the pilgrimage, recognizing Martin Luther King Jr. as a minister of one of their "constituent communions." Lee viewed the event as "consonant with the demonstration already made of the strength of spiritual power and nonviolent action" and a correct response "in this time of crisis."[73]

In contrast to the enthusiastic response the pilgrimage cochairmen received from the progressive religious community, Joseph Jackson's absence spoke volumes for the conservative faction. Did this prefigure the eventual split between the National Baptist Convention and the Progressive National Baptist Convention over the issue of civil rights? Even though Randolph's efforts to draw Jackson into his political causes failed, his success in drawing the young Martin Luther King to his liberal religious causes in the North may have foreshadowed the split between the National Baptists. Jackson politely declined Randolph's invitation to the April 5 planning meeting. Roy Wilkins also asked Jackson to speak at the pilgrimage, and Kilgore offered to make him an honorary cochairman with the six other influential black leaders. Jackson refused them both. Randolph's communications with Jackson by telegram and telephone reveal how much he wanted Jackson to participate, to show the unified support of the whole black community in the battle for integration. In fact, Randolph credited Jackson for taking the "initiative in giving to the nation the idea of memorializing the 17th of May with prayer." But Jackson interpreted the National Baptist Convention's resolution much more narrowly than Randolph did: "I can serve the cause best by being associated wholly with the prayer idea as expressed by our convention, and leave the work of the pilgrimage to be directed and guided by others." Jackson's repeated rejections of Randolph's overtures caused Randolph to look increasingly to Martin Luther King to carry out his liberal religious agenda and revealed the tensions beginning between the conservative and progressive factions of the National Baptist Convention.[74]

From his New York Brotherhood office, Randolph concentrated on rallying the local labor community, while Kilgore organized the Protestant and Catholic ministers for a planning meeting to mobilize New York's citizens scheduled for April 18. Addressing the workers as "devoted champions" in the struggle for human rights, Randolph emphasized the connection with the civil rights bill pending in Congress. He felt that for the first time in eighty years, there was a real possibility that Congress would pass civil rights legislation. Randolph called this a "moment of great decision" for all "decent thinking Americans" to "protest the unspeakable outrages occurring in the South: bombings of churches and homes, violent attacks on women and children, and repression of the NAACP."[75]

For one planning meeting held in the New York Brotherhood office, the pilgrimage staff wrote a memorandum of seven talking points that they wanted Randolph to cover. At the top of their list was Randolph's explanation of why this was a "pilgrimage" and not a "march on Washington" and if "the Pilgrimage lifted pressure from the President, where pressure should [then] be exerted." Staff memos show that the pilgrimage organizers believed that with the American labor movement contributing funds and workers for the event, it would be possible to attract fifty thousand people to Washington. Randolph urged Boyd Wilson of the United Steelworkers of America, who had participated in the initial April 5 meeting, "to have as many members, Negro and white, as possible, to be present in Washington and at the Lincoln Memorial on noon of May 17." Since the pilgrimage budget was close to $25,000, Randolph successfully solicited funds from local labor organizations to join Randolph's "crusade for First Class Citizenship for all Americans."[76]

As Randolph and Kilgore worked to fulfill New York's quota of ten thousand pilgrims, Adam Clayton Powell Jr. read the official call of the prayer pilgrimage for freedom into the *Congressional Record*, using the event's slogan, "To arouse the conscience of the nation." Included was information regarding the special New York church mobilization by such ministers as David Licorish, Claude L. Franklyn from Brooklyn, and George L. Payne from the Bronx. Powell's entire congressional staffs in both Washington and New York were assigned to work with the ministers' "Operation New York" project, headed by the Abyssinian pastor David Licorish. Designed to promote the pilgrimage in churches and fraternal groups, the project called on New York City Mayor Robert Wagner to designate May 17 as "Prayer Pilgrimage for Freedom Day in New York." Licorish invited Roy Wilkins to a luncheon meeting at the Abyssinian Church on May 3 "to solidify movement of ministers to Washington." Not only was Pastor Powell on the program, but the press and TV also would be present. Wilkins, busy with getting a civil rights bill through Congress, diplomatically declined Licorish's invitation but reminded him that for "nearly half-century of existence the NAACP [had] enjoyed the support of the church and its ministers." Wilkins commended Licorish and other New York ministers for "giving inspiring leadership to New York on the prayer pilgrimage."[77]

New York's black religious community responded enthusiastically to the call for a national demonstration for civil rights. In his letters to the New York ministers, Kilgore reminded them that "our people look to the Church for continued leadership in the struggle for freedom, justice and first-class citizenship" and that black churches must remain "in the vanguard of the liberation movement as we march forward together under the banner of the brotherhood of man and the Fatherhood of God." These were the same themes that Randolph had been reiterating for more than thirty years. Kilgore underscored the urgency felt by all organizers of the demonstration: "Yes, the time is now—and we must rise, with courage and conviction, to the occasion." Six days before the Washington pilgrimage, Kilgore and David Licorish invited Randolph to a Saturday noon rally, where they reserved a place for him on the podium in the hope he would make a few remarks. Kilgore and Licorish believed that "a few hours of open air prayer" would do much to "arouse the conscience of the nation toward the plight of 17 million of its loyal citizens." But apparently Randolph was busy mobilizing others in the New York community for the pilgrimage.[78]

Through his friend Jerome Davis, Randolph revived his old ties with the Religion and Labor Foundation. After Martin Luther King Jr. addressed a Religion and Labor Foundation luncheon in support of the event, Davis asked Randolph about distributing thousands of printed postcards with a poem by Rev. Claud D. Nelson of the Religious Liberty Department of the National Council of Churches. On the back side of the postcard was an invitation to join the American Civil Liberties Union. Randolph offered to distribute one hundred to "our local divisions" but warned Davis that he did not have the "machinery to distribute the cards" at the pilgrimage. Nelson's poem, "Proclaim Liberty throughout the Land," based on Leviticus 25:10, had a liberal and ecumenical religious message:

> LET FREEDOM RING!
> For East, for West, for White, for Black.
> For Moslem, Hindu, Christian, Jew.
> For Workers with hand and head and heart.

No Pharaoh can ring those bells, no
profiteer, imperialist, thought controller,
book burner, monopolist, nor any self-
righteous man—only he that has clean
hands and a pure heart.

LET MY PEOPLE GO!
Freedom without—
from want, ignorance, exploitation,
oppression, discrimination.
Freedom within—
from fear, hate, superstition,
greed, pride.

THE TRUTH—WHICH IS LOVE
SHALL MAKE YOU FREE!
And the only road to peace is for you to
enlarge the areas of freedom, within
you, around you, till all men are free—
and the nations have peace.[79]

Randolph also heard from other friends and activists from his old
MOWM days. Charles Wesley Burton, still connected with the South
Congregational Church in Chicago, suggested several ideas for the pilgrimage, including appropriate hymns and speakers. Burton recommended Dr. Mordecai Johnson, "one of our best ministers," as a good
speaker "if he could be limited to 25 or 30 minutes." Burton thought the
Howard University choir would be a good choice for music, as long as
"Negro spirituals will be its major concern." Finally, Burton urged Randolph not to let his "usual modesty" prevent him from "giving the dynamic address of the occasion." He believed that Randolph's speech
should be "twice as long as the second longest" and its content appro-
priately arousing, since the main purpose of the event was "placed on the
spiritual side of our fight and struggles for freedom." Rev. John Nance, of
the Washington Tabernacle Baptist Church in St Louis, wrote Randolph
that "Missouri is planning to be well represented at the National prayer
pilgrimage." As president of the Missionary Baptist State Convention,
Nance intended to lead a sizable delegation to Washington. As Burton
had, Nance related Randolph's current leadership role in this "noble purpose" to his past religious activism: Since "the dark days of the Pullman

Porters fight our Church . . . went all out for the principle for which you were fighting and continuing to fight for justice." Indeed, colleagues of Burton and Nance saw the pilgrimage as part of an old tradition of Randolph's religious activism.[80]

The NAACP headquarters in New York City, on 20 West Fortieth Street, was the nerve center for the prayer pilgrimage. Its files on the prayer pilgrimage show that the New York office notified all NAACP branches, youth councils, and college chapters; monitored the response or lack of response from prospective pilgrims from various regions of the nation; and organized regional delegations to get the word out. The NAACP's Washington bureau carefully coordinated the buses, "Freedom Trains," car caravans, and planes from New York, Detroit, Chicago, Montgomery, Atlanta, and Los Angeles. NAACP branches in Virginia planned a motorcade of two hundred cars for the event. The NAACP files also show the close coordination of the black ministers and churches with the local NAACP branches in San Francisco, Oakland, Richmond, and Los Angeles, from which round-trip flights from California to Washington, D.C., averaged $175.00.[81]

At last the momentous day arrived. The three-hour program, from 12 noon to 3 P.M., went off as planned. Henry Lee Moon, the NAACP's director of public relations, reminded Randolph, Wilkins, and King to be at the Lincoln Memorial at least two hours before the program was to begin, for live television interviews with CBS. The same morning, the three cochairmen were to be presented with the "keys to the District." Randolph's, Wilkins's, and King's speeches were placed in each of the hours of the three-hour program, with Randolph giving the opening speech in the first hour, Wilkins in the second, and King ending the program with his "Give us the ballot" speech. Interspersed throughout the program were the five honorary chairmen representing the black church. Bishop Sherman L. Greene of Atlanta, senior bishop of the AME Church, gave the invocation. Both Bishop William J. Walls of Chicago's AMEZ Church and Bishop William Y. Bell of the Third Episcopal District of the CME Church in South Boston, Virginia, gave scriptural readings in the first hour. Rev. Dr. William M. Jernagin, the Baptist president of the Fraternal Council of Negro Churches, and Bishop Robert C. Lawson, affiliated with New York City's Pentecostal-based Refuge Church of Our Lord, gave scriptural readings in the last hour. Representing the broader Christian and Jewish communities were Ross A. Weston, from a Unitarian church in Arlington, Virginia, and Rabbi Norman Gerstenfeld of the

Speaker's platform for the prayer pilgrimage for freedom, at the steps of the Lincoln Memorial in Washington, D.C., on May 17, 1957, marking the third anniversary of the *Brown* decision. Seated from left to right: Roy Wilkins of the NAACP; Randolph, conversing with Wilkins; Rev. Thomas Kilgore, national director of the pilgrimage; and Martin Luther King Jr. Reproduced from the Collections of the Library of Congress.

Washington Hebrew Congregation, both of whom offered brief prayers. Finally, Rev. Timothy M. Chambers from Zion Hill Baptist Church in Los Angeles gave the benediction.[82]

At the center of the program were four reports from the "southern freedom fighters": William H. Borders from Atlanta, C. K. Steele from Tallahassee, Fred Shuttlesworth from Birmingham, and A. L. Davis from New Zion Baptist Church in New Orleans. The spotlight on them may have contributed to the concern felt by several participants that the program was "heavily weighted with Baptists." As Roy Wilkins wrote to one of the Baptist ministers on the program, "There has been a little grumbling from the Methodists that the Baptists are on all the committees, have most of the staff jobs, and are more numerous on the program than any other denomination."[83]

The second hour of the program, when Roy Wilkins spoke, balanced somewhat the dominant religious tone of the meeting with a political message: support the civil rights bill that Congress was considering. After the demonstration, Henry Lee Moon complained to NAACP board members that the "loud and incessant helicopter drone . . . prevented the 27,000 persons present from hearing" Wilkins's remarks, suggesting that it was done on purpose, since "Mr. Wilkins was the only speaker subjected to this kind of competition throughout his address." Although Senators Paul H. Douglas and Jacob Javits failed to appear as scheduled, black Congressmen Charles Diggs and Adam Clayton Powell both delivered speeches. Mahalia Jackson's performances throughout the service and the congregational singing, including "Lift Every Voice and Sing" and "The Integration Song" sung to the tune "When We All Get to Heaven," represented a broad range of traditional and modern music from the black church tradition. Two women appeared on the podium: Irene McCoy Gaines of the National Association of Colored Women and Vivian Carter Mason from the National Council of Negro Women, although in the program her name is listed as Mrs. William Mason. Two youngsters from Clay, Kentucky, plaintiffs in one of the desegregation court cases, laid a wreath at the foot of the statue of Lincoln. Another dramatic moment was Randolph's announcement of Rev. Milton Perry's 230 mile-long walk to get to the pilgrimage. During the program, those in the audience who pledged to keep fighting for civil rights raised their hands and signed a Freedom bond to show that they did take part in and contribute to the success of the prayer pilgrimage.[84]

As the first of the three cochairmen to speak, Randolph's speech summed up the reasons that had brought blacks and whites, Jews and Gentiles, Protestants and Catholics to gather "at the monument of Abraham Lincoln, the Great Emancipator." Above all, it was to "tell the story of our long night of trial and trouble and our renewal of faith in and consecration to the sacred cause of a rebirth of freedom and human dignity." Repeating the phrases "we have come," "we are here," and "we have assembled," Randolph reminded his audience that the third anniversary of the *Brown* decision demonstrated the unity between the black community and "their allies, labor, liberal and the Church." In support of the civil rights bills now before Congress, Randolph warned the northern liberal, religious, educational, labor, and business forces that if this legislation failed to pass, "irrational racial legislation" could ban the "B'nai B'rith, the AFL-CIO, and some sections of the National Council of the Church of Christ in the U.S.A., tomorrow." Randolph singled out Martin Luther King Jr., "a great church leader and prophet of our times," for his inspired leadership in the Montgomery struggle but made no mention of E. D. Nixon's role.[85]

Like the Orchestra Hall speech commemorating the second anniversary of *Brown*, Randolph's prayer pilgrimage speech referred to his own deeply held religious beliefs with its emphasis on the "value and dignity of the personality of every human being, regardless of race, color, religion, national origin or ancestry." He reasoned that civil rights had a "moral and spiritual basis," for they gave force to "our human rights . . . because we have been created human beings by God." Randolph stressed that the current civil rights crisis was not white against black but slavery against freedom, truth against error, justice against injustice, love against hate, good against evil, and law and order against mob rule.

> We like to think that God is on the side of our American way of life but this will only be true to the extent that our American way of life is on the side of God, who said: "I am the way, the truth and the light."[*sic*] Hence, in the eyes of God there is neither black nor white, nor red nor yellow, nor Jew nor Gentile, nor barbarian nor Scythian, but all are brothers in Christ Jesus. "By this will all men know that you are my disciples, if you have love one for another."[86]

Randolph's speech and his influential role in the early civil rights movement that culminated in the 1963 March on Washington have been eclipsed in the popular imagination of the civil rights movement by the rising popularity of the young, charismatic Martin Luther King Jr. Typical of the enthusiastic responses from the participants that Randolph received after the prayer pilgrimage was a letter from a Brooklyn woman who called it "one of the most inspiring experiences of my life." She also asked for a copy of King's speech, which she called "one of the milestones of American history," but expressed no interest in Randolph's speech.[87]

But Randolph had deliberately designed the program so that King would deliver the keynote address, scheduled at the very end of the long three-hour program. Roy Wilkins agreed with that decision. King's prayer pilgrimage speech "Give us the ballot" was the most important speech he delivered until his "I have a dream" speech six years later at the

1963 March on Washington. Bayard Rustin recalled Randolph's influence in suggesting that King speak on a political topic. Randolph "drew
out of Martin what he himself sought," a "great church leader" making
a political statement on an important national issue that affected all people in a democratic society. The "Give us the ballot" speech was a "tactical speech, and presented Martin King to the nation as a tactician,"
Rustin explained. King called on black leaders, Catholics, Protestants,
and Jews, with their headquarters and wealth in the north, to join together and fight for the vote, that is, black political rights.[88]

The young Reverend King emerged from the prayer pilgrimage as the
new star of the civil rights movement, a position that only intensified with
his assassination eleven years later. Again, when King's "I have a dream"
speech became the highlight of the 1963 March on Washington, Rustin
observed that the march then became "Dr. King's March" and that the
public "assumed that Dr. King organized the march." But "this never worried Mr. Randolph," who just felt lucky that "Martin's speech . . . struck
such a chord that the march will be known forever in American history."
Rustin attributed Randolph's attitude to his characteristic graciousness,
but it probably reflected Randolph's admiration of a preacher who could
energize thousands of people in the heart of the South, reviving the modern civil rights movement that he had begun generations earlier.[89]

King's popularity placed a considerable strain on the carefully planned
unity of civil rights organizations. The black press's extensive coverage of
the pilgrimage emphasized King's role as the "new voice" of black America. James Hicks, a journalist for the *Amsterdam News*, heralded King as
the "number one" black leader and accused Randolph and Wilkins of not
throwing the full weight of their organizations behind the pilgrimage.
Hicks's article prompted Thomas Kilgore, Bayard Rustin, and Ella Baker
to set the record straight: that the pilgrimage had originated from clear
directives from their respective organizations to plan a large civil rights
demonstration. According to them, the prayer pilgrimage synthesized the
best of the ideas presented by the three, with the basic notion that the situation at this time needed a spiritual undergirding of their common struggle. In response to Hicks's accusation that the NAACP and the BSCP half-
heartedly supported the event, the organizers listed the jobs that each organization contributed, such as office space, secretarial help, financial
contributions, and publicity.[90]

Outraged at Hicks's article, Roy Wilkins complained that it had incited
personality fights, suspicion, and jealousy at a time when unity was es-

sential. Wilkins sent the *Amsterdam News* a list of thirty ways in which the NAACP had contributed to the success of the national event. In fact, it took the NAACP several years to pay off all the debts incurred. Wilkins and Randolph remained on friendly terms, with Wilkins describing Randolph's speech as "in the Randolph tradition, a cogent statement of the issues out of your scholarship and your rich experience over the years." Despite the problems and personality conflicts that the prayer pilgrimage revealed, it still set a pattern of civil rights activism that lasted until 1963. According to Rustin, once Randolph persuaded King to come north for the 1957 prayer pilgrimage, it was repeated year after year: with the Youth March for Integrated Schools in 1958, the second youth march in 1959, and the 1960 Democratic and Republican conventions, all with Dr. King playing the central role. Ending with the final dramatic demonstration leading to the 1963 March on Washington, Rustin asserted that "this was all largely under Randolph and Wilkins' direction."[91]

In the months after the prayer pilgrimage, the momentum of the civil rights movement helped Randolph's efforts to meet with President Eisenhower. Randolph wrote again to him asking for a meeting for himself and fifteen other black leaders. One month after the pilgrimage, Randolph heard from E. Frederick Morrow, the first black to serve in an executive position on a president's staff at the White House, who invited Randolph to discuss his meeting with the president.[92]

Randolph, however, made little headway in his attempts to influence the executive branch of government during the Eisenhower administration, whose civil rights policy was, at best, cautious. Equally disappointing to Randolph was the Civil Rights Act of 1957, the first civil rights legislation since Reconstruction. In the end, Randolph regarded it as "worse than no bill at all," since the amendments added to the bill while in the Senate greatly weakened it. Nonetheless, Randolph continued in his public role to repeat the basic theme since the prayer pilgrimage, that the black community remained "united behind the civil rights fight, and they have the cooperation of organized labor and also the Catholic, Protestant and Jewish religious communities in the interest of making the idea of the brotherhood of man a reality."[93]

In the weeks following the prayer pilgrimage, Randolph heard from many friends and colleagues from the old MOWM days, congratulating him on his contribution to an event that drew almost thirty thousand people to the Lincoln Memorial. Septima Clark of the Highlander School in Newark, New Jersey, described to Randolph her feelings as she approached the crowd: "As a sufferer in the cause for real freedom I wept tears of joy to see those people of all nationalities and backgrounds with banners waving marching across that green turf to stand in front of the Lincoln Memorial." Walking toward the program, Clark heard Randolph "speaking and those resonant tones gave us all a lift." Layle Lane, who drove to Washington with several activists of the old MOWM, wrote to Randolph that the pilgrimage convinced her that blacks were "sufficiently united to demand a civil rights measure now."[94]

Another enthusiastic pilgrim was the Reverend George Singleton, an African Methodist minister and former editor of the *AME Church Review* in Philadelphia, the birthplace of African Methodism. Singleton described how he felt standing "in the vast throng" witnessing the "most impressive" service of his life. Singleton asked for a copy of Randolph's speech for publication in the *AME Church Review*, "for the benefit of the many who were not present." Singleton, identifying Randolph as part of the AME Church family, wrote, "Mr. Randolph, we are proud of you." On his travels on church business, Singleton frequently referred to Randolph in his talks and featured his picture in the Quadrennial Report to our General Conference at Miami. Singleton and Randolph had been acquainted with each other for several years. Touched by Singleton's remarks, Randolph commented on his pride in belonging to the AME Church and in the fact that his forebears were members of a "religious institution founded by our people."[95]

Jervis Anderson, Randolph's biographer, recalled the morning in March 1956 when Randolph arrived in his office and noticed on the top of the day's mail a copy of Singleton's book *The Romance of African Methodism: A Study of the African Methodist Episcopal Church*. Anderson assumed that it was a gift for Randolph's upcoming sixty-seventh birthday. Because Randolph did not usually accept gifts from people, Anderson explained this exception because

> as much as anything else, Randolph liked to read the history of religious movements. None interested him more deeply than the rise of Protestantism in Europe and the spread of Methodism in America; and no aspect of Methodism in this country appealed to him quite as much as the story of the African Methodist Episcopal church.[96]

Singleton described his book, which traced the "story of the rise, expansion, and development of the African M.E. Church in the United

States," as "another thrilling chapter in the *Acts of the Apostles.*" Singleton's 1952 study was part of a scholarly tradition from W. E. B. Du Bois to C. Eric Lincoln that had long associated African Methodist history in twentieth-century America with "romance." Du Bois first noted the "tinge of romance" surrounding the history of the AME Church in America from the moment that Richard Allen and Absalom Jones and "a crowd of followers, refused to worship except in their accustomed places, and finally left the [St. George's Methodist] church in a body." C. Eric Lincoln wrote in his own description of the two-hundred year "romance" between African Americans and Methodism: "There was something about Methodism that was uniquely attractive to black Christians." Similarly, Singleton traced the voluntary segregation in black Methodist churches in the United States, before, during, and after the Civil War, showing that the AME Church was not a "segregated or Jim Crow institution" but, first and foremost, a "protest against segregation." Both Randolph and Singleton agreed on the "romance" of African Methodism, when Richard Allen walked out of his church in protest of black rights. Hadn't Randolph done the same thing? As Singleton's inscription reads:

> The Hon. A. Philip Randolph—Distinguished son of the church which stems from Richard Allen who was born a slave Feb. 24, 1760. As he struck a telling blow for religious freedom in 1787 when he left the Methodist Church as a protest against segregation you are incessantly waging a battle for the political emancipation of our people of African descent.[97]

Rev. Singleton's birthday present arrived in March 1956 when the Montgomery bus boycott was in its fourth month and Randolph and the In Friendship group were organizing their southern brothers and sisters in their fight against Jim Crow. The 1954 *Brown* decision was the first of a series of events that eventually outlawed legal segregation in the South. As Randolph unsuccessfully tried to use the old conference method of gaining President Eisenhower's attention, the successful alliance of a southern black church-based social movement in Montgomery and other urban centers in the south with a northern network of labor and liberal religious groups backed by the NAACP sparked a decade-long period of reform in America. The speeches, the rallies, and the strategic planning all resulted in the first national demonstration, the prayer pilgrimage, the test run for the later 1963 March on Washington. The pilgrimage did contribute to the Civil Rights Act of 1957, albeit a flawed first attempt at civil rights legislation.

After three years of intense activism, culminating in the prayer pilgrimage, Randolph acknowledged what a spectacular "prayer protest" it had been. As he rested before the next round of civil rights protests, Randolph paused at the end of 1957 to write to his In Friendship colleague Rev. Hildebrand, requesting membership in the Bethel AME Church. At sixty-eight, Randolph finally rejoined the church of his father, and in its recovery of its militant social conscience, the black church had joined him.

Epilogue
The Old Gentleman

In 1979, when Bayard Rustin sat down to write a memorial to honor his mentor, A. Philip Randolph, whom he called his "father, uncle, adviser, defender," he described the day that the tax examiner came to Randolph's apartment to assess his worth. Except for a broken television set that could be repaired, the tax examiner estimated the price of all his earthly goods to be no more than $500. Rustin decided that Randolph's most valued possession was an old battered watch presented to him years before by the Pullman porters. Randolph "lived a simple life, a life totally unconcerned with material possessions," and although he left little in worldly goods, Rustin believed that he "left all of us the wealth of his wisdom acquired in the pursuit of truth." Rustin then turned to a letter he had received from an old friend named Jim Farrell. Farrell told Rustin about a conversation he had had with a Pullman porter on a Chicago-bound train. It was more than ten years ago, about the time that Randolph was retiring from the presidency of the BSCP. Farrell told the porter that he personally knew Randolph. Thrilled to hear this, the porter told Farrell, "The old gentleman took care of us when we needed it, when we could not take care of ourselves. Now he's old and he needs to be taken care of. And we'll take care of the old gentleman."[1]

In the years after the prayer pilgrimage, the "old gentleman" faced several personal crises that slowed him down considerably. After his wife Lucille, his closest friend and companion of fifty years, died, just a few months before the 1963 March on Washington, Randolph was left alone without any immediate family. As his old friend Chandler Owen noted at the time, Randolph had faithfully cared for Lucille during a long convalescence, just as she had supported him throughout all the difficult years of his social activism. Randolph's biographer, Jervis Anderson, stated that Randolph was "unstinting in his personal attentions to his ailing wife," seeing to her comfort, watching her diet, and reading to her from newspapers, the Bible, or Shakespeare in his evenings at home. Even after her death, he continued to sit in her room by the bed, reading to himself. In the summer of 1968, after Randolph was mugged by three young assailants outside his apartment, Rustin moved him into a cooperative house owned by the International Ladies' Garment Workers Union (ILGWU), an appropriate place given Randolph's long association with the trade union movement. Despite his personal problems, Randolph continued working with the same religious communities as he had in the past.[2]

Randolph continued to support Martin Luther King Jr.'s new black ecumenical organization, the Southern Christian Leadership Conference (SCLC). He hoped the liberal coalition formed behind the church-led civil rights movement begun in Montgomery would remain united. But after the 1963 march, other political forces, such as the black power movement, emerged in the mid-1960s, fragmenting the carefully orchestrated unity of this early phase of the civil rights movement. From this time on, Randolph and his generation were increasingly perceived by younger radical activists as "Uncle Toms." But until that time, Martin Luther King Jr. was the civil rights leader for his generation, culminating in his "I have a dream" speech to the 250,000 people at the August 28, 1963, March on Washington.[3]

On that summer day in 1963, A. Philip Randolph's old dream had come true: a peaceful march on the nation's capital, demanding first-class citizenship. As the assembly slowly dispersed from the Lincoln Memorial, Rustin saw the tired "old gentleman" standing alone on the podium, looking out on the departing crowds. As Rustin walked up to Randolph, he was surprised to find "tears streaming down his cheeks," the first time he had ever seen Randolph show his emotions. Indeed, Randolph was so overcome with the power of that one-day event, in which the black community and the white liberal community came together in their demand for equal treatment under the law, that he "could not hold back his feelings." Less than a year later, President Lyndon Johnson signed the 1964 Civil Rights Act, understood by American blacks as their "second emancipation" and a reinforcement of their Fourteenth Amendment rights. In 1964, the SCLC's principal program was still "nonviolent direct action" when its eighth annual convention confirmed "its allegiance to the time honored tactics and strategies that have served us so well in the past ten years," especially its encouragement of "sit-in's, pray-in's, boycott's, picket lines, marches, civil disobedience and any form of protest and demonstrations that are non-violently conceived and executed." These were the same tactics and strategies that Randolph had pioneered in his own religious activism for more than fifty years.[4]

In his last years, Randolph's most ambitious undertaking was the establishment of the A. Philip Randolph Institute, under the directorship of Bayard Rustin. In 1966, the institute launched its ambitious "freedom budget for all Americans," a $185-billion economic program supported by varying degrees of commitment by all civil rights organizations. Once again, it reflected Randolph's lifetime conviction that until the African American community had achieved economic freedom, its political freedom would not be complete. Although the freedom budget failed to win the support of the government or the nation, which were preoccupied with the Vietnam War, it did signal Randolph's continuing interest in building a political coalition between the black community and the labor movement, with its demands for democratic social change.[5]

The "freedom budget" received support from the Christian press. Henry B. Clark of the Division of Christ Life and Mission of the National Council of Churches called it a welcome symbol at this particular moment in the nation's history, "of the resurrection of the liberal coalition disrupted by the black power controversy." He was particularly impressed with the "almost 200 blue-ribbon personages—from Stokely Carmichael, Floyd McKissick and Michael Harrington of the left to John Kenneth Galbraith, Reinhold Niebuhr, Ralph Bunche and John Courtney Murray of the establishment" who signed and supported the "freedom from want" document. Even at this stage in his life, Randolph still associated black economic power with its moral and spiritual base.[6]

Randolph also continued his relationships with white liberal Protestant ministers in New York. When he neared his retirement from the BSCP, he accepted the chairmanship of the Protestant Council of the City of New York, the first black to serve in that capacity. The Protestant Council regarded Randolph as a religious leader, even though he was a layman, because the only black who had served on the council's executive committee, eight years earlier, was Brooklyn's Rev. Gardner C. Taylor, a minister influential in the formation of the Progressive National Baptist Convention. Along with the organization's president, Norman Vincent Peale, Randolph worked with sixty-two other board members to make top-level decisions for more than seventeen hundred local Protestant congregations. Randolph, known as a prominent Methodist layman and an active member of Bethel AME Church, was elected with two black ministers in New York: Rev. M. L. Wilson of Convent Avenue Baptist Church and Rev. Walter Jacobs of St. Augustine's Episcopal Church in Brooklyn. Appointed for a one-year term, Randolph enjoyed his tenure on the Protestant Council, which met every two months. After his term, Norman Vincent Peale kept in touch with Randolph, seeking his advice on the "broader community participation in the Council's work and program." Although retirement and ill health limited his participation, Randolph offered his counsel to the Protestant Council for several years.[7]

In 1962, the year before the big march, Randolph prepared a long address to the Diamond Jubilee Celebration of an AME conference in Hamilton, Bermuda. Entitled "African Methodism and the Negro in the Western World," it traced thousands of years of Western history, from the ancient civilizations of Egypt, Babylon, and Greece to Jesus Christ and his "revolutionary ministry of the brotherhood of man." Randolph described how Jesus, "with a universal injunction of Christian humanism . . . brought hope to the multitudes with the things of the body, as well as the things of the spirit." With the "early giants" of the medieval church"—John Huss, Martin Luther, Calvin, Wycliffe, Melanchthon, and Wesley—Randolph included Richard Allen and the establishment of the first AME church. Randolph regarded African Methodism as the "religious reflection of the deep revolutionary currents set in motion by the French Revolution which had given rise to the doctrine of the Rights of Man." His comment that for "Richard Allen, the dignity of the human personality was sacred" reflected Randolph's own Christian humanist and personalist perspective. To him, Richard Allen's walking out of the segregated Methodist church was the opening act of the civil rights movement.

> On that day, and by that deed, Richard Allen broke down the iniquitous partition wall of racial proscription and segregation in the Christian Church, not only in the United States but throughout the world. Verily, the test of Christianity is the test of the color line, as the test of democracy is the test of the color line.[8]

A. Philip Randolph accomplished the mission given him by his African Methodist parents: to work for the economic and spiritual well-being of his race. Randolph left the oppressive atmosphere of the Jim Crow South and migrated north to participate in the vitality and challenge of the

Harlem Renaissance. There, as he struggled to fight Jim Crow, he blended the spiritual message of African Methodism with the economic principles of Marxist-inspired socialist theories. Frustrated with the Negro Church's accommodation to second-class citizenship, he boldly attacked the church for failing to live up to its prophetic role to challenge discrimination in white social, political, and religious institutions.

Recognizing that his radicalism splintered the black community, Randolph pragmatically set about building alliances with progressive-minded black ministers and their congregations. He used this tactic repeatedly in his labor activism when he organized the Pullman porters and in the early modern civil rights movement. Finally, when the progressive, socially conscious wing of the black church emerged as the mainstream in the 1950s with Martin Luther King Jr. and the black ecumenical movement of the SCLC, Randolph rejoined an AME church. He was neither irreligious nor antireligious. Rather, his religiosity was a blend of an African Methodist social gospel and a Christian humanist perspective informed by a philosophical belief in the sacredness of the human personality. Randolph drew on this complex religious nature as a source of spiritual strength throughout his seventy years of civil rights activism in order to respond to an oppressive and indifferent Christian nation, which in practice fell far short of its liberal and democratic ideals.

Notes

Notes to the Introduction

1. Edwin R. Embree, *13 against the Odds* (New York: Viking Press, 1944), 2, 211–12, 215. Embree also served as the executive director of the Rosenwald Fund, which gave liberally to black educational institutions.

2. Roi Ottley, *"New World A-Coming": Inside Black America* (Cleveland: World, 1943), 248–49 (italics in original).

3. Embree, *13 against the Odds*, 222.

4. Theodore Kornweibel Jr., *"Seeing Red": Federal Campaign against Black Militancy, 1919–1925* (Bloomington: Indiana University Press, 1998), 77. Larry Tye, *Rising from the Rails: Pullman Porters and the Making of the Black Middle Class* (New York: Henry Holt, 2004), 263.

5. Randolph played an active role in several of the most significant periods of African American history. The major works on Randolph's radical career as a black journalist during World War I and the Harlem Renaissance include Philip S. Foner's *American Socialism and Black Americans: From the Age of Jackson to the World War II* (1977); Theodore Kornweibel's *No Crystal Stair: Black Life and the* Messenger *, 1917–1928* (1975) and *"Seeing Red": Federal Campaigns against Black Militancy, 1919–1925* (1998); and Sondra K. Wilson's *The* Messenger *Reader: Stories, Poetry and Essays from the* Messenger *Magazine* (2000). On Randolph's labor activism in the 1930s, the period most explored by scholars, the main works are Brailsford R. Brazeal's *The Brotherhood of Sleeping Car Porters: Its Origin and Development* (1946); William H. Harris's *Keeping the Faith: A. Philip Randolph, Milton P. Webster and the Brotherhood of Sleeping Car Porters, 1925–1937* (1977); and Jack Santino's *Miles of Smiles, Years of Struggle: The Untold History of the Black Pullman Porter* (1989). Recent studies such as Beth Tompkins Bates's *Pullman Porters and the Rise of Protest in Black America, 1925–1945* (2001); and Eric Arnesen's *Brotherhoods of Color: Black Railroad Workers and the Struggle for Equality* (2001) make the historical connection between Randolph's labor and civil rights activism. Larry Tye's *Rising from the Rails: Pullman Porters and the Making of the Black Middle Class* (2004) further expands Randolph's labor leadership into its wider sociological

context. Finally, Randolph's pioneering role as a modern African American civil rights leader during World War II is explored in Herbert Garfinkel's *When Negroes March: The March on Washington Movement in the Organizational Politics for FEPC* (1959); and Paula F. Pfeffer's *A. Philip Randolph: Pioneer of the Civil Rights Movement* (1990). Note also Jervis Anderson's biography, *A. Philip Randolph: A Biographical Portrait* (1972). Anderson had extensive access to Randolph himself in the last years of his life.

NOTES TO CHAPTER 1

1. The Reminiscences of A. Philip Randolph, in the Columbia University Oral History Research Office Collection (hereafter cited as CUOHROC), 1972, 18 69–71. Phyl Garland, "A. Philip Randolph: Labor's Grand Old Man," *Ebony*, May 1969, 32. Jervis Anderson, *A. Philip Randolph: A Biographical Portrait* (New York: Harcourt Brace Jovanovich, 1973), 42.

2. CUOHROC, 69. Anderson, *A. Philip Randolph*, 50–52. A. Philip Randolph, "African Methodism and the Negro in the Western World," May 30, 1962, in A. Philip Randolph Papers (hereafter cited as APR), box 36.

3. CUOHROC, 45, 78–79.

4. Samuel Proctor, "Prelude to the New Florida, 1877–1919," in *The New History of Florida*, edited by Michael Gannon (Gainesville: University Press of Florida, 1996), 272, 275–76. Edmund F. Kallina Jr., *Claude Kirk and the Politics of Confrontation* (Gainesville: University Press of Florida, 1993), 8–10. Edward C. Williamson, *Florida Politics in the Gilded Age, 1877–1893* (Gainesville: University Press of Florida, 1976), 160. Maxine D. Jones, "The African-American Experience in Twentieth Century Florida," in *The New History of Florida*, edited by Michael Gannon (Gainesville: University Press of Florida, 1996), 374.

5. George E. Buker, *Jacksonville: Riverport—Seaport* (Columbia: University of South Carolina Press, 1992). Abel A. Bartley, *Keeping the Faith: Race, Politics, and Social Development in Jacksonville, Florida, 1940–1970* (Westport, Conn.: Greenwood Press, 2000), 1–5.

6. Bartley, *Keeping the Faith*, 2. Edward Akins, "When a Minority Becomes a Majority: Blacks in Jacksonville Politics 1887–1907," *Florida Historical Quarterly* 53 (October 1974): 123–45. Williamson, *Florida Politics in the Gilded Age*, 190–94. Proctor, "Prelude to the New Florida," 272–75. C. Vann Woodward, *The Strange Career of Jim Crow*, 2nd rev. ed. (Oxford: Oxford University Press, 1966), 33, 43, 45, 69, 71. Howard N. Rabinowitz, "More Than the Woodward Thesis: Assessing *The Strange Career of Jim Crow*," *Journal of American History*, December 1988, 842–56. Waldo E. Martin Jr., ed., *Brown v. Board of Education: A Brief History with Documents* (Boston: Bedford/St. Martin's, 1998), 3, 5.

7. CUOHROC, 76.

8. CUOHROC, 47.

9. CUOHROC, 72, 77. See Anderson, *A. Philip Randolph*, 39–40.

10. Proctor, "Prelude to the New Florida," 266–71, 283. Michael Gannon, *Florida: A Short History* (Gainesville: University Press of Florida, 1993), 53. John T. Foster and Sarah Whitmer Foster, *Beechers, Stowes, and Yankee Strangers: The Transformation of Florida* (Gainesville: University Press of Florida, 1999), xii, 115.

11. Randolph to Arthur Garvin and James Parker, November 5, 1963, APR, box 2.

12. Bishop Wesley J. Gaines, *African Methodism in the South: Twenty-five Years of Freedom* (1890; repr., Chicago: Afro-Am Press, 1969). Rev. Charles Sumner Long, *History of The A.M.E. Church in Florida* (Palatka, Fl.: A.M.E. Book Concern, 1939), 125–26. W. E. B. Du Bois, ed., *The Negro Church: Report of a Social Study Made under the Direction of Atlanta University; Together with the Proceedings of the Eighth Conference for the Study of the Negro Problem, Held at Atlanta University, May 26, 1903* (Atlanta: Atlanta University Press, 1903), 123.

13. Du Bois, *The Negro Church*, 123–25. A. Philip Randolph, "African Methodism and the Negro in the Western World. Thomas R. Frazier, "Historians and Afro-American Religion," *Journal of the Interdenominational Theological Center* 13, no. 1 (fall 1985): 7. George A. Singleton, *The Romance of African Methodism: A Study of the African Methodist Episcopal Church* (New York: Exposition Press, 1952). C. Eric Lincoln, "Black Methodists and the Methodist Romance," in *Wesleyan Theology Today: A Bicentennial Theological Consultation*, edited by Theodore Runyon, 215–16 (Nashville: Kingswood Books, 1985).

14. Katharine L. Dvorak, *An African-American Exodus: The Segregation of the Southern Churches* (New York: Carlson, 1991), 49–68. William E. Montgomery, *Under Their Own Vine and Fig Tree: The African-American Church in the South, 1865–1900* (Baton Rouge: Louisiana State University Press, 1993), 38–96. Clarence E. Walker, *A Rock in a Weary Land: The African Methodist Episcopal Church during the Civil War and Reconstruction* (Baton Rouge: Louisiana State University Press, 1982), 61–63. Singleton, *The Romance of African Methodism*, xix, 111. Singleton's study of the AME Church clearly distinguishes the voluntary segregation in the black church during and right after the war from the later twentieth-century policies of strict Jim Crow segregation.

15. Walker, *A Rock in a Weary Land*, 65–66.

16. Long, *History of The A.M.E. Church in Florida*, 52, 55.

17. Ibid., 56–57.

18. Ibid., 57.

19. Anderson, *A. Philip Randolph*, 29.

20. Anderson, *A. Philip Randolph*, 30–32. CUOHROC, 29.

21. CUOHROC, 5, 9–10. Anderson, *A. Philip Randolph*, 37.

22. CUOHROC, 10. Anderson, *A. Philip Randolph*, 31–32.

23. CUOHROC, 41, 43, 45, 49. Anderson, *A. Philip Randolph*, 37.

24. CUOHROC, 27, 37, 46, 58. Anderson, *A. Philip Randolph*, 35–39.

25. CUOHROC, 9, 27–28. Anderson, *A. Philip Randolph*, 31, 33, 37–38, 40.

26. CUOHROC, 47–48. Harry V. Richardson, *Dark Salvation: The Story of Methodism as It Developed among Blacks in America* (New York: Anchor Books, 1976), 200. Writing in the 1970s, Richardson remarked that "the Dollar Plan was an adequate source of income" until recently (200). Anderson, *A. Philip Randolph*, citing W. E. B. Du Bois's *Economic Cooperation among Negro Americans*, 60. C. Eric Lincoln and Lawrence H. Mamiya described the complex Methodist polity of an episcopal structure of general and annual conferences in their *The Black Church in the African American Experience* (Durham, N.C.: Duke University Press, 1990), 68–71. See also Henry McNeal Turner, *The Genius and Theory of Methodist Polity* (1885; repr. Northbrook, Ill.: Metro Books, 1972).

27. CUOHROC, 26. Benjamin E. Mays and Joseph W. Nicholson, *The Negro's Church* (New York: Institute of Social and Religious Research, 1933), 10–11, 40–41. W. A. Daniel, *The Education of Negro Ministers* (New York: George H. Doran, 1925), 104. Daniel's study shows that by the mid-1920s many ministerial students still conformed to their religious communities' conceptions of what constituted a valid call to the ministry. The "proof" of a divine call was a requirement for many Negro congregations, and it kept several conscientious men from entering the ministry. Daniel also noted that the "call-to-the-ministry belief" tended to conveniently "discount the importance of a high-grade theological education" (104).

28. CUOHROC, 18. A. Philip Randolph, "My Father's Politics," n.d., APR, box 37. Anderson, *A. Philip Randolph*, 41.

29. CUOHROC, 30, 49. Anderson, *A. Philip Randolph*, 32, 40.

30. CUOHROC, 28–29. Anderson, *A. Philip Randolph*, 32–33. Studies of "P.K.s" (preachers' kids) reveal how often ministers' children lived a "goldfish bowl" existence. Randolph's experience differed from this norm. For studies of P.K.s, see Edith Feiner, *The Long Shadow of the Parsonage: Some Light from the Dark Memories of a P.K.* (Los Angeles: Sky Line Writer Publications, 1996).

31. CUOHROC, 44–46, 49.

32. CUOHROC, 13–14, 19. Anderson, *A. Philip Randolph*, 29.

33. CUOHROC, 43, 75. Frazier, *The Negro in the United States*, 351–52. Hortense Powdermaker, *After Freedom: A Cultural Study in the Deep South* (New York: Russell & Russell, 1968), 253–73. Powdermaker's 1939 anthropological study of southern culture devotes four chapters to religion. The chapter entitled "Getting Religion" explores Negro revival meetings.

34. CUOHROC, 13, 18. Randolph, "My Father's Politics," n.d., APR, box 37. Anderson, *A. Philip Randolph*, 39.

35. Anderson, *A. Philip Randolph*, 44–46. Foster and Foster, *Beechers, Stowes, and Yankee Strangers*, 80–81, 126–27. The Fosters mention that Cookman gave its students an "excellent" preparation and that they went on to leadership positions "in all sections of the South" and beyond. As an example, the Fosters mention that "the famous civil rights leader A. Philip Randolph graduated from an academic program in 1907" (81). See also Anderson, *A. Philip Randolph*, 44. For Cookman's early history, see Jay S. Stowell, *Methodist Adventures in Negro Education* (New York: Methodist Book Concern, 1922).

36. CUOHROC, 14, 17, 19, 50. Anderson, *A. Philip Randolph*, 46.

37. Anderson, *A. Philip Randolph*, 50–51.

38. CUOHROC, 54, 79–81.

39. CUOHROC, 105. Carter Godwin Woodson, *A Century of Negro Migration* (Washington, D.C.: Association for the Study of Negro Life and History, 1918), 147–66. Gilbert Osofsky, *Harlem: The Making of a Ghetto: Negro New York, 1890–1930*, 2nd ed. (New York: Harper & Row, 1971), 17, 20. Joe William Trotter Jr., "Black Migration in Historical Perspective: A Review of the Literature," in *The Great Migration in Historical Perspective*, edited by Joe William Trotter Jr. (Bloomington: Indiana University Press, 1991), 6, 13–14. For Trotter's further critique of this literature, see "Afro-American Urban History: A Critique of the Literature," in his *Black Milwaukee: The Making of an Industrial Proletariat, 1915–45* (Urbana: University of Illinois Press, 1985), 264–91.

40. Adam Clayton Powell Sr., *Against the Tide: An Autobiography* (New York: Arno Press, 1938), 67–70. For information on Manhattan's Negro churches, see Osofsky, *Harlem*, 8–14, 82–91, 113–17, 245. Seth M. Scheiner, *Negro Mecca: A History of the Negro in New York City, 1865–1920* (New York: New York University Press, 1965), 87. See also Greater New York Federation of Churches, *Negro Churches in Manhattan* (New York: Federation of Churches, 1930), 17–21. Anderson, *A. Philip Randolph*, 55. Seth M. Scheiner, "The Negro Church and the Northern City, 1890–1930," in *Seven on Black: Reflections on the Negro Experience in America*, edited by William G. Shade and Roy C. Herrenkohl (Philadelphia: Lippincott, 1969), 98.

41. CUOHROC, 105, 127. Anderson, *A. Philip Randolph*, 59–60.

42. CUOHROC, 127.

43. CUOHROC, 112, 209.

44. Irving Howe, *Socialism and America* (New York: Harcourt Brace Jovanovich, 1985), 6.

45. Jacob H. Dorn, ed., *Socialism and Christianity in Early 20th Century America* (Westport, Conn.: Greenwood Press, 1998), xiii. Jacob H Dorn, "'In Spiritual Communion': Eugene V. Debs and the Socialist Christians," *Journal of the Gilded Age and Progressive Era*, July 2003, 2. James Darsey, *The Prophetic Tradition and Radical Rhetoric in America* (New York: New York University Press, 1997), 85–108.

46. CUOHROC, 113–14. A. Philip Randolph, "Eugene V. Debs," *Messenger,* November 1926, 337.

47. CUOHROC, 113–14, 122. Anderson, *A. Philip Randolph,* 106–8.

48. Manning Marable, "A. Philip Randolph & the Foundations of Black American Socialism, *Radical America* 14, no. 2 (1980): 8, 11–12.

49. CUOHROC, 152–53. Jeffrey Babcock Perry, "Hubert Henry Harrison, the Father of Harlem Radicalism": The Early Years—1883 through the Founding of the Liberty League and *The Voice* in 1917" (Ph.D. diss., Columbia University, 1987), 54–62, 76–78. For more on Harrison, see Philip S. Foner, *American Socialism and Black Americans: From the Age of Jackson to World War II* (Westport, Conn.: Greenwood Press, 1977), 207–18.

50. CUOHROC, 152. Perry, "Hubert Henry Harrison," 54.

51. CUOHROC, 154, 156. Perry, "Hubert Henry Harrison," 76–78.

52. CUOHROC, 149, 155, 234. Anderson, *A. Philip Randolph,* 62.

53. A. Philip Randolph, "Reply to the Industrial Defense Association, Inc. Boston, Mass," n.d., APR, box 10. Randolph, "African Methodism and the Negro in the Western World," May 30, 1962, APR, box 36.

54. Regarding African American religious humanism, see Anthony B. Pinn, *Varieties of African American Religious Experience* (Minneapolis: Fortress Press, 1998), 175; *Why Lord? Suffering and Evil in Black Theology* (New York: Continuum, 1995), 141; and *By These Hands: A Documentary History of African American Humanism* (New York: New York University Press, 2001), 150. Cornel West, *Prophesy Deliverance: An Afro-American Revolutionary Christianity* (Philadelphia: Westminster Press, 1982), 40, 89, 137, 140. Rufus Burrow Jr., *Personalism: A Critical Introduction* (St. Louis: Chalice Press, 1999), 12, 76–89.

55. CUOHROC, 155–56, 158.

56. Anderson, *A. Philip Randolph,* 92–95; Irving Howe, *World of Our Fathers* (New York: Harcourt Brace Jovanovich, 1976), 55, 527–33. CUOHROC, 173.

57. CUOHROC, 179, 183–84.

58. CUOHROC, 179.

59. CUOHROC, 143, 174, 200, 220–21. Roi Ottley and William J. Weatherby, *The Negro in New York: An Informal Social History* (New York: New York Public Library, 1967), 225.

60. CUOHROC, 181–82, 186.

61. CUOHROC, 183–84, 186.

62. CUOHROC, 184, 186, 215.

63. Randolph, "My Father's Politics." Marable, "A. Philip Randolph," 12.

NOTES TO CHAPTER 2

1. Roi Ottley and William J. Weatherby, *The Negro in New York: An Informal Social History* (New York: New York Public Library, 1967), 225–28. The

Reminiscences of A. Philip Randolph, in the Columbia University Oral History Research Office Collection, 1972, 18 (hereafter cited as CUOHROC), 211.

2. Ottley and Weatherby, *The Negro in New York*, 225–28.

3. CUOHROC, 211. Theodore Kornweibel Jr., *No Crystal Stair: Black Life and the* Messenger, *1917–1928* (Westport, Conn.: Greenwood Press, 1975), 50–55.

4. "The New Patriotism," *Messenger*, November 1917, 36. This statement was reprinted in the March 1919 issue. The editors, "The *Messenger* Is the Only Magazine of Scientific Radicalism in the World Published by Negroes," *Messenger*, November 1917, 21.

5. A. Philip Randolph and Chandler Owen, "The Negro—A Menace to Radicalism," *Messenger*, May–June 1919, 20. Editorial, "The United Brotherhood of Elevator and Switchboard Operators of New York," *Messenger*, November 1917, 12.

6. CUOHROC, 185. Editorial, "The Negro in Politics," *Messenger*, July 1918, 18. Randolph and Owen, "The Negro—A Menace to Radicalism," 20.

7. Walter Everette Hawkins, "Credo," *Messenger*, suppl., March 1919, 2. Hawkins's book *Chords and Discords*, published in 1920, was advertised several times in the *Messenger*.

8. Walter Everette Hawkins, "Too Much Religion," and "Here and Hereafter," *Messenger*, November 1917, 27. Benjamin E. Mays, *The Negro's God as Reflected in His Literature* (Boston: Chapman & Grimes, 1938): 206–9, 218. Significantly, Mays did not place Hawkins's religious poetry in his section "Ideas of God Involving Frustration, Doubt, God's Impotence and His Non-Existence." In another section, Mays cited other poems by Hawkins that stressed God's universality and impartiality, similar in tone to Howard Thurman's notion that God does not discriminate but unites all humankind. In "God Unites All Human Kind," Hawkins's first stanza reads: "Islam and Buddha and Christ, all but tend Toward the same goal,—these but means toward an end."

9. Claude McKay, "J'Accuse," *Messenger*, October 1919, 33. Several of McKay's poems appeared in the *Messenger* in these early years: "Labor Day" *Messenger*, September 1919, 31; "Birds of Prey" *Messenger* 2 (December 1919): 23; and, printed as part of an editorial, his famous "If We Must Die" *Messenger*, September 1919, 4. "If We Must Die" appeared again in an editorial on the Tulsa riot, *Messenger*, July 1921, 218.

10. Bertuccio Dantino to editors, March 14, 1919, *Messenger*, May–June 1919, 28, 30. C. L. Dellums, "The International President of the Brotherhood of Sleeping Car Porters and Civil Rights Leader," typescript of an oral history conducted in 1970 and 1971 by Joyce Henderson, Regional Oral History Office, Bancroft Library, University of California at Berkeley, 1973, 28.

11. The *Messenger* regularly endorsed the *Crucible* from July 1919 to February 1920. Beginning in August 1920, the two ads were combined to advertise

both the bookstore and the *Crucible*. The bookstore featured Annie Besant's *Marriage: As It Was, Is, and Should Be*, which was originally published in 1879, during the time when Ms. Besant became an active and influential speaker for the freethought movement in England. Affiliated with the National Secular League, she wrote on the subordinate role of women. See Bertuccio Dantino, "A Bronzed God—A Story," *Messenger*, March 1920, 9, and "A Bronzed God— Part 2," *Messenger*, April–May 1920, 11–12.

12. CUOHROC, 221. Robert Ingersoll, "Ingersoll's Vision of the Future," *Messenger*, May–June 1919, 26. For other references to Ingersoll, see *Messenger*, December 1920, 177. Lovett Fort-Whiteman, "The Eternal Magdalene," *Messenger*, January 1918, 25. Mark Solomon, *The Cry Was Unity: Communists and African Americans, 1917–36* (Jackson: University Press of Mississippi: 1998), 46–47.

13. "Suggestions for Good Reading," *Messenger*, September 1919, 14. "Who's Who—Scott Nearing," *Messenger*, March 1919, 23–24.

14. Upton Sinclair, *Profits of Religion: An Essay in Economic Interpretation* (Pasadena, Calif.: Author, 1918). On Sinclair's religious disillusionment, see Martin E. Marty, *The Noise of Conflict, 1919–1941*, vol. 2 of *Modern American Religion* (Chicago: University of Chicago Press, 1991), 70. Simon N. Patten, *The Social Basis of Religion* (New York: Macmillan, 1911). For background on Simon N. Patten, see John Everett Rutherford, *Religion in Economics: A Study of John Bates Clark, Richard T. Ely, and Simon N. Patten* (New York: King's Crown Press, 1946). R. Laurence Moore, "Secularization: Religion and the Social Sciences," in *Between the Times: The Travail of the Protestant Establishment in America, 1900–1960*, edited by William R. Hutchison (Cambridge: Cambridge University Press, 1989), 234. Donald Meyer, *The Protestant Search for Political Realism, 1919–1941*, 2nd ed. (Middletown, Conn.: Wesleyan University Press, 1988), 2.

15. For an overview of the complex relationship between Christianity and socialism, see Robert T. Handy, "Christianity and Socialism in America, 1900–1920," in *Protestantism and Social Christianity*, vol. 6 of *Modern American Protestantism and Its World*, edited by Martin E. Marty (Munich: K. G. Saur, 1992), 83–98. Jacob H. Dorn, ed., *Socialism and Christianity in Early 20th Century America* (Westport, Conn.: Greenwood Press, 1998).

16. W. A. Domingo, "Socialism: The Negroes' Hope," *Messenger*, July 1919, 22. Domingo's views corresponded to those of the black socialist preacher Rev. George Washington Woodbey. See Philip S. Foner, *American Socialism and Black Americans: From the Age of Jackson to World War II* (Westport, Conn.: Greenwood Press, 1977), 162. Solomon, *The Cry Was Unity*, 4, 9, 27.

17. Domingo, "Socialism: The Negroes' Hope," 22.

18. For Randolph and Owen's series "Why Negroes Should Be Socialists," see *Messenger* issues of October 1919, 15; December 1919, 13; and

October 1920, 106–7. CUOHROC, 178–79. Announcement of the National Brotherhood Association Convention, *Messenger*, September 1919, 22. According to one *Messenger* editorial, the Brotherhood was a "Negro Federation of Labor . . . composed of Negro unions of all kinds from Florida to New York." Editorial, "The National Brotherhood Association," *Messenger*, August 1919, 7.

19. Chandler Owen, "The Failure of Negro Leaders," *Messenger*, January 1918, 23. At this point, Owen named W. E. B. Du Bois, Kelly Miller, William Pickens, Archibald Grimké, James W. Johnson, Robert Russamoton, Fred R. Moore, William H Lewis, and Charles W. Anderson as the "old crowd Negroes." Editorial, "New Leadership for the Negro," *Messenger*, May–June 1919, 9. Chandler Owen, "What Will Be the Real Status of the Negro after the War?" *Messenger*, March 1919, 13–17.

20. Owen, "What Will Be the Real Status of the Negro," 16. The editors, "The Cause of and Remedy for Race Riots," *Messenger*, September 1919, 19. Editorial, *Messenger*, October 1921, 257. To see how this issue lingered on in *Messenger* editorials, see Chandler Owen, "A Voice from the Dead," *Messenger*, April 1922, 391.

21. A. Philip Randolph, "A New Crowd—A New Negro," *Messenger*, May–June 1919, 26–27.

22. Advertisement for September *Messenger*, August 1919, 33. "Notice to the Public," *Messenger*, September 1919, 34. W. A. Domingo, "If We Must Die," *Messenger*, September 1919, 4. For background on the critical year of 1919, see Kornweibel, *No Crystal Stair*, 66–104, especially his third chapter, "Black Radicalism and the Red Scare." See also Kornweibel's *"Seeing Red": Federal Campaigns against Black Militancy, 1919–1925* (Bloomington: Indiana University Press, 1998), 76–99. The fifth chapter, "The Most Dangerous of All the Negro Publications," concentrates on the radical years from 1918 to 1919, when radicalism and violence peaked in the fall of 1919. John Hope Franklin and Alfred A. Moss Jr., *From Slavery to Freedom: A History of Negro Americans*, 6th ed. (New York: Knopf, 1988), 313.

23. The editors, "A Report on the Chicago Riot by an Eyewitness Account," *Messenger*, September 1919, 11–12.

24. The editors, "The Cause and Remedy for Race Riots," 16–17.

25. The editors, "The Cause of and Remedy for Race Riots," 19.

26. The editors, "The Cause of and Remedy for Race Riots," 21. For more on the battle between the federal authorities and the *Messenger* editors, see Kornweibel, *Seeing Red*, 89, 92.

27. Editorial, "The Failure of the Negro Church," *Messenger*, October 1919, 6.

28. Ibid.

29. Ibid.

30. Ibid.

31. George E. Haynes, *The Trend of the Races* (New York: Council of Women for Home Missions and Missionary Education Movement of the United States and Canada, 1922), 14.

32. Editorial, "The Trend of the Times—Pickens," *Messenger*, March 1920, 11. Editorial, "The *Messenger* Lecture," *Messenger*, March 1920, 5. Editorial, "*Messenger* Editors Receive Ovation," *Messenger*, March 1920, 13. For the notices advertising *Messenger* lectures, see *Messenger* issues of August 1919, 20; September 1919, 21; and October 1919, 31. Philip S. Foner, *American Socialism and Black Americans: From the Age of Jackson to World War II* (Westport, Conn.: Greenwood Press, 1977), 266.

33. Editorial, "The Messenger Lecture," *Messenger*, March 1920, 5.

34. Editorial, "Some Negro Ministers," *Messenger*, March 1920, 3.

35. Editorial, "The Friends of Negro Freedom," *Messenger*, April–May 1920, 3–5. Editorial "The Open Forum," *Messenger*, April–May 1920, 16.

36. Editorial, "The Friends of Negro Freedom," 4.

37. Editorial, "The Friends of Negro Freedom," 4. Editorial, "The Friends of Negro Freedom," *Messenger*, August 1920, 1. "Resolutions of the Convention of the Friends of Negro Freedom," *Messenger*, September 1920, 88–90. Editorial, *Messenger*, November 1920, 128. Editorial, "The Friends of Negro Freedom," *Messenger*, December 1920, 163.

38. For background on the religious aspects of Garveyism, see Randall K. Burkett's *Garveyism as a Religious Movement: The Institutionalization of a Black Civil Religion* (Metuchen, N.J.: Scarecrow Press, 1978), and *Black Redemption: Churchmen Speak for the Garvey Movement* (Philadelphia: Temple University Press, 1978). For religious and cultural aspects of the Ku Klux Klan in the 1920s, see Stanley Coben, *Rebellion against Victorianism: The Impetus for Cultural Change in 1920s America* (New York: Oxford University Press, 1991); David H. Bennett, *The Party of Fear: From Nativist Movements to the New Right in American History* (Chapel Hill: University of North Carolina Press, 1988); David M. Chalmers, *Hooded Americanism: The First Century of the Ku Klux Klan, 1865–1965* (New York: Doubleday, 1965); Shawn Lay, ed., *The Invisible Empire in the West: Toward a New Historical Appraisal of the Ku Klux Klan of the 1920s* (Urbana: University of Illinois Press, 1992).

39. Editorial, "The Garvey Movement: A Promise or a Menace to Negroes," *Messenger*, October 1920, 114–15. Editorial, "The Garvey Movement: A Promise or a Menace," *Messenger*, December 1920, 170–72. A. Philip Randolph, "Garveyism," *Messenger*, September 1921, 250–52. Editorial, "Garvey's Social Equality Cables," *Messenger*, October 1921, 259. For more background on Garvey's link to the Ku Klux Klan, see John White, *Black Leadership in America: From Booker T. Washington to Jesse Jackson*, 2nd ed. (London: Longman, 1985), 88–89. White's fourth chapter, "Marcus Garvey: Jamaican Mes-

siah," provides a succinct overview of Garvey's movement in the United States. In his essay "The Virtuoso Illusionist: Marcus Garvey," Clarence E. Walker argues that "Garvey's call for black emigration to Africa was endorsed by the Ku Klux Klan and the Anglo-Saxon Clubs, two racist organizations flourishing in postwar America. In Garvey, the Klan and Anglo-Saxon Clubs found an answer to their prayers," and for his part, Garvey admired these racist organizations for their honesty in portraying "the true racial sensibilities of white America." Clarence E. Walker, *Deromanticizing Black History: Critical Essays and Reappraisals* (Knoxville: University of Tennessee Press, 1991), 53.

40. W. H. Tibbs, "The Ku Klux Klan in Chicago," *Messenger*, December 1919, 27. Editorial, "The American Legion—Our National Ku Klux Klan," *Messenger*, February 1920, 4, 9–10. Editorial, "Americanism," *Messenger*, September 1920, 80. "An Open Letter to America on the Ku Klux Klan," *Messenger*, December 1920, 167. One *Messenger* editorial remarked that Tibbs, a champion of black rights in Chicago, had been harassed by A. Mitchell Palmer and Woodrow Wilson, and consequently the *Messenger* tried to establish a Negro Radical Defense Fund for Tibbs and other radicals who needed the support from such persecution. See Editorial, "Persecuted Negro Radicals," *Messenger*, March 1920, 5.

41. Editorial, "Coming Race Riots," *Messenger*, July 1921, 210. Editorial, "Mob Violence and the Ku Klux Klan," *Messenger*, September 1921, 244–46.

42. Editorial, "W. H. Moses," *Messenger*, October 1921, 264–66.

43. Editorial, "The Friends of Negro Freedom," *Messenger*, November 1921, 274.

44. Editorial, "Twelve Smallest Persons in America," *Messenger*, November 1922, 517. Editorial, "A Negro Almost as Low as Garvey," *Messenger*, November 1922, 519–20 (italics in original).

45. "An Open Letter to America on the Ku Klux Klan," 168.

46. Editorial, "United Front against the Ku Klux Menace," *Messenger*, September 1922, 478–79. Editorial, "Episcopalians Assail Ku Klux," *Messenger*, October 1922, 497–98.

47. Editorial, "Episcopalians Assail Ku Klux," 498. During this period, Randolph wrote two articles on the "The Invisible Government of Negro Institutions" for the *Messenger*. According to Randolph, the Negro church, an integral part of this invisible government, was "usually the tool of the ruling class . . . a mental chloroform with which the masses are lulled to sleep." Although references to religious institutions remained positive, the *Messenger* still at times criticized its perceived shortcomings. See Editors, "Economic Interpretation of Leadership," *Messenger*, October 1920, 107–9; Editors, "The Invisible Government of Negro Institutions," *Messenger*, September 1920, 90–91.

48. Sondra Kathryn Wilson, ed., *The* Messenger *Reader: Stories, Poetry, and Essays from the* Messenger *Magazine* (New York: Modern Library, 2000). Wil-

son places the *Messenger* in the context of the Harlem Renaissance and traces its contribution to this cultural movement, just as the NAACP's *Crisis* and the NUL's *Opportunity* magazines did. "The *Messenger*'s connection to the Harlem Renaissance was not forged systematically but rather was a product of African Americans' response to zealous radical voices crusading for socialism. Though most African-Americans rejected the journal's philosophy of socialism, many race leaders accepted the major elements of its message" (xxiv). See also Kornweibel's chapter in *No Crystal Stair*, "The *Messenger* and the Harlem Renaissance," 105–31.

49. "Plan Tablet in Memory of Leaders," *Messenger*, January 1925, 53–59, and February 1925, 82, 105–9. In his 1973 reminiscences, Randolph made several admiring references to the artist H. O. Tanner.

50. Editorial, "A Ray of Hope," *Messenger*, June 1924, 179. Other editorials commented on church conventions and meetings. One commended the election to the bishopric of such "high types" as J. A. Gregg, Reverdy Ransom, and A. L. Gaines. Another editorial stated, "Up to the present time, for the larger part, the average Negro convention has been little more than *oratory applied to social problems*" (italics in original). See editorials, "The A.M.E. Conference," and "Coming Conventions," *Messenger*, July 1924, 211–12.

51. "Olivet—A Community-Serving Church in Chicago," *Messenger*, September 1924, 282.

52. Robert W. Bagnall, review of *The History of the Negro Church*, by Carter G. Woodson, *Messenger*, May 1923, 724.

53. Carter G. Woodson, *The History of the Negro Church* (Washington, D.C.: Associated Publishers, 1921). Bagnall, review.

54. Woodson, *The History of the Negro Church*, 242, 248–50, 254, 282. Editorial, "The Friends of Negro Freedom," *Messenger*, May 1922, 411. "The Open Forum," *Messenger*, April–May 1920, 16. Editorial, "Who's Who: Carter G. Woodson," *Messenger*, September 1922, 489. Editorial, "The Journal of Negro History," *Messenger*, January 1924, 6.

55. Editorial, "Bishop Charles Williams and George Frazier Miller," *Messenger*, July 1921, 213. The Editors, "The Negro Radicals—Part 2," *Messenger*, December 1919, 21. Editorial, "A Record of the Darker Races," *Messenger*, September 1920, 84. Editorial, "Some Negro Ministers," *Messenger*, March 1920, 3. Miller's articles are in the *Messenger*, March 1919, 12–13; May–June 1919, 13–14; July 1919, 23; August 1919, 21; September 1919, 30–31; and October 1919, 19, 24, 31. Regarding Rev. Miller's connection to Randolph's socialist magazine, historian Clarence Taylor wrote, "By ideologically connecting socialism and Christianity, he attempted to put the black church in the vanguard of addressing economic concerns of blacks." Clarence Taylor, *The Black Churches of Brooklyn* (New York: Columbia University Press, 1994), 122–23.

56. Editorial, "The Fundamentalists vs. the Modernists," *Messenger*, Febru-

ary 1924, 40. Marty, *The Noise of Conflict*, 155–214. Marty's chapter "The Protestant House Divided" provides historical background on this critical religious debate in American Protestant history.

57. CUOHROC, 189, 192.

58. William Pickens, "Church Wars," *Messenger*, January 1924, 30. See editorial, "Some Negro Ministers," *Messenger*, March 1920, 3. William Pickens, "Things Nobody Believes: A Lesson in Religion," *Messenger*, February 1923, 614 (italics in original).

59. Pickens, "Things Nobody Believes," 615 (italics in original).

60. Advertisement, *Messenger*, March 1923, 624.

61. Henry Ward Beecher (1813–87) famed Brooklyn, New York, Congregational minister and spokesman for liberal Protestantism. Although Pickens never cited his source for Beecher's renunciation of a material heaven and hell, published sermons show that Pickens's interpretation of Beecher's views was accurate. For example, in October 1870, Beecher delivered two Sunday sermons, "The Heavenly State" and "Future Punishment," which expressed the views described by Pickens. See Henry Ward Beecher, *The Original Plymouth Pulpit: Sermons by Henry Ward Beecher* (Boston: Pilgrim Press, 1871), vol. 5, 75–113. Pickens believed that Beecher "deserved the love of the colored people of the United States," probably because of Beecher's well-known antislavery position before and after the Civil War. Beecher's thought prefigured the emergence of Protestant modernism, or liberal Protestantism, a radical readjustment of Protestant theology in light of new intellectual and scientific developments. For background on Beecher's life and thought as representing nineteenth-century Victorian America, see Clifford E. Clark Jr., *Henry Ward Beecher: Spokesman for a Middle-Class America* (Urbana: University of Illinois Press, 1978); and William G. McLoughlin, *The Meaning of Henry Ward Beecher: An Essay on the Shifting Values of Mid-Victorian America, 1840–1870* (New York: Knopf, 1970).

62. William Pickens, "Intelligent Christianity: Not the Fear of Hell," *Messenger*, April 1923, 668–69.

63. John C. Carroll, "Things Everybody Believes," *Messenger*, April 1923, 673.

64. Ibid., 674.

65. Ibid.

66. Editorial, "The Fundamentalists vs. the Modernists," *Messenger*, February 1924, 40.

67. William Pickens, "Speaking of Miracles," *Messenger*, June 1923, 745. E. Ethelred Brown, "The God of an Eternal Penitentiary," *Messenger*, June 1923, 745–46. Gilbert Osofsky, *Harlem: The Making of a Ghetto: Negro New York, 1890–1930*, 2nd ed. (New York: Harper & Row, 1971), 132. Osofsky mentioned Brown's West Indian background. For more on Brown's contribution to "Black Humanism and the Unitarians," see Anthony B. Pinn, *Varieties of*

African American Religious Experience (Minneapolis: Fortress Press, 1998), 175–79.

68. Kelly Miller Jr., "Science and Religion," *Messenger*, October 1923, 848. William Pickens, "Church Wars," *Messenger*, January 1924, 30. George S. Schuyler, "Shafts and Darts," *Messenger*, February 1924, 4. J. A. Rogers, "Critical Excursions and Reflections," *Messenger*, February 1924, 51. J. A. Rogers, "Science Versus Superstition.," *Messenger*, March 1925, 138. See editorial, "Religious Reaction," *Messenger*, August 1922, 458. Also George S. Schuyler and Theophilus Lewis, "Shafts and Darts: A Page of Calumny and Satire," *Messenger*, January 1925, 36. Historian Martin Marty presented John Roach Straton as an "extreme fundamentalist." See Marty, *The Noise of Conflict*, 164–76. See also Jeffrey P. Moran, "Reading Race into the Scopes Trial: African American Elites, Science, and Fundamentalism," *Journal of American History*, December 2003, 891–911.

69. Advertisement, "Next Month! Is Christianity a Menace to the Negro? $10 for Best Answer," *Messenger*, February 1927, 34 (italics in original).

70. Schuyler and Lewis, "Shafts and Darts," 35. Schuyler claimed that he and Theophilus Lewis "are both atheists." Because of the sarcastic and irreverent tone of Schuyler's writings in the *Messenger*, it is often difficult to assess the sincerity of his statements. John W. Baddy, "Is Christianity a Menace to the Negro?" *Messenger*, March 1927, 66, 86. Editorial, "The Aframerican Digest" *Messenger*, December 1927, 362.

71. Abram L. Harris, at this time a promising black intellectual and a contributing editor to the *Messenger*, later coauthored with Sterling D. Spero the classic early study on black labor: *The Black Worker: The Negro and the Labor Movement* (New York: Columbia University Press, 1931).

72. John Haynes Holmes to Randolph, January 13, 1926, A. Philip Randolph Papers, box 36 (hereafter cited as APR), 1. Holmes and Randolph were lifelong friends. For more information on "labor churches" and other prolabor Protestant ministers, see Meyer, *The Protestant Search for Political Realism*, 76–81, 126–27. For the two announcements of the debate," see "Orthodox Christianity!" and "Does Orthodox Christianity Handicap Negro Progress?" *Messenger*, May 1927, 140, 171. On how the *Messenger* staff viewed the debate as an important aspect of their educational mission, see "Messenger Gossip," *Messenger*, May 1927, 160. "Messenger Gossip," *Messenger*, June 1927, 174. "This Month," *Messenger*, June 1927, 190.

73. For the *Messenger*'s three religious perspectives, see advertisement, "Next Month! Is Christianity a Menace to the Negro?" 34.

74. See Philip Abbott, *Leftward Ho!: V. F. Calverton and American Radicalism* (Westport, Conn.: Greenwood Press, 1993). The *Modern Quarterly* ads in the *Messenger* appeared regularly from May 1926 to July 1927. V. F. Calverton, "Orthodox Religion: Does It Handicap Negro Progress?" *Messenger*, July 1927, 221.

75. Calverton, "Orthodox Religion," 236.

76. John Baddy to George Schuyler, "Open Forum," *Messenger*, July 1927, 222. For this column, Baddy, curious about public reaction to his essay, wrote Schuyler asking, "Have you had much comment on my essay?" See also John W. Baddy, "Error of Kelly Miller and Calverton," *Messenger*, October 1927, 297; V. F. Calverton, "The Negro and Religion, or Errors and Mr. Baddy," *Messenger*, January 1928, 5; John W. Baddy, "More Errors of Mr. Calverton," *Messenger*, February 1928, 43. See Abbott, *Leftward Ho!* 198–201, 217. One of Niebuhr's biographers provides background to the debate among Niebuhr, Hooks, and Calverton which took place on December 12, 1934. See Richard W. Fox, *Reinhold Niebuhr: A Biography* (New York: Pantheon Books, 1985), 169. V. F. Calverton, *The Passing of the Gods* (New York: Modern Library, 1934).

77. Editorial, "Who's Who—Kelly Miller," *Messenger*, March 1919, 22–23. Kelly Miller Jr., "Science and Religion," *Messenger*, October 1923, 848. Randolph's editorial comment can be found in *Messenger*, July 1927, 236.

78. Kelly Miller Jr., "Orthodox Christianity: Does It Handicap Negro Progress?" *Messenger*, August 1927, 254.

79. Miller, "Orthodox Christianity." For St. Clair Drake's treatment of the American Negro's providential role in Africa's redemption, see his *Redemption of Africa and Black Religion* (Chicago: Third World Press, 1970). Between November 1922 and February 1923, Randolph wrote a series of articles in the *Messenger* entitled "The Only Way to Redeem Africa," which reveal his deep awareness of this fundamental concept of African American religion.

80. Miller, "Orthodox Christianity," 255.

81. Ibid.

82. Raymond Gavins, *The Perils and Prospects of Southern Black Leadership: Gordon Blaine Hancock, 1884–1970* (Durham, N.C.: Duke University Press, 1977), 34, 189. CUOHROC, 144. Gavins depicts Hancock as an effective Baptist preacher and black leader before the civil rights movement, albeit hampered by the limitations of his times. In his insistence that the "church wage war against prejudice and work for racial uplift, Hancock actualized the social gospel and spaded valuable ground for the seeds of present day black theology" (189). Hancock's position in Richmond's black community brought him "prestige normally accorded only the pastors of First African and Ebenezer, Richmond's silk-stocking Negro Baptist churches" (34).

83. Gavins, *The Perils and Prospects of Southern Black Leadership*, 26, 30. Harris earned his Ph.D. in economics from Columbia and held professorships at Howard and the University of Chicago. A few years later, Harris surfaced as a strong critic of Randolph's effectiveness as a labor leader. In their 1931 book *The Black Worker*, Harris and Sterling Spero attacked Randolph's leadership of the Brotherhood in the early 1930s. Critical of the way that Randolph handled the 1928 strike, they wrote, "The failure of the Brotherhood has been laid at

Randolph's door. The extraordinary extent to which he dominated the move-ment and the insistence with which he kept his personality and name in the fore-ground of all its activities make such judgment inevitable. Perhaps the most striking shortcoming of Randolph's tactics was his hunger for publicity. He seemed possessed of the notion that publicity was a good in itself which would in some mystical manner win victory for the porters" (459–60).

84. Gordon B. Hancock, "Orthodox Christianity: Does It Handicap Negro Progress? Yes and No," *Messenger*, September 1927, 278.

85. Ibid.

86. Ibid., 278–79.

87. A. Philip Randolph, "The State and Policy of the Brotherhood," *Messen-ger*, June 1926, 185. Methodist Federation for Social Service, "The Social Ser-vice Bulletin," *Messenger*, May 1927, 164.

88. A. Philip Randolph, "Randolph's Reply to Perry Howard" *Messenger*, October–November 1925, 352.

89. A Philip Randolph, "A. Philip Randolph Answers New Questions for Perry Howard," *Messenger*, December 1925, 400, 402.

90. A. Philip Randolph, "A Reply to Joe D. 'Blibb,' 'Idiot-or' of the Chicago 'Flip,' Misnamed the Whip," *Messenger*, December 1925, 379.

91. A. Philip Randolph, "Reply to the Industrial Defense Association, Inc. Boston, Mass." n.d., APR, box 10.

92. Ibid.

93. Peter W. Williams, *America's Religions: Traditions and Cultures* (Urbana: University of Illinois Press, 1998), 409. See also Martin E. Marty, *The Infidel: Freethought and American Religion* (Cleveland: Meridian Books, 1961).

NOTES TO CHAPTER 3

1. "Pullman Porter in Mysterious Death in Georgia," *New York Age*, April 12, 1930, 1. "Brotherhood Member Lynched in Georgia," *Black Worker*, April 1, 1930, 1. "Lynch Pullman Porter—The Body Hung to Tree," *Chicago De-fender*, April 12, 1930, 1.

2. "Brotherhood Member Lynched in Georgia," 1.

3. A. Philip Randolph, "The Case of the Pullman Porter," *Messenger*, July 1925, 254–55. A. Philip Randolph, "Pullman Porters Need Own Union," *Mes-senger*, August 1925, 289. A. Philip Randolph, "The Pullman Company and the Pullman Porter," *Messenger*, September 1925, 312.

4. William H. Harris, *Keeping the Faith: A. Philip Randolph, Milton P. Web-ster, and the Brotherhood of Sleeping Car Porters, 1925–1937* (Urbana: Univer-sity of Illinois Press, 1977), 20–21. "Big Protest Mass Meeting," *Black Worker*, April 1, 1930, 1.

5. Citizens Committee, "Citizens Back Porters' Fight," *Black Worker*, July 1, 1930, 3.

6. "Wife of Lynched Pullman Porter Is Left Penniless," *Black Worker*, June 1, 1930, 3. "Some Donors to the Wilkins Fund," *Black Worker*, July 1, 1930, 1. "Division Notes—New York," *Black Worker*, July 1, 1930, 2. "Division Notes—Oakland," *Black Worker*, July 1, 1930, 4. "Division Notes—Chicago," *Black Worker*, August 1, 1930, 2.

7. "PPBA Memorial Services Fall Flat," *Black Worker*, July 1, 1930, 1.

8. Ashley L. Totten, "Strange Christians," *Black Worker*, July 1, 1930, 2.

9. A. Philip Randolph, "Negro Labor and the Church," in *Labor Speaks for Itself on Religion: A Symposium of Labor Leaders throughout the World*, edited by Jerome Davis (New York: Macmillan, 1929), 79.

10. "The Pullman Wage Conference Farce," *Messenger*, March 1926, 80. A. Philip Randolph, "Notes of the Brotherhood of Sleeping Car Porters," *Messenger*, January 1926, 15. Tampa Division Questionnaire, n.d., in A. Philip Randolph Papers (hereafter cited as APR), box 10.

11. The cartoons lampooning both prominent ministers and leaders as Uncle Tom figures and Negro churches are in *Messenger* issues December 1925, 382; January 1926, 11, 14; February 1926, 36; May 1926, 153; and April 1927, 128.

12. The Reminiscences of A. Philip Randolph, in the Columbia University Oral History Research Office Collection (hereafter cited as CUOHROC), 1972, 18, 276–77. Harris, *Keeping the Faith*, 20–21. Randolph, "Negro Labor and the Church," 82–83.

13. Webster to Randolph, August 20, 1928, Brotherhood of Sleeping Car Porters Papers, Chicago Division Operating Files, 1925–44 (boxes 1–6), Chicago Historical Society, box 3, folder 7 (hereafter cited as BSCP). Randolph to Webster, August 23, 1928, BSCP, box 3, folder 7.

14. Randolph, "Negro Labor and the Church," 81. Editorial, "Chisum," *Messenger*, February 1926, 54, 60.

15. Editorial, "Chisum," *Messenger*, February 1926, 54. Randolph, "Notes of the Brotherhood of Sleeping Car Porters," *Messenger*, January 1926, 25. Editorial, "Pullman Company's Conference in Washington, D.C.," *Messenger*, December 1925, 389.

16. Editorial, "Chisum," *Messenger*, February 1926, 54, 60. Randolph, "Negro Labor and the Church," 81.

17. Randolph, "Negro Labor and the Church," 79–80.

18. Ransom to Randolph, dated December 17, 1925, *Messenger*, March 1926, 93–94. Randolph, "Negro Labor and the Church," 82.

19. Ransom to Randolph, 93–94.

20. George S. Schuyler, "Shafts and Darts," *Messenger*, May 1926, 143. Untitled cartoon, *Messenger*, April 1927, 128. "Silenced," *Messenger*, January 1927,

22. Editorial, "A New Bishop-Politician," *Messenger*, June 1927, 190–91. Editorial, "Bishop A. J. Carey Indicted," *Black Worker*, November 15, 1929, 4.

21. Randolph to Webster, August 27, 1928, BSCP, box 3, folder 7. A. Philip Randolph, "Reply to the Industrial Defense Association, Inc. Boston, Mass.," n.d., APR, box 10.

22. Randolph, "Notes of the Brotherhood of Sleeping Car Porters," January 1926, 24–25. John J. Leary Jr., "The Porter Wants More Than a Tip," March 24, 1934, APR, box 54.

23. Ibid.

24. A. Philip Randolph, "The State and Policy of the Brotherhood," *Messenger*, June 1926, 186.

25. Randolph, "Negro Labor and the Church," 80. David W. Wills, An Enduring Distance: Black Americans and the Establishment," in *Between the Times: The Travail of the Protestant Establishment in America, 1900–1960*, edited by William R. Hutchison (Cambridge: Cambridge University Press, 1989), 171.

26. "Porters Hold Unemployment Conference," *Black Worker*, April 1, 1930, 1. A. Philip Randolph, "The Truth about the Brotherhood of Sleeping Car Porters," *Messenger*, February 1926, 37. Randolph, "Notes of the Brotherhood of Sleeping Car Porters," January 1926, 15, 24–25, 31. Randolph, "Negro Labor and the Church," 81.

27. Randolph, "Notes of the Brotherhood of Sleeping Car Porters," January 1926, 24. Harris, *Keeping the Faith*, 4. According to Harris, establishing the BSCP on the same par as the other four major railway unions was considered essential by Randolph and BSCP strategists. The "Big Four" were the Brotherhood of Locomotive Engineers, the Order of Railway conductors, the Brotherhood of Locomotive Firemen, and the Brotherhood of Railway Trainmen. Randolph, CUOHROC, 263. Editorial, "A New Bishop-Politician," *Messenger*, July 1927, 190–91. A. Philip Randolph, "Open Letter to the Pullman Company," *Messenger*, July 1927, 240.

28. Randolph, "Notes of the Brotherhood of Sleeping Car Porters," January 1926, 24. A. Philip Randolph, "Notes of the Brotherhood," *Messenger*, July 1926, 221.

29. Randolph to Webster, January 8, 1927, BSCP, box 1, folder 14. Randolph to Webster, September 26, 1926, BSCP, box 1, folder 10. The Boston Citizens' Committee, "The Pullman Porters' Struggle (The Story of a Race's Exploitation)," n.d., APR, box 10.

30. CUOHROC, 271.

31. Editorial, "A New Bishop-Politician," 190–91. Randolph, "An Open Letter to the Pullman Company," 240.

32. Randolph, "Notes of the Brotherhood," July 1926, 221. A. Philip Randolph, "Ye Pioneer Brotherhood Men," *Messenger*, April 1927, 129. New York

Leading Negro Ministers Endorse Pullman Porter Union, March 13, 1927, BSCP, box 2, folder 2. Randolph, "Open Letter to the Pullman Company," 240.

33. Randolph, "Notes of the Brotherhood of Sleeping Car Porters," January 1926, 25.

34. E. J. Bradley, "Some of My Early Experiences Organizing Pullman Porters in St. Louis," n.d., APR, box 10. Editorial, "E. J. Bradley," *Messenger*, January 1927, 24.

35. Bradley, "Some of My Early Experiences." Randolph to Roy Lancaster, August 3, 1927, APR, box 7.

36. A. Philip Randolph, "Notes on the Brotherhood of Sleeping Car Porters—Kansas City," *Messenger*, January 1926, 25. Randolph to Webster, September 26, 1926, BSCP, box 1, folder 10. A. Philip Randolph, "Notes of the Brotherhood," *Messenger*, December 1926, 370. Bennie Smith to Ashley Totten, May 24, 1935, APR, box 1.

37. Randolph, "Notes of the Brotherhood of Sleeping Car Porters," January 1926, 2. A. Philip Randolph, "Notes of the Brotherhood," *Messenger*, July 1926, 220.

38. "Report of Proceedings of the Fourth Triennial Convention and Thirty-seventh Anniversary of the Brotherhood of Sleeping Car Porters," 1962, APR, box 14.

39. Randolph, "Notes of the Brotherhood of Sleeping Car Porters," January 1926, 24–25. Randolph, "Negro Labor and the Church," 80.

40. Webster to Ida B. Wells-Barnett, September 15, 1926, BSCP, box 1, folder 10. Benjamin E. Mays and Joseph W. Nicholson, *The Negro's Church* (New York: Institute of Social and Religious Research), 35–36. Ida B. Wells, *Crusade for Justice: The Autobiography of Ida B. Wells*, edited by Alfreda M. Duster (Chicago: University of Chicago Press, 1970), xxvi, xxx, 297–98.

41. "APR Personal—BSCP Organization," December 21, 1925, APR, box 7.

42. Randolph, "Notes of the Brotherhood of Sleeping Car Porters," January 1926, 25. Webster to Randolph, March 5, 1928, BSCP, box 3, folder 3. Wells, *Crusade for Justice*, xxx. "APR Personal—BSCP Organization."

43. Webster to Randolph, September 8, 1926, BSCP, box 1, folder 10. Webster to Randolph, September 16, 1926, BSCP, box 1, folder 10. Webster to Ida B. Well-Barnett, September 15, 1926, box 1, folder 10. Speech of Donald R. Richberg, *Messenger*, December 1926, 373. Speech Made by Mary McDowell, *Messenger*, December 1926, 375. Webster to Randolph, October 13, 1926, BSCP, box 1, folder 11. Editorial, "Twelve Smallest Persons in America," *Messenger*, November 1922, 517. Harris, *Keeping the Faith*, 224.

44. A. Philip Randolph, "The Brotherhood of Sleeping Car Porters: Activities of the Month," *Messenger*, December 1927, 358.

45. Webster to Dad Moore, November 6, 1927, BSCP, box 2, folder 9. Webster to Randolph, November 11, 1927, BSCP, box 2, folder 9. Randolph to Web-

ster, November 2, 1927, BSCP, box 2, folder 9. Randolph to Webster, November 21, 1927, BSCP, box 2, folder 9.

46. A. Philip Randolph, "Notes of the Brotherhood," *Messenger*, March 1926, 89. A. Philip Randolph, "The Organization Tour West," *Messenger*, April 1926, 122. Paul L. Caldwell, "Our Local Struggle to Organize St. Paul, Minnesota," *Messenger*, January 1927, 25.

47. Ibid.

48. Randolph, "Notes of the Brotherhood," *Messenger*, December 1926, 370.

49. Frank R. Crosswaith, "Crusading for the Brotherhood," *Messenger*, June 1926,173.

50. Frank R. Crosswaith, "Crusading for the Brotherhood," 173.

51. Ibid., 174.

52. Horace A. White, "Who Owns the Negro Churches?" *Christian Century*, February 9, 1938, 176–77. Randolph to Rev. Horace White, n.d., APR, box 3. Later, Rev. White actively supported Randolph's march on Washington movement, and Randolph called on him to organize picketing activities in Detroit.

53. Editorial, "Two Spokes in the Wheel: Dad Moore and Clarence E. Ivey," *Messenger*, June 1926, 191. For BSCP activity in the Pacific Northwest, see Randolph, "The Organization Tour West," 122. A. Philip Randolph, "Notes on the Brotherhood," *Messenger*, October 1926, 314.

54. For Bay Area BSCP activities, see Randolph, "The Organization Tour West," 122–23. Randolph, "Notes on the Brotherhood," *Messenger*, October 1926, 314. BSCP Activities of the Month, *Messenger*, December 1927, 358. BSCP Activities of the Month, *Messenger*, March 1928, 65. BSCP Activities of the Month, *Messenger*, April 1928, 89. BSCP Activities of the Month, *Messenger*, May–June 1928, 113.

55. Dad Moore to Webster, March 26, 1927 BSCP, box 2, folder 1. C. L. Dellums, "The International President of the Brotherhood of Sleeping Car Porters and Civil Rights Leader," typescript of an oral history conducted in 1970 and 1971 by Joyce Henderson, Regional Oral History Office, Bancroft Library, University of California at Berkeley, 1973, 26–27.

56. Dellums, "The International President," 36.

57. Ibid., 28–29, 36–37 (italics in original).

58. Randolph, "Notes on the Brotherhood," *Messenger*, July 1926, 220. Brotherhood Activities, *Messenger*, August 1927, 260. BSCP Monthly Activities, *Messenger*, October 1927, 307.

59. Randolph, "Notes on the Brotherhood," *Messenger*, July 1926, 220. Randolph, "Notes on the Brotherhood," *Messenger*, October 1926, 314. Randolph, "Negro Labor and the Church," 81.

60. Randolph, "The Brotherhood's Anniversary," *Messenger*, September

1926, 264–65. Randolph, "The State of the Brotherhood," *Messenger*, February 1927, 56. Randolph, "Reply to the Industrial Defense Association."

61. "Ad for 'Religion and the Working Class,'" *Messenger*, November 1927, 328. George S. Grant, "Religion and the Working Class," *Messenger*, February 1928, 33, 47. George S. Grant, "A Black Mother's Blessing," *Messenger*, November 1927, 338.

62. Randolph to Webster, January 8, 1927, BSCP, box 1, folder 14. Randolph to Webster, February 4, 1927, BSCP, box 1, folder 15. Randolph to Webster, February 17, 1927, BSCP, box 1, folder 15. "Instructions for Giving the Password to a Brother," n.d., BSCP, box 1, folder 15. "Oath of Fealty to the Brotherhood of Sleeping Car Porters," n.d., BSCP, box 1, folder 15.

63. Editorial, "The Menace of Rumors," *Black Worker*, March 15, 1930, 4. "Kansas City Stools Commend Brotherhood," *Black Worker*, June 1, 1930, 2. Ashley L. Totten, "The Voice Is the Voice of Jacob but the Hand Is the Hand of Esau," *Black Worker*, August 1, 1930, 1–2. Ashley L. Totten, "Sample's Nocturnal Visit," *Black Worker*, August 1, 1930. 2. A. Sagittarius, "Study the Bible as an Aid to Your Problems," *Black Worker* July 1, 1930, 2–3. Randolph to Webster, October 4, 1928, BSCP, box 3, folder 8.

64. Oscar Walters, "Am I My Brother's Keeper," *Black Worker*, July 1, 1930, 4.

65. A. Philip Randolph, "Brotherhood and Our Struggle Today," *Black Worker*, November 15, 1929, 1, 3. A. Philip Randolph, "The Brotherhood, the Finest Fruitage of the Fighting Faith of Black Men," *Black Worker*, March 15, 1930, 1. A. Philip Randolph, "Salvation from Within," *Black Worker*, April 1, 1930, 1.

66. A. Philip Randolph, "The Brotherhood and Victory," *Black Worker*, January 15, 1930, 1. A. Philip Randolph, "The Brotherhood Makes Progress toward Goal," *Black Worker*, May 1, 1930, 1. A. Philip Randolph, "Pullman Porters and Industrial Progress," *Black Worker*, January 1, 1930, 1. A. Philip Randolph, "The Brotherhood and the New Year," *Black Worker*, December 15, 1930, 2.

67. Jerome Davis, ed., *Labor Speaks for Itself on Religion: A Symposium of Labor Leaders throughout the World* (New York: Macmillan, 1929), 7–11. Randolph, "Negro Labor and the Church," 74–76.

68. Dennis C. Dickerson, "African American Religious Intellectuals and the Theological Foundations of the Civil Rights Movement, 1930–1955," *Church History* 74:2 (June 2005), 220. Jerome Davis, "A Study of Protestant Church Boards of Control," *American Journal of Sociology*, November 1932, 418–31. Programme of the Biennial Convention and Fifteenth Anniversary Celebration of the Brotherhood of Sleeping Car Porters, September 15–19, 1940, APR, box 5. Dr. Willard Uphaus to Randolph, September 1, 1950, APR, box 5. The Pullman Porters Injunction Fund, September 1, 1931, APR, box 54. Mays and Nicholson, *The Negro's Church*, 100.

69. Lee H. Butler Jr., "African American Christian Churches: The Faith Tradition of a Resistance Culture," in *The Ties That Bind: African American and Hispanic American/Latino/a Theologies in Dialogue*, edited by Anthony Pinn and Benjamin Valentin (New York: Continuum, 2001), 223–33. Randolph, "Negro Labor and the Church," 74–76.

70. Randolph, "Negro Labor and the Church," 76, 78–79.

71. Ibid., 83.

72. Gayraud Wilmore, *Black Religion and Black Radicalism: An Interpretation of the Religious History of Afro-American People*, 2nd ed. (Maryknoll, N.Y.: Orbis Books, 1995), 135–66.

73. The Negro Labor Conference, *Messenger*, January 1928, 13, 21.

74. Randolph to Webster, November 22, 1927, BSCP, box 2, folder 9. George S. Schuyler, "Business & Industry," *Messenger*, January 1928, 14. Memorandum on the Sleeping Car Porters, June 19, 1929, APR, box 10. Editorial, "Negro Labor Conferences," *Messenger*, March 1928, 61, 71. Randolph to John Fitzpatrick, December 16, 1927, BSCP, box 2, folder 10.

75. Resolutions Adopted by Third Negro Labor Conference of Washington, D.C., January 9, 1928, APR, box 10. Third Negro Labor Conference Agenda, January 9, 1928 APR, box 10. "Why Every Porter Should Join the Brotherhood and Pay Dues," n.d., APR, box 54. Speech Delivered over Radio Station WCFL, *Messenger*, March 1928, 66. Martin E. Marty, *The Noise of Conflict, 1919–1941*, vol. 2 of *Modern American Religion* (Chicago: University of Chicago Press, 1991), 362–72.

76. Editorial, "National Negro Labor Conference," *Black Worker*, November 15, 1929, 4. Editorial, "White and Black Leaders Back National Negro Labor Conference," *Black Worker*, January 15, 1930, 1. Editorial, "The National Negro Labor Conference," *Black Worker*, January 15, 1930, 4. "National Negro Labor Conference Epochal Success," *Black Worker*, February 1, 1930, 1. Editorial, "Achievement of Labor Conference," *Black Worker*, February 15, 1930, 4.

77. M. P. Webster, "Sidelights on the National Negro Labor Conference," *Black Worker*, March 1, 1930, 1–2. "Notes of Divisions," *Black Worker*, December 1, 1929, 2.

78. Publicity and Propaganda, APR, box 10, BSCP 7th Biennial Convention, Twenty-fifth Anniversary, 1950, APR, box 5. Webster to Victor Olander, January 6, 1931, BSCP, box 4, folder 1. Labor Conference Program, February 28–March 5, 1940, BSCP, box 5, folder 9.

79. Publicity and Propaganda, n.d., APR, box 10. "Why Every Porter Should Join the Brotherhood and Pay Dues," n.d., APR, box 54. "Brotherhood's Achievements," *Black Worker*, June 1, 1930, 3. Editorial, "Brotherhood's Fifth Anniversary," *Black Worker*, September 1, 1930, 4. A. Philip Randolph, "The

Brotherhood and the New Year," *Black Worker*, December 15, 1929, 1–2. Webster to Randolph, September 21, 1928, BSCP, box 3, folder 8.

80. Webster to Randolph, March 5, 1928, BSCP, box 3, folder 3. Webster to Randolph, March 9, 1928, BSCP, box 3, folder 3. Randolph to Webster, June 25, 1928, BSCP, box 3, folder 6. The Methodist Federation for Social Service, "The Social Service Bulletin," *Messenger*, May 1927, 164–66. Eldon Ernst, "The Interchurch World Movement and the Great Steel Strike of 1919–1920," in *Protestantism and Social Christianity*, vol. 6 of *Modern American Protestantism and Its World*, edited by Martin E. Marty (Munich: K.G. Saur, 1992), 220. For more on the MFSS as evidence for the rise of social gospel radicalism in the 1920s and the flourishing of Christian radicalism in the 1930s, see William McGuire King, "The Emergence of Social Gospel Radicalism: The Methodist Case," in *Protestantism and Social Christianity*, vol. 6 of *Modern American Protestantism and Its World*, edited by Martin E. Marty (Munich: K. G. Saur, 1992), 220–33.

81. Randolph to Webster, August 8, 1928, BSCP, box 3, folder 7. Webster to Randolph, September 4, 1928, BSCP, box 3, folder 8. Randolph to Webster, September 7, 1928, BSCP, box 3, folder 8. Randolph to Webster, September 21, 1928, BSCP, box 3, folder 8.

82. Editorial, "Wall Street Crash and Tips," *Black Worker*, January 1, 1930, 4. Editorial, "The Problem of Unemployment," *Black Worker*, January 15, 1930, 4. Editorial, "Unemployment and Trade Unions, *Black Worker*, April 1, 1930, 4.

83. "Chief of Employment Bureau of New York to Address Unemployment Conference," *Black Worker*, March 15, 1930, 1.

84. "Preachers Endorse Brotherhood," *Black Worker*, March 21, 1932, 1.

85. "Some Pullman Porters' Grievances," *Black Worker*, March 21, 1932, 1. "Porters' Leaders Address White Forums," *Black Worker*, March 21, 1932, 3.

86. Eric Arnesen, *Brotherhoods of Color: Black Railroad Workers and the Struggle for Equality* (Cambridge, Mass.: Harvard University Press, 2001), 101. Mays and Nicholson, *The Negro's Church*, 279. Horace A. White, "Who Owns the Negro Churches?" *Christian Century*, February 9, 1938, 176–77.

87. Mary R. Sawyer, *Black Ecumenism: Implementing the Demands of Justice* (Valley Forge, Pa.: Trinity Press International, 1994), 15, 17, 19.

88. National Negro Congress Official Proceedings—Resolutions on the Negro Church, 1936, APR, box 29.

89. Sawyer, *Black Ecumenism*, 17. Samuel Kelton Roberts, "Crucible for a Vision: The Work of George Edmund Haynes and the Commission on Race Relations" (Ph.D. diss., Columbia University, 1974), 233–40. For the cooperation between George E. Haynes and Randolph, see Wills, "An Enduring Distance," 178–79.

90. A. Philip Randolph, "Story of the Porter—A Saga in Trade Unionism," September 10, 1950, APR, box 5.

NOTES TO CHAPTER 4

1. Ted Posten, "Porters Re-Elect Randolph," *Pittsburgh Courier*, September 28, 1940, 1, 4. Ashley Totten, "Brotherhood's 15th Anniversary," n.d., in A. Philip Randolph Papers (hereafter cited as APR), box 5.

2. Florence Murray, *The Negro Handbook* (New York: W. Malliet, 1942), 60. Vera Chandler Foster and Jessie P. Guzman, "The Negro Press," in *Negro Year Book, 1941–1946* (Atlanta: Foote and Davies, 1947), 386–87.

3. Allan Morrison, "A. Philip Randolph: Dean of Negro Leaders," *Ebony*, November 1958, 102–16. Walter White, *A Man Called White: The Autobiography of Walter White* (New York: Viking Press, 1948), 186.

4. Editorial, "White House Blesses Jim Crow," *Crisis*, November 1940, 350. Morgen S. Jensen, "Trio of Leaders Deny Approving Segregated Army," *Pittsburgh Courier*, October 19, 1940, 1, 5. Editorial, "Negro Officers in the Army," *Pittsburgh Courier*, October 19, 1940, 5. "Urban League Condemns Army Segregation," *Chicago Defender*, October 26, 1940, 3. "Charge White House Trickery: Here Is What Committee Asked for and Here Is What They Were Given," *Pittsburgh Courier*, October 19, 1940, 1.

5. Editorial, "F.D.R. Regrets That Army Policy Was 'Misinterpreted,'" *Crisis*, December 1940, 390. "Leaders at A.F. of L. Confab [in New Orleans]," *Pittsburgh Courier*, November 30, 1940, 3. Jervis Anderson, *A. Philip Randolph: A Biographical Portrait* (New York: Harcourt Brace Jovanovich, 1973), 248–50. E. E. Williams, "Origin of the March on Washington Movement," June 11, 1942, APR, box 25.

6. A. Philip Randolph, "Let's March on Capital 10,000 Strong, Urges Leader of Porters," *Pittsburgh Courier*, January 25, 1941, 13.

7. Editorial, "A. Philip Randolph," *Chicago Defender*, February 8, 1941, 14.

8. Editorial, "Speaking for All Negroes," *Pittsburgh Courier*, February 15, 1941, 6. Editorial, "Slightly Effective Embarrassment," *Pittsburgh Courier*, May 24, 1941, 10. Editorial, "That March on Washington," *Pittsburgh Courier*, June 14, 1941, 5. Charley Cherokee, "Coxey's Army," *Chicago Defender*, May 31, 1941, 5. After the postponement of the march, the *Defender* stated, "The Courier was the sole Negro newspaper to oppose the March-on-Washington which alone was responsible for the President's executive order and for more progress in breaking down discrimination than any other single thing." See "Walter White Blasts Newspaper Critics," *Chicago Defender*, July 12, 1941, 9.

9. Editorial, "A.P. Randolph in Appeal to FDR on Bias," *Chicago Defender*, April 12, 1941, 9. "Randolph Assumes Charge of the Job March," *Pittsburgh*

Courier, May 31, 1941, 4. "South Rallies to Job March on Washington—Randolph Mobilizes Citizens for Tour," *Pittsburgh Courier*, May 24, 1941, 23.

10. "50,000 to Hit at U.S. Defense Discrimination," *Chicago Defender*, May 17, 1941, 3. "Group Issues Call for Job March on Nation's Capital for July 1," *Pittsburgh Courier*, May 17, 1941, 1.

11. Editorial, "That March on Washington," *Pittsburgh Courier*, June 14, 1941, 5. Eleanor Roosevelt, "First Lady Says Group Will Make Serious Mistake," *Pittsburgh Courier*, June 21, 1941, 4.

12. Editorial, "End Job Bias—Roosevelt: Nation's Chief Executive Orders OPM to Halt Discrimination in All US Defense Industries," *Pittsburgh Courier*, June 21, 1941, 1, 2. "FDR Breaks Silence; Urges OPM to Smash Defense Job Race Ban," *Chicago Defender*, June 21, 1941, 1. "Roosevelt Opposed to March on Washington—Cabinet Members at White House Parley; Committee Is Named," *Pittsburgh Courier*, June 28, 1941, 1,4. "FD Names Body to Study Defense Bias," *Chicago Defender*, June 28, 1941, 1.

13. "New York Youth Division to the National Executive Committee," June 28, 1941, APR, box 24. "Act to 'Fool-Proof' FDR Ban on Jim Crow—Leaders Seek Enforcement in Entirety," *Chicago Defender*, July 12, 1941, 7. Herbert Garfinkel, *When Negroes March: The March on Washington Movement in the Organizational Politics for FEPC* (Glencoe, Ill.: Free Press), 63, 78, 117. The Spingarn medal was established by the NAACP in 1915 and was the most important award in the black community. It usually was given to a scientist, scholar, or artist. Randolph, chosen specifically for the establishment of the FEPC, was significant for honoring a protest leader.

14. Garfinkel, *When Negroes March*, 77–96. Paula F. Pfeffer, *A. Philip Randolph: Pioneer of the Civil Rights Movement* (Baton Rouge: Louisiana State University Press, 1990), 51–55.

15. Randolph to Rev. S. T. Eldridge, March 31, 1942, APR, box 24.

16. Ibid.

17. Randolph to Rev. T. B. Harten, April 16, 1942, APR, box 24. Randolph to Rev. George Sims, April 16, 1942, APR, box 25.

18. BSCP Staff, "Charles Wesley Burton," 1950, APR, box 5. James Adair to Rev. Charles Wesley Burton, September 27, 1941, APR, box 26. Charles Wesley Burton, "Negro March-on Washington Committee, Chicago Division," March 16, 1942, APR, box 24. Minutes of BSCP Meeting, Chicago Division, May 29, 1942, BSCP, box 6, folder 5.

19. Charles Wesley Burton to Randolph, April 29, 1942, APR, box 24. Chairman Committee Names and Designations, n.d., APR, box 26. The many lists of the Chicagoans who participated in the MOWM were not available for the New York and St. Louis rallies.

20. Neva Ryan to Randolph, May 13, 1942, APR, box 25. Rev. Ross D.

Brown to Randolph, June 26, 1942, APR, box 24. Neva Ryan to Randolph, n.d., APR, box 24.

21. Charles Wesley Burton to "Dear Reverend," June 11, 1942, APR, box 24.

22. Neva Ryan to Randolph, March 16, 1942, APR, box 25. Randolph to Neva Ryan, March 20, 1942, APR, box 25. Randolph replied, "I think it would be well to invite Pearl Buck to speak at the meeting."

23. Neva Ryan to Randolph, April 27, 1942, APR, box 25. Ethel Payne to Randolph, May 10, 1942, APR, box 25. Neva Ryan to Randolph, May 13, 1942, APR, box 25.

24. Charles Wesley Burton to Randolph, April 29, 1942, APR, box 24. Randolph to Ethel Payne, October 8, 1942, APR, box 25. Neva Ryan to Randolph, April 26, 1942, APR, box 25.

25. Burton to Randolph, April 29, 1942, APR, box 24. Neva Ryan to Randolph, April 27, 1942, APR, box 25. Randolph to Neva Ryan, May 22, 1942 APR, box 24. Randolph to Neva Ryan, June 16, 1942, APR, box 25.

26. Charles Wesley Burton to "Dear Reverend," June 11, 1942, APR, box 24.

27. Randolph to Charles Wesley Burton, June 10, 1942, APR, box 24. "Calling All Negroes in Chicago," n.d., APR, box 24. Randolph to Neva Ryan, June 15, 1942, APR, box 25.

28. "MOW St Louis and Second Group of Instructions," n.d., APR, box 26. Randolph to Lawrence Erwin, July 25, 1942, APR, box 24. Randolph to T. D. McNeal, July 21, 1942, APR, box 24. Program for St. Louis Mass Meeting, August 14, 1942, APR, box 27.

29. Theophilus Lewis, "Plays and a Point of View," July 1942, APR, box 27. Garfinkel, *When Negroes March*, 92. Pfeffer, *A. Philip Randolph*, 52–53.

30. Lewis, "Plays and a Point of View."

31. Randolph to Herbert Garfinkel, November 28, 1955, APR, box 27. Garfinkel, *When Negroes March*, 94. Pfeffer, *A. Philip Randolph*, 85.

32. *March on Washington Movement: Proceedings of Conference Held in Detroit September 26–27, 1942*, APR, box 24.

33. John LaFarge, *The Manner Is Ordinary* (New York: Harcourt, Brace, 1954), 349–50. John LaFarge, "The Spiritual Front," *Interracial Review* 15 (1942): 107–8. Martin A. Zielinski, "Working for Interracial Justice: The Catholic Interracial Council of New York, 1934–1964," *U.S. Catholic Historian* 7 (spring/summer 1988), 243. David W. Southern, *John LaFarge and the Limits of Catholic Interracialism, 1911–1963* (Baton Rouge: Louisiana State University, 1996), 201, 244, 249–50. John McGreevy, *Parish Boundaries: The Catholic Encounter with Race in the Twentieth-Century Urban North* (Chicago: University of Chicago Press, 1996), 171.

34. Zielinski, "Working for Interracial Justice," 242–43. *Interracial News Service: A Digest of Trends and Development in Human Relations*, vol. 12, nos. 3 and 4 (New York Commission on Religion and Race: National Council of

Churches in Christ in the U.S.A., 1941). Garfinkel, *When Negroes March*, 133. Randolph, "Father John LaFarge," n.d., APR, box 38.

35. T. D. McNeal to Randolph, August 22, 1942, APR, box 24. Mass Prayer Service, October 18, 1942, APR, box 26. T. D. McNeal to Randolph, October 28, 1942, APR, box 24. Garfinkel, *When Negroes March*, 133–34, 207. "2000 Attend Mass Meeting," *Pittsburgh Courier*, October 3, 1942, 23.

36. David Grant, "The 'March on Washington Players,' St. Louis Unit Presents a Biblical Narration Taken from the 2nd Book of Moses called 'Exodus,'" n.d., APR, box 26. T. D. McNeal to Randolph, October 28, 1942, APR, box 24.

37. Grant, "The 'March on Washington Players.'"

38. Mass Prayer Service, October 18, 1942, APR, box 26.

39. T. D. McNeal to Randolph, October 28, 1942, APR, box 24. Mass Meeting Sponsored by March on Washington Movement, October 27, 1942, APR, box 27. "2,000 Attend Mass Meeting," *Pittsburgh Courier*, October 3, 1942, 23.

40. T. D. McNeal to Randolph, August 22, 1942, APR, box 24. Enoc P. Waters, "Two Lynched Boys Were Ace Scrap Iron Collectors in Mississippi Town—Part 1," *Chicago Defender*, March 6, 1943, 13. Enoc P. Waters, "Ignorance and War Hysteria Found Underlying Causes of 2 Lynchings—Part 2," *Chicago Defender*, March 13, 1943, 13.

41. Randolph to Dr. Charles Wesley Burton, October 26, 1942, APR, box 3. Randolph to Charles Wesley Burton, October 22, 1942, APR, by 24. Wittie Anna Biggins, "LaGuardia Fails to Halt Prayer against Lynching," *People's Voice*, November 14, 1942, 8. On the dissension in the Chicago march movement after the Chicago Coliseum rally, see David Wilburn to Charles W. Burton, August 25, 1942, APR, box 25. David Wilburn et al. to Randolph, August 30, 1942, APR, box 25. "List of Grievances," August 28, 1942, APR, box 25. David Wilburn to Randolph, September 22, 1942, APR, box 25.

42. Randolph to "My Dear Reverend," October 24, 1942, APR, box 25. Randolph to Rev. Harry Emerson Fosdick, October 27, 1942, APR, box 24. Randolph to Rev. Allan Knight Chalmers, October 30, 1942, APR, box 24. Randolph to Rev. John Paul Jones, November 7, 1942 APR, box 24. Randolph to "Dear Sir," November 4, 1942, APR, box 25.

43. Randolph to Rev. John E. Johnson, October 27, 1942, APR, box 24. Randolph to "My Dear Reverend," October 28, 1942 APR, box 25. Eugenie Settles to Rev. William Lloyd Imes, October 30, 1942, APR, box 25. William Lloyd Imes to Randolph, October 29, 1942, APR, box 24. "Randolph Organizes Canadian Porters," *Pittsburgh Courier*, November 14, 1942, 24.

44. Randolph to "My Dear Reverend," October 24, 1942, APR, box 25. Rev. James B. Adams to Randolph, November 6, 1942 APR, box 24. Ministers and Members of the Baptist Church from James E. Lee, October 27, 1942 APR, box 24.

45. Rev. Shelton Hale Bishop to Randolph, June 23, 1942, APR, box 24.

46. Randolph to "My Dear Reverend," October 24, 1942, APR, box 25. Randolph to Rev. John E. Johnson, October 27, 1942, APR, box 24. Randolph to "My Dear Reverend," October 28, 1942 APR, box 25.

47. Randolph to Rev. Charles Young Trigg, October 27, 1942 APR, box 25.

48. Randolph to "My Dear Reverend," October 24, 1942, APR, box 25. Randolph to Rev. John E. Johnson, October 27, 1942, APR, box 24. Randolph to "My Dear Reverend," October 28, 1942 APR, 25. Randolph to Rev. Allan Knight Chalmers, October 30, 1942, APR, box 24. Randolph to Rev. John Paul Jones, November 7, 1942 APR, box 24. Randolph to Rev. Harry Emerson Fosdick, October 27, 1942, APR, box 24. Harry Emerson Fosdick to Randolph, October 29, 1942, APR, box 24. Randolph to Harry Emerson Fosdick, November 19, 1942, APR, box 24.

49. Allan Knight Chalmers to Randolph, October 31, 1942, APR, box 24. Later Chalmers cochaired the National Council for a Permanent FEPC with Randolph. Pfeffer, *A. Philip Randolph*, 98. Randolph to Rev. Dr. David de Sola Pool, October 30, 1942, APR, box 24. Dr. D. de Sola Pool to Randolph, November 4, 1942, APR, box 24. David and Tamar De Sola Pool, *An Old Faith in the New World: Portrait of Shearith Israel, 1654–1954* (New York: Columbia University Press, 1955), 204, 337–38.For the historical background of the Spanish and Portuguese synagogue, Shearith Israel, see Sydney E. Ahlstrom, *A Religious History of the American People* (New Haven, Conn.: Yale University Press, 1972), 569–73. Eugenie Settles to Rev. S. T. Eldridge," November 5, 1942, APR, box 25. Ministers participating in the Public Prayer, n.d., APR, box 26.

50. "Program of the Public Prayer," November 9, 1942, APR, box 26. Reverend S.T. Eldridge to Rev. Wm. Lloyd Imes, November 6, 1942, APR, box 24. Rev. S. T. Eldridge to Rev. John Paul Jones, November 7, 1942, APR, box 24. Rev. S. T. Eldridge to Rev. David de Sola Pool, November 7, 1942, APR, box 24. Rev. S. T. Eldridge to Rev. S. M. Sweeney, November 7, 1942 APR, box 24.

51. Lawrence Ervin to Randolph, October 31, 1942, APR, box 24. Lawrence Ervin to Randolph, November 5, 1942, APR, box 24. Lawrence Ervin to Fiorello LaGuardia, November 8, 1942, APR, box 24.

52. Lawrence Ervin to Randolph, November 1942, APR, box 1.

53. Iona Morris to Randolph, December 15, 1942, APR, box 24. Randolph to Rev. S. M. Sweeney, November 7, 1942, APR, box 25. Randolph to Rev. David de Sola Pool, November 27, 1942, APR, box 24. Randolph to Rev. Shelton Hale Bishop, November 27, 1942, APR, box 24. Randolph to Rev. William Lloyd Imes, November 27, 1942, APR, box 24. Randolph to Rev. John Paul Jones, November 28, 1942, APR, box 24.

54. Garfinkel, *When Negroes March*, 134, 207. Wittie Anna Biggins, "LaGuardia Fails to Halt Prayer against Lynching," *People's Voice*, November 14, 1942, 8.

55. Editorial, "The Messenger," *Messenger*, November 1917, 21.

56. A. Philip Randolph, "A Reply to My Critics," *Chicago Defender*, June 12, 1943, 13. Garfinkel, *When Negroes March*, 136. Randolph to Paula Pfeffer, September 29, 1972, APR, box 42.

57. Editorial, "'March' Plans Big Parley in Chicago," *Chicago Defender*, May 1, 1943, 7. "May March to Save Nation's Soul—Randolph," *Pittsburgh Courier*, December 19, 1942. "Randolph Flays Negro Baiters at Loop Meet," *Chicago Defender*, January 9, 1943, 13. Randolph to Rev. James Lafayette Horace, January 2, 1943, APR, box 27.

58. *March on Washington Movement: Proceedings of Conference Held in Detroit September 26–27, 1942*, APR, box 24. "Randolph Makes Plea for India," *Chicago Defender*, October 24, 1942, 8. Pauli Murray to A. Philip Randolph, August 9, 1942, APR, box 24.

59. "March Movement to Get New Executive," December 14, 1942, APR, box 27.

60. "March on Washington May Conference Will Ponder Program of Civil Disobedience and Non-cooperation," December 30, 1942, APR, box 27. "Randolph to Adopt Gandhi Technique," *Chicago Defender*, January 9, 1943, 4.

61. "Randolph Blasts Courier as 'Bitter Voice of Defeatism,'" *Chicago Defender*, June 12, 1943, 13.

62. "Randolph Tells Philosophy behind 'March' Movement," *Chicago Defender*, June 19, 1943, 13.

63. E. Pauline Myers, "The March on Washington Movement and Non-Violent Civil Disobedience," February 23, 1943, APR, box 26. A. Philip Randolph and E. Pauline Myers, "National March on Washington Movement—Policies and Directives," n.d., APR, box 27. In *A Theology of Liberation*, Gustavo Gutiérrez writes, "In the language of the Bible, we are in a *kairos*, a propitious and demanding time in which the Lord challenges us and we are called upon to bear a very specific witness. During the *kairos* Latin American Christians are experiencing a tense and intense period of *solidarity*, *reflection* and *martyrdom*" (italics in original). Gustavo Gutiérrez, *A Theology of Liberation* (New York: Orbis Books, 1988), xx.

64. Myers, "The March on Washington Movement and Non-Violent Civil Disobedience." Randolph and Myers, "Policies and Directives."

65. Myers, "The March on Washington Movement and Non-Violent Civil Disobedience."

66. A. Philip Randolph, "The March on Washington Movement and the War," January 29, 1943, APR, box 27.

67. "Randolph Refutes Cry of 'Calamity Howlers,'" *Chicago Defender*, February 6, 1943, 6. "Citizen Repudiates Non-violence Program," *Pittsburgh Courier*, April 24, 1943, 4.

68. Randolph, "The March on Washington Movement and the War." "Randolph Refutes Cry of 'Calamity Howlers.'"

69. Pauli Murray to Randolph, May 13, 1943, APR, box 27. Myers, "The March on Washington Movement and Non-Violent Civil Disobedience." A. J. Muste to Randolph, January 11, 1943, APR, box 27. Randolph to Muste, January 25, 1943, APR, box 27. Outline of Summer Training Course in Non-Violent Direct Action, n.d., APR, box 26.

70. George M. Houser, *Erasing the Color Line* (New York: Fellowship Publications, 1945), 7.

71. J. Holmes Smith to Randolph, June 27, 1943, APR, box 27. Memo on the pilgrimage to the Lincoln Memorial, n.d., in *The Papers of Bayard Rustin* (hereafter cited as BRP), edited by John Bracey Jr. and August Meier (Bethesda, Md.: University Publications of America, 1990), reel 4, 1035. August Meier and Elliott Rudwick, *CORE: A Study in the Civil Rights Movement, 1942–1968* (New York: Oxford University Press, 1973), 14.

72. "Great Missionary Dr. E. Stanley Jones to Speak at MOWM Meet," May 6, 1943, APR, box 26. E. Stanley Jones to Randolph, May 18, 1943, APR, box 27. Randolph to Rev. E. Stanley Jones, May 25, 1943, APR, box 27. "E. Stanley Jones Expounds Non-Violent Technique at MOWM Conference," July 19, 1943, APR, box 26. David Bundy, "The Theology of the Kingdom of God in E. Stanley Jones," http://wesley.nnu.edu/WesleyanTheology/theojrnl/21–25/23-04.htm.

73. MOWM press release, April 13, 1943, APR, box 26. "Prominent Negroes Sign Call for MOWM Conference," May 1, 1943, APR, box 26. Randolph to Charles Wesley Burton, March 17, 1943, APR, box 27. Randolph to Horace White, March 17, 1943, APR, box 27. Randolph to Rev. James E. Cook, March 17, 1943, APR, box 27. Randolph to Bishop John A. Gregg, March 26, 1943, APR, box 27. Randolph to D. V. Jemison, March 26, 1943, APR, box 27. Call to We Are Americans, Too Conference, n.d., APR, box 27. George E. DeMar to Randolph, February 16, 1943, box 27. Randolph to Robert P. Johnson, March 11, 1943, APR, box 27.

74. D. V. Jemison to Randolph, March 31, 1943, APR, box 27. D. V. Jemison to Randolph, April 3, 1943, APR, box 27. Randolph to Jemison, April 6, 1943, APR, box 27. Randolph to Jemison, April 9, 1943, APR, box 27. Randolph to D. V. Jemison, May 19, 1943, APR, box 27. Randolph to Pauli Murray, May 17, 1943, APR, box 27.

75. R. R. Wright to Randolph, March 18, 1943, APR, box 27. Randolph to Bishop R. R. Wright, n.d., APR, box 27. R. R. Wright to Randolph, March 31, 1943, APR, box 27. R. R. Wright to Randolph, April 10, 1943, APR, box 27. Randolph to R. R. Wright, April 13, 1943, APR, box 27. William Jernigan to Randolph, April 1, 1943, APR, box 27. Bishop James A. Bray to Randolph, March 31, 1943, APR, box 27.

76. Lawrence Ervin to "Dear Reverend," January 15, 1943, APR, box 27. "Clerics Ask President to Revive FEPC," *Chicago Defender*, February 6, 1943, 2.

77. Randolph to S. T. Eldridge, January 21, 1943, APR, box 27. "Save FEPC Conference Planned in Washington February 5," January 30, 1943, APR, box 27. Rev. John H. Johnson to Randolph, April 1, 1943, APR, box 27.

78. Burton to Randolph, March 20, 1943, APR, box 27. Burton to Randolph, March 22, 1943, APR, box 27. Burton to "Dear Member," April 1, 1943, APR, box 27. Burton to Randolph, March 16, 1943, APR, box 27. Burton to Randolph, April 21, 1943, APR, box 27. Randolph to Burton, April 22, 1943, APR, box 27.

79. Burton to Randolph, May 2, 1943, APR, box 27. Ethel Payne to Randolph, June 5, 1943, APR, box 27. Randolph to Burton, June 3, 1943, APR, box 27.

80. John R. Williams, "Race Riots Sweep Nation," *Pittsburgh Courier*, June 26, 1943, 1. Burton to Randolph, May 2, 1943, APR, box 27. E. Pauline Myers to Local Units of March on Washington Movement, July 20, 1943, APR, box 24. MOW We Are Americans, Too program, June 30–July 4, 1943, APR, boxes 24 and 26. "Randolph Blames Roosevelt for U.S. Wave of Rioting," *Chicago Defender*, July 10, 1943, 1.

81. Advertisement, "Our Fellow Americans . . . Negroes Are Americans Too!" *Washington Evening Star*, July 7, 1943, B-19. Randolph to William Lloyd Imes, July 18, 1943, APR, box 27.

82. John Robert Badger, "World View," *Chicago Defender*, July 17 and 24, 1943, 15. Editorial, "Confirmation," *Pittsburgh Courier*, July 17, 1943, 6.

83. Nancy MacDonald and Dwight MacDonald, "Memo: Two Outsiders Look at the M.O.W.," June 20, 1943, APR, box 27.

84. Ibid.

85. MacDonald and MacDonald, "Memo." Program for Symposium: Mapping a Broad National Program in the Interest of Abolishing Jim Crow in America, July 1, 1943, APR, box 24.

86. Randolph to Mr. and Mrs. Dwight MacDonald, July 20, 1943, APR, box 27. Randolph to Burton, July 8, 1943, APR, box 27. E. Pauline Myers to Dr. William Stuart Nelson, July 27, 1943, APR, box 27. David M. Grant to Layle Lane, July 13, 1943, APR, box 27.

87. Pfeffer, *A. Philip Randolph*, 137. For background on UCC minister Allan Knight Chalmers, see http://www.bwayucc.org/History2.html.

88. Nathaniel Cooper to Randolph, January 30, 1953, APR, box 1.

NOTES TO CHAPTER 5

1. Jervis Anderson, *A. Philip Randolph: A Biographical Portrait* (New York: Harcourt Brace Jovanovich, 1973), 25–26.

2. Richard Allen Hildebrand to Randolph, July 2, 1959, A. Philip Randolph Papers (hereafter cited as APR), box 4. Randolph to Dr. Hildebrand, July 8, 1959, APR, box 4.

3. Randolph to Hildebrand, January 1, 1960, APR, box 4. Bishop Frank Madison Reid to Randolph, June 28, 1958, APR, box 4. Hildebrand to Randolph, December 11, 1958, APR, box 4. Randolph to Hildebrand, April 15, 1960, APR, box 4. Hildebrand to Randolph, April 23, 1960, APR, box 4.

4. "The Memorial Services for Asa Philip Randolph, 1889–1979: Bethel AME Church, 52 West 132nd Street in Harlem, Henderson R. Hughes, Minister" (Berkeley: University of California, Bancroft Library, 1979), 1–4.

5. Ella Baker to Monseigneur Cornelius Drew, October 9, 1956, APR, box 23. Statement by A. Philip Randolph to the Prayer Pilgrimage for Freedom at the Lincoln Memorial, May 17, 1957, APR, box 35.

6. Bayard Rustin, "Reminiscences of Bayard Rustin," transcript of an interview by Ed Edwin (New York: Columbia University Oral History Research Office Collection, 1985/86) (hereafter cited as BRCUOH), 458–59, 516–17.

7. Ibid., 477–78.

8. Ibid., 459–61, 464.

9. A. Philip Randolph, "Negro Labor and the Church," in *Labor Speaks for Itself on Religion: A Symposium of Labor Leaders throughout the World*, edited by Jerome Davis (New York: Macmillan, 1929), 76.

10. Randolph to President Eisenhower, August 31, 1955, APR, box 31. Randolph to Roy Wilkins, August 31, 1955, APR, box 31.

11. Ibid.

12. Minutes of National Action Committee on "In Friendship," February 24, 1956, APR, box 23. Randolph to Rabbi Edward E. Klein," March 15, 1956, APR, box 23. Randolph to Ella Baker, March 7, 1956, APR, box 23. John D'Emilio, *Lost Prophet: The Life and Times of Bayard Rustin* (New York: Free Press, 2003), 224.

13. Randolph to Rabbi Edward Klein, March 15, 1956, APR, box 23.

14. Monseigneur Cornelius Drew to Randolph, February 25, 1956, APR, box 23. Letterhead to "In Friendship"—Welfare Aid to Victims of Racism, August 29, 1956, APR, box 23. "Quotable Quotes from Rev. King," in *The Papers of Martin Luther King, Jr.* , edited by Clayborne Carson (Berkeley: University of California Press, 2000) (hereafter cited as MLK), vol. 3, 209.

15. Nathaniel Evans to Randolph, March 21, 1956, APR, box 2. Randolph to Nathaniel Evans, April 10, 1956, APR, box 2.

16. Randolph to Dr. George D. Cannon, June 21, 1956, APR, box 2.

17. D'Emilio, *Lost Prophet*, 153–60.

18. Bayard Rustin, "Memories of A. Philip Randolph," BRP, reel 19, 99–100.

19. August Meier to Bayard Rustin, April 20, 1973, BRP, reel 23, 39.

20. D'Emilio, *Lost Prophet*, 184–205.

21. BRCUOH, 183.

22. BRCUOH, 137. D'Emilio, *Lost Prophet*, 227–28. Taylor Branch, *Parting*

the Waters: America in the King Years, 1954–63 (New York: Simon & Schuster, 1988), 176.

23. "How It Started by E. D. Nixon," n.d., BRP, reel 4, 260–62. Larry Tye, *Rising from the Rails: Pullman Porters and the Making of the Black Middle Class* (New York: Henry Holt, 2004), 199–227. Tye's chapter "Train to Freedom" focuses on Nixon's key role in the Montgomery bus boycott.

24. E. D. Nixon to Randolph, January 7, 1974, APR, box 3. Randolph to E. D. Nixon, February 23, 1956, Martin Luther King Jr. Papers, Boston University, box 91, folders 4 and 5.

25. John Swomley to Wilson Riles, February 21, 1956 BRP, reel 4, 229. John Swomley to Charles Walker, n.d., BRP, reel 4, 231. Glenn Smiley to John Swomley and Al Hassler, February 29, 1956, BRP, reel 4, 232.

26. Swomley to Smiley, February 29, 1956, BRP, reel 4, 235–36. Swomley to Smiley, March 1, 1956, BRP, reel 4, 237. Glenn Smiley to John Swomley and Al Hassler, February 29, 1956, BRP, reel 4, 232.

27. Swomley to Smiley, February 29, 1956, BRP, reel 4, 236. Smiley to Swomley, March 2, 1956, BRP, reel 4, 239–42.

28. Glenn Smiley to John Swomley and Al Hassler, February 29, 1956, BRP, reel 4, 232. Smiley to Swomley, March 2, 1956, BRP, reel 4, 239–42. D'Emilio, *Lost Prophet*, 227–28.

29. Smiley to Swomley, March 2, 1956, BRP, reel 4, 242.

30. Bayard Rustin, "How Outsiders Can Strengthen the Montgomery Nonviolent Protest," March 7, 1956, BRP, reel 4, 342–44.

31. BRCUOH, 319–20. D'Emilio, *Lost Prophet*, 238. John Swomley to Glenn Smiley, February 29, 1956, BRP, reel 4, 235.

32. Robert McAfee Brown, *Liberation Theology: An Introductory Guide* (Louisville: Westminster/John Knox Press, 1993), 103.

33. A. Philip Randolph, Statement at Fifty-first Anniversary Luncheon of the League of Industrial Democracy, April 14, 1956, APR, box 35.

34. A. Philip Randolph, Statement at the State of the Race Conference, April 24, 1956, APR, box 35. Paula F. Pfeffer, *A. Philip Randolph: Pioneer of the Civil Rights Movement* (Baton Rouge: Louisiana State University Press, 1990), 174–75.

35. Pfeffer, *A. Philip Randolph*, 174–75. Randolph to Martin Luther King Jr. April 19, 1956, MLK, vol. 3, 216–17.

36. Randolph, Statement at the State of the Race Conference, April 24, 1956, APR, box 35.

37. Randolph, Statement at Fifty-first Anniversary Luncheon of the League of Industrial Democracy, April 14, 1956, APR, box 35. Randolph, Statement at the State of the Race Conference, April 24, 1956, APR, box 35.

38. Randolph, Statement at the State of the Race Conference, April 24, 1956, APR, box 35.

39. Randolph, Statement at the State of the Race Conference. "Hundreds Sign Negro Manifesto—Answer to Law-Makers Who Defy Supreme Court," *Pittsburgh Courier*, April 7, 1956, 6. During April and May 1956, the *Courier* kept its readers informed about the individuals who supported its "Negro manifesto." See *Pittsburgh Courier*, April 14, 1956, 7; April 21, 1956, 8; April 28, 1956, 14; May 5, 1956, sec. 2, 6; and May 12, 1956, sec. 2, 6.

40. Martin Luther King Jr. to B. F. McLaurin, May 6, 1956, MLK, vol. 3, 246–47. Ella Baker, "That You Might Know—A Brief Digest of the Activities of 'In Friendship,'" March 6, 1957, APR, box 23. D'Emilio, *Lost Prophet*, 239–40.

41. Randolph to Martin Luther King Jr., May 7, 1956, MLK, vol. 3, 247–48. King to Randolph, May 10, 1956, MLK, vol. 3, 253.

42. A. Philip Randolph, "Madison Square Garden Civil Rights Rally," May 24, 1956, APR, box 35.

43. Randolph, "Madison Square Garden Civil Rights Rally." Will Herberg, *Protestant, Catholic, Jew: An Essay in American Religious Sociology* (New York: Doubleday, 1955). "Rummel Hits at Jim Crow Directive," *Pittsburgh Courier*, March 3, 1956, 14.

44. Frank McCallister to Randolph, May 21, 1956, APR, box 2. Randolph to Frank McCallister, May 28, 1956, APR, box 2.

45. A. Philip Randolph, "Civil Rights and the Negro," May 17, 1956, APR, box 35.

46. Rufus Burrow Jr., *Personalism: A Critical Introduction* (St. Louis: Chalice Press, 1999), 3, 76–85. John Macquarrie, *Twentieth-Century Religious Thought*, 4th ed. (London: SCM Press, 1989), 65–68, 188. David J. Garrow, *Bearing the Cross: Martin Luther King, Jr., and the Southern Christian Leadership Conference* (New York: Vintage Books, 1986), 44.

47. Burrow, *Personalism*, 76–85.

48. A. Philip Randolph, "Labor and the Struggle for a Better Tomorrow," September 2, 1956, APR, box 35.

49. In Friendship—Minutes of Executive Committee, July 19, 1956, APR, box 23. Randolph, "Labor and the Struggle for a Better Tomorrow."

50. Randolph, "Civil Rights and the Negro," May 17, 1956, APR, box 35.

51. Randolph to the president, February 2, 1956, APR, box 31. Randolph to the president, May 8, 1956, APR, box 31.

52. Randolph to the president, May 31, 1956, APR, box 31. Randolph to the president, December 29, 1956, APR, box 31. Persons invited to participate in conference with the president, n.d., APR, box 31. Randolph to Martin Luther King, January 4, 1957, MLK, vol. 4, 90. Martin Luther King to Randolph, January 7, 1957, APR, box 31. J. H. Jackson to Randolph, January 8, 1957, APR, box 31.

53. Branch, *Parting the Waters*, 195.

54. Martin Luther King Jr., "Our Struggle," MLK, vol. 3, 237–38.

55. Bayard Rustin to King, March 8, 1956, MLK, vol. 3, 163–64.

56. Randolph to Martin Luther King Sr., n.d., APR, box 35. Garrow, *Bearing the Cross*, 90.

57. The Southern Negro Leaders' Conference on Transportation and Nonviolent Integration, APR, box 35.

58. Randolph to Stanley Levison, January 4, 1957, APR, box 2. Jack Clareman to Randolph, February 5, 1957, APR, box 2. Randolph to Clareman, February 20, 1957, APR, box 2. John O. Neustadt to Randolph, January 5, 1957, APR, box 2. Randolph to John O. Neustadt, January 2, 1957, APR, box 2. Trip to African and India based on 54 journey for three, n.d., APR, box 2.

59. Thomas Kilgore, Bayard Rustin, and Ella Baker to James Hicks, June 4, 1957, APR, box 30. Garrow, *Bearing the Cross*, 91.

60. "NAACP News—West Coast Regional Office," April 29, 1957, in *Papers of the NAACP, Part 21: NAACP Relations with the Modern Civil Rights Movement* (Bethesda, Md.: University Publications of America) (hereafter cited as NP21), reel 20, 658. John A. Morsell to Mrs. Latta R. Thomas, April 22, 1957, NP21, reel 20, 673.

61. Kivie Kaplan to Roy Wilkins, May 13, 1957, NP21, reel 20, 928. Press release, May 10, 1957, NP21, reel 20, 842. Thomas Kilgore, Bayard Rustin, and Ella Baker to James Hicks, June 4, 1957, APR, box 30.

62. Clarence Mitchell to Roy Wilkins, April 22, 1957, NP21, reel 20, 652. Secure Lincoln Memorial for prayer pilgrimage, April 25, 1957, NP21, reel 20, 653.

63. Wilkins, Randolph, and King to Sol Hurok, April 12, 1957, NP21, reel 20, 656. Marian Anderson to Roy Wilkins, April 26, 1957, NP21, reel 20, 655. Roy Wilkins to Robert Ming, May 1, 1957, NP21, reel 20, 754. E. Franklin Frazier, *The Negro Church in America* (New York: Schocken Books, 1964), 72–75.

64. Ella J. Baker to Dear Committee Member, May 2, 1957, NP21, reel 20, 831. Staff, n.d., NP21, reel 20,721. Memo regarding prayer pilgrimage, n.d., APR, box 30 (italics in original).

65. Memo regarding prayer pilgrimage, n.d., APR, box 30.

66. Ibid.

67. Ibid.

68. Call to prayer pilgrimage for freedom, April 5, 1957, APR, box 30. BR-CUOH, 516. Thomas Kilgore to Gloster B. Current, April 16, 1957, NP21, reel 20, 727. Gloster B. Current to local NAACP officials, April 17, 1957, NP21, reel 20, 659–71. Ella J. Baker to Dear Committee Member, May 2, 1957, NP21, reel 20, 831.

69. Bayard Rustin to Wilkins, Randolph, King, and Kilgore, April 23, 1957, NP21, reel 20, 648–50.

70. Ibid.

71. Ibid.

72. Call to prayer pilgrimage for freedom, April 5, 1957, APR, box 30.

73. William Herbert King to Martin Luther King, April 2, 1957, APR, box 30. Rev. William Holmes Borders to Martin Luther King, April 6, 1957, APR, box 30. Reinhold Niebuhr to Martin Luther King, Roy Wilkins, and A. Philip Randolph, May 3, 1957, NP21, reel 20, 762. Henry C. Koch, "Resolution of the Washington Federation of Churches," May 3, 1957, NP21, reel 20, 783. James A. Pike to King, Wilkins, and Randolph, May 6, 1957, NP21, reel 20, 789. John LaFarge to Randolph, May 6, 1957, NP21, reel 20, 790. NAACP press release on prayer pilgrimage for freedom, May 8, 1957, NP21, reel 20, 812. "3 Top Clergymen Back Pilgrimage," *Pittsburgh Courier*, May 18, 1957, 6. Oscar Lee to Martin Luther King, May 9, 1957, NP21, reel 20, 837. Eugene Carson Blake to King, Wilkins, and Randolph, May 10, 1957, NP21, reel 20, 854.

74. Randolph to J. H. Jackson, April 17, 1957, APR, box 30. Roy Wilkins to J. H. Jackson, NP21, reel 20, 760. Rev. J. H. Jackson to Randolph, April 12, 1957, APR, box 30.

75. Randolph to Dear Brother Co-Worker, n.d., APR, box 30. Thomas Kilgore to Dear Fellow Minister, n.d., APR, box 30. Prayer pilgrimage for freedom New York organizational meeting, April 18, 1957, APR, box 30.

76. Memo regarding prayer pilgrimage, n.d., APR, box 30. Randolph to Boyd Wilson, April 23, 1957, APR, box 30. Ezra Parrett to Randolph, May 9, 1957, APR, box 30.

77. *Congressional Record*, May 2, 1957, APR, box 30. Ministers' mobilization of the prayer pilgrimage for freedom, May 3, 1957, NP21, reel 20, 782. Ministers' "Operation New York' Project," May 2, 1957, NP21, reel 20, 781. David Licorish to Roy Wilkins, May 1, 1957, NP21, reel 20, 756. Roy Wilkins to David Licorish, May 3, 1957, NP21, reel 20, 777.

78. Thomas Kilgore Jr. to Dear Fellow Minister, n.d., APR, box 30. Rev. David N. Licorish and Rev. Thomas Kilgore to Randolph, May 7, 1957, APR, box 30.

79. Jerome Davis to Randolph, April 25, 1957, APR, box 30. Randolph to Jerome Davis, April 30, 1957, APR, box 30. "Proclaim Liberty throughout the Land," n.d., APR, box 30.

80. Charles Wesley Burton to Randolph, May 1, 1957, APR, box 30. Rev. John E. Nance to Randolph, May 7, 1957, APR, box 30 (italics in original).

81. BRCUOH, 458. To NAACP branches, youth councils, and college chapters regarding the prayer pilgrimage, April 12, 1957, NP21, reel 20, 642. Notes on scheduled departures for prayer pilgrimage," May 14, 1957, NP21, reel 20, 933. "Rain or Shine Virginians," May 2, 1957, NP21, reel 20, 681. Planning committee in Los Angeles, California, May 2, 1957, NP21, reel 20, 757. NAACP West Coast region, May 2, 1957, NP21, reel 20, 759. P. T. Robinson to Roy Wilkins, May 6, 1957, NP21, reel 20, 784.

82. Henry Lee Moon to Randolph, May 15, 1957, APR, box 30. Prayer pilgrimage for freedom—timed program, May 17, 1957, APR, box 30.

83. Prayer pilgrimage for freedom—timed program, May 17, 1957, APR, box 30. Roy Wilkins to T. M. Chambers, May 14, 1957, NP21, reel 20, 946–47.

84. Chairman's notes on program, n.d., APR, box 30. Suggested program, n.d., APR, box 30. Proposal for Freedom bond, n.d., APR, box 30. "Lift Every Voice and Sing, the Integration Song," n.d., APR, box 30. Memorandum from Henry Lee Moon to the NAACP national officers, board members and field staff, May 23, 1957, NP21, reel 21, 126.

85. Statement by A. Philip Randolph to the prayer pilgrimage for freedom at the Lincoln Memorial, May 17, 1957, APR, box 35.

86. Ibid.

87. Faith Wallstrom to Randolph, May 23, 1957, APR, box 30. Randolph to Faith Wallstrom, June 4, 1957, APR, box 29.

88. BRCUOH, 460–61, 464.

89. BRCUOH, 382.

90. James Hicks, "King Emerges as Top Negro Leader," *New York Amsterdam News*, June 1, 1957. Alfred Duckett, "The Old Pro vs. the New Voice," *Chicago Defender*, June 1, 1957.

91. Roy Wilkins to C. B. Powell, June 4, 1957, APR, box 30. Thomas Kilgore, Bayard Rustin, and Ella Baker to James Hicks, June 4, 1957, APR, box 30. Memo to the NAACP board of directors, June 5, 1957, APR, box 30. Roy Wilkins to Randolph, August 9, 1957, APR, box 30. Randolph to Eugene Davison, August 12, 1957, APR, box 30. Thomas Kilgore Jr. to Randolph, May 27, 1957, APR, box 30. Randolph to Thomas Kilgore Jr., June 3, 1957, APR, box 30. Roy Wilkins to Randolph, May 23, 1957, APR, box 30. BRCUOH, 478.

92. Randolph to the president, June 10, 1957, APR, box 31. E. Frederic Morrow to Randolph, June 25, 1957, APR, box 31.

93. Maxwell Rabb to Randolph, August 20, 1957, APR, box 2. Richard Nixon to Randolph, August 12, 1957, APR, box 31. Radio program—*As We See It*, October 13, 1957, APR, box 35.

94. Septima Clark to Randolph, May 21, 1957, APR, box 30. Randolph to Septima Clark, June 4, 1957, APR, box 30. Layle Lane to Randolph, May 19, 1957, APR, box 30. Randolph to Layle Lane, May 24, 1957, APR, box 30.

95. George Singleton to Randolph, May 21, 1957, APR, box 30. Randolph to Rev. George Singleton, June 4, 1957, APR, box 30.

96. Anderson, *A. Philip Randolph*, 24.

97. George A. Singleton, *The Romance of African Methodism: A Study of the African Methodist Episcopal Church* (New York: Exposition Press, 1952), xix–xv, 111. W. E. B. Du Bois, ed., *The Negro Church: Report of a Social Study Made under the Direction of Atlanta University, Together with the Proceedings*

of the Eighth Conference for the Study of the Negro Problem, Held at Atlanta
University, May 26, 1903 (Atlanta: Atlanta University Press, 1903), 123–24. C.
Eric Lincoln, "Black Methodists and the Methodist Romance," in *Wesleyan
Theology Today: A Bicentennial Theological Consultation*, edited by Theodore
Runyon (Nashville: Kingswood Books, 1985), 215–16. Anderson, *A. Philip
Randolph*, 23–24.

NOTES TO THE EPILOGUE

1. Bayard Rustin, "In Memory of A. Philip Randolph," June 1979, BRP, reel
19, 90–91.
2. Chandler Owen to Randolph, April 16, 1963, in A. Philip Randolph Papers (hereafter cited as APR), box 2. Jervis Anderson, *A. Philip Randolph: A Biographical Portrait* (New York: Harcourt Brace Jovanovich, 1973), 18–20.
3. Annual Report of SCLC Eighth Annual Convention in Savannah, Georgia,
September 28 to October 2, 1964, APR, box 2.
4. Ibid.
5. Anderson, *A. Philip Randolph*, 330.
6. Henry B. Clark, "The Freedom Budget," *Christianity and Crisis*, November 28, 1966, 263–64.
7. "Protestant Post to Randolph," *New York Amsterdam News*, April 2,
1966, 1. Norman Vincent Peale to Randolph, April 17, 1969, APR, box 3. Randolph to Norman Vincent Peale, April, 1969 APR, box 3.
8. A. Philip Randolph, "African Methodism and the Negro in the Western
World," May 30, 1962, APR, box 36.

Selected Bibliography

Abbott, Philip. *Leftward Ho!: V.F. Calverton and American Radicalism.* Westport, Conn.: Greenwood Press, 1993.

Anderson, Jervis. *A. Philip Randolph: A Biographical Portrait.* New York: Harcourt Brace Jovanovich, 1973.

_____. *This Was Harlem, 1900–1950.* New York: Farrar, Straus & Giroux, 1981.

Arnesen, Eric. *Brotherhoods of Color: Black Railroad Workers and the Struggle for Equality.* Cambridge, Mass.: Harvard University Press, 2001.

Baer, Hans A., and Merrill Singer. *African-American Religion in the Twentieth Century: Varieties of Protest and Accommodation.* Knoxville: University of Tennessee Press, 1992.

Bainbridge, William Sims. *The Sociology of Religious Movements.* New York: Routledge, 1997.

Bates, Beth Tompkins. *Pullman Porters and the Rise of Protest in Black America, 1925–1945.* Chapel Hill: University of North Carolina Press, 2001.

Beckford, James A. *Religion and Advanced Industrial Societies.* London: Unwin-Hyman, 1989.

Branch, Taylor. *Parting the Waters: America in the King Years, 1954–63.* New York: Simon & Schuster, 1988.

Brazeal, Brailsford R. *The Brotherhood of Sleeping Car Porters: Its Origin and Development.* New York: Harper Bros., 1946.

Burkett, Randall K. *Black Redemption: Churchmen Speak for the Garvey Movement.* Philadelphia: Temple University Press, 1978.

_____. *Garveyism as a Religious Movement.* Metuchen, N.J.: Scarecrow Press, 1978.

Burrow, Rufus Jr. *Personalism: A Critical Introduction.* St. Louis: Chalice Press, 1999.

Carson, Clayborne, ed. *The Papers of Martin Luther King, Jr.* Vols. 3 and 4. Berkeley: University of California Press, 2000.

Chapman, Mark L. *Christianity on Trial: African-American Religious Thought before and after Black Power.* Maryknoll, N.Y.: Orbis Books, 1996.

Chateauvert, Melinda. *Marching Together: Women of the Brotherhood of Sleeping Car Porters.* Urbana: University of Illinois Press, 1998.

Cone, James H. *A Black Theology of Liberation*. 2nd ed. Maryknoll, N.Y.: Orbis Books, 1993.

Darsey, James. *The Prophetic and Radical Rhetoric in America*. New York: New York University Press, 1997.

Davis, Jerome, ed. *Labor Speaks for Itself on Religion: A Symposium of Labor Leaders throughout the World*. New York: Macmillan, 1929.

Dellums, C. L. "The International President of The Brotherhood of Sleeping Car Porters and Civil Rights Leader." Typescript of an oral history conducted in 1970 and 1971 by Joyce Henderson. Berkeley: University of California, Regional Oral History Office, Bancroft Library, 1973.

D'Emilio, John. *Lost Prophet: The Life and Times of Bayard Rustin*. New York: Free Press, 2003.

Dickerson, Dennis C. "African American Religious Intellectuals and the Theological Foundations of the Civil Rights Movement, 1930–1955," *Church History* 74: 2 (June 2005): 220.

Dorn, Jacob. H., ed. *Socialism and Christianity in Early 20th Century America*. Westport, Conn.: Greenwood Press, 1998.

Drake, St. Clair. *The Redemption of Africa and Black Religion*. Chicago: Third World Press, 1970.

Drake, St. Clair, and Horace R. Cayton. *Black Metropolis: A Study of Negro Life in a Northern City*. New York: Harcourt, Brace, 1945.

Du Bois, W. E. B. *The Negro Church: Report of a Social Study Made under the Direction of Atlanta University; Together with the Proceedings of the Eighth Conference for the Study of the Negro Problem, Held at Atlanta University, May 26, 1903*. Atlanta: Atlanta University Press, 1903.

———. *The Souls of Black Folk*. 1903. Reprint, New York: Penguin Books, 1989.

Dvorak, Katharine L. *An African-American Exodus: The Segregation of the Southern Churches*. New York: Carlson, 1991.

Egerton, John. *Speak Now against the Day: The Generation before the Civil Rights Movement in the South*. Chapel Hill: University of North Carolina Press, 1994.

Ernst, Eldon. "The Interchurch World Movement and the Great Stell Strike of 1919–1920." In *Protestantism and Social Christianity*. Vol. 6 of *Modern American Protestantism and Its World*, edited by Martin E. Marty. Munich: K. G. Saur, 1992.

Fairclough, Adam. *To Redeem the Soul of America: The Southern Christian Leadership and Martin Luther King, Jr*. Athens: University of Georgia Press, 1987.

Fauset, Arthur Huff. *Black Gods of the Metropolis*. Philadelphia: University of Pennsylvania Press. 1944.

Foner, Eric. *Reconstruction: America's Unfinished Revolution, 1863–1877*. New York: Harper & Row, 1988.

Foner, Philip S. *American Socialism and Black Americans: From the Age of Jackson to World War II*. Westport, Conn.: Greenwood Press, 1977.

Foster, John T., and Sarah Whitmer Foster. *Beechers, Stowes and Yankee Strangers: The Transformation of Florida*. Gainesville: University Press of Florida, 1999.

Fox, Richard W. *Reinhold Niebuhr: A Biography*. New York: Pantheon Books, 1985.

Frazier, E. Franklin. *The Negro Church in America*. New York: Schocken Books, 1963.

Freeman, Jo, ed. *Social Movements of the Sixties and Seventies*. New York: Longman, 1983.

Fulop, Timothy E., and Albert J. Raboteau. *African-American Religion: Interpretive Essays in History and Culture*. New York: Routledge, 1997.

Garfinkel, Herbert. *When Negroes March: The March on Washington Movement in the Organization Politics for FEPC*. Glencoe, Ill.: Free Press, 1959.

Garrow, David J. *Bearing the Cross: Martin Luther King, Jr., and the Southern Christian Leadership Conference*. New York: Vintage Books, 1986.

Gavins, Raymond. *The Perils and Prospects of Southern Black Leadership: Gordon Blaine Hancock, 1884–1970*. Durham, N.C.: Duke University Press, 1977.

Goldberg, Robert A. *Grassroots Resistance: Social Movements in Twentieth Century America*. Belmont, Calif.: Wadsworth, 1991.

Harris, William H. *Keeping the Faith: A. Philip Randolph, Milton P. Webster, and the Brotherhood of Sleeping Car Porters, 1925–1937*. Urbana: University of Illinois Press, 1977.

Harvey, Paul. *Redeeming the South: Religious Cultures and Racial Identities among Southern Baptists, 1865–1925*. Chapel Hill: University of North Carolina Press, 1997.

Haynes, George E. *The Trend of the Races*. New York: Council of Women for Home Missions, 1922.

Herberg, Will. *Protestant-Catholic-Jew: An Essay in American Religious Sociology*. Garden City, N.Y.: Doubleday, 1955.

Houser, George M. *Erasing the Color Line*. New York: Fellowship Publications, 1945.

Howe, Irving. *Socialism and America*. San Diego: Harcourt Brace Jovanovich, 1985.

Hutchison, William R. *The Modernist Impulse in American Protestantism*. Durham, N.C.: Duke University Press, 1992.

————, ed. *Between the Times: The Travail of the Protestant Establishment in America, 1900–1960*. Cambridge: Cambridge University Press, 1989.

Jones, William R. "Religious Humanism: Its Problems and Prospects in Black

Religion and Culture." *Journal of the Interdenominational Theological Center* 7 (spring 1980): 169–86.

Juster, Susan, and Lisa MacFarlane, eds. *A Mighty Baptism: Race, Gender and the Creation of American Protestantism.* Ithaca, N.Y.: Cornell University Press, 1996.

King, William McGuire. "The Emergence of Social Gospel Radicalism: The Methodist Case." In *Protestantism and Social Christianity.* Vol. 6 of *Modern American Protestantism and Its World,* edited by Martin E. Marty. Munich: K. G. Saur, 1992.

Kornweibel, Theodore Jr. *No Crystal Stair: Black Life and the Messenger, 1917–1928.* Westport, Conn.: Greenwood Press, 1975.

———. *"Seeing Red": Federal Campaigns against Black Militancy, 1919–1925.* Bloomington: Indiana University Press, 1998.

LaFarge, John. *The Manner Is Ordinary.* New York: Harcourt, Brace, 1954.

Larana, Enrique, Hank Johnston, and Joseph R. Gusfield, eds. *New Social Movements: From Ideology to Identity.* Philadelphia: Temple University Press, 1994.

Lay, Shawn, ed. *The Invisible Empire in the West: Toward a New Historical Appraisal of the Ku Klux Klan of the 1920s.* Urbana: University of Illinois Press, 1992.

Lewis, David Levering. *W. E. B. Du Bois: Biography of a Race, 1868–1919.* New York: Henry Holt, 1993.

Lincoln, C. Eric. *The Black Church since Frazier.* New York: Schocken Books, 1974.

———. "Black Methodists and the Methodist Romance." In *Wesleyan Theology Today: A Bicentennial Theological Consultation,* edited by Theodore Runyon. Nashville: Kingswood Books, 1985.

Lincoln, C. Eric, ed. *The Black Experience in Religion.* Garden City, N.Y.: Anchor Books, 1974.

Lincoln, C. Eric, and Lawrence H. Mamiya. *The Black Church in the African American Experience.* Durham, N.C.: Duke University Press, 1990.

Litwack, Leon F. *Been in the Storm So Long: The Aftermath of Slavery.* New York: Vintage Books, 1979.

———. *North of Slavery: The Negro in the Free States, 1790–1860.* Chicago: University of Chicago Press, 1961.

Long, Charles Sumner. *History of the A.M.E. Church in Florida.* Palatka, Fl.: A.M.E. Book Concern, 1939.

Luker, Ralph E. *The Social Gospel, Black & White: American Racial Reform, 1885–1912.* Chapel Hill: University of North Carolina Press, 1991.

Macquarrie, John. *Twentieth-Century Religious Thought.* 4th ed. London: SCM Press, 1989.

Marable, Manning. "A. Philip Randolph & the Foundations of Black American Socialism." *Radical America* 14, no. 2 (1980): 6–32.

Marsden, George M. *Fundamentalism and American Culture: The Shaping of the Twentieth-Century Evangelicalism: 1870–1925.* Oxford: Oxford University Press, 1980.

Martin, Waldo Jr. *Brown v. Board of Education: A Brief History with Documents.* Boston: Bedford/St. Martin's, 1998.

Marty, Martin E. *The Infidel: Freethought and American Religion.* Cleveland: Meridian Books, 1961.

———. *The Irony of It All, 1893–1919.* Vol. 1 of *Modern American Religion.* Chicago: University of Chicago Press, 1986.

———. *The Noise of Conflict, 1919–1941.* Vol. 2 of *Modern American Religion.* Chicago: University of Chicago Press, 1991.

———. *Under God, Indivisible, 1941–1960.* Vol. 3 of *Modern American Religion.* Chicago: University of Chicago Press, 1996.

Mays, Benjamin E. *The Negro's God as Reflected in His Literature.* Boston: Chapman & Grimes, 1938.

Mays, Benjamin E., and Joseph W. Nicholson. *The Negro's Church.* New York: Institute of Social and Religious Research, 1933.

McGreevy, John. *Parish Boundaries: The Catholic Encounter with Race in the Twentieth-Century Urban North.* Chicago: University of Chicago Press, 1996.

McLouglin, William G. *Revivals, Awakenings, and Reform: An Essay on Religion and Social Change in America, 1607–1977.* Chicago: University of Chicago Press, 1978.

Meier, August, and Elliott Rudwick. *CORE: A Study in the Civil Rights Movement, 1942–1968.* New York: Oxford University Press, 1973.

Meyer, Donald. *The Protestant Search for Political Realism, 1919–1941.* 2nd ed. Middletown, Conn.: Wesleyan University Press, 1988.

Montgomery, William E. *Under Their Own Vine and Fig Tree: The African-American Church in the South, 1865–1900.* Baton Rouge: Louisiana State University Press, 1993.

Moore, R. Laurence. *Religious Outsiders and the Making of Americans.* New York: Oxford University Press, 1986.

Morris, Aldon D. *The Origins of the Civil Rights Movement: Black Communities Organizing for Change.* New York: Free Press, 1984.

Morris, Aldon D., and Carol McClurg Mueller, eds. *Frontiers in Social Movement Theory.* New Haven, Conn.: Yale University Press, 1992.

Myrdal, Gunnar. *An American Dilemma: The Negro Problem and Modern Democracy.* New York: Harper & Row, 1944.

Oberschall, Anthony. *Social Conflict and Social Movements.* Englewood Cliffs, N.J.: Prentice-Hall, 1973.

Osofsky, Gilbert. *Harlem: The Making of a Ghetto: Negro New York, 1890–1930*. 2nd ed. New York: Harper & Row, 1971.

Ottley, Roi. *"New World a-Coming": Inside Black America*. Cleveland: World, 1943.

Paris, Peter J. *The Social Teaching of the Black Churches*. Philadelphia: Fortress Books, 1985.

Patten, Simon N. *The Social Basis of Religion*. New York: Macmillan, 1911.

Perry, Jeffrey Babcock. "Herbert Henry Harrison, 'The Father of Harlem Radicalism': The Early Years—1883 through the Founding of the Liberty League and *The Voice* in 1917." Ph.D. diss., Columbia University, 1986.

Pfeffer, Paula F. "A. Philip Randolph and Bayard Rustin after 1960." In *Black Conservatism*, edited by Peter Eisendtadt. New York: Garland, 1999.

———. *A. Philip Randolph: Pioneer of the Civil Rights Movement*. Baton Rouge: Louisiana State University Press, 1990.

Pinn, Anthony B. *The Black Church in the Post–Civil Rights Era*. Maryknoll, N.Y.: Orbis Books, 2002.

———. *Varieties of African American Religious Experience*. Minneapolis: Fortress Press, 1998.

———, ed. *By These Hands: A Documentary History of African American Humanism*. New York: New York University Press, 2001.

Pinn, Anthony B., and Benjamin Valentin, eds. *The Ties That Bind: African American and Hispanic American/Latino/a Theologies in Dialogue*. New York: Continuum, 2001.

Piven, Frances Fox, and Richard A. Cloward. *Poor People's Movements: How They Succeed, How They Fail*. New York: Pantheon Books, 1977.

Raboteau, Albert J. *Slave Religion: The Invisible Institution in the Antebellum South*. Oxford: Oxford University Press, 1978.

Raboteau, Albert J., and David Wills, with Randall K. Burkett, Will B. Gravely, and James Melvin Washington. "Retelling Carter Woodson's Story: Archival Sources for Afro-American Church History." In *Religious Diversity and American Religious History: Studies in Traditions and Cultures*, edited by Walter Conser and Sumner Twiss. Athens: University of Georgia Press, 1997.

Randolph, A. Philip. "Negro Labor and the Church." In *Labor Speaks for Itself on Religion: A Symposium of Labor Leaders throughout the World*, edited by Jerome Davis. New York: Macmillan, 1929.

———. *The Papers of A. Philip Randolph*. Edited by August Meier and John Bracey Jr. Bethesda, Md.: University Publications of America, 1990 (35 reels).

———. "The Reminiscences of A. Philip Randolph." Transcript of interview by Wendell Wray, 1972. New York: Columbia University, Oral History Research Office Collection.

Randolph, A. Philip, and Chandler Owen, eds. *Messenger*. Vols. 1–10. New York: Messenger Publishing, November 1917–June 1928.

Richardson, Harry V. *Dark Salvation: The Story of Methodism as It Developed among Blacks in America*. New York: Anchor Books, 1976.

Roberts, Samuel Kelton. "Crucible for a Vision: The Work of George Edmund Haynes and the Commission on Race Relations." Ph.D. diss., Columbia University, 1974.

Rustin, Bayard. "A. Philip Randolph: Dean of Civil Rights." *Crisis* 76, no. 4 (1969): 170–73.

_____. *The Papers of Bayard Rustin*. Edited by John Bracey Jr. and August Meier. Bethesda, Md.: University Publications of America, 1990 (23 reels).

_____. "Reminiscences of Bayard Rustin." Transcript of interview by Ed Edwin, 1985/86. New York: Columbia University, Oral History Research Office Collection.

_____. "The Total Vision of A. Philip Randolph." In *Down the Line: The Collected Writings of Bayard Rustin*, edited by C. Vann Woodward. Chicago: Quadrangle, 1971.

Santino, Jack. *Miles of Smiles, Years of Struggles: The Untold History of the Black Pullman Porter*. Urbana: University of Illinois, Press, 1989.

Sawyer, Mary R. *Black Ecumenism: Implementing the Demands of Justice*. Valley Forge, Pa.: Trinity Press International, 1994.

Scheiner, Seth M. *Negro Mecca: A History of the Negro in New York City, 1865–1920*. New York: New York University Press, 1965.

Scott, Alan. *Ideology and the New Social Movements*. London: Unwin-Hyman, 1990.

Sernett, Milton C. *Bound for the Promised Land: African American Religion and the Great Migration*. Durham, N.C.: Duke University Press, 1997.

Singleton, George A. *The Romance of African Methodism: A Study of the African Methodist Episcopal Church*. New York: Exposition Press, 1952.

Smith, Christian. *Disruptive Religion: The Force of Faith in Social-Movement Activism*. New York: Routledge, 1996.

_____. *The Emergence of Liberation Theology: Radical Religion and Social Movement Theory*. Chicago: University of Chicago Press, 1991.

Solomon, Mark. *The Cry Was Unity: Communists and African Americans, 1917–1936*. Jackson: University Press of Mississippi, 1998.

Southern, David W. *John LaFarge and the Limits of Catholic Interracialism, 1911–1963*. Baton Rouge: Louisiana State University Press, 1996.

Spero, Sterling D., and Abram L. Harris. *The Black Worker: The Negro and the Labor Movement*. New York: Columbia University Press, 1931.

Tarrow, Sidney. *Power in Movement: Social Movements, Collective Action and Politics*. Cambridge: Cambridge University Press, 1994.

Taylor, Clarence. *The Black Churches of Brooklyn*. New York: Columbia University Press, 1994.

————. *Black Religious Intellectuals: The Fight for Equality from Jim Crow to the Twenty-first Century*. New York: Routledge, 2002.

Trotter, Joe William Jr. *The Great Migration in Historical Perspective*. Bloomington: Indiana University Press, 1991.

Turner, James. *Without God, without Creed: The Origins of Unbelief in America*. Baltimore: Johns Hopkins University Press, 1985.

Tye, Larry. *Rising from the Rails: Pullman Porters and the Making of the Black Middle Class*. New York: Henry Holt, 2004.

Walker, Clarence E. *A Rock in a Weary Land: The African Methodist Episcopal Church during the Civil War and Reconstruction*. Baton Rouge: Louisiana State University Press, 1982.

Wells, Ida B. *Crusade for Justice: The Autobiography of Ida B. Wells*. Edited by Alfreda M. Duster. Chicago: University of Chicago Press, 1970.

White, Ron C. Jr. *Liberty and Justice for All: Racial Reform and the Social Gospel, 1877–1925*. San Francisco: Harper & Row, 1990.

White, Walter. *A Man Called White: The Autobiography of Walter White*. New York: Knopf, 1948.

Williams, Peter W. *America's Religions: Traditions and Culture*. Urbana: University of Illinois Press, 1998.

Williamson, Edward C. *Florida Politics in the Gilded Age, 1877–1893*. Gainesville: University Press of Florida, 1976.

Wills, David W. "Beyond Commonality and Plurality: Persistent Racial Polarity in American Religion and Politics." In *Religion & American Politics: From the Colonial Period to the 1980s*, edited by Mark A. Noll. New York: Oxford University Press, 1990.

————."An Enduring Distance: Black Americans and the Establishment." In *Between the Times: The Travail of the Protestant Establishment in America, 1900–1960*, edited by William R. Hutchison. Cambridge: Cambridge University Press, 1989.

Wilmore, Gayraud. *Black Religion and Black Radicalism: An Interpretation of the Religious History of Afro-American People*. 2nd ed. Maryknoll, N.Y.: Orbis Books, 1995.

Wilson, Sondra K., ed. *The* Messenger *Reader: Stories, Poetry and Essays from the* Messenger *Magazine*. New York: Modern Library, 2000.

Wintz, Cary D., ed. *African American Political Thought, 1890–1930: Washington, Du Bois, Garvey and Randolph*. Armonk, N.Y.: Sharpe, 1996.

Woodson, Carter G. *A Century of Negro Migration*. Washington, D.C.: Association for the Study of Negro Life and History, 1918.

————. *History of the Negro Church*. Washington, D.C.: Associated Publishers, 1921.

Woodward, C. Vann. *The Strange Career of Jim Crow*. 2nd rev. ed. Oxford: Oxford University Press, 1966.

Index

Abernathy, Ralph, 183, 185–86, 205
Abolition/abolition movement, 57, 97, 103
Abrams, Samuel J., 98
Abyssinian Baptist Church, 182, 199. *See also* Baptist churches
Acts of the Apostles, 219
Aframerican Digest, 71
Africa/Africans, 76–77; African animism, 117; "redemption" of Africa, 76–77, 241n. 79
African American religion, 2–4, 13, 21, 31–32, 44, 73, 75, 117, 175, 241n. 79
African Methodism, 2–3, 6–7, 13–14, 16, 20–21, 24, 26, 31, 36, 218–19, 224–25; AME bishops, 21, 23, 60, 238n. 50; and religious reformism, 28–29, 60; revivalism, 22–23, 230n. 33; the "romance," 13, 218–19; in the South, 12, 14–17, 19, 21. *See also* Randolph, A. Philip
African Methodist Episcopal Church (AME), 8, 13, 17–18, 21–22, 26, 56, 82, 84, 117, 127, 159, 166, 176–77, 199, 212, 218–19, 224; Bishops' Council, 177; and the BSCP, 87, 89, 93, 102, 123; Christian Endeavor League, 22, 26; "dollar money law," 19, 230n. 26;

General Conference, 61; Mother Bethel (Philadelphia), 60; Mount Olive Church (Jacksonville), 10, 22; St. Stephen's, 138–39
African Methodist Episcopal Zion Church (AMEZ), 123, 147, 189, 212; Mother Zion Church, 26, 123
Agnosticism, 40, 43
Allen, Richard, 11, 13, 15, 60–61, 127, 219, 224
AME Church Review, 218
America, 144
American Civil Liberties Union (ACLU), 210
American Federation of Labor. *See* Labor movement
American Friends Service Committee, 201
American Jewish Committee, 181
American Jewish Congress, 174, 181, 194
American Revolution, 12
American Veterans Committee, 181
Amsterdam News, 216–17
Anderson, Jervis, 176, 218, 221, 228n. 5
Anderson, Marion, 132, 203
Anti-Catholicism, 57–59, 144–45
Anti-clericalism, 44
Anti-religion or anti-church, 2, 33, 35, 38, 55–56, 118

120–121; and the Chicago
MOWM, 138, 140–41; and the
fundamentalist-modernist debate,
66; and the Garvey movement,
57–58; ministerial alliances for the
BSCP, 87, 89, 96, 98–99, 106–7,
112–13, 121, 123; ministerial alliances for the MOWM, 152, 156,
166–68, 170; and the Montgomery
bus boycott, 178, 183–84, 187,
199–200; and the National Negro
Congress, 124–26; and the New
York MOWM, 135–37, 168; and
the New York MOWM prayer
protest, 151–54, 156–57; and the
prayer pilgrimage, 201–18; progressive ministers, 53–55, 63–65,
70, 95, 98, 225; and Pullman
porters, 186, 188, 191, 194;
"southern freedom fighters," 213;
and the St. Louis MOWM,
141–42, 146–50; and the Wilkins
Fund, 88. *See also* Southern Christian Leadership Conference (SCLC);
White ministers
Black power movement, 222
Black press, 39, 139, 184, 199, 207,
216; and the BSCP, 92, 104–5,
111, 121; and the MOWM, 128,
130, 132–33, 141, 161, 164. See
also *Chicago Defender*; *Messenger*;
Pittsburgh Courier
Black theology. *See* March on Washington Movement (MOWM)
Black Worker, 2, 87–88, 114–15,
122–23
Blake, Eugene Carson, 208
B'nai Brith, 215
Borders, William Holmes, 199, 207,
213
Bowen, John Wesley Edward, 196
Bowne, Borden Parker, 196

Boylan Home Industrial Training
School for Girls, 9
Bradley, E. J., 99–100
Bray, James A., 168
"Breaking Partitions" sermon,
149–50; walls of Jericho, 141–42,
148–49. *See also* Segregation
Bridges, William, 34
Briggs, Cyril, 34, 45
Brightman, Edgar S., 196
Brooks, William Henry, 30
Brotherhood of Sleeping Car Porters
(BSCP), 1, 5, 38, 70, 72, 79, 82,
127, 130, 141, 152, 189, 199, 203,
216, 221, 244n. 27; citizens' committee, 97–98, 136, 141; divisions
on the East Coast, 96–99; divisions
in the Midwest, 99–105; divisions
in the Northeast, 105–9; divisions
in the West, 109–12; early union
organization, 86–96; fifteenth anniversary convention (1940),
128–29, 133; In Friendship, 181;
labor conferences, 95, 118–21,
170, 173; Montgomery bus boycott, 186; the MOWM, 132, 135,
137; and the prayer pilgrimage,
178; progressive black ministers,
124; "State of the Race" convention, 189–93, 195, 197–98; unemployment conferences, 122–23
Brotherhood religion, 113–14. *See
also* Randolph, A. Philip; Working-
class religion/black proletariat
Brotherhood Workers, 46, 235n. 18
Brown, Ethelred, 69, 239n. 67
Brown, John, 79
Brown, Robert McAfee, 190
Brown, Russell, 106
Brown v. Board of Education, 5,
177–80, 190–95, 198, 201–2,
206–8, 214–15, 219

39, 55, 72, 83; forum for social scientific thought, 39–40, 44–45, 47, 50–52, 56, 64; and the Fundamentalist-Modernist Debate, 64–70; "Garvey Must Go" campaign, 56–59, 103–4; and Negro journalism of the 1920s, 62; the "New" Negro, 40, 47–49, 51, 57, 60, 64, 200; and orthodox Christianity, 73–80, 83, 105; radical critique of the Negro Church, 50–53, 55, 83; radical period, 38–56, 78, 238n. 48; and religious liberty, 57, 59; socialist magazine, 33–37, 43

Methodism and Methodists, 23, 96, 141, 151, 156, 166, 182, 213, 218–19, 223

Methodist churches, 49, 61, 80, 87, 108, 112, 121, 128, 152, 154, 170, 196

Methodist Episcopal Church, South, 13–14

Methodist Federation for Social Service (MFSS), 59, 122, 249n. 80

Metropolitan Community Church, 94, 102–3, 121, 170. *See also* Brotherhood of Sleeping Car Porters (BSCP); Chicago (BSCP Headquarters); March on Washington Movement (MOWM)

Meyer, Donald, 72

Meyers, Dr. James, 168

Miller, George Frazier, 34, 46, 55, 63–64, 99, 238n. 55

Miller, Kelly, 34–35, 67, 72–73, 75, 78, 80

Miller, Loren, 199

Mitchell, Clarence, 203

Mitchell slush fund, 47. *See also* Black ministers

Modern Quarterly, 73, 240n. 74

Montgomery, Alabama, 5, 175; "headquarters of the Old Confederacy," 192

Montgomery bus boycott, 177–79, 181, 183, 185–89, 191–95, 198–200, 219, 222; BSCP rally at Madison Square Garden, 189, 193, 195, 197; and the nonviolent, goodwill direct action, 177–78, 183, 185–88, 191–92, 195, 200; northern agitators and communists, 183, 187–89; Montgomery Improvement Association (MIA), 186, 193–94, 199; MIA's "Institute on Nonviolence and Social Change," 199–201

Monticello, Florida, 16

Moon, Henry Lee, 37, 174, 212, 214

Moore, Dad, 110

Moore, Richard B., 34

Mormons, 112

Morris, Iona, 157

Morrow, E. Frederick, 217

Murphy, Carl, 54, 199

Murray, John Courtney, 223

Murray, Pauli, 159–60, 164, 174

Muste, A. J., 74, 165, 169–70, 185

Myers, E. Pauline, 160, 169, 171, 173–74

Nance, John E., 150, 211–12

National Association for the Advancement of Colored People (NAACP), 30, 33, 62, 64, 86, 105, 108, 123, 129, 132, 134, 174, 178, 180–81, 189, 193–94, 197–99, 219, 238n. 48; prayer pilgrimage for freedom, 202–7, 208–10, 212–14, 216–17

National Association of Colored Women, 214

National Baptist Convention (NBC), 91, 166–67, 180, 182, 189, 192,

Nonviolent, goodwill direct action. *See* March on Washington Movement (MOWM); Montgomery bus boycott

Northern agitators, 183. *See* Montgomery bus boycott

Odom, L. Sylvester, 202

Office of Production Management (OPM), 133

O'Keefe, Father Thomas M., 30

Old Testament imagery, 114, 210; Moses and the Exodus, 2, 147–48, 210–11; the patriarchs, 191, 195; the prophets, 41, 126, 195, 198

Olivet Baptist Church, 61–62. *See also* Social gospel

Orchestra Hall speech. *See* Randolph, A. Philip

Orth, Professor John, 97

Orthodox Christianity, 70–80; attack on traditional religion, 39, 41–43, 45–46, 50, 64–70; liberal orthodoxy vs. conservative heterodoxy, 78–80; new religions in California, 70; science and religion, 75. *See also* Christian doctrine; Protestantism

Ottley, Roi, 1–2, 37–38

Owen, Chandler, 3, 29, 33–36, 221; and the demise of radicalism, 56–57, 63–64, 78; radical journalist, 37–39, 43–44, 46–47, 49–55, 116, 184–85

Owens, Robert, 111

Pacifism, 174, 185. *See also* March on Washington Movement (MOWM); Quakers

Paine, Thomas, 44

Palmer, A. Mitchell, 37, 237n. 40

Parker, Perry, 89–90

Parker, Theodore, 72

Parks, Rosa, 177, 185, 194

Parrish, Richard, 132

Passing of the Gods, 74

Patten, Simon N., 45

Patterson, F. D., 199

Payne, Daniel, 12

Payne, Ethel, 138–40, 170

Payne, George L., 209

Peale, Norman Vincent, 223–24

Pearl Harbor, 3, 128, 136, 161

Penn, Garland I., 89–90

Pentecostal churches, 151, 212

People's Voice, 151

Perry, Milton, 214

Personalism, 31–32, 68, 196–97. *See also* Randolph, A. Philip

Pfeffer, Paula, 3

Phelps-Stokes Fund, 199

Phillips, Wendell, 103

Phyllis Wheatley Community Center, 105; Phyllis Wheatley YWCA, 160

Pickens, William, 64–69, 71, 80

Pike, James A., 207–8

Pittsburgh Courier, 129; antagonism of, to the MOWM, 131, 161, 163–64, 172, 250n. 8; "Double V" campaign, 129; "Negro manifesto" of, 193

Politics, 172

Poll tax, 8–9, 131, 166

Pool, David de Sola, 154–55

Post War World Council, 160

Powell, Adam Clayton, Jr., 143, 157–58, 174, 189, 194, 209, 214

Powell, Adam Clayton, Sr., 25, 87–88, 98

Powell, C. B., 199

Prayer pilgrimage for freedom (1957), 6, 158, 178–79, 189, 199, 210–20; alliance between NAACP, BSCP, and SCLC, 180, 201–2, 203–5,

Wells-Barnett, Ida B., 102–4
West, Paul E., 128
West Indies/West Indians, 34–35, 69–70
Weston, Ross A., 212
Wheeler, La Verne F. (Bertuccio Dantino), 43–44
White, Horace, 108–9, 167, 246n. 52
White, L. S., 182
White, Walter, 86, 123, 129, 132–133
White Citizens Council, 191–94
White House conferences, 179–81, 198–99, 219. *See also* Eisenhower, Dwight D.; Roosevelt, Franklin D.; Truman, Harry
White ministers, 72; black and white religious leaders, 158, 166, 168; In Friendship supporters, 181–82; Montgomery bus boycott, 200; MOWM supporters, 154–56, 164; Protestant Council of the City of New York, 223–24; Southern progressive ministers, 59; BSCP supporters, 81, 121, 123–24. *See also* Black ministers; Protestantism
Wilkins, John H., 85–86, 114, 123; Wilkins Lynching Investigation Defense Fund, 87–88, 123
Wilkins, Roy, 178, 180, 194, 199; role in prayer pilgrimage for freedom, 201–6, 208–9, 212–17. *See also* National Association for the Advancement of Colored People (NAACP)
Willet, Dr. Herbert L., 121
Williams, E. E., 130

Williams, Lacey Kirk, 62, 91
Wilmore, Gayraud, 118. *See also* "Deradicalization thesis"
Wilson, Boyd (United Steel Workers), 209
Women activists in the MOWM. See Eason, Georgia; March on Washington Movement (MOWM); Payne, Ethel; Ryan, Neva
Woodbey, Rev. George Washington, 234n. 16
Woodson, Carter G., 25, 54, 62–63, 95–96, 116
Workers Defense League, 181
Working-class religion/black proletariat, 95, 113–14, 116–18. *See* March on Washington Movement (MOWM); Randolph, A. Philip
World War I, 3, 25, 30–31, 34, 36–37, 52, 56, 69, 80, 98, 147, 199, 227n. 5
World War II, 128–29, 145, 150–52, 159, 193, 228n. 5; Battle of England, 131; black morale and wartime patriotism, 157–58, 160, 163–64; national defense, 129–32; segregation in the military, 129; wartime hysteria, 151
Wright, Richard, 37
Wright, R. R., 167

Yale Divinity School, 115–16
Yankee schoolteachers, 11–12, 24, 97–98
Y.M.C.A., 105, 120, 147, 156
Youth March for Integrated Schools, 217

About the Author

Professor Cynthia Taylor received her doctorate in American religious history at the Graduate Theological Union in Berkeley, California. She has taught American history at several Bay Area colleges in the past decade and is currently teaching American history and religion in the humanities department of Dominican University of California.